EUGENE O'NEILL'S AMERICA

Eugene O'Neill's America

DESIRE UNDER DEMOCRACY

John Patrick Diggins

The University of Chicago Press   Chicago and London

JOHN PATRICK DIGGINS is Distinguished Professor in the Graduate Center of the City University of New York and the author of a number of books, including *The Rise and Fall of the American Left* (1992), *The Proud Decades: America in War and in Peace, 1941–1960* (1988), *The Lost Soul of American Politics* (1984), and *The Promise of Pragmatism* (1994), the last published by the University of Chicago Press.

The University of Chicago Press, Chicago 60637
The University of Chicago Press, Ltd., London
© 2007 by The University of Chicago
All rights reserved. Published 2007
Printed in the United States of America

16 15 14 13 12 11 10 09 08 07   1 2 3 4 5

ISBN-13: 978-0-226-14880-9 (cloth)
ISBN-10: 0-226-14880-7 (cloth)

Library of Congress Cataloging-in Publication Data

Diggins, John P.
  Eugene O'Neill's America : desire under democracy / John Patrick Diggins
      p. cm.
  Includes index.
  ISBN-13: 978-0-226-14880-9 (cloth : alk. paper)
  ISBN-10: 0-226-14880-7 (cloth : alk. paper)
    1. O'Neill, Eugene, 1888–1953. 2. O'Neill, Eugene, 1888–1953 — Criticism and interpretation. 3. Dramatists, American — 20th century — Biography. 4. Dramatists, American — 20th century — Family relationships. 5. Dramatists, American — 20th century — Psychology. 6. America — In literature. I. Title.
PS3529.N5Z6275 2007
812'.52 — dc22
[B]

                                                          2006051409

Dedicated to the memory of

Colleen Dewhurst, Jason Robards, Paul Robeson, Jose Quintero

The only thing in us that is unconditional is desire.
SIMONE WEIL

This is the use of Memory:
For liberation is not loss of love but expanding
Of love beyond desire, and so liberation
From the future as well as the past.
T. S. ELIOT

Every satisfied desire gives birth to a new one.
ARTHUR SCHOPENHAUER

He who possesses is possessed.
FRIEDRICH NIETZSCHE

To come to possess all, desire the possession of nothing.
ST. JOHN OF THE CROSS

Who is your literary idol?
The answer to that is in one word—Nietzsche.
EUGENE O'NEILL

Contents

Preface and Acknowledgments

It was late afternoon on October 9, 1946, a strange hour for a Broadway stage play to raise its curtain. Eugene O'Neill's *The Iceman Cometh* opened at the Martin Beck Theatre in New York City to much attention and controversy. The play started at 4:30 and, with a long intermission to allow some to scramble for dinner, ended a little after 10 in the evening. Critics from all over the world came to see the literary event, and before curtain time the press could only speculate what was in store since rehearsals for the "mysterious play mysteriously titled" were carried out behind locked doors.[1] What was one to make of an author who had silenced himself for twelve years after having won three Pulitzer awards (and later a posthumous fourth) and the Nobel Prize, the only American playwright so honored? O'Neill had high hopes for his play. "There are moments in it," he wrote to a friend in 1940, "that suddenly strip the secret of the soul of a man stark naked, not in cruelty or moral superiority, but with an understanding compassion which sees him as a victim of the ironies of life and of himself. Those moments are for me the depth of tragedy, with nothing more that can possibly be said."[2] He had written the work five years earlier, but it was withheld from production during the war years because, as he told his friend, "a New York audience could neither see nor hear its meaning. The pity and tragedy of defensive pipe dreams would be deemed downright unpatriotic. . . . But after the war is over, I am afraid . . . that American audiences will understand *The Iceman Cometh* only too well."[3]

Not well enough. Two weeks after the play opened, *Time* had O'Neill on its cover and James Agee wrote the feature essay hailing the return of

America's master playwright. But the play itself seemed to settle for the theatrically effective, with actors avoiding searching their own emotional pasts and the playwright unable to probe the depths of real people. "As drama," wrote *Time,* "for all its brooding, *The Iceman* was scarcely deeper than a puddle."[4]

A decade later, O'Neill's play had a highly successful run off-Broadway, and in our own day it enjoyed a spectacular success, in a London production that moved on to New York to open to equally ecstatic reviews. Directed by Howard Davies and starring Kevin Spacey, the production of *Iceman* in 2000 was hailed as a "landmark" that "may be making theater history." O'Neill won praise for his "psychological precision" in giving depth to characters who, on first glance, seem little more than a bunch of bums. Drama critics described audiences sitting in stunned silence, riveted to every scene for more than four hours. "When was the last time you heard that kind of hush in a theater?" asked critic Ben Brantley.[5] How, then, can we account for the confused and negative receptions that *Iceman* suffered in its 1946 debut?

The setting for the play is the back room of Harry Hope's saloon in the year 1912, a dive that attracts down and out has-beens. While relying on liquor grudgingly furnished by the proprietor, they await the arrival of Theodore Hickman (Hickey), a salesman who periodically turns up to throw them a party with free drinks and good cheer. The failures include former radical activists, hookers, a police captain fired for corruption, veteran military officers of the Boer War, a public relations man dismissed for drinking on the job, a circus performer, a black man who once lived high as a gambling house proprietor, and a Harvard Law School graduate and son of a wealthy criminal. The mood of the play is gloomy with loneliness, death, suicide, murder, guilt, pity, and the need for illusion. The existential theme of being asked to face life when there is no meaningful life to be found may have been too much for the postwar American audience. Yet there are historical and political reasons why the play left that audience perplexed and disappointed.

After the Depression and World War II, an era in which Americans experienced the paralysis of economic stagnation and then went on to victorious achievement on the battlefield, people did not want to hear about defeat and failure. Had not President Franklin Roosevelt reassured Americans in declaring "the only thing we have to fear is fear itself"? The American people had overcome adversity, and they did not want to look back. Yet the characters in O'Neill's play look back in hope and sorrow. All of them have seen better days, and all that is left is to fantasize about the future as the return of a past perhaps more imagined than true. Nostalgic about the flush times of yesterday, O'Neill's characters are unable to act upon anything to do with the present. But the American people themselves, in the postwar world, looked forward rather than backward as the economy was about to embark on a massive expansion never before seen in American history. What the country was moving toward, a life of endless material abundance, O'Neill saw almost as a biblical curse. In a well-publicized press interview held shortly after the play opened, O'Neill complained that "there are no values to live by today" and that "anything is permissible if you know the angles."

> I feel, in that sense, that America is the greatest failure in history. It was given everything, more than any other country in history, but we squandered our soul by trying to possess something outside it, and we'll end up as that game usually does, by losing our soul and the thing outside it too. But why go on — the Bible said it much better: "For what shall it profit a man if he gain the whole world, and lose his own soul?"[6]

With O'Neill's discouraging outlook, one can understand *Time*'s disappointment in the play. A few years earlier the magazine's editor Henry Luce had coined the term "The American Century," believing that the rest of the twentieth century would belong to America if only the country's ideals might be better embraced and articulated. "We are not happy about ourselves in relation to America," he complained. Luce sought to inspire his readers and persuade them to accept America's historical mission, the manifest destiny of the American people to "do their mysterious work of lifting the life of mankind."[7]

In 1946, as America moved beyond the ordeals of the Depression and the sacrifices of World War II, the public had little patience with O'Neill's pessimistic outlook. History, however, failed to provide "The American Century" that publisher Luce had promised. Instead America would have to face "The Communist Century." Withing a few years all of Eastern Europe and soon most of Asia fell to communist dictatorships. One wonders whether O'Neill's play might have enjoyed a better reception if it had appeared as the cold war suddenly emerged to shake America's confidence in itself. Two years after the play opened, *Time* featured Reinhold Niebuhr on its cover with a long essay that had been composed by Agee and the ex-communist Whittaker Chambers. Under the cover photo of Niebuhr the headline read: "Man's Story Is Not a Success Story." Niebuhr sought to warn America that human nature is fallen, cursed with original sin, and susceptible to the Christian sin of pride. Years earlier O'Neill had cautioned: "Man is born broken. He lives by mending. The grace of God is glue." America's greatest modern theologian and its greatest playwright saw history as tragic, ironic, full of pathos and sorrow.

Aware of how the Greek theater of classical antiquity depicted conflict as inexorable, both thinkers saw that attempts to relieve the human condition by communist political means would only lead to catastrophe.[8]

Much of America was prepared to listen to Niebuhr after the experiences of Hitler and Stalin. The settings of many of O'Neill's plays, however, took place in the historical past before the rise of totalitarianism (although a few of his unfinished plays addressed the subject). O'Neill had been in the forefront of the Greenwich Village "Lyrical Left" when the Bolshevik Revolution struck the rebels like a message from the messiah. "I have been over into the future," wrote the popular journalist Lincoln Steffens upon returning from Russia in 1921, "and it works!" Yet O'Neill was one of the few American writers who knew that communism would not work, that indeed it would turn out to be the cruelest of illusions, the "pipe dream" of the Left, the "opium of the intellectuals" that would later overtake China and much of Southeast Asia, whose leaders had studied Marxism-Leninism in Paris. Moreover, Eugene O'Neill was the only major writer, in Europe as well as America, who identified with the Left and yet remained profoundly skeptical of communism even before the Bolsheviks came to power in 1917. Playwrights in particular no longer quarreled with history, as they had in previous centuries; on the contrary, they eagerly submitted to it as the theater of heroic action. American playwrights were sympathetic to Soviet Russia (Clifford Odets, John Howard Lawson, Arthur Miller); their European counterparts wildly enthusiastic (Bertolt Brecht, Sean O'Casey, George Bernard Shaw). O'Neill alone realized that the promise of politics had simply replaced the promise of religion in claiming to save the world from sin and corruption.

In 1946, with the first disappointing performance of *Iceman,* the cold war had yet to become a reality and a victorious America was cocky about its role in the world. In 2000, with the successful performance of the play, the country's relation to the rest of the world had grown worrisome, especially with the rise of Islamic fundamentalism and terrorism. Many of the subjects that O'Neill had dealt with in his plays (family, religion, youth, men and power, women and feminism, race and justice, non-Western cultures abroad, and political terrorism and the desperate delusions of anarchism) have become urgent matters in recent American life and in world history.

At our present critical point in American history, a study of Eugene O'Neill tells us some things about ourselves that most politicians would dare not utter. Not since the *Federalist* authors of the eighteenth century, and Nathaniel Hawthorne and Herman Melville of the nineteenth, has an author told the unpleasant truths about human nature; not since the philosopher Friedrich Nietzsche has a playwright dramatized how democracy can turn into a culture of complaint and resentment; and not since the ancient Greeks has a thinker pondered how our desires choose and control us.

It has been said that American history lacks a sense of tragedy. In classical terms, tragedy called for the hero to be a man of high rank brought down by some inner character flaw. Abraham Lincoln, however, saw tragedy everywhere as the Civil War erupted and North and South fought each other for the survival of liberty or of slavery. In his famous debates with Stephen Douglas, Lincoln denied the idea of "popular sovereignty" that would allow the western territories to vote to become slave states, thereby permitting "a people the right to do wrong." O'Neill depicted the American character doing just that in *Mourning Becomes Electra* — indeed, resorting to classical tragedy for analogues — where the killings on the battlefield of the Civil War serve as a rehearsal for the murders in the Mannon household. Both melancholic thinkers saw American history as tragic, the terrain in which the present becomes aware of itself as opposing forces struggle to prevail. Conventional wisdom sees democracy arising to control power. Democracy, however, affords equality of opportunity for those with the will to dominate and control. Reading the speeches of Lincoln and the plays of O'Neill, one arrives at the same conclusion. Both the president and the playwright wanted America to see the perils of pride so that we would not, in seeing power as virtue, "lose our own soul."

ACKNOWLEDGMENTS

I wish to express my gratitude for the helpful criticisms on the manuscript offered by Stephen A. Black, Robert Brustein, John Rodden, and the late Thomas Flanagan. I am also in debt to the thoughtful copyediting of Richard Audet, the encouragement of editor Doug Mitchell, and the steady support of fellow writer Elizabeth Harlan. The Bogliasco Foundation in Italy provided the environment that stimulated my early thoughts on this book, and the staff at Yale University's Beinecke Library helped me work through the O'Neill materials and decipher the playwright's handwriting. As a latecomer to the subject, I also appreciate the welcome I received from members of the Eugene O'Neill Society.

The book is dedicated to four figures of the American stage whose arrangements and performances dramatized O'Neill's genius for elevating autobiographical intensity to the level of metaphysical curiosity.

Introduction:
Knowers Unknown to Ourselves

"The theatre," instructed Eugene O'Neill, "should reveal to us who we are." Action on the stage can provide "a better understanding of ourselves and a better understanding of one another." A possibility, to be sure. Yet one wonders whether the audience attends the theater rather to be entertained than take the plunge into the depths of self-knowledge. In classical thought it was assumed that "a man is at least known to himself" (Cicero). In the milieu of modern thought in which O'Neill wrote, a recipe turns into a riddle. "We knowers are unknown to ourselves," observed Nietzsche, "and for a good reason; how can we ever hope to find what we have never looked for?"[1]

O'Neill may have believed that the theater would help us recognize ourselves in our emotions and desires. Curiously, however, his characters rarely do so. Instead, they feel the tug of a divided self that eludes the mind. Believing in reason, they respond to emotion; hungering for freedom, they are haunted by memory; defeated by reality, they are driven by illusion. While the characters fret and struggle, they remain unaware of who they truly might be and thus incapable of realizing their individual nature and destiny. In conventional wisdom, to obtain knowledge of one's self was both the counsel of the Delphic oracle of Greek philosophy and the imperative of Ralph Waldo Emerson: "Know thyself. Every heart vibrates to that string." But O'Neill's heart remained unmoved. "'Know thyself!' What a mortal bore life would become if you did," O'Neill wrote to his young sweetheart Beatrice Ashe in 1914. "It is the unexpected whims which change one's perspective" and "make life fascinating."[2]

One of our most introspective playwrights suggests that the mind comes alive by turning outward and responding to change and contingency. O'Neill almost seems to be claiming that in the encounter with life one learns from experiences that enrich one's perspectives. That view, however, was one he expressed as a youth. When O'Neill wrote his more mature scripts, many of his characters remain inert, passive, incapable of changing and opening up to experience. As we follow them on the stage, we know what Nietzsche meant when he said that we are "strangers to ourselves." If O'Neill aimed to give us "a better understanding of ourselves," it seemed that he wanted to show Americans how tempting it was to flee from one's self rather than face the challenge of self-realization. One character bears the nickname "Jimmy Tomorrow." Unknown to himself, he awaits the future under the illusion that he will find what has eluded him in the past.

*

O'Neill may have been critical of America, but in no other country could his plays have found such resonance. A nation of immigrants, America is the land of desire, the place where people come to fulfill their wishes as the very definition of who they are. At least that is the storybook tale that America has inculcated in its youngsters. O'Neill, however, shared the conviction held by the New England Transcendentalists Ralph Waldo Emerson and Henry David Thoreau, writers who were the first to demonstrate how America had become alienated and lost its soul without knowing it. The poets and philosophers tried to awaken the country to the conventions that strangled society and left its members leading "lives of quiet desperation." In *More Stately Mansions,* O'Neill would have us know what we have done to ourselves when we allow society to shape the self. "It is the idealistic fallacy which is responsible for all the confusions in our minds," declares Simon Harford, "for the blundering of our desires which are disciplined to covet what they don't want and be afraid to crave what they wish for in truth." The idealistic fallacy is to deny, for reasons of conventional morality, what one prefers to seek, and to settle for what one neither needs nor desires. This is, as both Emerson and Nietzsche put it, to "castrate the ego." The playwright Henrik Ibsen also protested against an "idealism" of moral hypocrisy and self-deceit that society imposes on the individual.

Ancient Greek thinkers believed in the self-revelatory potential of the theater. On the stage philosophy steps aside to allow the "dark underside" of desire to express itself. Reason may hide us from ourselves by providing excuses and rationalizations, whereas the emotions reveal before our very eyes what we need to see about ourselves. O'Neill's plays turn on what has been experienced, and they call up a whole swarm of memories, desires, and fears associated with that experience. On the stage he lays bare the agonies of the soul, the secrets of the family, the cruelties of history, the traumas of youth — all residing in memory. Not those who forget the past but those who remember it are condemned to repeat it.

O'Neill's Nietzschean reading of American history envisioned the will to power leading to a chaos of warring desires that aim to appropriate and subdue. Desire, defined as the self's longing for an object that compels it, or even a vague yearning that has no clear object, plays havoc with freedom. To be free is to be a self-determining subject; the existence of desire, in contrast, implies that our will is determined by something other than itself. In the first instance, we are inner directed; in the second, driven from without. The Transcendentalists wrestled with this dichotomy, as does the modern playwright, and thus the American character can embrace both Ralph Emerson and Willy Loman, the seeker of the "Oversoul" who wanted to think for himself, and the traveling salesman who thought only of others in order to be well liked.

*

Long before Nietzsche, the American Founders well knew that human nature possessed a drive toward power. This inexorable propensity was one of the "springs of action" that would, if left unrestrained, "vex and oppress" others. Thus the *Federalist* authors framed a constitution of checks and balances that aimed to control power. But O'Neill's plays demonstrate how power escaped authority and its political institutions and imposes itself on almost every aspect of life. "In America," we are told in *More Stately Mansions,* "you are free to take what you want," and for O'Neill the acquisitive instinct resides in the American character as a curse that allows freedom to play itself out as power. Yet the human condition may be weak and timid even more than strong and assertive. For power cannot stand still; it must keep alive by increasing and augmenting itself. Moreover, the will may have a failure of nerve and be incapable of fulfilling its own desire for autonomy and mastery. In Nietzsche, the will to power is equivalent to "the instinct for freedom," but it also falters, loses the spirit of struggle as the will atrophies. Modern humanity succumbs to complacency, envy, and resentment. O'Neill's characters are lonely, in need of pity and the protection of identity, and fearful of the religious reminder of death and damnation. In a democracy the masses tend to acquiesce to society and simply live for today and passively react to the world instead of passionately acting upon it. Nietzsche made

O'Neill aware of the distinction between freedom and democracy, between the potential strength of the self and the actual weakness of the people. The observation was made earlier by Alexis de Tocqueville, who saw the authority of government yielding to the sovereignty of society and its citizens cowering before the "tyranny of the majority." The American people conform and follow the majority in its restless pursuit of material happiness and its "petty pleasures." Like Tocqueville, O'Neill was trying to make sense of the modern condition, and America offered the setting in which to meditate on desire and its discontents. "Americans," a character remarks in *Days Without End,* "no longer know what they want the country to be, what they want it to become, where they want it to go. They have lost the ideal of the Land of the Free. Freedom demands initiative, courage, the need to decide what life must mean to oneself."

If O'Neill seemed harsh on America, he was even harsher on himself and on his family. What he was asking from America he knew very well he would not find in the members of his family or himself. Neither mother, father, nor brother was capable of deciding "what life must mean to oneself." With few exceptions, such as perhaps Anna Christie, none of O'Neill's characters are capable of so deciding. In his plays desire is either dead, as in *The Iceman Cometh,* or it is so alive that it controls the character's every mood, as in *More Stately Mansions.* Desire can mean the need to revenge a wrong, the demand for social recognition, the urge to escape society, the greed for a piece of property, the lust for another's body, or the genuine romantic attraction to another person ("lovesickness")—or all six, as in *Desire Under the Elms* and *A Touch of the Poet.* Yet desire cannot be all negative, for without it there is no motive to act, no reason why explorers would set out to discover a new world—the subjects of O'Neill's *The Fountain* and *Marco Millions.*

O'Neill was carrying on the classical tradition in seeing desire as a form of blindness and carrying on in the Christian tradition in finding in desire what the mind is helpless to command. The emotion, when out of control, obscures why it is we want what we want, compelling us to pursue that which cannot be satisfied (Seneca) and succumbing to the "slimy desires of the flesh" (Saint Augustine). O'Neill's father, whose counterpart confesses how this riddle affected his own life in *Long Day's Journey into Night,* failed to recognize it in his son's own plays. Even though steeped in Shakespeare, he never quite grasped what the son was trying to say in his plays. James O'Neill delighted in the success of *Beyond the Horizon,* though not in its substance. "People come to the theater to forget their troubles, not to be reminded of them," he admonished his son after the play's opening. "What are you trying to do—send them home to commit suicide?"[3]

Brought up in his early years on the teachings of Roman Catholicism,

Eugene O'Neill later looked to the mystical vitality of Greek paganism for the tragic pathos of frailty and suffering that he saw as the universal human condition. As the director Dudley Nichols put it as early as 1928: "Eugene O'Neill is our most modern dramatist in the sense that he alone has succeeded in breasting back across that ocean of two thousand years and more which rolls between our time and the ancient Greeks. He is like Euripides, with a certain difference; for, transmigrating from Athens the old to America the new, the rebel Greek has dallied in the spirit of Jesus, Tolstoy, Ibsen, Strindberg, Wedekind, Nietzsche, Freud and all the other pioneers and rebels."[4] O'Neill's pioneering role was to be the first American playwright to draw upon the Greek theater of classical antiquity to dramatize the realities of American democracy.

While O'Neill sought to bring Greek tragedy forward to modern times, he had to leave Greek philosophy behind. Aristotle's conviction that rational deliberation can govern human action, and thus enable the mind to choose freely, makes no appearance in O'Neill's plays. O'Neill's father figure, James Tyrone, was not the only O'Neill character who remained frustrated and confused, trying to give a reason for why he did what he came to regret. In need of sympathy, Tyrone wishes to be understood before he can be intelligible to himself by assigning motives for his actions. Nor can he understand the acts of others. In *Long Day's Journey into Night,* the father responds angrily when the son reminds him that he had tried to commit suicide. "You weren't in your right mind. No son of mine would ever—you were drunk." The son replies: "I was stone cold sober. That was the trouble. I'd stop to think too long."

To think, mind's highest activity, is no help to Yank of *The Hairy Ape,* a happy-go-lucky stoker content with putting his muscle to work for the modern industrial machine, until he receives a shock to his senses and tries to think through who he is and where he belongs, even striking the pose of Rodin's *The Thinker,* and then goes to pieces. Aristotle promised that thinking itself would clarify fears and emotions and put them to rest. O'Neill's Americans are rarely at rest.

*

This book represents an attempt to appreciate O'Neill beyond the aesthetic criteria of dramaturgy or the neurotic symptoms of psychology. It is a study not so much of the plays themselves as the ideas in the plays and their implications for social and political philosophy and intellectual history. Many drama critics, and most audiences that have viewed the plays, looked to the performances as a window into the meaning of the playwright's personal history. Those schooled in Freudian psychoanalysis use O'Neill's texts to get at the meaning of his life that had been "over-determined" by childhood experiences with his dysfunctional family. Though entirely valid, such an exercise risks a double reductionism. First, O'Neill's literary output is explained in light of his life, and then his life is reduced to the story of his family and his early experiences within a household charged with tension and torment. Had O'Neill been a writer of literary naturalism, perhaps he would have had no objection to seeing his *oeuvre* reduced to the forces of heredity and environment. Yet O'Neill was influenced by thinkers who defied fate and challenged the political, religious, and social conventions they had inherited. Thus the same plays that may afford insight into O'Neill's personal life also illuminate the meaning of America, particularly as seen by a playwright who had much to say about class, religion, gender, race, family, and power, as well as tragedy and the yearning for transcendence, society at the higher reaches and the lower depths, and even the discovery of America during age of exploration in the fifteenth century.

Some drama critics, instead of appreciating such subjects, are under-standably severe about the inadequacies of O'Neill's language and dia-logue, which supposedly explain the limitations of his plays as works of art. O'Neill has been likened to Theodore Dreiser, the novelist who gave us compelling characters and stories but in the end failed to write ex-quisite prose. My interest is not in how O'Neill's characters expressed themselves and their allegedly clunky dialogue. Rather my concern is with the subject matter that the playwright addressed as issues in Ameri-can history. Perhaps the point might be better made by comparing Eu-gene O'Neill's America to that of the French social philosopher Alexis de Tocqueville, author of the classic *Democracy in America,* published in the 1830s, the time frame of several of O'Neill's plays.

Neither the French philosopher nor the American playwright believed that the future of the United States depended on its political institutions. On the contrary, it rested on the character of the people themselves, their social *moeurs,* attitudes, and mental outlooks, what the French thinker called "habits of the heart." Both writers saw America threatened by an all-devouring materialism, the pervasiveness of *egoisme,* the frantic pur-suit of happiness as a way of denying the shadow of death. Tocqueville hoped that a narcissistic "vicious materialism" might be held in check by "self-interest rightly understood," a materialism governed by reflection rather than passion. Hence Tocqueville considered four institutions that might help America avoid democracy's decline into decadence as a result of unfettered desire.

He looked to religion to keep Americans focused on their soul rather than the self; to law to keep them obedient to objective principles of justice; to commerce to turn their passions toward grainy practical affairs; and to the work ethic to keep them honoring honest labor as a way of life. Many readers of Tocqueville seize on his expression "habits of the heart" to claim he was optimistic about America. Actually, Tocqueville was apprehensive about the young republic, almost as though experiencing an anxiety attack in thinking about his subject. "This whole book," he stated in the introduction to *Democracy*, "has been written under the impulse of religious dread."[5] Tocqueville was haunted by the prospect that the future would spell the decadence of an American democracy incapable of disciplining its desires, a free people thinking they are in control when actually they are being controlled. What was potential in the nineteenth century became actual in the twentieth: Tocqueville's America became O'Neill's America; one thinker's worries became the other's realities.

The tentative hopes that Tocqueville had for America — the role of religion in saving people from "vicious materialism," the institution of law to inculcate respect for justice, the advent of commerce to make people prudent, and the presence of the work ethic to honor labor — are not to be found in O'Neill's outlook on America. Nor can they be found in Henry Adams and other anguished minds disinherited from the American past, such as the novelist John Dos Passos, the poet T. S. Eliot, or the political philosopher Walter Lippmann. In O'Neill's *The Hairy Ape* and in other plays, the worker is incapable not only of rising to class consciousness but of commanding any respect whatsoever; religion is indifferent to sin and guilt; economics fails to perform the civic role assigned to it; and the legal profession speaks in the voice of Caiaphas, who urged that Jesus be condemned to die on the cross. The rich and powerful strut down New York's posh Fifth Avenue in top hats and bible in hand, the paragons of respectability in a society that worships wealth without work. Religion, instead of compelling the powerful to know themselves, insulates them from reality and delivers them from what Christianity had assumed it had implanted in a fallen human nature: guilt for its sins. Christianity had taught the poor and powerless to invent a morality of meekness the better to control the mighty, as though an ethical sense would keep the ruling class in awe of the Ten Commandments. But the rich stroll down Fifth Avenue as though passing through the eye of the needle with no worry at all, completely free of "the bite of conscience" (Nietzsche).

*

Eugene O'Neill is the great dramatist of American democracy, but unlike the poet Walt Whitman, who sang its praises, the playwright probed its soul and found a betrayal of its own professed values. "Take your idiotic conscience to hell out of here," the husband says to his greedy wife in *More Stately Mansions*. "The possession of power is the only freedom, and your pretended disgust with it is a lie."

The rationalizing self that lies to itself will never know itself, particularly when it feigns disgust with its deepest desires. Many of O'Neill's characters are too weak to seek power, and those who do are too hypocritical to admit it. "Skin upon skin of the self must be peeled off if egotism is to be overcome," wrote a great theologian of tragedy, who, with O'Neill, tried to warn us that "the culture of every society seeks to obscure the brutalities upon which it rest."[6] O'Neill saw the same sins of self-deceit in America as he tended to see within himself and his own family. In *Long Day's Journey into Night,* the mother tells Edmund that his brother "can't help being what the past has made him. Anymore than your father can. Or you. Or I." But Edmund knows that his weakness is to try to deny what must be faced:

> Who wants to see life as it is, if they can help it? That's what I wanted — to be alone with myself in another world where truth is untrue and life can hide from itself.

O'Neill would have America see life as it is, even though we may need illusions to hide from ourselves. Americans cannot count on their political leaders to speak truth to pride. It was up to the playwright to do so by revealing to us who we are. Dealing with democracy and its driving ambitions, the playwright put on the stage what the social philosopher had put into a book. "This constant strife," wrote Tocqueville in *Democracy in America,* "between the desires inspired by equality and the means it supplies to satisfy them harasses and wearies the mind."[7] Tocqueville, too, dealt with desire under democracy, and the sociologist as well as the playwright observed how the mind can suffer from freedom as much as from oppression. In America, the conditions of freedom enabled people to do what they wanted, if only they knew what they wanted to do based on a grasp of who they really are. O'Neill saw, as had Tocqueville, that Americans live through the opinion of others and look upon themselves as others do. What was lost to modernity was the ancient Greeks' trust in the exercise of rational reflection as a means of knowing thyself. But in Tocqueville's democratic America, the gratification of desire becomes possible only to experience anxiety at its every hindrance and frustration. And in Eugene O'Neill's modern America, democracy leaves the mind uninformed of any conception of the desirable and with no easy means of self-identification. The specter that haunts democracy is desire, that mysteriously spontaneous emotional force that the will cannot govern and the mind cannot command. Faced with this modern human condition that threatens our sovereignty, the playwright may help us understand how difficult it is to come to know ourselves and become who we are, how difficult it is for America to be truly "the Land of the Free." A study of O'Neill's wrestling with the deceits of desire and power may also help us understand why our country allowed itself to believe it could bring democracy to the rest of the world even by means of military conquest. To be blind to our own follies is one definition of tragedy.

1

The Misery of the Misbegotten

IRISH ANCESTRY

The story of Eugene O'Neill's ancestry and that of his immediate family suggests how the emotion of desire could arise from the experience of desolation. The Irish came to America determined not to talk about the conditions that drove them from their home country. Family members knew that the past left an unspoken trauma on their lives, and when O'Neill's father James for once tried to break through and talk about the awful ordeals faced by his mother, the story of grief might almost have served as the beginning of healing. It was not to be. The O'Neill family carried the "curse of the misbegotten" to the grave. Reflecting on his decision to give up Shakespeare to earn a fortune acting in the popular theater, James continually asked himself, "What was it I wanted?" Material success proved inadequate to satisfy a deeper spiritual longing. Each O'Neill family member knew, in different ways, the meaning of unfulfilled desire, and each knew that in a competitive democracy frustrated desire only "harasses and wearies the mind" (Tocqueville).

*

"The critics have missed the most important thing about me and my work," Eugene O'Neill remarked to his son, Eugene Jr., in 1946: "the fact that I am Irish." The playwright took pride in his Irish ancestry and often would remind friends that in Gaelic the name O'Neill meant "champion." He suggested to the novelist James T. Farrell that he read Sean O'Faolain's

The Great O'Neill, a historical biography of Hugh O'Neill, the legendary Gaelic chief who ruled northern Ulster in the Elizabethan age.[1]

A far different matter troubled Eugene Jr. Why had his younger stepbrother, Shane O'Neill, become so alienated from their father, the eminent playwright? Was Shane following in the father's footsteps, as though the O'Neill family carried a genetic curse? Responding to his son's concern, O'Neill denied any such pattern:

> There was no other influence pulling me away from my father. My family's quarrels and tragedy were within. To the outer world we maintained an indomitably united front and lied and lied for each other. A typical pure Irish family. The same loyalty occurs, of course, in all kinds of families, but there is, I think, among Irish still close to, or born in Ireland, a strange mixture of fight and hate and forgive, a clannish pride before the world, that is particularly its own.

O'Neill went on to blame Shane's difficulties on his ex-wife Agnes Boulton, who allegedly used the substantial alimony she received from O'Neill to spoil the son. Shane the dropout and drifter was an embarrassment to O'Neill, and he explained to Eugene Jr. that his stepbrother had none of the "clannish pride" of the Irish:

> There is nothing like that in Shane's past. He has a background all torn apart, without inner or outer decency, the Boulton background — a laziness, a grafting, in which nothing is ever finished, a slow decay, spite, unscrupulousness, envy, ridiculous social aspirations, a hatred of anyone who succeeds. Bohemianism at its nasty silliest.[2]

To attribute fault and blame, such would be the hell that was the O'Neill family, a "strange mixture of fight and hate and forgive." Shane would go from alcohol to marijuana to morphine to heroin, and when not arrested as a junkie, was in and out of mental hospitals. Shane's plight brought back memories of O'Neill's own mother and her addiction years earlier. The other son, Eugene Jr., would start drinking heavily in the late forties, lose his professorship at Princeton, show up to a television show disheveled and incoherent, and commit suicide in 1950, a dreaded destiny that also awaited son Shane. The fate of the sons could not help but remind O'Neill of his old friend Terry Carlin, the Greenwich Village anarchist and mystic who, hoping to initiate O'Neill into Eastern religion, urged him to read *The Path to the Light* and absorb the advice "Desire only that which is in you. Desire only that which is beyond you. Desire only that which is unattainable."[3] Carlin, too, represented "Bohemianism at its nasty silliest," the Dionysian figure wild and furious rebelling against all reason and limitation. At one time handsome, talented, and witty, Carlin wasted his life away and ended up the model for one of the derelicts in *The Iceman Cometh*. So many people in O'Neill's life, consumed by desires that could be put out of mind only by drink or drugs, allowed their memory to destroy them. Only the human species permits itself to be tortured by the past, Nietzsche observed in *The Genealogy of Morals*. "A thing is branded on the memory to make it stay there; only what goes on hurting will stick."[4]

O'Neill's Irish background carried as much pain as pride. As with many Irish immigrants of the nineteenth century, the older O'Neill family was haunted by memories of the potato famine of the 1840s, and like other Irish Americans, the father James O'Neill saw the Irish as victims of British policy and all but defeated and dispossessed by history. The Irish immigrant experience is portrayed in all its poignant truth in O'Neill's autobiographical *Long Day's Journey into Night*. In recounting his childhood to his son Edmund, father Tyrone recalls:

My mother was left, a stranger in a strange land, with four small children, me and a sister a little older and two younger than me. My two older brothers had moved to other parts. They couldn't help. They were hard put to keep themselves alive. There was no damned romance in our poverty. Twice we were evicted from the miserable hovel we called home, with my mother's few sticks of furniture thrown out in the street, and my mother and sisters crying. I cried, too, though I tried hard not to, because I was the man of the family. At ten years old! There was no more school for me. I worked twelve hours a day in a machine shop, learning to make files. A dirty barn of a place where rain dripped through the roof, where you roasted in summer, and there was no stove in winter, and your hands got numb with cold, where only the light came through two small filthy windows, so on grey days I'd have to sit bent over with my eyes almost touching the files in order to see! You talk of work! And what do you think I got for it? Fifty cents a week! . . . And my poor mother washed and scrubbed for the Yanks by the day, and my sister sewed. . . . We never had clothes enough to wear, nor enough food to eat. Well I remember one Thanksgiving, or maybe it was Christmas, when some Yank in whose house mother had been scrubbing gave her a dollar extra for a present, and on the way home she spent it all on food. I can remember her hugging and kissing us and saying with tears of joy running down her tired face: "Glory be to God, for once in our lives we'll have enough for each of us!" (*He wipes tears from his eyes.*) A fine, brave, sweet woman. There never was a braver or finer.

Edmund agrees with his father that his mother was a rare miracle. After the father continues to recall his hardships—forever keeping the wolf from the door, investing in land rather than in unreliable banks, giving up a promising acting career in high culture out of fear of ending up back in the poorhouse—the son replies, "I'm glad you've told me this, Papa. I know you a lot better now."

Occasionally young O'Neill himself could feel such compassion toward his father. But in the autobiographical play, the father, named James Tyrone, comes off as a tightwad. The audience sees him standing on a chair unscrewing a lightbulb to save on the electricity bill, yet his stinginess seems understandable in view of the deprivations of his childhood. For the most part, however, the son remained unforgiving toward the father. James O'Neill behaved badly when he seemed reluctant to find the best medical care for his wife, and he also preferred to send his son to a state sanitarium to be treated for tuberculosis rather than to a private hospital. Above all, the father seemed to have embodied something that went wrong with America itself. Having to eke out an existence of brute struggle and bare sustenance, the father somehow managed to study acting, and when he rose to fame in the American theater in the 1870s, he played alongside Edwin Booth and alternated the roles of Brutus and Cassius, Iago and Othello. But from young Eugene's point of view, the fall from grace came in the following decade, when O'Neill senior made the momentous decision to forsake becoming America's most important Shakespearean actor in order to take on the lead role in *The Count of Monte Cristo*. The father, tall and handsome, performed almost nightly in that role for a quarter-century, making a fortune and at the same time sacrificing a reputation. He knew what he had done to himself. "I lost the talent I once had through years of easy repetition."

A matinee idol, James performed *Monte Cristo* thousands of times throughout the country, often taking his family on the road. Occasionally young O'Neill and his brother would play minor characters or work the props, and the budding playwright would come to hate the swashbuckling grandiloquence of the theater of that era. Yet some of that tradition would turn up in several of O'Neill's early plays, stagy with their histrionic characters, hyperbolic speech, and mannered affectations.

The family affected the playwright in many ways. Fear of poverty led O'Neill's father to seek financial security. To young O'Neill, however, the father's behavior could only be lamented for preferring fortune to fame.

Hence the family, particularly as headed by his father James O'Neill, becomes much like the story of American history itself. The father's "selling out" could be seen as symptomatic of the country's own yielding of its convictions for the sake of comfort. The study of the family bears many similarities to the study of history. We are born into our family, and we have no choice of who or what our parents are. History, the weight of the past, is inherited without the consent of the inheritors, and a country that once started out with the youthful high hopes of the colonial era continues to succumb to the compromises of maturity based upon old fears of scarcity. O'Neill's father made decisions based on felt needs, and the country too would see itself responding to need, as though the realm of necessity could never pass over into the realm of freedom. And freedom seems to express itself, to use Santayana's formulation, in wanting what we want rather than in being who we are. O'Neill sees America as a study in declension. The emotion of desire may have once had the potential for having a romantic or even a spiritual object, but historically it becomes lost to economics and the idolization of wealth. The father O'Neill only knew he wanted to make money, but he could not remember why or what he wanted to do with it.

The idea of tragedy in O'Neill is Hegelian as well as classical, not simply a fatal flaw of character or right against wrong but the conflict of right against right. Abraham Lincoln knew well the meaning of this form of tragedy during the Civil War, when saving the Union could have entailed sacrificing the cause of black emancipation. It was right that the Union be preserved and right that black Americans be freed. In the case of O'Neill's father, and of American history itself, the forsaking of earlier ideals to achieve material well-being could be justified as a rags-to-riches success story that helped bring the country into the world of modernity. But young O'Neill felt justified in protesting a country too willing to settle for less than the imagination demanded of history. One recalls the romantic imagination evoked in the conclusion of F. Scott Fitzgerald's *The Great Gatsby*. We are asked to ponder what America might have been like when the Dutch sailed up the Hudson River and saw the "fresh green breast of the New World," and "for a transitory and enchanted moment man must have held his breath in the presence of this continent, compelled into an aesthetic he neither understood nor desired, face to face for the last time in history with something commensurate to his capacity for wonder." Fitzgerald's American Dream lived on in the remote past, perhaps more imagined than real. To O'Neill, the promise of American life had been compromised from the very beginning, with the first landing of Spaniards, who spoke of God while searching for gold. He would hardly be enchanted by Fitzgerald's Dutch sailors. O'Neill's seventeenth-century explorers to the New World brought the sins of the Old World with them. On the playwright's stage prowled the specter of corruption.

"WHY THE DEVIL WAS I EVER BORN AT ALL?"

O'Neill's troubled emotions remained with him almost from birth to death, as though he entered the world as a crime and left it with a curse. And his struggles with his self took place in the family before O'Neill perceived the tragic character of American history. Leo Tolstoi instructed us to look not to the normalcy of everyday life, where all happy families are the same, but to the sad spectacle of unhappy families, where each family is uniquely unhappy in its own way. Democracy may offer the possibility of freedom, but domesticity is often the setting for what an O'Neill character called "the idealistic fallacy," the commandment to be good even if it meant the suffocation of the self.

Why did O'Neill feel that the most important fact about himself was his Irish nationality and ethnic identity? The immigration experience seemed to have remained in his genes. James O'Neill was born in County Kilkenny in Ireland, and in 1849, at the age of five, he came to America. Many of his people who arrived in the nineteenth century saw themselves as exiles, and one historian has described the Irish as "the most homesick of all the immigrants." Longing for the old country, the Irish looked upon America as the country in which they could reach levels of achievement but only at the cost of betraying their original identity. After several generations many Irish exiles surmounted poverty and prejudice to achieve status and respectability and even assimilation. But for some Americanization seemed the result of compulsion rather than decision, and the Irish-American mentality remained torn between pride and self-pity. As late as 1900, Irish-American Catholic neighborhoods were still marked by what a historian has called a "self-indulgent community morbidity." The journals of immigrants sag with anguish and insecurity, and fathers would remind sons of what O'Neill senior called "the value of the dollar and the fear of the poorhouse." Success seldom brought ease and confidence, and the Irish character was often "ravaged by an alcoholism born of crippling self-doubt."[5]

Eugene O'Neill, skeptical that there would be any place he truly belonged, bore the burden of the Irish immigrant experience in yet more personal terms. To Yankee Americans the availability of land represented the great promise of American life, and private property became synonymous with political liberty. Yet in O'Neill's plays, property becomes either a matter of deprivation or desperation, a plot of land from which a family is about to be evicted (*Moon for the Misbegotten*) or a farm that the sons cannot wait to seize from the father (*Desire Under the Elms*). Doubts that one could ever enjoy property accompanied the arriving Irish immigrants, driven off the land in the old country.

Young O'Neill could also not forget that his grandfather had abandoned his wife and eight children to return to Ireland. Deserted women and widows were as common to this community as Irish men hanging out in taverns to the late hours of the night. Few of O'Neill's characters would look to their home as a haven in a heartless world. O'Neill had read Emerson and Thoreau but he wondered whether he would ever "know thyself" or even if there was a core self to know. When he thought about his family, he felt a certain helplessness and guilt for the pitiful condition of its members. And having lost his Catholic faith, he had little to fall back on to ease his torments, as did other children of Irish immigrants who could clear their conscience by going to confession. O'Neill had to live with the restless striving of his own soul. Whether it derived from his personal experience, he readily universalized his sense of the human condition and projected it onto those who were far from Irish immigrants. In *The Great God Brown* the playwright dramatized, and perhaps exaggerated, the ordeal of the divided self, utterly disoriented yet holding on to sanity. One character, Dion, asks with what is described as a "suffering bewilderment,"

> Why am I afraid to dance, I who love music and rhythm and grace and song and laughter? Why am I afraid to live, I who love life and the beauty of the flesh and the living colors of earth and sky and sea? Why am I afraid of love, I who love love? Why am I afraid, I who am not afraid? Why must I pretend to scorn in order to pity? Why must I hide myself in self-contempt in order to understand? Why must I be so ashamed of my strength, so proud of my weakness? Why must I live in a cage like a criminal, defying and hating, I who love peace and friendship? Why was I born without a skin, O God, that I must wear armor in order to touch or to be touched? . . . why the devil was I ever born at all?

The Irish immigrant experience cannot possibly offer a complete explanation of O'Neill's life of anguish and torment. For most people memories of material deprivation rarely lead to metaphysical *angst*. As George Orwell noted, it is only in good times that "cosmic despair" flourishes among the intellectual class, as though alienation is the luxury of the fortunate few.[6] What the experience does explain is why O'Neill was determined never to follow in his father's footsteps by accepting life as a compromise and regarding his literary craft as an economic opportunity. In other respects O'Neill's background is no different from that of many ethnic groups that emerge from the traumas of history with a sense of survivor's guilt. But not all survivors are blessed with genius.[7]

*

Eugene O'Neill was born in a New York City hotel, on Broadway and 43rd Street, on October 16, 1888. The acting career of his father kept the family on continuous road tours living out of a suitcase and a wardrobe trunk. But the father dressed handsomely, something of a "dandy" and "Broadway sport." The mother, Mary Ellen Quinlan (known as Ella), a graduate of a convent academy in Indiana, was pious, demure, lovely, and perhaps too fragile for the rough life with an actor on the move from city to city. In later life she reminisced about having wanted to become a nun, only to have met the handsome, irresistible actor James O'Neill. Possibly pregnant at the time of their marriage in 1877, not long afterwards she gave birth to James Jr. Ten years older than Eugene, he was a precocious youth who would go on to waste his talents on drinking and whoring, a pathetic, haunting figure whom O'Neill would depict in two of his last plays, a mother's pet who could never grow up to break free of his emotional bondage — and yet, as O'Neill's first wife Agnes Boulton remembered him, Jamie was a *bon vivant* who saw life as a joke he wanted to share with everyone. "The world was his oyster," she recalled, "and he had eaten it, and that was that."[8]

After James a second son, Edmund, was born in 1884 and died a year and a half later, having caught the flu from Jamie, leaving all the family members feeling somehow responsible. When Eugene himself was born, the delivery was so painful for Ella that the doctor prescribed morphine. Years later O'Neill's mother would become addicted to the drug, and the son could hardly forgive himself for having entered the world so hurtfully. After repressing for almost a half-century his anguished memory of his family members, O'Neill recalled them in *Long Day's Journey into Night,* a play written, he told his wife, in "blood and tears." He also requested that the work be kept from the public until twenty-five years after his death.

Many scholars contend that to know the mind and thought of Eugene O'Neill is to understand how his character and temperament had been shaped by the painfully troubled conditions of his early family background. Surrounded by a disgruntled father who regretted what he himself had become, a weak older brother who was drinking himself to death and trying to drag his younger brother down with him, and a fragile mother who neglected her son as she succumbed to reverie and daily doses of morphine, young O'Neill had three strikes against him before he stepped up to the plate. The posthumous production of *Long Day's Journey* in 1956, staged only three years after O'Neill's death, made Americans aware of what their greatest playwright had been struggling with as he faced the demons of memory. The play is indeed an open wound that raises one of the most intriguing questions in the history of culture. Is there a connection between pain and creativity?

No doubt pain resided deeply in O'Neill's psyche. The rapid sequence of deaths of family members and friends established the persistent condition of mourning and grief that runs through O'Neill's plays and constitutes their leitmotif of sorrow.[9] The psychological understanding of creativity born of suffering also resonated in ancient classical literature, a subject that intrigued O'Neill and led him to regret that he never learned Greek.

With O'Neill, however, it is difficult to separate the personal from the social. The playwright focused on society as well as the self, and he perceived the masses of humanity leading lives of "pipe dreams" and escapist enchantment. O'Neill also delved into subjects that rarely came up within the circle of his family, especially politics, the working class, and sympathy for the oppressed; race, the ghetto, and the plight of black Americans; women, feminism, free love, and gender identity; and history itself, from Marco Polo to Ponce de Leon to the America of Andrew Jackson and Abraham Lincoln. O'Neill was too wide ranging a thinker to have his thoughts reduced to childhood determinants. Moreover, he himself could never forget the turmoil of his family background while at the same time remaining uncertain whether it explained much beyond the family. Self-knowledge would remain a mystery to O'Neill. "I am a great believer in all we don't know about ourselves, but inclined to skepticism about what we think we know."[10] Those who know they know, or think they do, may well remain unknown to themselves. Sean O'Casey agreed with the critic George Jean Nathan that O'Neill had surpassed him and George Bernard Shaw in plumbing the depths of human emotion. The Irish playwright then added: "I've often envied him this gift. I've pondered his plays, & tried to discover how he came by it, & of course, never could; for the man doesn't know himself."[11]

"OH GOD — THOSE OLD DAYS": THE EARLY YEARS

O'Neill attended prep schools in Connecticut and entered Princeton University in 1903, only to be expelled for campus pranks and cutting class. He could have returned to Princeton the following year, but the life of a student had little appeal to him. He became a secretary in a New York mail-ordering house while spending his spare time reading and talking enthusiastically to his roommates about Schopenhauer. In the summer of 1909, on a double date, he became involved with Kathleen Jenkins and soon found himself in a sexual affair more casual for him than for her. Learning of her pregnancy caused O'Neill to come close to panic, and his friends urged him to wed her immediately. Kathleen's parents went to see the O'Neills, and the Catholic conscience of all four looked to marriage as the only solution. O'Neill's father, however, had suspicions that the less well-off Jenkins family saw Eugene as a good catch, and understanding that his son had no real love for Kathleen, he suggested buying her off. Eugene knew that Kathleen would be offended, and he concluded he had to go down the aisle with the woman he had no intention of living with or seeing again. Right after the marriage, his father helped him find work as a deckhand on a steamer bound for Honduras, and he eagerly shipped out leaving behind an expectant wife.

O'Neill's father hoped his wayward son would straighten out in South America and return having made a man of himself. While prospecting for gold excited the youth, the muddy trails and mosquitoes wore him down, as did the sights of poverty and filth. Back in America he drifted around in New England for several months and then signed on as an able-bodied seaman on a Norwegian vessel headed to Buenos Aires. On this voyage, and on another to London, the discovery of the sea proved a mystical experience for O'Neill and its beckoning presence would be felt in several of his future plays. "I became drunk with the beauty and singing rhythm of it," he recalled in his plays of the rolling ocean and its flying spray, "and for a moment I lost myself—actually lost my life." He felt "peace and unity and wild joy." He "belonged to Life itself! To God, if you want to put it that way."

In Buenos Aires he held respectable, though temporary, office jobs and soon found himself seeking companions among the denizens of the waterfront and often sleeping on park benches, experiencing the life of a sailor "on the beach." He enjoyed the camaraderie with seamen and thought of Joseph Conrad and of sailors so loyal and generous that they would give one the shirt off their back. O'Neill was at home with the renegades of the world. "I landed in Buenos Aires a gentleman so-called, and wound up a bum on the docks in fact."[12]

In 1911, back in America, he hung out at "Jimmy the Priest's," a run-down saloon and rooming house on lower New York's Fulton Street. O'Neill paid $3 a month for a room upstairs, in case he wanted to escape the backroom where heads reclined asleep on the tables, a place of rest bought for the cost of a five-cent schooner of beer. Waterfront taverns resembling this din of iniquity would be the setting of several of his plays. It was a scene of sorrow and pity, the habitues even more desperate than Edward Hopper's "nighthawks," whom the artist drew at least sipping coffee. The characters O'Neill knew were dissolute, bottomed out on the bottle. "No one ever wanted to go to bed," recalls O'Neill's friend Dorothy Day of the scene in Jimmy the Priest's, "and no one ever wished to be alone."[13]

The following year O'Neill arranged to be in a room with a prostitute, feigning adultery in order to establish grounds for his divorce from Kathleen Jenkins, now the mother of the son he had never seen. A decade passed before O'Neill met his son, Eugene O'Neill Jr., by then eleven years old. Both father and son were nervous as they shook hands, but they hit it off and O'Neill let Kathleen know he would pay for the boy's education. Eugene Jr. remained close to his father and years later became a professor of classics at Yale. But, alas, he too would have a sad ending.

The year 1912, the "Lyric Year" to the bohemians of the exciting Greenwich Village rebellion, was the winter of despair for O'Neill. Ill, emaciated, drunk on cheap liquor, "blotto whenever I could be," he hit bottom. From a pharmacist he bought veronal tablets, went up to his room at Jimmy the Priest's and swallowed them down, determined to commit suicide. Semi-conscious, he heard knocks at the door, not knowing whether he was alive or "not dead yet, but on my way." Then a "horrible thought" hit him, suggestive of Schopenhauer's idea of the irrepressible will to live and Nietzsche's of the eternal return. "I was dead, of course, *and death was nothing but a continuation of life as it had been when one left it!* A wheel that turned endlessly round and round back to the same old situation. This was what purgatory was — or was it hell itself? My body was dead, but *I* was there too." His downstairs cronies broke into the room and revived him by standing him up and forcing him to walk. Then they went back down to the flophouse bar to celebrate his return from the dead. The gang at Jimmy the Priest's, who also knew that death was no escape from life, would become the characters of *The Iceman Cometh*, the living dead who would keep on drinking to find peace once the mind ceased thinking. *"Oh God—those old days,"* O'Neill told Agnes Boulton. *"Nobody'd believe it. Nobody'd understand it."*[14]

In December 1912, O'Neill entered a sanitarium with tuberculosis, and during his convalescence at the Gaylord Farm in Connecticut he started to read omnivorously "the Greeks and the Elizabethans — practically all the classics — and of course all the moderns. Ibsen and Strindberg, especially Strindberg." Sleeping outdoors and swimming in his beloved ocean, O'Neill began to recover and to write a series of one-act plays and some poetry. In the sanitarium he had a brief romance with fellow patient Catherine Mackay, who became the subject of the play *The Web*. In 1914 he went to Harvard to enroll in George Pierce Baker's famous course in playwrighting, announcing as he stepped into Professor Baker's office, "I want to be a writer or nothing." The work O'Neill developed in the course did little to impress Baker, but the student would always remember that his teacher encouraged him to believe in his work and continue with confidence. "He helped us to hope," O'Neill later said of Baker at the time of his death, "and for that we owe him all the finest we have in memory of gratitude and friendship."[15]

*

Neither the esteemed professor nor the budding playwright could look to his own country as a source of inspiration. The early American stage remained too cheerful to be a training ground for young O'Neill. During the nineteenth century the audience had sat through a repertoire of polite plots, adolescent melodrama, swashbuckling romance, chirpy choruses, burlesque and farce, and an occasional play about a prostitute or "fallen" woman that reassured America of its own virtue. Perhaps the one serious moment was New York City's three-day Astor Place riot of 1849: the British Shakespearean William Macready had allegedly sneered at American actors, leading to scuffles in the newly constructed Astor Place Opera House. The notorious gangs of New York showed up to turn a cultural event into class warfare.

In the decades after the Civil War, the theater returned to its commercial norms, and O'Neill's father, James O'Neill, having once starred as Hamlet and Othello, became the protagonist in *The Count of Monte Cristo*. Night after night for almost twenty years he performed the role no less than six thousand times and earned $40,000 annually (about $800,000 in today's dollar value), though at the end of his life he regarded the play as a "curse." With *Monte Cristo* and other popular plays, the spectators of the late nineteenth century bought their tickets and took their seats expecting to be entertained and even flattered. They were.

Then, coming out of nowhere, Eugene O'Neill appeared upon the scene in 1916, producing a one-act play that might have been titled, in view of its existential dread, "As He Lay Dying" (the actual title was *Bound East for Cardiff*). The American theater would never be the same, and it would never look back for guidance and direction. So thin and bland had been the older American drama that O'Neill had to draw his inspiration from Europeans, adopting some of the daring plots of Scandinavian playwrights, the philosophical perspectives of German thinkers, and the political passions of Russian anarchists. From such sources O'Neill went on to become arguably America's greatest playwright, winning four Pulitzer awards and the Nobel Prize.

The modern theater stands as the great cultural surprise of American history. The Puritans had banished plays and music as distractions to the soul, and later thinkers doubted that democracy itself could produce titans of talent. In the nineteenth century, Emerson and Tocqueville worried about a mass society mired in mediocrity and an egalitarian democracy that sought its revenge on those who dared to be different. Quoting Aristotle's observation "that no great genius was ever without some mixture of madness," Emerson wondered how America would recognize such an "agitated soul" and how a democracy could look upon Shakespeare as anything other than "miraculous." Writing in the 1830s, Tocqueville advised that "if you want advance knowledge of the literature of a people which is turning toward democracy, pay attention to the theatre." Although different social classes might intermingle within the audience, Tocqueville doubted democracy could rise to high culture since spectators think only of the present and wish to see no one but themselves on the stage. "Democratic peoples have but little reverence for learning and scarcely bother at all about what happened in Rome and Athens."[16]

Twentieth-century intellectuals similarly sensed the limitations of American culture as "the lost generation" of writers fled to Europe. O'Neill knew some of the members of that generation, particularly the critic Malcolm Cowley and the poet Hart Crane. *Civilization in the United States,* a manifesto of the future expatriates mapped out and edited by Harold Stearn in 1920, was a collection of essays by various authors in different fields who each judged America harshly for failing to produce a culture hospitable to the creative mind. Yet in that same year America applauded the performance of a new play *Beyond the Horizon* and awarded its author the Pulitzer. O'Neill had accomplished what Emerson thought improbable: he brought the "hopeless commiseration" and "paralyzing terror" of Greek tragedy to an America a little too content with itself:[17]

I have been accused of unmitigated gloom. Is this a pessimistic view of life? I do not think so. There is skin deep optimism and another higher optimism, not skin deep, which is usually confounded with pessimism. To me, the tragic alone has that significant beauty which is truth. It is the meaning of life — and the hope. The noblest is eternally the most tragic. The people who succeed and do not push on to a greater failure are the spiritual middle classes. Their stopping at success is proof of their compromising insignificance. How petty their dreams have been! The man who pursues the mere attainable should be sentenced to get it — and keep it. . . . Only through the unattainable does man achieve a hope worth living and dying for—and so attain himself. He with the spiritual guerdon of a hope in hopelessness, is nearest to the stars and the rainbow's feet.[18]

Thus spoke Eugene Gladstone O'Neill.

*

During the years 1915–1916 O'Neill lived in New York's Greenwich Village and in the fishing village of Provincetown, Massachusetts. He found companions and drinking partners among the radicals of the labor movement, particularly the anarcho-syndicalists of the I.W.W., the Industrial Workers of the World, known as the Wobblies. He became a close friend of John Reed, who would play an important role as the founding father of American communism and the author of *The Ten Days That Shook the World.* The quiet, brooding O'Neill was attracted to Reed's wild exuberance. He also had a brief affair with Reed's wife, Louise Bryant, who accompanied Reed to Russia to observe the Bolsheviks in power. While Reed was writing about political struggles, O'Neill was pondering the world, depicting man in relation to the mysterious forces of nature, in short, demanding the meaning of existence. Then on July 28, 1916, American drama had its modern birth.

"THEN WE KNEW WHAT WE WERE FOR!"

On that evening the Provincetown Players performed O'Neill's *Bound East for Cardiff,* a one-act play that tells of a dying sailor on a tramp freighter and the stark loneliness that overcomes the sailor's friend upon his death. All dialogue and no action, the play forces the audience to face the fear of life running out, fighting the despair of annihilation and the possible nothingness that follows. "It's hard to ship on this voyage I'm goin on—alone!" murmurs Yank, who imagines he is visited by a "pretty lady dressed in black" right before he dies.

This early existential theme was far removed from the mawkish sentimentality and escapist romanticism that had characterized the American theater until O'Neill arrived on the scene. Days before the performance, when members of the Provincetown Players read the script, they suddenly realized that the search for the appropriate playwright to bring America into the modern world had ended. "Then we knew," said the playwright Susan Glaspell, "what we were for!"[19]

*

Father O'Neill had no reason to expect that his son would go onto fame and even fortune. In 1914 James O'Neill had paid for the cost of publishing a volume of his son's one-act plays. Subsequently, during World War I, young O'Neill wrote a series of plays set on the high seas as well as some subversive poems and sketches for future dramatic treatment. He met the writer Agnes Boulton and married her in 1918, spending the following year at his wife's home in New Jersey recording further ideas for plays. In 1920 his *Beyond the Horizon* appeared on Broadway and won him the Pulitzer. His father was in the audience on opening night, and legend has it that the elder O'Neill wept when the performance concluded, at last seeing his son a success and not the boozer and wastrel that he feared he would become.

But O'Neill himself continued to drink, perhaps to escape the personal problems that would plague him. The slow, cancerous death of his father in 1920 soon after *Horizon*'s debut was followed by his mother's death in 1922. So distraught was O'Neill that on the opening night of his success, *The Hairy Ape,* he could not bring himself to go to the railroad station to meet his mother's coffin on its arrival from Los Angeles and instead spent the night walking the streets of New York. A year later his brother Jamie, who had been in and out of sanitariums, died as a consequence of a life of alcoholism.

In the mid-1920s O'Neill continued to win praise for plays that dealt with a variety of subjects, from race relations, love and marriage, and the working class, to modern science and religion and the early exploration of the American continent. He ceased his heavy drinking and smoking, convinced that such abuses had killed his brother. The abstinence helped him overcome his insomnia and to enjoy long swims in the ocean. He became something of a public figure interviewed in the press and mentioned in society columns. His plays also enjoyed the respect of leading literary intellectuals such as George Jean Nathan, Edmund Wilson, T. S. Eliot, Joseph Wood Krutch, and Lionel Trilling. In the same decade America witnessed the rise of the Hollywood film industry, and some intellectuals complained of the lavish spectacle and expense that aimed to draw the masses to the movie box office, all at the cost of genuine dramatic art. "Someday," wrote the acerbic H. L. Mencken, "someone with an authentic movie mind will make a cheap and simple picture that will arrest the notice of the civilized minority as it was arrested by the early plays of Eugene O'Neill."[20]

Although born right in New York City's Times Square, the hub of the commercial theater, O'Neill was continually drawn away from the city's polluted rivers and toward the reinvigorating ocean, what Herman Melville called "the watery parts of the world." For several years he spent the summer and fall with his wife living in an abandoned Coast Guard station on Cape Cod, so isolated on the dunes that his shack could not be reached by car, so desolate that occasionally he could count only on a porpoise for a swimming companion. In the late 1920s Agnes and Eugene moved to Bermuda and took up residence in a beach cottage at Spithead, with the clear, blue-green crystalline tropical Atlantic lapping at its bulkhead.

Back in New York, overseeing the rehearsals of *Strange Interlude* and *Marco Millions,* O'Neill became involved with the attractive actress Carlotta Monterey, who years earlier had played a minor role in *The Hairy Ape.* Carlotta had been married to her third husband and living at the Hotel des Artistes when one evening she returned unexpectedly from an out-of-town play and found her husband in bed with another woman. Her affair with O'Neill commencing after her divorce, Carlotta was the opposite of the more aloof and intellectual Agnes. Named "Miss California" as a teenager in 1907, she was born Hazel Nielson Tharsing, later assuming the more striking name of Carlotta Monterey. Sultry, high strung, overly dramatic, Carlotta nevertheless found herself absorbed in O'Neill and dedicated to his work. O'Neill's breakup with Agnes was drawn out and costly both emotionally and financially. But upon their marriage, O'Neill and Carlotta moved to Sea Island, Georgia, where he wrote his only popular comedy, *Ah, Wilderness!,* a play that strikingly showed another side of the playwright, his longing for a normal and nurturing family and a comfortable childhood.

It is hard to imagine O'Neill choosing the life of the youth depicted in his single comedy, for he was given to a tragic view of life. He saw humanity at the mercy of mysterious forces, whether unconscious, repressed drives, as in Freud's theory of the emotions; or the external movements of nature that snub humanity with their indifference, as in Herman Melville's outlook; or the human will to accept the conflicting conditions of life and yet triumph over despair, as in the Greeks, Shakespeare, and Nietzsche. O'Neill would be remembered instead for such a play as *Mourning Becomes Electra,* which helped win him the Nobel Prize in 1936. His natural theme was tragedy, a subject that could be elevated, if properly handled, to give meaning and significance to life. With O'Neill, political philosophy reverses its original premise: we are born fated, and everywhere we struggle to be free, and in that struggle lies a certain nobility. O'Neill's plays may rock with some laughter, but he was not cut out for comedy. "This world is a comedy to those who think," observed Horace Walpole, "a tragedy to those who feel."

O'Neill's earlier raucous drinking bouts could bring out the humorous side of the playwright as he took to the piano to pound out risqué ditties. No doubt he would smile at the graffiti in the working-class Irish bar: "I'd rather have a bottle in front of me than a frontal lobotomy." His early seedy life in waterfront dives masked his actual good looks, which developed in the twenties after he settled down. O'Neill was tall, slender, handsome, often tan, with high cheekbones and dark, piercing eyes staring with luminous intensity. His silent stillness intimidated the actress Ingrid Bergman. "One hardly dared to speak to him. Then, as he came closer, I saw those eyes. They were the most beautiful eyes I have seen in my whole life. They were like wells; you just fell into them." Others were struck by his severe gauntness. "Everything about him seems to be long and thin," observed journalist Mary B. Mullett, even his hands and fingers, "the longest I have ever seen . . . the type of hands that go with a dreamer temperament." Our contemporary writer John McPhee, looking at a striking merchant marine sailor, observed: "He had the metabolism of Eugene O'Neill; six feet tall and weightless." O'Neill was not known to roar with laughter but when he smiled he radiated delight and at least a momentary happiness. More often O'Neill's spirits sagged with worry and depression. He took life seriously, perhaps too seriously, but like his hero Nietzsche he could find a certain joy in tragedy, and as with the philosopher so with the playwright — neither could forget that without Christianity life ceases to have meaning. One of O'Neill's final unfinished plays, "The Last Conquest," has Satan and Christ in a dialogue, each realizing they need one another to remind the world that good and evil exist and that life is not about comfort and pleasure but conflict and struggle. A fellow Greenwich Village rebel, Max Eastman, tellingly described O'Neill as "darkly handsome but somber and sallow, as a down-and-outer brought to Jesus by the Salvation Army.[21]

"GOD DAMMIT, DIED IN A HOTEL ROOM": THE LAST YEARS

In the mid-1930s O'Neill's health, both mental and physical, began to weaken, and doctors advised him to take a rest in order to avoid a nervous breakdown. His most recent play, *Days Without End*, where he seemed to be considering returning to the Catholic faith, had been a critical failure when it appeared in 1934. For twelve years O'Neill would produce nothing for the stage and remain in reclusion at Tao House, which he and Carlotta purchased in the East Bay across from San Francisco. Husband and wife busied themselves expanding the dwelling: she purchased Oriental furniture, he supervised the building of a swimming pool. O'Neill, an old comrade of the working class, discovered his wife growling when having to deal with electricians and plumbers and convincing herself that the growing strength of labor unions, thanks to Franklin Roosevelt, spelled the decline of America. But the O'Neills enjoyed the Bay Area, and Eugene would travel to Berkeley to watch the Saturday football games, delighted and amused that he could sit among fifty thousand spectators without being recognized.

Although little heard from, O'Neill was far from idle. During this period of withdrawal he had begun to work on an eleven-play cycle, though the scheme of its continuity began to elude him as he discovered he had difficulty making clear when the plot of one play ended and the next began. One play did see its way to completion, *A Touch of the Poet,* and was successfully produced posthumously years later in 1957. But after the war *The Iceman Cometh* had a mixed reception, and *A Moon for the Misbegotten* closed during its road tour in 1947 before it even reached Broadway.

The post–World War II years, following the defeat of Hitler and the end of the Great Depression, brightened for most Americans but not for O'Neill and his family. The playwright's health gravely deteriorated. Suffering from something similar to Parkinson's disease, he developed a neurological disorder that caused his hands to tremble so violently he could barely hold a pencil. O'Neill dreaded that he might never be able to write again, and he tried dictating his scripts, to no avail. Family matters only deepened his depression. His teenage daughter Oona had fallen in love with Charlie Chaplin, and O'Neill disapproved of her marrying a man three times her age, especially a Hollywood actor with a reputation for womanizing. His relation to Carlotta, always rocky — they were at once attracted to one another and repelled by their mutual need — deteriorated into quarrels and recriminations. One of O'Neill's sons, Shane, had taken to drugs and was always asking for bail money; the other, Eugene Jr., a classics professor, committed suicide in 1950. When a friend phoned to try to inform O'Neill, Carlotta flew into a rage, exclaiming "How dare you invade our privacy!" Carlotta told her husband instead that his son was "very ill," but O'Neill knew the worst and withdrew into further grief and reclusion as the two agreed to live apart.[22]

In his last years, 1951–1953, O'Neill lived in Boston and reconciled with Carlotta, who kept him isolated from his old friends. Debilitated by illness, he ordered Carlotta to destroy the remaining unfinished plays in his cycle, some of which had been trashed earlier. On February 5, 1951, Eugene and Carlotta had a bitter fight and he rushed out of the house into the winter snow. Did he intend to jump into the icy Charles River nearby and, with the suicide of his son in mind, take his own life? Whatever his intent, he slipped on the sidewalk and broke his leg. In pain and freezing from the cold, he called out to Carlotta. He later told a close friend that Carlotta opened the door, looked down, and spoke in vengeance. "How the mighty have fallen! The master is lying low! Now where is all your greatness!" She shut the door and he passed out. Someone called a doctor, who carried the frail O'Neill back into the house, and he was later rushed to Salem Hospital. The next night the police found Carlotta walking the streets talking irrationally. She was taken to the same hospital for a psychiatric examination.[23]

Most of their friends thought the marriage was over. But O'Neill and Carlotta dropped their divorce proceedings, reconciled again, and took a suite in a hotel. Coming down with pneumonia, O'Neill, now sixty-five, spent much of his time in bed. Carlotta would carry his emaciated body to the window where he could look down at the Charles River and see the water that had once reinvigorated his body. Hotel guests and staff heard some ferocious quarrels coming from their room. While O'Neill could barely cope with his helplessness, Carlotta became increasingly hostile, even to the point of hurling anti-Semitic remarks at one of O'Neill's closest friends. Perhaps the only good news came from daughter Oona, who wrote to say she had given birth to her second son, named Eugene after her father. Oona and Charles Chaplin would have eight children and a long, happy, loving marriage. The playwright, alas, would know nothing of it.

On November 27, 1953, Eugene O'Neill died in the Hotel Shelton in Boston and was buried in a private ceremony at Forest Hills Cemetery. Among his last words were "Born in a hotel room and, god dammit, died in a hotel room."

*

O'Neill had written his most famous play, *Long Day's Journey into Night,* in 1940, the year after World War II erupted in Europe, and he deposited a sealed copy of it with publishers at Random House in 1945, the year the war ended, on the condition it would not be opened until twenty-five years after his death and stipulating that while it could be published, it should never be produced as a play. Three years after his death Carlotta thought better of her husband's will and released the play to Stockholm's Royal Dramatic Theatre, where it opened on February 2, 1956. In the fall of the year it opened on Broadway and won for O'Neill his fourth Pulitzer Prize.

Long Day's Journey is considered by many critics as among the greatest plays in modern drama. It is also O'Neill's most sincere and authentic work, and certainly his most personal. The Tyrones' house is the house young Eugene lived in in New London, Connecticut, with fog wafting and foghorns sounding on the stage as they had in real life. As were the members of his own family, the play's characters are unfulfilled, resentful, divided human beings. It is this play more than any other that has come to identify O'Neill as part of a family whose psychic effects he could never escape. In the play characters are at each other's throats, hissing hurtful judgments. The family becomes the setting for tragedy, the house of the damned whose members are weak, possessive, chronically needy, unable to feel deeply for anyone other than themselves; the miracle of love that might have moved them dies stillborn. They are lost in the fog, asking why their lives have come to this, and why has no answer. There is something Irish in the sight of suffering that is more mystical than reasonable. One thinks of Daniel Patrick Moynihan's remark upon hearing of the assassination of John Fitzgerald Kennedy: "What's the use of being Irish unless you know that eventually life will break your heart."

The personal torments of *Long Day's Journey into Night* have left a deep impression among those who have seen the play in the past half-century. It seems that we are witnessing a theater of therapy for O'Neill to work out his own emotional problems with his family. But it was not only his family that left O'Neill in anguish. It was also the human condition and the narrative of American history itself. O'Neill went beyond his own biography to help Americans understand themselves, and he addressed many issues that rarely came up within the O'Neill family. Still, he could never forget his father who, like America itself, everyone regarded as a success story. O'Neill thought otherwise of his father and of his country:

> My father died broken, unhappy, intensely bitter, feeling that life was "a damned hard billet to chew." His last words to me—when his speech had almost failed him—were: "Eugene—I'm going to a better sort of life. This sort of life—here—all froth—no good—rottenness!" This after seventy-six years of what the mob undoubtedly regard as a highly successful career! It furnishes food for thought, what? I have quoted his words verbatim. They are written indelibly—seared on my brain—a warning from the Beyond to remain true to the best that is in me though the heavens fall.[24]

O'Neill's idol Friedrich Nietzsche well understood that settling for ordinary life besmirches the highest ideals of which humankind is capable, and hence, as in *Thus Spoke Zarathustra,* the sin of the father must be expiated:

> What was silent in the father speaks in the son; and often I found the son unveiled in the secret of the father.

2

The Playwright as Thinker

O'NEILL AND HIS CRITICS:
HIGH AND LOW CULTURE

The playwright's role in history cannot be appreciated apart from that of the critic and of the public. The vicissitudes of authors' reputations may be as telling as the criticisms made of their works. During O'Neill's productive years, few readers were aware of the writings of Alexis de Tocqueville, who was not really discovered in America until after World War II, and hence the public continued to see American democracy as a morally healthy proposition and in no need of a severe analysis by a brooding literary intellectual. Even fewer Americans had read Friedrich Nietzsche, and those who did knew that his reputation had fallen on hard times with the rise of Nazism. After victory in war the American people could hardly be expected to understand what the German philosopher meant when he claimed that democracy has a rendezvous with decadence as well as destiny; or, for that matter, what the French thinker meant when he described desire in America as knowing no bounds and democracy's "soul" as knowing no rest. Nor could Americans readily understand what was bothering Eugene O'Neill.

That was surely the case with the first production of *The Iceman Cometh* in 1946. Critics panned the play, and the audience left the theater confused and weary after the five-hour ordeal. While its author may have had no intention of making Americans happy about themselves and their country, he did wish to help Americans understand themselves. "The people in that saloon were the best friends I've ever known," he said about the seventeen characters in the play. "Their weakness was not an evil. It is a weakness found in all men."[1]

The play was one of the last O'Neill completed and the very last of his enduring works that he lived to see produced on stage. We shall return to it in the concluding chapter of this text as his final statement of the pessimism and nihilism that came to dominate his brooding, penetrating mind. But first it is necessary to address the critics who have dismissed O'Neill as a playwright without a serious intellect.

The Iceman Cometh's unsuccessful debut may have had less to do with the promising social conditions of the time than with the shortcomings of the director and the actors involved in the first production. When it was revived off-Broadway in 1956, produced by Theodore Mann, directed by Jose Quintero, and starring Jason Robards as Hickey, the play was a great success and won critical praise as a work of dramatic art. The earlier production, however, left critics confused if not downright hostile. Mary McCarthy complained that O'Neill had no idea of how real drunks behave: no slobbering, no shakes, no hangovers, no "semi-schizoid silences, no obscurity of thought, no dark innuendoes, no flashes of hatred . . . none of the terror of drink" that culminate in the "destruction of personality." McCarthy also assailed O'Neill for trying to situate his nihilistic philosophical outlook in the lower depths of dereliction. "His intention is symbolic and philosophical, but unfortunately you cannot write Platonic dialogues in the style of *Casey at the Bat.*"[2]

Criticisms of O'Neill's plays long antedated the performance of his post–World War II productions. Francis Ferguson, who would write the influential *The Idea of a Theatre,* assaulted O'Neill's earlier plays as too melodramatic and full of childish sentimentality. He was especially severe on O'Neill for using Harlem as a setting for drama. Dismissing the Nietzschean themes in one of the plays, Ferguson concluded: "Mr. O'Neill is not a thinker, and we need not attempt to investigate his thought any longer." Bernard De Voto, upset that O'Neill won the Nobel Prize in 1936, could barely restrain his outrage. He anticipated Mary McCarthy's criticism by suggesting that important thoughts cannot possibly come forth from common people. "You may add a new volume to the Rover Boys series by setting the action in the unconscious mind, but they will still be the Rover Boys." Where O'Neill strove for classical themes, as in *Mourning Becomes Electra,* De Voto saw only stylistic "dodges and devices" instead of any deep penetration into the human heart. "Wherein is his wisdom?" protested De Voto, who called O'Neill "the biggest wind machine in our theatrical history."[3]

The consensus of the critics held O'Neill to be an over-stylized dramatist devoid of depth. In *The Playwright as Thinker,* Eric Bentley reached an even more severe conclusion: "He is no thinker, and therefore he appeals to [his admirers] even more. A great playwright need not be "a great metaphysician," but he must have "a great mind," and O'Neill, whatever his gifts for character and plot, "has yet to show us he has a mind." Bentley's idea of great minds were those of Bertolt Brecht and George Bernard Shaw, who wrote the true "drama of ideas."[4]

One literary critic who never doubted that O'Neill had an intellect was Harold Bloom, yet he wondered how such a tortured mind could be appreciated within the tradition of American poetry, prose, and philosophy. Referring to *Long Day's Journey into Night,* Bloom asked: "Can it stand intellectually with the crucial essays of Emerson and of William James?"[5] One wonders if O'Neill needs to stand as high as such thinkers, or may he stand opposed to them? O'Neill read Emerson, and he too saw nature as superior to society and chose to mock the hypocrisies of democratic politics. But most of O'Neill's characters are too weak to practice Emerson's doctrine of self-reliance, as the poet feared was true for Americans generally, and the few who are strong act only for reasons of power and manipulation. As to James, he offered the philosophy of pragmatism to show us how trust in the "will to believe" can overcome doubt and the inability to decide and to act, and how truth need not be an ultimate concern when knowledge finds its verification in the world of practice and experience. O'Neill's characters, however, had no free will to set belief in motion, and experience, that is, memories of what has happened, were so painful that the characters could barely face the future. Emerson, James, and many other thinkers looked to the intellect to find the way to redeem America, to make their country right. O'Neill sought to know where it went wrong.

*

No doubt many of O'Neill's plays, particularly the early ones, reek of melodrama, and the dialogue seldom rises above the prosaic. But some of the criticism of his plays reflects an elitist bias that denies genuine thought and feeling to the lower classes. Philosophical discourse is supposed to take place in the refined literary salon, far removed from the disreputable saloon and its low street life. During the heyday of the "New York Intellectuals," roughly the forties and fifties, the distinction between "high" and "low" culture remained an abiding principle that would supposedly save America from the mediocrity of mass society. O'Neill had boldly defied that conceited convention, and *The Iceman Cometh* demonstrates that the life of the mind could be invoked through lowlife characters who symbolize the force of ideas. In the figure of Hickey, O'Neill hints of the disturbing presence of Mikhail Bakunin, the nineteenth-century Russian anarchist and nihilist, the destroyer of all illusions, false faiths, and pitiful pipe dreams. "Wake up Comrades!"

shouts Larry Slade, the aging, disillusioned veteran of the older radical "movement" of the previous century. He is exhorting the character Hugo Kalmer, in real life the Czech-American anarchist Hippolyte Havel, who had spent years in jail for his political ideas but now so depressed he can only drink and sleep:

> Here's the Revolution starting on all sides of you and you're sleeping through it! Be God, it's not to Bakunin's ghost you ought to pray in your dreams, but to the great Nihilist! Hickey! He's started a movement that'll blow up the world!

The movement would do so by stripping the world of its illusions, even the promises of revolutionary socialism itself. A century earlier Bakunin had warned that man alienates himself by projecting onto God his own desires for perfection and that the socialists seek the same salvation in the working class. But O'Neill suggests that Hickey is the real nihilist who sees, with Nietzsche, what is troubling the barroom drunk and his guilty mind. "Powerless against what has been done, he is an angry spectator of all that is past," observed Nietzsche of the whiners of the world. History breeds resentment, not revolution. The anarchist and the nihilist will not allow the masses to see themselves as victims of the past, the very premise that Karl Marx hoped would lead to class consciousness. Bukunin's aim was to arouse and provoke: his "ability to charm and command," wrote Edmund Wilson, "together with his enthusiasm and grandiose presence, enabled him to perform miracles of persuasion."[6] Bakunin, who once declared that to "destroy" is to "create," also shared a tendency with other nihilists such as Hickey—a professed love for humanity and a deep hatred for the world. Bakunin protested against the "everlasting theoretical insanity" of Marx, who would leave the future of history to be worked out by the "awful ponderosities of German metaphysics." Philosophy, however, has come to an end, for history cannot be undone. "The will cannot will backwards," wrote Nietzsche, and thus humanity "cannot break time and time's covetousness, that is the Will's lonelist melancholy."[7] In Harry Hope's dive, O'Neill presents beings who suppress themselves, creatures of memory for whom thinking can only invoke self-reproach. There is no regaining of time lost, no possibility that life affords a second act. To drink and to sleep, such are the escapes from the "Will's loneliest melancholy."

Unlike Brecht and Shaw, O'Neill saw that the dreams of radicalism simply perpetuate illusions rather than dispel them. In contrast to generations of American literary figures, from the teens to the thirties, O'Neill was the only major writer on the Left who did not share its rapturous embrace of communism. His close friend John Reed went off to Russia to witness the Revolution firsthand, and having written the breathtaking *Ten Days That Shook the World,* returned home to organize the American Communist Party. But O'Neill doubted, as did some older anarchists, that freedom could simply be a matter of political organization, that authority would disappear with the "withering away of the state," and that the riddle of power would "resolve itself," as Marx put it, in the act of revolution.

O'Neill's Nietzschean perspective played havoc with the socialist assumption that the masses were capable of rising to class consciousness. Even Karl Marx acknowledged, in *The German Ideology,* that capitalism puts the mind to sleep, resting quietly undisturbed among "phantoms formed in the human brain," and it is only when reveries end that the world's movement toward revolution can begin. But the dozing, drunken derelicts in *The Iceman Cometh* suggest this would be a long wait, and in the meantime the characters struggle with their own being, wondering, when sober, where it is and how they lost it.

The entire edifice of socialism rests on the premise that humanity is the *animal laborans,* the worker who finds fulfillment in producing and making. But how can the worker believe in the joy of labor when he or she has experienced it as oppressive? In *The Iceman Cometh,* O'Neill has the one black character, Joe Mott, deliver a streetwise dissertation on the claims of those who feel they have a right to be the beneficiary of the labor of others:

> If dere's one ting more'n anudder I cares nuttin' about, it's de sucker game you and Hugo call de Movement. (*He chuckles — reminiscently*) Reminds me of damn fool argument me and Mose Porter has de udder night. He's drunk and I'm drunker. He says, "Socialist and Anarchist, we ought to shoot dem dead. Dey's all no-good sons of bitches." I says, "Hold on, you talk 's if Anarchists and Socialists was de same." "Dey is," he says. "Dey's both no-good bastards." "No dey ain't," I says. "I'll explain the difference. De Anarchist he never works. He drinks but he never buys, and if he do ever get a nickel, he blows it on bombs, and he wouldn't give you nothin'. So go ahead and shoot him. But de Socialist, sometimes, he's got a job, and if he gets ten bucks, he's bound by his religion to split fifty-fifty wid you. You say — how about my cut, Comrade? And you gets de five. So you don't shoot no Socialists while I'm around. Dat is, not if dey got anything. Of course, if dey's broke, den dey's no good bastards, too." (*He laughs, immensely tickled.*)

He has earned his right to laugh. A descendant of plantation slaves, Joe Mott is the appropriate person to be skeptical of the labor theory of value. He also expresses what Oscar Wilde pointed out in *The Soul of Man Under Socialism:* those at the bottom of the social ladder can think of nothing but money, which is the tragedy of being poor. Marx may have regarded the presence of money as the cause of alienation, but Joe Mott can only long to return to running a gambling house in Harlem. The faith in class consciousness is more hopeless than betting on a long shot—the "sucker game" of the intellectuals.

Contrary to the critics, O'Neill was a dramatist of ideas, and the philosophical outlooks of Freidrich Nietzsche, Arthur Schopenhauer, Oswald Spengler, and others run through his plays. His characters are compelled to express to themselves, if not to others, the reasons for doing what they wish to do. Thus Nina Leeds of *Strange Interlude* voices Zarathustra's warning of the need to be free of the needs of others unless we can bend them to our will. "My three men! . . . I feel their desires converge on me!" In *More Stately Mansions,* Simon Harford warns his wife Sara that his mother has the will to power and controls everyone whether or not they are aware of it:

SIMON: I must confess I cannot believe your possessive adjectives are more than a boast. I always have the feeling at home that, although Mother has relinquished all outward show of ownership and authority, she has managed to keep in possession.
SARA: (*resentfully*) Well, you're wrong. I have the only say about everything, and she's happy to let me have it.
SIMON: Yes, Mother has always had a subtle talent for contriving it so that others must desire what she desires—and then generously giving them their way!

With Nietzsche and Schopenhauer, O'Neill sensed that "God is dead" and truth dead as well, that the mind would have to cope with the presence of others and the forces shaping history, and that desire seeks to dominate others because power itself is desirable. It is a world of strife and struggle where the self cannot live with itself and must appropriate the will of others by deceit or persuasion. Even in a democratically free world, power still operates in human relations, particularly beyond the political institutions that liberalism had established to control the human passions. In the ancient world, power was, like wealth, an aspect of possession that can never be satisfied but must always augment itself, and hence citizens must be taught to be aware of it. In America, the Founders assumed they had resolved the problem of power by creating countervailing mechanisms that would master it through its system of "checks and balances." But O'Neill scarcely wrote about liberal politics, and he saw power as the expression of the human desire to control and dominate that has more to do with social relations than political institutions.

The distinction between high and low culture misleads us into assuming that profound thoughts need to be elegantly expressed and that we can hardly expect significant reflections when history is treated from below. Yet O'Neill, having shipped out on tramp steamers and labored in mines in Honduras, was intimately acquainted with the working class and was hardly above endowing his characters with philosophical utterances, however mumbled their expression of them. In *The Hairy Ape,* Yank conveys Schopenhauer's pessimism in the idiom of the waterfront sailor who senses he can be held responsible for matters that have no cause or reason:

YANK: Sure! Lock me up! Put me in a cage! Dat's the only answer you know. G'wan, lock me up!

POLICEMAN: What you been doin'?

YANK: Enuf to gimme life for! I was born, see? Sure, dat's de charge. Write it in the blotter. I was born, get me?

O'Neill scarcely needed to write esoteric Platonic dialogues to convey the modern philosopher's view that life is pointless when existence itself mocks our search for meaning and purpose. The proletarian Yank needed no college education to recognize that one can be sentenced to life for simply living it. The primitive, sympathetic stoker tries to tell his shipmates that the world scarcely owes them anything, particularly the fulfillment of their socialist dreams of a better society. Then he himself takes a blow to his identity, and the striving and suffering begin.

*

O'Neill empathized with his characters, whether the salesman as a Bakuninite nihilist, the high-society woman as a Nietzschean life spirit, or the stoker as a Schopenhaurean subject buffeted by the incomprehensible forces of history. For O'Neill, as for the modern philosopher, existence may have no meaning, yet the rage to live is stronger than the reason for life.

Modern German philosophy dovetailed with some of the older Jansenist-Pascal themes that were taught, in simplified versions, in the Catholic schools that young O'Neill attended. The message that "you are miserable" until you save your soul and can look forward to death and the afterlife was so traumatic that humanity can only flee to "divertisissements," as Pascal put it, explaining the self-deception of not thinking about the inexorability of death. In O'Neill's one-act play *Hughie,* Erie Smith lingers in the hotel lobby talking to the night clerk (whose eyes are so dead that "they had even forgotten how it feels to be bored"), escaping into diversions as he rambles on about racetracks, shooting craps, blondes, nagging housewives, Mercedes roadsters, booze, heroin—anything to take the mind away from thinking the unthinkable: "We all gotta croak. Here today, gone tomorrow." O'Neill may use the language of the Rover Boys, but he shows that even the inarticulate man anticipates his own death as an act of reflection.

Asked what he thought about the rage for French existentialism that had spread across American shores after the Second World War, O'Neill replied that his favorite thinkers still remained the Germans Nietzsche, Schopenhauer, and Spengler. Although he never acknowledged any indebtedness to Sigmund Freud, his "elective affinities" led him to accept the philosophical implications of the repressed unconscious regardless of its psychoanalytic explanations. While Nietzsche looked to the will as the agent of knowledge and liberation, at times O'Neill seemed closer to Schopenhauer in seeing the will as preventing the rise to consciousness of emotions that, if fully felt, would arouse feelings of humiliation, confusion, and shame. Against William James and the American pragmatists, O'Neill could hardly look upon "the will to believe" as itself an instrument of freedom since it is neither self-determining nor capable of realizing its desires. In his essay on Schopenhauer, Thomas Mann explains why the will knows not what it wants. "Will, as the opposite pole of passive satisfaction, is naturally a fundamental unhappiness, it is unrest, a striving for *something*—it is want, craving, avidity, demand, suffering; and a world of will can be nothing else but a world of suffering."[8] The will to live survives the anxieties of existence, but the drives of the will make it impossible to flee the determinants of desire. Nietzsche carried forward Schopenhauer's idea of suffering as a moral vocation, but he would not allow his fellow German philosopher to kill the will to desire. Yet the will is so torturously divided against itself in Nietzsche's philosophy that the idea of free will can become, for the weak in the thrall of religion, "the hangman's metaphysics."

O'Neill carried over into the American theater the unresolved tensions of modern German philosophy. He looked to drama to give suffering its stage, pain its voice, desire its despair. European scholars have pointed to the final passage in O'Neill's *Mourning Becomes Electra* as the playwright's way of opposing the "pessimism of Schopenhauer to the optimism of Aeschylus." The culmination of tragedy does not lead to recognition and understanding, as in the Greek play, but to the clarifying deception of life and the finality of death. Daughter Lavina Mannon, burdened by the suicide of the mother she hated and the suicide of the brother she loved, accepts her fate:

> I'm the last Mannon. I've got to punish myself! Living alone here with the dead is a worse act of justice than death or prison! I'll never go out or see anyone! I'll have the shutters nailed closed so no sunlight will ever get in. I'll live alone with the dead, and keep their secrets, and let them hound me, until the curse is paid out and the last Mannon is let die! (*With a strange cruel smile of gloating over the years of self-torture*) I know they will see to it I live for a long time! It takes the Mannons to punish themselves for being born!

Schopenhauer believed that the "sin of being born" is the "crime of existence itself."[9] The Catholic Church called it "original sin" and asked for vows of obedience, a demand to which young O'Neill refused to submit. Try teaching the Ten Commandments to the anarchist!

*

In regard to ideas, O'Neill denied that he was influenced by Sigmund Freud while acknowledging that he was impressed by Carl G. Jung. He believed that one could learn more about the unconscious from Greek tragedy than from psychoanalytic theory (Freud would not have disagreed). He seemed less interested in the mechanics of repression than in the awakening of memory that could cause history to be reenacted in the imagination. In *The Emperor Jones,* memories of things past, even if not actually lived but carried on in the collective unconscious, could trigger fear, panic, and tragic disintegration. Brutus Jones suffers no guilt from having led a life of crime — he simply emulated "rich white folk." His motives are not hidden, as in Freud, but the weight of his history lingers to surface as fear and terror of the buried memory of ancestral slavery:

> What you all doin', white folks? What's all dis? What you all lookin' at me fo? What you doin' wid me, anyhow? (*Suddenly convulsed with raging hatred and fear*) Is dis a auction? Is you sellin' me like dey uster befo' de war? (*Jerking out his revolver just as the Auctioneer knocks him down to one of the planters — glaring from him to the purchaser*) And *you* sells me? And *you* buys me? I shows you I'se a free nigger, damn yo' souls!

O'Neill's characters carry the burden of history as though it were as inescapable as original sin. The burden may stem from the playwright's Irish heritage perhaps even more than from any psychoanalytic theory. As in the troubled thoughts of other Irish writers (Beckett, Joyce, Yeats), history stalks O'Neill's stories and never leaves the present to itself. What happened in the past is so strong that life becomes reactive, repetitive, repressive. Yet at least Joyce tried to awaken from the "nightmare" that is history; the characters in *The Iceman Cometh* seek only to stay asleep. Few of O'Neill's drowsy, drunken figures can confidently exclaim the conclusion of *Finnegan's Wake:* "BussoffTheeMememormee!" In *The Iceman Cometh* the weight of history has killed the passion for life, and even the death of desire cannot eliminate the fear of death.

O'Neill shares with Joyce a passion to find larger meanings in small things, to make the rut of everyday existence resound with meaning and significance. As Edmund Wilson put it, O'Neill makes us appreciate "his gift for drawing music from humble people."[10] O'Neill also shared with Joyce a concern that has obsessed the literary imagination, the problem of consciousness. How does the writer truly know what others are thinking? As a novelist, Joyce explored the consciousness of his characters through interior monologue, the counterpart to the playwright's soliloquy. As a dramatist, O'Neill had to confine himself to dialogue alone, and we are tempted to think of the old adage that we are given speech to hide our thoughts. But O'Neill goes beyond the spoken word to deal with the presence of memory, the basis of feelings and the causes of emotions, and the association of ideas with objects. In several plays he experiments with masks and long asides to probe the inner recesses of the mind through uncoerced, unspoken thoughts free of judgment or shame. While the problem of consciousness requires that we think ourselves into the mind of another, our own thoughts can also be projected into the being of another character. With Joyce, Virginia Woolf, and other masters of the internal narrative, the voice of the character is often that of the author, and so it is in O'Neill. One of his characters recalls, in vivid detail, his first trip to a brothel twenty-five years earlier. The young O'Neill had in fact been taken there by his older, more adventuresome brother. He found the experience so frightening and disgusting that he was never able to write about sex as a fulfilling pleasure — most of his male characters are more seduced than seducing.

Nietzsche had warned that desire is bound up with the will to power and to try to eliminate either would mean "to *castrate* the intellect." O'Neill fully understood that there can be no object of desire without the mind seeing the object as desirable. In many of his plays it is the female character who sets out to fulfill her desires. The drunken men in bar scenes are, if not mindless, certainly will-less and, hence, castrated.

The melodramatic excesses of O'Neill's early plays tend to conceal the more philosophical reflections of his later ones. His admirer and editor, the drama critic George Jean Nathan, attributed this weakness to O'Neill's attempt to emulate his hero August Strindberg, the Swedish playwright of black moods and bright hopes, of the deadly trivia of everyday life and the rare moments of romantic ecstasy. O'Neill, according to Nathan, had no genius for words that would allow dialogue to soar; instead he substituted dramatic scenes for aesthetic substance, pounding out ideas from which sparks fail to fly:

> Now and again one discerns something that looks vaguely like a spark, but on closer inspection it turns out to be only an imitation lighting-bug that has been cunningly concealed in the actors' sleeves. O'Neill, in such instances, always goes aground on the rocks of exaggeration and overemphasis. His philosophical melodrama is so full of psychological revolver shots, jumps off the Brooklyn bridge, incendiary Chinamen, galloping hose carts, forest fires, wild locomotives, sawmills, dynamite kegs, time fuses, mechanical infernal machines, battles under the sea, mine explosions, Italian black-handers, last minute pardons, sinking ocean liners, and fights to the death on rafts, that the effect is akin to trying to read a treatise on the theme of bump-the-bumps. He rolls up his sleeves and piles on the agony with the assiduity of a coal heaver. He misjudges, it seems to me completely, the Strindberg method. That method is the intensification of a theme from within. O'Neill intensifies his theme from without. He piles psychological and physical situation on situation until the structure topples over with a burlesque clatter. Strindberg magnified the psyche of his characters. O'Neill magnifies their action.[11]

One of O'Neill's greatest admirers offers here a perceptive aesthetic criticism of his works. O'Neill did make use of rather trite scenarios and characters, whether it be a tire blowout confused for a suicide by revolver, or a prostitute opening up her heart of gold. The corny melodrama may appear to sacrifice psychic depth to dramatic action, and in his early plays O'Neill did carry over the hammy burlesque antics of the stage on which his father performed. Nathan's verdict holds — for the early plays.

O'Neill told a friend that he had been "haunted by history," and the past does indeed hover over the scenes so that his themes are intensified from without rather than from within. History becomes synonymous with memory as the psyche walks the stage. As with Nietzsche, O'Neill held that the will, however free, is helpless to change the past that lingers in memory. His plays often deal with had happened before the curtain rises, what remains unalterable, "the curse of the misbegotten." Overdetermined, the characters are cursed with a deficiency, a lacking and sense of wanting, a neediness needing to be fulfilled. It is the incessant drive of desire that dramatizes life under the conditions of democracy, in which Tocqueville described people who "clutch everything but hold nothing fast, and so lose grip as they hurry after some new delight."[12] And in a democracy we are supposed to live as we wish, if only we know what we want.

What, then, is the object of desire?[13] Is desire a lack, a deprivation demanding to be satisfied? Or is it an excess, an insatiable emotion that, once fulfilled, sets off in pursuit of a new object? Is it born of frustration or fantasy? Schopenhauer believed that suffering is the essence of life and the only possible relief lies in the extinction of desire. In *The Iceman Cometh* Hickey seeks to arouse the sots from their sleep and reignite their immediate desires to better dispel their comforting "pipe dreams," which leaves them dreaming about tomorrow and incapable of acting today. If Hickey's Bakuninite message is heard, the world may well blow up, for the mind would be without belief or illusion and need neither booze nor the Bible. Both classical philosophy and Christian religion had hoped to overcome desire by educating citizens and the young to do good by thinking the right thoughts, whether through the discipline of reason or the doctrine of faith. But what if it is the case that certain minds refuse to be bounded by right reason and religious authority, that indeed they identify desire with freedom and power?

Greek philosophy counsels us that the "unexamined life" is not worth living. No American playwright examined the conditions of modern life so thoroughly and comprehensively as O'Neill, but in his case a life of questioning and probing hardly led to the happy life promised by Aristotle. Democracy gave America the conditions of freedom without the concepts to guide its decisions. To be free is to be on one's own, whereas in the past philosophy or theology offered a reference point beyond the self and its longings. Greek philosophy believed in reason and saw life inflicting punishment on the irrational. Greek playwrights, in contrast to philosophers, had less faith in reason, and their idea of tragedy promised to purge us of our misery by enabling us to feel the emotions of terror and pity. "As to Aristotle's purging," O'Neill wrote to Brooks Atkinson in 1931,

> I think it is about time we purged his purging out of modern criticism, candidly speaking! What modern audience was ever purged by pity and terror by witnessing a Greek tragedy or what modern mind by reading one? It can't be done! We are too far away, we are in a world of different

values! As Spengler points out, their art had an entirely different life-impulse and life-belief than ours. We can admire while we pretend to understand — but our understanding is always a pretense! And Greek criticism is as remote from us as the art it criticizes. What we need is a definition of Modern and not Classical Tragedy by which to guide our judgments. If we had Gods or a God, if we had a Faith, if we had some healing subterfuge by which to conquer Death, then the Aristotelian criterion might apply in part to our Tragedy. But our tragedy is just that we have only ourselves, that there is nothing to be purged into except a belief in the guts of man, good or evil, who faces unflinchingly the black mystery of his own soul.[14]

Many scholars of Eugene O'Neill insist that his plays have their origins in his personal background. True enough. But when it comes to the many subjects his plays dealt with, particularly the central theme of desire and its objects and obstacles, political philosophy may be as important as personal psychology in understanding O'Neill. As much as he was grappling with the conditions of childhood and family, he was also dealing with the political culture of modern liberalism and its restless inquietude. O'Neill's characters have their fantasies and jealousies, and some are even narcissistic personalities preoccupied with themselves alone. But they also inhabit a liberal environment that had led history to believe that it is the nature of humankind to seek freedom, and freedom is the ability to choose as an inalienable right. Yet the presence of desire confounds the ability to choose. Nowhere was the dilemma better dramatized than in the life of O'Neill's father James, and subsequently in his stage persona of James Tyrone. He would continually ask himself, sometimes in front of his sons, what was his motive in choosing to do what he had done with his life — or to his life. To young Edmund, O'Neill's counterpart, the father recounts (in *Long Day's Journey*) how he had been of one of America's leading Shakespearean actors at the age of twenty-seven and happily married to Edmund's mother:

Her love was an added incentive to ambition. But a few years later my good bad luck made me find the big money-maker [the popular play *The Count of Monte Cristo*]. It wasn't that in my eyes at first. It was a great romantic part I knew I could play better than anyone. But it was a great box office success from the start — and then life had me where it wanted me — at from thirty five to forty thousand net profit for a season! A fortune in those days — or even in these. (*Bitterly.*) What the hell was it I wanted to buy, I wonder, that was worth — Well, no matter. It's a late day for regrets.

Having sacrificed his artistic aspirations for commercial success, old Tyrone convinces himself that he cannot remember exactly what caused him to make such a momentous decision, and he is too regretful of the self-centered materialist he has become to blame himself for the choices he has made. Instead he insists that "life had me where it wanted me," as though his mind had come to be commanded by a force other than itself. James Tyrone is not entirely false to his condition. For the essence of the phenomenon of desire is its mysterious occurrence. It enters our mind unsought, imposes itself as a suddenly felt need, and leaves us wondering why we want what we want. In recent times, the subject has been explored by psychoanalysts, but the phenomenon goes back to the Greeks, who believed that desire could be disciplined by reason, and to Christianity, which taught that it could be overcome by faith. It is only with the dawn of modern liberalism that desire becomes an ineradicable aspect of the human condition.

The seventeenth-century English philosopher John Locke, whose values and anxieties permeated the early American landscape, saw the human mind plagued by "the uneasiness of desire." Unlike classical and Christian thinkers, Locke saw the presence of desire as positive, the emotion that enables humankind no longer to submit to authority but to defy it by regarding the self as autonomous, a productive agent determined to transform the environment. Man has a natural right to labor on the earth for the sake of self-preservation, but he dreads, above all, death, "for if man were creator of himself, someone who would give himself being, who could bring himself into the world, he would also have granted himself an eternal duration for his existence."[15] In the face of death "we have only ourselves," observed O'Neill when thinking about the meaning of tragedy. In contrast to Lockean liberalism, O'Neill recognized the emotional force of desire but regarded it as leading not to "life, liberty, and property" but to illusion, despair, and an insatiable quest for the impossible. Simon Harford, of *More Stately Mansions,* understands that under democracy desire is free to dream its dream of freedom, one that ends up enslaving the mind to something other than itself:

> What a damned fool a man can make of himself by clinging to the irresponsible, sentimental dreams of his youth long after he has outgrown them and experience has proven how stupidly impractical they are! Keep on deliberately denying what he knows himself to be a fact, and encourage a continual conflict in his mind, so that he lives split into opposites and divided against himself! All in the name of Freedom! As if Freedom could ever exist in Reality! As if at the end of every dream of liberty one did not find the slave, oneself, to whom oneself, the Master, is enslaved!

O'Neill saw in the will to want and to claim and acquire the playing out of "the tragedy of the possessive — the pitiful longing of man to build his own heaven here on earth by glutting his sense of power with ownership and land, people, money—but principally the land and other people's lives."[16] In *Desire Under the Elms* O'Neill depicts the coveting of someone else's property and of the wife of another man as stemming from greed, lust, resentment, righteous vengeance, and even from romantic love itself. Under the conditions of modern democracy desire knows no restraint or limitation, no cessation or fulfillment, except the frustration of seeking immortality, which is unattainable. O'Neill probed this theme in *Lazarus Laughed,* where he mocked the fear of death as the "root of all evil, the cause of man's blundering unhappiness" and his everlasting submission to authority.[17]

Many of O'Neill's characters are discontent with desire. Nina Leeds, the protagonist in *Strange Interlude,* has lost her lover in World War I and, assuming that somehow he can be brought back to life, she decides to achieve this by having a baby by another man. Her desire expresses itself as dominance, in forcing things to be as she would have them be. Yet desire carries the seeds of its own failure since it cannot resist appropriating the Other. "My having a son was a failure, wasn't it?" she remarks at the conclusion of the play. "He couldn't give me happiness. Sons are always their father. They pass through the mother to become their father again. The Sons of the Fathers have all been failures!" With the maternal womb unable to control even its own creation, the desiring self is helpless to realize its desires.

In O'Neill's America there is no clear presence of authority, no firm voice informing people what they should do or not do. Historically both Christianity and classical philosophy stood as forces of morality, each opposing the advent of trade and commerce, selfishness freeing itself from shame, and possessiveness born of the irrationalities of desire. It was the Calvinists, as Max Weber demonstrated, who broke the bonds of these traditions, especially with the New England Puritans and the Yankee Ben Franklin. But the Puritan sense of conscience and Franklin's sense of civic duty had petered out by the nineteenth century, leaving a culture of acquisitiveness without virtue or guilt. O'Neill dealt with an environment of avarice in his plays that had their setting in that century, particularly *Desire Under the Elms, A Touch of the Poet,* and *More Stately Mansions.* In each there is no remnant of religious principles or classical ideals to withstand the drive toward power, status, and wealth.

In the twentieth century, in O'Neill's own time, another "ism" had come to prominence in taking a stand against capitalism and the corruptions of greed. When O'Neill came of political age in the pre–World

War I era, Marxist socialism emerged as the prevailing ideology of the Left. If Christianity and classical philosophy infused its brethren and citizens with a sense of guilt for chasing after material pleasure, Karl Marx taught his followers that they could have their materialism and munch it too. Workers and intellectuals, exhorted Marx, must draw their "poetry" from the future and look forward to history's final stage, the end of "prehistory," when property and possessiveness would give way to revolution and human solidarity. But in *The Hairy Ape* O'Neill sought to demonstrate that the dream of socialism has more to do with the past than the future. While other shipmates expressed their hatred of the wealthy classes and looked forward to a classless society free of struggle and strife, the stoker Paddy realizes that the dream of paradise is long gone, having disappeared with the passing of the old clipper ships where sailors allowed the winds to do the work and felt that they were "sons of the sea as it 'twas the mother bore them."

In much of today's academic discourse, the whole idea of genius or cultural excellence itself is derided as a "construction" that reflects the preferences of a "hierarchical social organization."[18] O'Neill, ironically, was a rebellious anarchist who scorned hierarchy and challenged the genteel traditions of the day. His plays, instead of reinforcing cultural hegemony, compelled the audience to listen to America talk about itself and to itself, even interrogating itself. O'Neill read Emerson and Thoreau as well as Nietzsche, and he agreed that the masses leading lives of smug satisfaction conceal a deeper desperation, the lack of identity and the need to belong in a democracy of conformity. Thus the character Con Melody, in *A Touch of the Poet,* forsakes his aristocratic pretensions as an individual and feels he is free "to jine the Democrats, and I'll vote for Andy Jackson, the friend av the commen men like me, God bless him!" Like the Greeks, O'Neill scrutinizes democracy rather than simply celebrating it.

"THE GENIUS OF O'NEILL"

Whatever critics think of O'Neill's shortcomings as a composer of dialogue, no one doubts his pioneering role in forging the American theater. During O'Neill's lifetime, however, the scholarship and critical analysis of his plays seemed far from encouraging. His wife Carlotta Monterey told the drama critic Joseph Wood Krutch that interpretations of her husband and his work missed the mark. "I know him fairly well," she wrote impatiently. "The junk that is written about him amazes me. The man and his work are one." The ever-sensitive wife, no doubt. But in O'Neill's lifetime critics seemed to have analyzed his works as though the playwright wrote for all persuasions. There were only two books of interpretation, O'Neill informed the Romanian director Petre Comanescu in 1947: one was "conceived from a strictly left-wing materialistic standpoint," the other "from a right-wing religious mystic standpoint. And both are, in general, favorable, if you can believe that!"[19] What mattered to O'Neill, actually a left-wing mystic, defied matter and aspired to the metaphysical.

*

"Whatever is unclear about Eugene O'Neill, one thing is certainly clear— his genius." The judgment is Lionel Trilling's, offered in an essay on the playwright, "The Genius of O'Neill," that appeared in *The New Republic* in 1936, the year he won the Noble Prize. The essay was written in the midst of "the red decade," when writers were asked to turn their faces to the barricades and write about social realism and the struggles of the workers and to take seriously the issues of class and class conflict. Trilling explained why O'Neill, though sympathetic to radical causes, chose to probe deeper issues:

> On the whole, our theatre, when it is serious, is social and realistic in the tradition of Moliere and Ibsen, and although this tradition may, obviously, lead both to profoundity and to poetry, it tends to avoid the ultimate problems of existence with which philosophy deals. O'Neill is least interesting when he occasionally concerns himself with social realism. His tradition is that of *Lear* and *Faust,* and if this need not be taken as indicative of his poetic stature it is at least indicative of the philosophic tendency of his work and of the dramatic form this tendency suggests. For though O'Neill had his beginnings in a movement of social protest, he is always looking beyond the social to the transcendental. He looks for the "meaning of life" and his dramatic technique must allow him to attempt equivalents to the scenes [of Shakespeare and Goethe]. Trying to solve the riddle of the universe, he needs wide room for his movements.[20]

The "wide room" O'Neill needed was supplied by American history. Several of his plays take place in the very environment of the pre–Civil War era that Tocqueville keenly analyzed in *Democracy in America,* wherein "the woof of time is ever being broken and the track of past generations lost. Those who have gone before are easily forgotten, and no one gives a thought to those who will follow. All a man's interests are limited to those near himself."[21] O'Neill's characters bear the same limitations of being incapable of thinking beyond themselves. Yet O'Neill himself could rarely separate his thoughts from those of others, and he scarcely forgot those who had preceded him, particularly members of his family and his Irish ancestry. Perhaps his interest in history had to do with his own preoccupation with memory and the return of the unconscious, the legacy of emotions that defy reason. O'Neill dramatized what Tocqueville had earlier depicted: an American character that sees itself as individualistic while succumbing to the gaze of others, a people proudly idealistic and caught up in its own possessive materialism, *egoisme*. As subsequent chapters will indicate, O'Neill's perspective on American history partakes not only of Tocqueville's sensibilities but of those of Nietzsche, Emerson, and Thoreau. The American character seeks to be free but depends on others for validation. The country that proudly issued its "Declaration of Independence" in a bold rebellion against political power, quietly submits to society and conforms to its ways.

But the problem that burdened O'Neill, the problem of time and memory, should not have been a problem for America. According to Tocqueville, America had no time for time:

> However powerful and impetuous the flow of time here, imagination anticipates it and is already taking possession of a new universe. The tableau is not big enough for it. There is no country in the world where man more confidently seizes the future, where he so proudly feels that his intelligence makes him master of the universe, that he can fashion it to his liking. It's an intellectual movement which can only be compared to that which led to the discovery of the new world three centuries ago; and one can really say that America has been discovered a second time. And let it not be supposed that such thoughts rise only in the minds of philosophers. They are as present to the artisan as to speculator, to the farmer as to the city dweller. They inhere in all objects, they are part of every sensation. They are palpable, visible, in a way felt; perceived by all the senses.[22]

In offering his country a glimpse of the tragic, O'Neill went against the American grain and wrote of a family that, instead of seizing the future, faces its own end. In *Mourning Becomes Electra* the ancestral home of the Mannons becomes the prison house of the past without a future, and it is only in the future, where things can be acted upon and changed, that freedom becomes possible. In the final scene the daughter of the murdered father takes on his ghostly spirit as she cohabits with the dead. Lavinia has all the shutters closed to the mansion, knowing that time has come to an end as life and death become one and the same.

Classical scholars have said of *Mourning Becomes Electra* that "it is the most defeatist, deterministic version of the *Oresteia* that we have."[23] Both plays, dating more than two thousand years apart, deal with the furies of desire and the passions of the heart that can find no rest. Whereas Tocqueville and other commentators saw America as having broken away from the Old World, O'Neill saw his country as carrying on its emotions, as though the collective unconscious stretched all the way from antiquity to the present. Rather than seeing "American exceptionalism" and praising the virtues of a unique new republic supposedly free of Old World vices, O'Neill saw his country as continuous with history and its burdens. The experience of continuity presupposes memory, and there would be no identity without a sense of the past. But in one respect America may have broken free of ancient conventions. Whereas the Greeks saw a healthy conflict between reason and desire, O'Neill tended to see desire expressing itself freely in modern American democracy. Is desire compatible with democracy?

Curiously, the word democracy, so much in the forefront of today's America's political culture, almost never came up among the members of the O'Neill family or in his barroom scenes. "Democracy begins in conversation," wrote the great philosopher John Dewey, who believed in the constructive activities of dialogue and the redemptive potential of social interaction, a point that has been elaborated by the influential neopragmatist Richard Rorty, who goes so far as to claim that philosophy has come to an end and thus the promise of thinking must continue as conversation as we speak and listen to the voices of humanity.[24] Philosophy has moved from mind to mouth. What would Nietzsche say, who believed that silence was more difficult than speech? O'Neill would also be amused, if not appalled, by this "linguistic turn" in modern thought.

For the O'Neill household, conversation could be a form of attack as well as defense; similarly, in O'Neill's waterfront dives, where there is a true democracy among the derelicts, dialogue serves only to disguise characters from one another and from themselves. Conversation is often hailed as a socializing instrument that elevates civility and mutual concern, but in the democracy of the barroom no one wants to listen, and the O'Neills themselves engaged in talk as though they were using weapons — the family's four members could find a quarrel in a straw when their identity was at stake. O'Neill takes us into the world of passion and feeling, the depths of consciousness, where the struggles of the heart try to cope with the long night of the soul.

*

O'Neill also takes us elsewhere. He was not only a playwright but a political philosopher. Not that he gave much attention to political institutions or saw much value in the vote. But he was keenly sensitive to the human condition in ways that put him far beyond liberalism or conservatism. Most liberals, from Locke to Emerson to Dewey, saw desire as good and healthy, and their aim was not to frustrate it but to provide opportunities for its fulfillment. Conservatives, on the other hand, saw desire as sinful, a lust or greediness that needed to be brought under control. Classical and Christian thinkers believed that man's natural impulses had to be subdued and renounced, either by reason or by religion. But O'Neill saw all authority as repressive and he would not submit to the will of his father or the commandments of his church. Indeed he found he could not subscribe even to the anarchism he once espoused.

In his early plays, O'Neill takes us into the world of politics, not the sedate electoral politics of the two-party system but the heyday of radical anarchism of the World War I years. This was "The Great War," a war that promised to end all wars and to "make the world safe for democracy." Competing with Woodrow Wilson's vision of a new world order was that of V. I. Lenin, the Russian leader of the Bolshevik party who promised to rid the world of all conflict and make it safe for socialism. Suddenly desire soared in the political winds of doctrine that erupted in the war years, and two forces, revolutionary socialism and democratic liberalism, would do battle for the soul of the West. Facing the "twilight of the idols," the playwright had to contend with the spell of illusion, the self-deceptions of both liberalism and communism, one convinced that war is the way to peace, the other that revolution is the way to freedom. Both promised to tame power. But could such a promise be fulfilled without desire denying its own object and relinquishing its own impulse to control and possess? O'Neill, the radical anarchist who had no lust to command and no wish to obey, addressed the revolutionary Wobblies of the World War I years, those anarcho-syndicalists who thought they could destroy power simply by seizing it.

3

Anarchism: The Politics of the "Long Loneliness"

Warren Beatty's popular 1981 film *Reds,* which deals with the Bolshevik Revolution and the formation of the American Communist Party, featured Jack Nicholson portraying Eugene O'Neill, Beatty as John Reed, and Diane Keaton as Louise Bryant. In one scene O'Neill is in his apartment at his desk when Bryant visits him. She asks to borrow money so that she can to travel to Russia and join Reed. Knowing O'Neill is taken by her, she can hardly admit she is traveling six thousand miles away for romantic reasons. Awkwardly, she mumbles something about the urgency of the political situation. O'Neill asks what she is getting at. "I want to bring back the message of the Revolution," she explains. At this point the camera swoops down directly on O'Neill's face as he looks up from his desk and responds, with a sarcastic grin, "Do you really think there's going to be a revolution in America?"

Many among the movie's audiences felt this question echoing in their own heads, for to a later generation the Greenwich Village rebels depicted in the film seemingly had lost their minds in reacting to the news coming from St. Petersburg. When Reed arrived there, Bertrand D. Wolfe later wrote, he thought he was celebrating a wedding, only to discover that he was attending a funeral.[1] To a 1980s film audience O'Neill spoke sense in penetrating the illusion of an epoch. A misleading impression holds that O'Neill was not interested in politics; it would be more accurate to say that, like George Orwell, he preferred to treat it as parody.

The amazing thing about Beatty's film is that the exchange between

O'Neill and Bryant captures perfectly, *avant la lettre,* the feelings he wrote to her in love letters that have only recently been discovered. "Perhaps if I had seen Russia in the throes as you have I might be aroused to a love for the human race, or at least some branch of it. As it is, humanity inspires me only with loathing," O'Neill grumbled. As to "the freedom of humanity," he exploded in response to Bryant's use of that expression, it "sounds to me like four words, hopelessly meaningless, which I might have read in Carlyle's French Revolution, quoted from a long-winded speech of Robespierre's. We are bound on the wheel. The old Gods remain. . . . What you write of the death of eight hundred out of a thousand children in Russia leaves me sad in as much as I deeply pity the two hundred who survived. And then — so many children are killed." O'Neill then explains why he and the love of his life exist in two different worlds. "If you feel 'empty and burnt out,' so do I; but I have my work to take the place of your love of Russia. In it I find what scattered moments of the joy of living are still vouchsaved to me. I work hard and, I trust, pass on gradually to better and bigger things."[2]

O'Neill's impatience with the siren of revolution would erupt in full fury in *The Iceman Cometh,* a text that he started writing in 1939, the year the Soviet Union and Nazi Germany signed their nonaggression pact, and was performed in 1946, the year Hitler was gone from history and Stalin remained in power at the start of a cold war that America would have to live with for almost a half-century. With his country at war in the forties, O'Neill worried that Americans would come to worship the state as they had during the First World War, and they would rationalize their doing so by saying, "of course, we can tell ourselves we are still a democracy, just as the Russians kid themselves [that] Stalinism is the proletariat delivered from bondage into ideal liberty!"[3] O'Neill's politics seem bewildering. When the Soviet Union invaded Finland in 1939, he found himself "wishing our government would break off all relations with Russia and outlaw the Communist Party in this country as a foreign-controlled, traitor organization."[4] He also feared that government would grow into a bureaucratic monstrosity that strangles individual liberty. The political positions O'Neill held in his last years would be the very positions espoused by Barry Goldwater and Ronald Reagan, the paragons of American conservatism. Yet in the years of the First World War, O'Neill stood with the radical Left, an anarchist in opposition to all authority, whether of church or state, the rebel against the materialist culture of capitalism and the tyranny of pettiness stifling bourgeois society.

*

"Politics in a work of literature," wrote Stendhal, "is like a pistol-shot in the middle of a concert, something loud and vulgar, and yet a thing to which it is impossible to refuse one's attention."[5] Several of O'Neill's early domestic plays ended with pistol shots, and if the sound was loud and vulgar, it rang with the finality of death — such as the last scene of *Recklessness,* where the wife, informed by her husband that her lover has died, goes upstairs to her bedroom and shoots herself. Does the melodrama at the curtain suggest that O'Neill's plays are too sentimental to take seriously as social criticism? O'Neill once remarked that his radical activist friends were at war with society while his quarrel was with God. The Left traditionally looked to the coming of the revolution as the historic event that would make possible what Karl Marx had foretold: "the essential unity of man with nature." But O'Neill was closer to Nietzsche in feeling humankind's estrangement not from nature but its deeper alienation from a God who is dead and who had died, as one of his characters put it, quoting Nietzsche, "out of pity for us." Where Marx exhorted humanity to draw its "poetry" from what was still to come, O'Neill depicted his characters as survivors of what had already been done.

Prisoners of the past, O'Neill's characters can readily be interpreted in psychological terms as carrying in their psyches the imprint of personal traumas. But the social-political basis of O'Neill's plays is just as telling. Although skeptical of the radical dreams that drove the American Left of his era, his mind was soaked in the emotions that fed them, and his characters would not hesitate to affirm Henry Adams' dictum that politics is the "systematic organization of hatreds." Some examples of the venom:

RICHARD: I don't believe in this silly celebrating the Fourth of July—all this lying talk about liberty—when there is no liberty!. . . The land of the free and the home of the brave! Home of the slave is what they ought to call it— the wage slave ground under the heel of the capitalist class, starving, crying for bread for his children, and all he gets is a stone! The Fourth of July is a stupid farce. I'll celebrate the day the people bring out the guillotine again and I see Pierpont Morgan being driven by a tumbril. . . .

MILLER: (*solemnly*) Son, if I didn't know it was you speaking, I'd think we had Emma Goldman with us.

—*Ah, Wilderness!*

HOGAN: But I couldn't bring myself to set foot on land bought with Standard Oil money that was stolen from the poor it ground in the dust beneath its dirty heel— land that is watered with the tears of starving widows and orphans.

—*Moon for the Misbegotten*

LONG: And who's ter blame, I arsks yer? We ain't. We wasn't born this rotten way. All men is born free and ekal. That's in the bleedin' Bible, maties. But what d'they care for the Bible — them lazy, bloated swine what travels first cabin? Them's the ones. They dragged us down 'til we're on'y wage slaves in the bowels of a bloody ship, sweatin', burnin' up, eatin' coal dust! Hit's them's ter blame — the damned Capitalist class!

—The Hairy Ape

Strong stuff. But the passages come from the mouths of the comical and ineffectual. The first babble is made by an adolescent out to shock his parents on a patriotic holiday and prove his worldly wisdom, a youth whose true feelings quickly turn to a summer's romantic crush; the second is uttered by an Irish peasant who actually lusts after the land whose owner he is denouncing; the third is the rage of a sailor who explodes with all the cliches of social conflict and class consciousness, even though he himself is unconscious of how history has left the working class behind, how the dream of socialism lies in the past and not over the horizon in the future.

In his early years, O'Neill shared the anarchist conviction that normal electoral politics make little difference and that voting has no consequences whatsoever. Although he admired Lincoln, he had no patience for the shining shibboleths of democracy. "Sure you don't need to fool all the people all the time," he reflected when thinking of the aphorism attributed to Lincoln, "but only a majority of them some of the time — in an election year — and that is easy."[6] Yet O'Neill was not completely apolitical; he could hardly stand above the fray and sneer at those struggling for a better world. Actually, he was sympathetic to the causes of the Left and befriended many comrades who took on the establishment. Here is another example of how O'Neill's mind and temperament cannot be reduced to emotions that return us to his troubled family. Neither his father, mother, nor older brother expressed any interest in radical politics or in the plight of the underprivileged. O'Neill did so, drawn as he was toward all sorts of rebels and bohemians at the lower depths of society. He once referred to himself as "a philosophical anarchist," which he defined as "Go to it, but leave me out of it!"

The playwright could be as disdainful of the overclass as he was respectful of the underclass, and here his critical attitude may have been part of his memories of his family's exclusion from New London's class pretensions. The sensitive young Gene felt the slings of snobbery even more than his thick-skinned father, though his early life style mocked the pretensions of propriety. As a freshman at Princeton, O'Neill kept a messy room, with clothes strewn on the floor and walls covered with pinup posters, playbills, and brassieres. His one-act play *Abortion,* set in an eastern university resembling Princeton, involves a tragic romance between an all-American football player and a poor working girl. When her brother discovers she has died during an abortion, he lashes out at the campus star who had callously arranged the operation: "I've always hated yuh since yuh first come to the house. I've always hated all your kind. Yus come here to school and yuh think yuh c'n do as yuh please with us town people. Yuh treat us like servants, an' what are *you,* I'd like to know?—a lot of lazy no-good dudes spongin' on your old men; and the goils, our goils, think yuh're grand!"

A little ironic, for O'Neill was also supported by his father James while attending Princeton and for a few years afterward. Like another Irish-American writer, F. Scott Fitzgerald, in his later years O'Neill would be as attracted to wealth and elegant surroundings despite his repeated warnings about their temptations. The playwright himself had no need for such worries. The better off he became financially the more he threw himself into his work. Unlike Fitzgerald, O'Neill's anxieties were metaphysical rather than social. The playwright suffered no "crack-up" about his identity and reputation and experienced no conflict between the dedicated craftsman and the moneyed celebrity. When it came to hard work, O'Neill was more of a Puritan than he would acknowledge.

While Fitzgerald often allowed himself to become enchanted with the rich and the glamorous, O'Neill frequently wrote from "the bottom up" as his own sentiments traveled from the top down and outward to the margins of society. He had, in his own words, "acute sympathy" for American Indians, having met some when he was ill with tuberculosis in the hospital. Later he protested the government's "treachery against the Indians" and hailed the Battle of Little Big Horn and the defeat of General Custer.[7] O'Neill had multicultural sympathies and transnational curiosities as evidenced by his writing about Asia and Africa. He befriended gamblers and racketeers as well as hobos and sots. He felt part of the brotherhood among sailors, and at his California estate in the thirties, Tao House at San Ramon, he framed on the wall of his study his able-bodied seaman certificate.

During his Greenwich Village days, O'Neill hung out at Jimmy the Priest's, a seedy tavern frequented by the down and outs who could barely afford the nickle for a sixteen-ounce schooner of beer or a shot of cheap whiskey. O'Neill joked that Jimmy the Priest's made Maxim Gorky's tavern settings "look like an ice cream parlor in comparison." Another O'Neill haunt in the twenties was the Golden Swan, which its habitues called the "Hell Hole." Along with the artists and writers who met there were the Hudson Dusters, a gang that terrorized the Village neighborhood and lived for drinking and brawling. When not working as truck drivers and stevedores, the Dusters would hijack their rivals' truckloads and dump ballot boxes in the river at the pay of Tammany Hall. A Duster O'Neill particularly liked was William Fernandez, known as Spanish Willie. The essayist Malcolm Cowley observed the way in which the playwright and the bootlegger respected one another. O'Neill never felt he was slumming when in the company of the Dusters. "He was just as grammatical, just as considerate if he were holding a conversation with Shakespeare or the Prince of Wales," remembered Cowley. "Perhaps this was the reason why all the West Side gorillas worshipped him, and even attended his plays."[8]

Interestingly, in his later years when he gave up drinking, O'Neill became something of a recluse, with his wife Carlotta serving as a watchguard to make sure the playwright could avoid unwelcome visitors. But in the teens and twenties he enjoyed a comaraderie completely free of condescension. Observations similar to those of Cowley were recorded by Dorothy Day. Before she converted to Catholicism and became a pacifist in the thirties, Day knew O'Neill in the Village while she worked for the *Liberator,* successor to the government-suppressed *The Masses.* She would later describe her search for God and the miracle of human kindness as similar to the anarchist's search for utopia and the miracle of human solidarity — "The Long Loneliness." O'Neill and Day never became intimate, and legend has it that O'Neill would invite her up to his room, serve several rounds of drinks, and recite "The Hound of Heaven," the heartbreaking Catholic poem by Francis Thompson. Then O'Neill would ask in a drunken slur, "Dorothy, are you prepared to lose your virginity?" But before she could reply, O'Neill would have passed out on the sofa. Whether or not the story is apocryphal, Day vividly remembered the respect with which O'Neill regarded the poet Maxwell Bodenheim and the anarchists Terry Carlin and Hippolyte Havel. "One of the fine things about Gene," Day records, "is that he took people seriously. He took Max seriously — as a poet, I mean. He took Terry Carlin seriously. He took Hippolyte seriously, and almost no one else did. After Hippolyte had a few drinks he would get up in the center of the room and whirl around, while the rest of us laughed. But not Gene. 'This man has been in every prison in Europe,' he used to say, 'He'd suffered for what he believes in.' Gene was very responsive to people who suffered."[9]

*

At the time the First World War broke out in August 1914, O'Neill had been absorbed in the writing of several one-act plays. It would be three years before the United States entered the war, and for a portion of that period O'Neill was at Harvard studying with Professor George Pierce Baker, who encouraged him despite the ineptitude of his first plays. When President Woodrow Wilson went before Congress, in April 1917, and asked for a declaration of war, O'Neill first thought of enlisting in the navy, but fear of a recurrence of tuberculosis dissuaded him. He then got caught up in the antiwar sentiments of the Village rebels and their anarchist and pacifist passions.

The outbreak of World War I loomed as the chastening crisis of the American Left. It had been an entire century since history had witnessed the world-shaking Napoleonic wars, and the twentieth century promised to continue peace and prosperity. Until the "Guns of August," the Left in particular could take encouragement from the belief that the workers of the world would oppose war and express their international solidarity. Yet in 1914 the unexpected happened. Workers proved militantly nationalistic, and the socialist parties of Europe voted in their respective parliaments to finance the war. The American Socialist Party stood almost alone in opposition to Wilson's declaration of war, although a number of leading intellectuals supported intervention, including old-time socialists like Jack London, the philosopher John Dewey, and the scourge of the leisure class, Thorstein Veblen. Before the war some of O'Neill's companions, particularly John Reed, regarded themselves as cultural nationalists, children of Walt Whitman as well as of Karl Marx. But with America deeply involved in the war, patriotism turned ugly and seemed to unleash a mob gone mad with hysteria. Antiwar dissidents were prosecuted and their papers suppressed. Emma Goldman and other alien anarchists would be rounded up and deported. Radicals everywhere sought to explain this unexpected development that left socialist theory in ruins and shattered anarchist hopes. Ironically, war did for the state what even the American Founders could not do: it turned the people to its side rather than against it as the public succumbed to an orgy of patriotic fervor. Conventional Jeffersonianism had been turned on its ear: that government is best which governs not least but most ferociously. "War is the health of the state," declared the rebel Randolph Bourne. In the socialist *The Call* in 1914, O'Neill reacted to the sorry spectacle in "Fratricide":

> What cause could be more asinine
> Than yours, ye slaves of bloody toil?
> Is not your bravery sublime
> Beneath a tropic sun to broil
> And bleed and groan — for Guggenheim!
> And give your lives for— Standard Oil! . . .

Comrades, awaken to new birth!
New values on the tables write!
What is your vaunted courage worth
Unless you rise up in your might
And cry: "All workers on the earth
Are brothers and WE WILL NOT FIGHT!"

Three years later, with America involved in the war, O'Neill was certain, as were others on the Left, that the war had been a conspiracy put over on the public by the creatures of capitalism. "My soul is a submarine," he wrote in a poem in *The Masses:*

My aspirations are torpedoes.
I will hide unseen
Beneath the surface of life
Watching for ships,
Dull, heavy-laden merchant ships,
Rust-eaten, grimy galleons of commerce
Wallowing with obese assurance,
Too sluggish to fear or wonder,
Mocked by the laughter of waves
And the spit of disdainful spray.

I will destroy them
Because the sea is beautiful.

One wonders what might have been the literary outcome had O'Neill followed John Reed in covering the war in Europe. A number of American writers saw action as ambulance drivers in the First World War, and a few, namely John Dos Passos, Ernest Hemingway, and e. e. cummings, wrote important war novels. O'Neill's isolation from "the Great War" may explain why his two war plays, *The Sniper* and *Shell Shock,* lack vividness and verisimilitude, the feeling of what it was like actually being there. The first play deals with the "rape" of Belgium at the opening of the war, namely Germany's unannounced invasion, occupation, and possible annexation, and the accompanying atrocities. The one-act play has a farmer trying to control his grief after his son has been shot on his wedding day. When he discovers his wife has also been killed, he refuses to heed the priest's warning and sets his sights on German troops approaching his farmhouse and fires away until he is overwhelmed and executed.

Shell Shock, set in New York's Harvard Club, brought the war home to America. A lieutenant recalls crawling out of a foxhole at Chateau Thierry, and he thinks he entered "no man's land" not in response to the crying wounded but to look for cigarettes among the corpses. It turns out that a man he rescued arrives at the Club, and the lieutenant, his amnesia now lifted, remembers that he acted honorably.

Both plays were written for the drama course O'Neill had been taking at Harvard. O'Neill allowed *The Sniper* to be performed as an antiwar play; *Shell Shock* he wisely withdrew from circulation. Failures as works of art, both plays nonetheless do offer a first glimpse at O'Neill's early political sentiments. The lieutenant is temporally disordered mentally for thinking he may have done the right thing but for the wrong reason, and he is wracked with a bad conscience — always a bad sign to those familiar with Nietzsche. A Nietzschean presence also hovers over the Belgian farmhouse as the priest tries to talk the farmer into putting down his rifle and trusting in God. "Come, come, it is hard, I know, but you must bear it like a man. God's will be done! He, too, had a Son who died for others. Pray to Him and he will comfort you in your affliction." As he faces the firing squad, the farmer shouts, "to hell with your prayers."

O'Neill may have failed to make a compelling analysis of the war or write a successful play that dramatized its horrors. But the role of the priest reaffirmed Nietzsche's view that Christianity, a religion that thinks it can relieve affliction by ignoring its causes, "may be called the great treasure house of ingenious means of consolation."[10]

THE APPEALS OF ANARCHISM

The philosopher Friedrich Nietzsche provoked the mind of the Lyrical Left of the Greenwich Village era. In rebellion against respectability, the Left took to a writer who called into question all established institutions and their comforting values and redefined life as a ceaseless war against complacency and mendacity. Randolph Bourne, a hero to the Lyrical Left for his opposition to America's entry into the First World War, drew upon Nietzsche for a critique of American Puritanism as a pseudo-morality that fears death and denies life. In May 1914, a few months before war would break out in Europe, O'Neill wrote to Jessica Ripin, a fellow New Londoner, providing a lecture on "the lofty ether of Nietzsche and Schopenhauer," noting that conventional moral categories must be turned inside out if we are ever to be free of sin and guilt. "Lord, hear my prayer!" he exclaimed. "Sin and punishment, virtue and its reward; piffle upon piffle until everything in the world is turned upside down and all that is delightful is dubbed 'Bad' and all that is disagreeable and ugly 'Good.'" Nietzsche enabled the intellectual to see that Christianity and its conventional moral judgments have no transcendent foundation in nature, reason, or divine revelation. For his part Schopenhauer taught that life consists in the blind striving of will that never gets what it wants or knows what it wants. "I seethe with longings; desire has me by the throat," O'Neill confessed to Ripkin. I may only "express the strivings of an impecunious young author to project the phantasmagoria of his own brain on paper," but I shall "keep on with my rainbow chasing," O'Neill concluded. To an anguished mind fleeing Catholicism, Nietzsche and Schopenhauer rescued O'Neill from the torments of hell by showing him that he was already living it.[11]

O'Neill's flirtation with Nietzscheism has been criticized by recent academic scholars, who claim that he and other bohemian rebels privileged the individual over the political, settling for personal liberation over social transformation.[12] But Nietzsche turned many rebels toward anarchism, a stance that prevented the Left from capitulating to capitalism or surrendering to bolshevism. Freedom finds itself not in voting or running for office or even identifying with a foreign revolution; on the contrary, people are free by virtue of taking responsibility for themselves. "The man who is truly free," wrote Nietzsche, "tramples underfoot the contemptible species of well-being dreamt of by shop-keepers, Christians, cows, women, Englishmen, and other democrats. The free man is a warrior."[13]

O'Neill might wince at the inclusion of women, but change warrior to sailor and we begin to get at the playwright's political outlook. If anarchism was incapable of realizing anything in the political realm, it was entirely capable of resisting what destroys freedom in the name of creating it. Much of twentieth-century intellectual history turned on whether freedom should be the domain of the individual or belong to the masses who are to be guided toward it by a revolutionary vanguard. On this issue Eugene O'Neill and John Reed part company, with the playwright remaining skeptical of bolshevism and the journalist espousing it. V. I. Lenin's *State and Revolution* (1915) did have a certain anarchist flavor; its author saw no possibility of reforming the Tsarist government and promised that under communism we would see "the withering away of the state." But when the Bolsheviks came to power two years later, the communist party replaced the state and, just as many anarchists had predicted, it became a despotic power machine as it eliminated opposition and crushed dissent. A revolution that had promised total freedom degenerated into total servitude. Emma Goldman wrote with brilliant prescience on the subject (as did Rosa Luxemburg in Europe), and her place in American history would be recognized by O'Neill as a haunting shadow, a figure who represents a political stance that cannot make its appearance on the stage of history. To the playwright Goldman remained a heroine who lives on in memory.

Whether O'Neill had spent any time with Goldman is unclear.[14] He did stay in contact with her close companion, the anarchist Alexander Berkman, who, while in the Soviet Union in the twenties, translated one of O'Neill's plays to be performed at the Moscow State Theatre. O'Neill knew Goldman's publication, *Mother Earth,* and both the playwright and the activist traveled in the same circles in Provincetown and New York. Goldman participated in the Little Theater movement and gave courses that were published as *The Social Significance of Modern Drama.* Whereas today Goldman is a heroine to feminists, O'Neill had other reasons for having her serve as the burden of memory in *The Iceman Cometh.*

O'Neill may have become intrigued with Goldman because he viewed her as embodying a paradox at the heart of anarchism. O'Neill, it will be recalled, saw the human condition as flawed by greed and possessiveness. As a feminist, Goldman saw jealously as malignant, an impulse to control the opposite sex through the historical custom of monogamy. Although she assumed that man's desire to possess women was tantamount to the desire to own property, Goldman, like O'Neill, could hardly escape the troubling thought that the irrationality of arbitrary desires may be an inexorable aspect of human nature. "Every relation between persons ultimately involves the question of possession," observed Reinhold Niebuhr.[15] Jean Paul Sartre reminds us that possession nullifies autonomy. "I am possessed by the Other, the Other's look fashions my body in its nakedness, causes it to be born, sculptures it, produces it as it is, sees it as I shall never see it. The Other holds a Secret—the Secret of what I am."[16]

Goldman may have renounced possessiveness in the name of socialism but she also upheld self-fulfillment in the name of anarchism. The paradox of anarchism is that it is based on the irreducible reality of egotism that makes the self as sacred as it is autonomous. Becoming aware of the Other risks surrendering the self to it, and thereby one's own self becomes conditioned by something alien. Even intimacy and romantic love may call into question the priority of the self when experiencing a passion brought about by another. Under the conditions of democracy, love is desire at its most passionate pitch as the self finds itself almost involuntarily wanting what it wants. Nietzsche warned the anarchists that the romantic state of mind could slide into resentment and hostility. In *The Iceman Cometh,* Hickey's love for his wife turns into hatred for himself and her as well. Desire can become complicit in its own destruction.

In "The Tragedy of Woman's Emancipation," Emma Goldman addressed such dilemmas. "How to be one's self and yet in oneness with others," she asked, "to feel deeply with all human beings and still retain one's own characteristic qualities?" Goldman had no real solution to the quandary of a self that desires to be free and yet aches for love. The challenge is "to give one's self boundlessly, in order to find one's self richer, deeper, better."[17]

Emma Goldman may have allowed her passions to sweep her away in her love affairs, but when O'Neill depicts her in *The Iceman Cometh,* she cannot give herself to anything other than her own political causes, a deprivation felt painfully by her (fictional) son. Perhaps O'Neill needed to make this point since he had also experienced the absence of his own mother's affections. Even those who claim to value freedom above all else can have their personal addictions: with Eugene, the son, it is the mother; with Ella, the mother, morphine; with Emma, the anarchist, "the movement."

*

Writing about O'Neill's politics presents an apparent contradiction. While the playwright's outlook on life was thoroughly pessimistic, his political sympathies flowed directly to the radical Left, the side of the political spectrum that typically radiated hope and optimism. Why did so gloomy a mind find anarchism attractive?

O'Neill was introduced to the philosophy of anarchism at the age of seventeen, having left prep school in Connecticut one weekend to visit New York City and the Village's Unique Book Shop, operated by Benjamin R. Tucker. In American history anarcho-libertarian sentiments can be traced back to the rationalist Tom Paine and the Transcendentalist Henry David Thoreau. In addition to these better-known figures, Tucker had been influenced by Joseph Warren and Stephen Pearl Andrews, writers who drew their inspiration from the emancipatory principles of the Declaration of Independence. But at the bookstore O'Neill had what might be called his "Germanic turn" as Tucker introduced him to Friedrich Nietzsche, Max Stirner, and Arthur Schopenhauer. Of Nietzsche's *Zarathustra* O'Neill said it had "influenced me more than any book I've ever read. . . . I've always possessed a copy . . . and every year or so I re-read it and am never disappointed, which is more than I can say for any other book." But O'Neill adds in a parenthesis: "That is, never disappointed in it as a work of art, aspects of its teaching I no longer concede."[18] It would be interesting to know which aspects of Nietzsche's thought he reconsidered and which he continued to accept as he compiled a folder of the philosopher's quotations. His earliest biographer, Barrett Clark, spotted O'Neill entering a rehearsal of *The Great God Brown* at the Greenwich Village Theatre with "a worn copy of Nietzsche's *The Birth of Tragedy*" halfway in his back pocket.

The former Catholic O'Neill took to Nietzsche, the dragon slayer of doctrines who wandered in a world without any truth to live by or a God to live for. Stirner, for his part, attacked every institution that stood in the way of the individual and justified the ego and its selfish pursuits. So upset was Karl Marx with Stirner's *Der Einzige und Sein Eigentum* (The Ego and Its Own) that he paused in *The German Ideology* to rebut it. Marx claimed that the solitary ego was an illusion and the self had no existence save in social interaction with others. It is difficult to see O'Neill's accepting unbridled egotism as salutary given that he regarded selfish possessiveness as the curse of humankind. Perhaps more congenial was Stirner's conviction that culture and its ideals are rationalizations of egoistic impulses. As for Schopenhauer, he saw life in ways that may have reinforced O'Neill's sense of existence. Each person exists alone in an illusionary world in which we cannot separate the past from our memory of it, or distinguish the real world from its unreliable representations. The only answer to a purposeless life in which happiness is destined to be frustrated is the release of reverie, or what O'Neill would term "pipe dreams."

Anarchism was a political proposition as much as a philosophical explanation of the possibilities of knowledge and its impediments. In the popular mind anarchism had been associated with street politics, mass demonstrations, chaos, violence, and terror. Emma Goldman seldom shied away from such tactics as "direct action," and she defended her lover Alexander Berkman after he tried to assassinate the industrial tycoon Henry C. Frick. Although Tucker and other anarchists distanced themselves from Goldman, O'Neill stayed in touch with Berkman and remained loyal to anarchism despite its record of abject failure as a political movement.

O'Neill was more attracted to anarchism than to revolutionary socialism because its hope for a better world was more moral than scientific and more personal than philosophical. Marxists looked to the "laws" of historical development as progressive and to the "dialectic" as the key to progress. The Marxist intellectual need not be troubled by the condition of the masses whose plight was destined to be remedied paradoxically by virtue of worsening, the so-called theory of the "immiseration" of the working class. Marx was fond of saying that capitalists were their own gravediggers since capitalism carried the seeds of its own "contradictions." But the proposition that the very condition of oppression would also be the condition of liberation carried its own contradiction that could be resolved only if one were a Hegelian and believed that anything that exists "negates" itself and becomes its opposite. Most anarchists had little use for Hegel's dialectical reasoning, and thus they looked to the people themselves to bring reason and justice into the world, without the redemptive illusions of science and philosophy and without the predictable stages of history. From this perspective people are as much the problem as the solution. O'Neill's pessimistic outlook resonated with the anarchist dictum that there are no tyrants but only slaves and that if there were no subjects there would be no state. As an ex-Catholic and a rebel against authority, O'Neill could be comfortable with those anarchists who wished neither to give orders nor to obey them. But the problem might be that the masses, whom the Marxists assumed would carry out the "mission" of history, remained obedient subjects. That the many allow themselves to be ruled by the few troubled O'Neill as much as it did Rousseau and Nietzsche. Marx promised that humanity could break free of its chains. O'Neill saw that it was more than chains that kept the masses in subjugation.

Significantly, neither radical Marxists nor conservative classicists have been troubled by the problem of desire. The former assumes revolution will overcome the alienation aching at the heart of the soul; the latter assumes the life of reason will discipline the unruly passions. But anarchists knew desire to be a riddle without a resolution. To wait for revolution is to wait for a "pipe dream," and the idea that reason can create a disinterested mind is to "castrate the intellect" and render it without a will of its own. The phenomenon of desire is inexpugnable since it lies within ourselves as we bestow upon objects or other people their value as desirable. As O'Neill put it in *More Stately Mansions,* "We are our desires." We are what we want even when we do not know why we want what we want. And we are responsible for those desires that compel us to act wrongly. To the anarchist, desire is the most problematic issue in political philosophy because it is aroused when we feel the need for someone or something other than ourselves. To lack what we want is to crave for what is alien to our own being.[19]

Many of the Village rebels of O'Neill's generation read Nietzsche much the same way they read Freud, not as the theoretician of tragedy but as the intellectual emancipator who would liberate culture from guilt and repression. O'Neill's first wife Agnes Boulton recalled in her memoirs how her husband kept Nietzsche's books by his side, the pages tattered and marked up with marginalia. In O'Neill's papers, in the Beinecke Library at Yale University, is a file of quotes by Nietzsche, though most of them have less to do with politics and history than with marriage and morals. But the genius of Nietzsche was to discern the psychological affinity of socialism to Christianity as doctrines of redemption, whether in this world or the hereafter. That the proletariat would fulfill the mission of history meant that the poor would inherit the earth. But neither in socialism nor in Christianity do poverty and exploitation lead to happiness and freedom. On the contrary, the masses assume they are morally superior to the upper classes by virtue of their lack of wealth and power. This false conceit, rather than leading to liberation, only creates more subtle, internalized forms of self-oppression. The pathos of O'Neill's working-class characters is their inability to rise to consciousness, to overcome a resignation to reality based on a hatred of it, leaving them only with a righteous resentment.

"LONG — LIVE — THE REVOLUTION!"

O'Neill wrote two plays that were meant to be observations on the state of radical politics, *The Personal Equation* and *The Hairy Ape*. Marx once observed that in the coming revolution philosophy would be at the "head" of the movement and the workers would shoulder its "body." O'Neill's first political play dealt with ideologues and intellectuals who were all mind, the second with workers who were all muscle. O'Neill rarely bothered thinking about the country's established two-party system. While the Democratic and Republican parties may vie with each other for the spoils of victory, the ideals of the Left promised more even if they could deliver less. Politics to O'Neill meant the fate of the working class in a bourgeois society. Many socialists were unable to face this dilemma. Instead, socialists assumed that the middle class would be replaced by the rising proletariat, under the inexorable logic of history's progressive stages. O'Neill used the theatrical stage to suggest that there may be no next stage in history. Having achieved liberty in the eighteenth century, America could never move beyond the liberalism of the twentieth century. But the anarchists thought otherwise, and in O'Neill's first political play a radical leader cites the words of Danton during the French Revolution: "It is necessary to dare, and again to dare, and still again to dare."

The Personal Equation was written in the spring of 1915, a year after the First World War broke out and a year after the breakout of class warfare in Colorado where, at the mining town of Ludlow, the National Guard set fire to tents and machine-gunned fleeing miners, killing more than forty workers, including twelve children. The Ludlow strike had been spearheaded by the I.W.W. A courageous brotherhood of hoboes and heroes, the Wobblies captured the imagination of the literary Left. The novelist John Dos Passos retained his sympathies toward the anarchist Wobblies even after he became a staunch conservative admired by William Buckley and Ronald Reagan. The appeal of anarchism lies in its stubborn integrity and unswerving dedication to freedom without compromise. Wobblies took to anarcho-syndicalism, which taught that autonomous industrial unions, workers and producers of all kinds, could alone lead the masses to socialism, without the necessity of a party vanguard — though perhaps a well-placed bomb would help. Having great faith in the spontaneous, creative character of the proletariat, Wobblies were often at odds with socialists, who preferred ballots to bombs, and with the Marxists, who looked to party leadership to guide the untutored consciousness of the workers. Anarchists suspected the rule of elites, and they thought giving workers the right to vote was, to paraphrase a lament, about as useful as giving a blind man a lantern.

The Personal Equation opens with a dialogue dealing with the tactical differences that divided the Left. Olga Tarnoff was perhaps modeled after Emma Goldman. Of Russian background, she makes fiery speeches at Union Square advocating birth control, free love, and a revolutionary politics opposed to melioristic reformism. In a room at the headquarters of the IWU, the Internal Workers Union in Hoboken, she complains to a fellow Wobbly:

> Oh, these Socialists! How I loathe their eternal platitudes, their milk-and-water radicalism, their cut-and-dried sermons for the humble voters. As if to vote were not also to acquiesce in the present order of things, to become a cog in the machine which grinds the voter himself to bits! Revolution by an act of Congress! The dolts!

Tom Perkins, Olga's lover, agrees with her denunciation of social democracy but he is so enthralled with her romantically that he is forever asking her to marry him. This would be a surrender, she sneers, to bourgeois conventions and its "enforced servitude" to possessiveness. "Do you want a signed certificate proving I am yours — like a house or a lot?"

After hearing an IWU official express fear that a war is to break out in Europe, Olga sees a general strike as the anarchist's ultimate dream. "Think what it would mean," she exclaims, voicing her anarcho-syndicalist conviction that workers have the potential of toppling the capitalist class and taking over the means of production: "No electricity, no cars, no trains, no steamers, the factories dark and deserted, no newspapers, no wireless, nothing. The whole world of workers on a holiday."

To instigate so massive a strike, IWU leaders decide to sabotage the plant of the Ocean Steamship Company. Tom has just been fired from the company for passing out pamphlets, but his father, Thomas Perkins, works for the company as an engineer on the vessel *San Francisco* and retains an almost mystical bond with the engines that power the ship. When Tom acknowledges to his father that he belongs to the Wobblies, the father, a decent if weak-willed person, is jolted:

PERKINS: But aren't they—don't they start strikes—and throw bombs—and blow up places with dynamite?
TOM: They use force when force is used against them, when they have to.

The father warns the son he will do anything to prevent anarchists from dynamiting his engines, unaware that Tom has already agreed to plant the bombs. Tom gives up trying to persuade his father to stay out of the way and, before rushing out the door, shouts that they live in two different worlds, leaving the father in despair.

In the final act, which takes place on the *San Francisco,* the now pregnant Olga, having sneaked aboard in disguise, has undergone a change as her militancy gives way to maternal instincts. She wants someone other than Tom to take on the dangerous assignment, telling him how much she looks forward to raising their child. But after anguished vacillation she agrees with Tom that he is the only one capable of the task.

The dockworkers, however, have been bought off by management and refuse to go on strike, and the man who was to deliver the dynamite has been arrested. The best that can be achieved now is to prevent the *San Francisco* from sailing by having the stokers smash its engines, thereby throwing off the ship's schedule and ruining the company's reputation. As the stokers make their move, Tom's father, in the ship's engine room guarding his beloved machines, takes out his gun, with Tom smirking contemptuously when his father threatens to shoot the first person who lays his hand on the engines. Tom then turns and smashes a gauge, and right after the tinkle of glass, a shot is heard and Tom's expression turns to bewilderment as he sags and slumps to the floor. "You've murdered him!" shouts a stoker. "But I pointed it over his head," gasps the father as he drops the revolver.

Three weeks later, Tom, having suffered a bullet to the head, will be, a physician advises, "like a little child for the rest of his life." The father, after some reluctance, agrees to share with Olga the caring for Tom, whose baby she is carrying. Then Wobbly leader Whitely enters the hospital room to tell Olga that he has decided to enlist in the army in order to join the crusade against Prussian militarism. To Olga, Whitely is betraying the anarchist commitment to social revolution; when Whitely inquires how she can continue her devotion to revolution after all that has happened, Olga responds:

You mean, after it has ruined my life? (*Whitely nods, a bit ashamed of what he has said. Olga's eyes flash.*) Oh, you fool! You blind fool! What am I? What is my small happiness worth in the light of so great a struggle? We fight, and at times like the present, it seems hopelessly. We fight and go down before the might of society; but the Revolution marches on over our bodies. It moves forward though we may not see it. We are the bridge. Our sacrifice is never in vain. . . . I have suffered and will suffer . . . and I am proud that I can still cry from the depths of my soul: It is well done. Long live the Revolution!

Had there been an audience, it would have assumed that Tom is comatose and has heard nothing of these strident political shibboleths. But Tom utters one last reflection, the sarcasm of which O'Neill underscores in the stage directions:

TOM: (*with a low, chuckling laugh—mimicking Olga*): Long—Live—the Revolution. (*His vacant eyes turn from one to the other of them. A stupid smile plays about his loose lips. Whitely turns away with a shudder. Olga stares at the figure in the bed with fascinated horror—then covers her face with her hands as The Curtain Falls*)

The Personal Equation disappeared from the O'Neill canon until recent years. The author never had it copyrighted, published, or produced on stage. Whatever its merits or limits as dramatic art, the play has political significance in American intellectual history. Eugene O'Neill was the only major intellectual on the Left who did not allow himself to be carried away by the Russian Revolution that took place two years after the play was written. His friend John Reed, the *Masses* editors Max Eastman and Floyd Dell, and even Emma Goldman went wild over the Bolshevik seizure of power in the fall of 1917. In O'Neill's play, it will be recalled, the socialists were scorned for being insufficiently revolutionary; now all radicals sought to prove their revolutionary credentials by identifying with the October Revolution that took place six thousand miles away in St. Petersburg. Reed's eyewitness account, *The Ten Days That Shook The World,* had the American Left believing that "Bolshevism was but the Russian name for the IWW." Not only Wobblies but democratic socialists waxed enthusiastic. "From the crown of my head to the soles of my feet," declared Eugene Debs, "I am a Bolshevik and proud of it." In *The Personal Equation* the shibboleth "Long—Live—the Revolution" is uttered in "a low, chuckling laugh" by the demented Tom whose condition has been reduced to that of "a little child." V. I. Lenin himself would later write a pamphlet accusing those who sought to perpetuate revolution indefinitely as suffering from "infantile disorder." In truth, today we know that Reed got the story completely wrong in seeing Wobbly dreams fulfilled under Lenin's dictatorship, which had no use for the anarchists' fantasy about spontaneity and direct action from below. Of the Greenwich Village rebels O'Neill stood alone in refusing to be seduced by the cult of revolution and the Marxist conviction that the mission of the proletariat is to bring about the transformation of history. That a cripple with the mind of a child mimics revolution as a fairy tale of the true believer brings politics face to face with nihilism, the state of recognizing that no idea has grounds for its existence. The revolution, Olga declares, "moves forward though we may not see it." O'Neill himself could not see it, and to appreciate his skeptical prescience we need to consider his second and far superior political play.

CLASS CONSCIOUSNESS AND THE STRUGGLE FOR RECOGNITION

O'Neill wrote *The Hairy Ape* "with a mad rush" in 1921, an eight-scene play that took him less than three weeks to compose. "The whole play just spilled forth without interruption save for writers cramp," he told drama critic George Jean Nathan.[20] Except for *The Emperor Jones,* all of O'Neill's plays of this era dealt with domestic themes, survival at sea, or the early age of exploration. But *The Hairy Ape* was decidedly political, which raises a question. If *The Personal Equation* concluded with the implication that the idea of revolution was little more than the desperate mystique of the intellectual class, where did that leave the working class? And why did O'Neill subtitle his play "A Comedy of Ancient and Modern Life in Eight Scenes"?

The Hairy Ape opens in the firemen's forecastle of a transatlantic cruise liner. O'Neill's stage directions are designed to make the audience see and feel the steamy, steely tumult in the bowels of the ship: "The brazen clang of the furnace doors as they are flung open or slammed shut, the grating, teeth-gritting grind of steel against steel, of crunching coal . . . the roar of leaping flames." The "monotonous throbbing beat of the engines" gives the rhythm of a mechanically regulated recurrence. The stokers, some stripped to the waist, are blackened in soot, and as they crouch to shovel coal "the ceiling crashes down upon the men's heads. They cannot stand upright," and thus the stooping posture "should resemble those pictures in which the appearance of the Neanderthal Man is guessed at." All the men are powerful figures with muscular arms "and low, receding brows above their small, fierce, resentful eyes."

This inferno of simian creatures is dominated by the mighty Yank, "more powerful, more sure of himself than the rest. They respect his superior strength — the grudging respect of fear. Then, too, he represents to them a self-expression, the very last word in what they want, their most highly developed individual." Yank expresses a force of indomitable conviction, the lord of the forecastle, all might and will, untroubled by doubt or drink. Without his shovel, nothing moves.

Yank is based on O'Neill's acquaintance with a Liverpool Irishman named Driscoll, whose person had also influenced previous plays. O'Neill described Driscoll as "a giant of a man. He thought a whole lot about himself, was a determined individualist. He was very proud of his strength, his capacity for grueling work. It seemed to give him mental poise to be able to dominate the stoke hole, do more than any of his mates. . . . He wasn't the type [to] just give up, and he loved life." In his days of bumming around waterfront bars O'Neill took pleasure in Driscoll's company. Then O'Neill heard that his tough, fierce companion "came to a strange end. He committed suicide by jumping overboard in mid- ocean. . . . Why? It was the why of Driscoll's suicide that gave me the germ of the idea" for the play.[21]

Yank, like Driscoll, symbolizes the strength and determination of the working class. In his figure we have a solid, resolute physical laborer who finds fulfillment in his demanding work and is at one with himself and completely at home in the modern world of machinery. Yank seems a paragon of what the proletariat should be. What, then, destroyed him?

The possibility that Yank might become the victim of capitalist exploitation, in the strict economic sense of the term, is dealt with at the outset. The stoker Long complains of the class system, with its privileges for the rich along with the plight of the poor and the sufferings of humanity — all in violation of the Bible. Other stokers have heard this radical rant once too often and respond with hisses and boos. Then the spotlight turns to Yank:

(standing up and glaring at Long)
Sit down before I knock yuh down! (Long makes haste to efface himself. Yank goes on contemptuously.) De Bible, huh? De Cap'tlist class, huh? Aw nix on dat Salvation Army-Socialist bull. Get a soapbox! Hire a hall! Come and be saved, huh? Jerk us to Jesus, huh? Aw g-wan! I've listened to lots of guys like you. . . . Wanter know what I t'ink? Yuh ain't no good for no one. Yuh're de bunk. Yuh ain't got no noive. . . . Say! What's dem slobs in de foist cabin got to do wit us? We're better men dan dey are, ain't we? Sure! One of us guys could clean up de whole mob wit one mit. Put one of 'em down here for one watch in de stokehole, what'd happen? Dey'd carry him off on a stretcher. Dem boids don't

amount to nothin'. Dey're just baggage. Who makes dis old tub run? Ain't it us guys? Well, den, we belong, don't we? We belong and dey don't. Dat's all.

Yank's outburst elicits a "loud chorus of approval" from the other stokers. But there is another, countering, voice, that of the Irishman Paddy, and while what he has to say is as poetic as it is disturbing, his thoughts have no effect on Yank. Drunken Paddy watches in a "blinking, melancholy daze" as Yank puts down Long's anticapitalist diatribes, and as Yank boasts, as though claiming the identity of a special class, that he and the workers below embody the power of steam and steel that drives modern society. All this machismo is too much for Paddy, who "suddenly cries out in a voice full of old sorrow":

We belong to this, you're saying? We make the ship to go, you're saying? Yerra then, that Almighty God have pity on us! (*His voice runs into the wail of a keen, he rocks back and forth on his bench. The men stare at him, startled and impressed in spite of themselves.*) Oh, to be back in the fine days of my youth, ochone! Oh, there was fine beautiful ships them days — clippers wid tall masts touching the sky — fine strong men in them — men that was sons of sea as it 'twas the mother that bore them.

The men who sailed the clipper ships were brave and bold and gave no thought to the passage of time, Paddy continues, "for we was free men — and I'm thinking 'tis only slaves to be giving heed to the day that's gone or the day to come — until they're old like me." Above deck, clipper sailors could enjoy the blazing moon and winking stars and during the day feel the warm sun, the bracing wind, and the ocean spray. But Paddy suddenly becomes mournful, knowing his thoughts are "a dead man's whisper," and he turns to Yank "resentfully":

'Twas them days men belonged to ships, not now. 'Twas them days a ship was part of the sea, and a man was part of a ship, and the sea joined all together and made it one. (*scornfully*) Is it one wid this you'd be, Yank — black smoke from the funnels smudging the sea, smudging the decks — the bloody engines pounding and throbbing and shaking — wid divil a sight of sun or a breath of clean air — choking our lungs wid coal dust — breaking our backs and hearts in the hell of a stokehole — feeding the bloody furnace — feeding our lives along wid the coal, I'm thinking— caged in by steel from a sight of the sky like bloody apes in the Zoo! . . . Is it to belong to that you're wishing? Is it a flesh and blood wheel of the engines you'd be?

Yank scorns Paddy's dreams of the past. If the stokehole is hell, "it takes a man to work in hell," and Yank relishes the challenge. "It's me makes it roar! It's me makes it move! Sure, on'y for me everything stops. It all goes dead, get me? . . . I'm at de bottom, get me? Dere ain't nothin' foither. I'm de end! I'm de start! . . . Slaves, hell! We run de whole woiks. All de rich guys dat tink dey're somep'n, dey ain't nothin'! Dey don't belong. But us guys, we're in de move, we're at de bottom, de whole ting is us!"

In the Marxist scenario, those at the bottom of society who are engaged in the productive activity of labor constitute the "driving force of history." The assumption of radicalism is that the proletariat's true class consciousness will rise to assault the "false consciousness" at the higher reaches of society. *The Hairy Ape* reverses this scenario. Yank's steadfast conviction about his identity and sense of belonging is shattered, not by the hard blows of the ruling class but by a glance of disgust leveled by a weak, frivolous woman.

THE SHOCK OF HUMILIATION

The scene that follows the one in the stokehole takes place on the first-class promenade, and O'Neill's disdain for the idle rich is nowhere better expressed. Mildred Douglas and her aunt languish in luxury while engaging in inane banter. Mildred, the granddaughter of a steel tycoon, is dressed all in white and looks as though "the vitality of her stock has been sapped before she had been conceived," her leisure-class life style all poise and no substance, an artifice more bought than made. Mildred likes to go slumming to see how the other half lives, and she has talked an officer into letting her visit the stokehole. She enters the room of blazing furnaces and watches horrified as Yank shovels coal and grunts taunts and threats to the other stokers. Noticing that they have stopped shoveling, he turns around to see Mildred, his eyes locking onto hers in a frozen trance. Mildred's body begins to slump and she is about to faint when she utters, "Take me away! Oh, the filthy beast." When she and the officer exit, the stunned Yank hurls a shovel at the slammed door and roars, "God damm yuh!" After that one slight he will never be the same.

The next act finds Yank sitting with his chin on his palm in the manner of Rodin's *The Thinker*. Accused by others of having been infatuated by the fleeting sight of Mildred, Yank lashes back. "Love, hell! Hate, dat's what. I've fallen in hate, get me?" But all the cocky bravado is gone. The radical Long lets him know that Mildred is related to the president of the steel trust that makes the ship's furnaces. "You and me, Comrade, we're 'is slaves." "Is all dat straight goods?" asks Yank, who at last realizes he is trapped in the iron cage of capitalism.

When the ship docks in New York, Yank sets out in search of Mildred to seek revenge for destroying his sense of self. He walks up swanky Fifth Avenue shouting to be recognized, only to be ignored by the wealthy, indifferent strollers. Those coming out of church are a "procession of gaudy marionnettes, yet with something of the relentless horror of Frankenstein in their detached, mechanistic unawareness." The capitalist and the Christian combine to form a community of zombies floating through life effortlessly while citing a "Doctor Caiaphas," presumably a clergyman whose name evokes the high priest who engineered the trial condemning Jesus to death. Trying desperately to get attention, Yank picks a fight with one of the high hats and is arrested, roughed up, and thrown in jail. There a cellmate tells him that if he wants to get back at society, he should joint the Wobblies. A newspaper is circulated, and a prisoner reads aloud a U.S. senator's warning about the I.W.W., a monologue indicating O'Neill's disdain for conventional American history and its celebration of liberal consensus:

> Like Cato I say to this Senate, the I.W.W. must be destroyed. For they represent an ever-present dagger pointed at the heart of the greatest nation the world has ever known, where all men are born free and equal, with equal opportunities for all, where the Founding Fathers have guaranteed to each one happiness, where Truth, Honor, Liberty, Justice, and the Brotherhood of Man are a religion absorbed with one's mother milk, taught at our father's knee, sealed, signed, and stamped upon in the glorious Constitution of these United States!

These words elicit from the prisoners "a perfect storm of hisses, catcalls, boos, and hard laughter."

Released from jail, Yank heads for the I.W.W. headquarters and starts to rave about dynamiting the Douglas steel plant. The officials regard him as a dangerous street crazy or a possible police agent, and he is thrown out the door. Rejected by his comrades, and mindful of Mildred's description of him, Yank makes his way to the monkey section of the city zoo. Looking at a gorilla, he opens the cage door thinking he can identify with the animal's strength and that both man and beast will "git even" with the society that has imprisoned him. But the gorilla suddenly crushes Yank, who grabs the bars of the cage and utters bewilderingly, "Even him didn't tink I belonged." On the floor the dying Yank has the play's final, terrifying line, "And perhaps the Hairy Ape at last belongs."

Whether or not O'Neill is suggesting that one "belongs" and returns to one's true self only in death, the political implications of the play far outweigh the metaphysical. How radical and politically revolutionary was the play? "Since my production of my *Hairy Ape* in Moscow," O'Neill wrote to the anarchist Alexander Berkman, referring to Russian critics, "they seem to regard me as a pure proletarian writer." The FBI agreed. "*The Hairy Ape* could lend itself to radical propaganda, and it is somewhat surprising that it has not already been used for this purpose," wrote a government agent. His report, which indicates a surveillance of O'Neill, continues with a warning about the play. "It possesses more inferential grounds for radical theories than *R.U.R.* [by Czech playwright Karl Capek], which has lately been adopted by the radical fraternity."[22]

The Hairy Ape was a success, and when the play immediately moved from Greenwich Village, where it opened, uptown to Broadway, the New York Police Department tried to close down the theater. America's finest law enforcers no more understood O'Neill's play than did the Soviet cultural commissars.

The play represents a curious convergence of drama and social theory. The years the play ran, 1922–1923, saw the publication of *History and Class Consciousness,* by the Hungarian philosopher Georg Lukacs. The text, then unknown except to Max Eastman and a few Village rebels who could read foreign languages, would become a bible to New Left activists when it came out in English in the sixties. So would the writings of Antonio Gramsci, the Italian Marxist who insisted that workers remained oppressed not simply by the economic and political power of capitalism but instead by its "hegemony," its influence over popular culture and public opinion. But 1922 was an ominous year, the time when Lenin was imposing his own control over communism throughout the world and fascism was rising in Italy. Yet while Gramsci called upon intellectuals to subvert the cultural hegemony of the upper classes, Lukacs the Hegelian claimed that freedom could be found residing within the instruments of control, and his book sought to prove that the proletariat had found its political fulfillment in Lenin's party dictatorship and that workers alone are capable of achieving the class consciousness necessary to the dissolution of bourgeois society.

Neither Lukacs nor his followers who extolled the working-class had much direct experience with working-class life, while Gramsci feared "Fordism" and "Taylorism," that is, the integration of workers into an industrial system based on scientific principles. Yank's identification with coal furnaces and steam power dramatizes the worker's worship of technology, but his breakdown after absorbing Mildred's scornful glance expresses what Gramsci meant by the power of cultural hegemony. The voice of Paddy also suggests it is false to look to machinery for deliverance. And when Yank looks upward above the turbines to see the opulent Mildred, her one gesture of disdain blows him away.

O'Neill did ship out on tramp steamers, labored in mines in Honduras, hung out in working-class dives in New York City, and hence knew the working class intimately. *The Hairy Ape* opens with Yank sure of himself because he resides where Marxist intellectuals tell us social consciousness begins: "I'm at de bottom, get me?" Yank is convinced that nothing can move until he moves into action. But is he frustrated by the forces of society or by his own limitations, by class oppression imposed from above or by a feeling of social inferiority felt from within?

Significantly, as the play progresses, Yank regresses, losing all confidence and sense of identity, and the other workers, stoking the engines that power the cruise ships of affluent society, know only the meaning of their own powerlessness. The notion of "false consciousness," which the Left sees as the sickness of the bourgeoisie alone, O'Neill recognizes as the plague of the proletariat as well. Yank assumes that he is society's life force, the co-agency of steel, coal, and turbines that drive the industrial world. O'Neill's play questions not just Marx's faith in the proletariat rising to consciousness but Hegel's faith in power relations that somehow dialectically reverse themselves so that in the course of history the slaves take over from the masters. Lukacs' book had been influenced by that Hegelian black magic. In Hegel's scheme of history, the master class can only consume and waste while the working classes produce and create; in the end, it is the slaves, bondsmen, and laborers who win the struggle for recognition. It is such a struggle that compels Yank to leave the ship and to try to seek revenge on a society that dubs him a "hairy" Neanderthal. But the wealthy leisure class promenades down Fifth Avenue serenely oblivious of Yank's pathetic presence. Hegel's promise was that we can become aware of ourselves only when others are conscious of us. Nietzsche, in reaction to Hegel, taught us why we should forget about others. O'Neill shows why Yank cannot forget when the wounds of insult bore so deeply into the psyche.

Yank is a rare character for O'Neill. Whereas many of his figures are driven by the will to power and possessiveness, Yanks seeks neither, and until he is inflicted with an insult that goes to the core of his being, he is at one with himself and his occupation. But once he is thrown into utter disorientation, the object of his desire is to wreak revenge on the society he hates. He is a strange proletarian figure, one who can cope with a life of exploitation but collapses into a question mark at the first touch of humiliation.

O'Neill had been thinking about the script for *The Hairy Ape* around the time his fellow Greenwich Village rebels were rejoicing in the Bolshevik Revolution. In western Europe as well, each country had a major philosopher who hailed the revolution in Russia as the beginning of a true world revolution that would liberate humanity from exploitation and oppression. So too did dramatists and poets such as Bertolt Brecht, George Bernard Shaw, and Louis Aragon. Humanity's deepest desire for recognition would be realized as the "I" and the "Other" were about to be reconciled, justice and freedom realized, and alienation overcome. But in America it was anarchists like Eugene O'Neill and Emma Goldman who remained skeptical of communism, and *The Hairy Ape* offered "A Comedy of Ancient and Modern Life in Eight Scenes," each scene moving further away from the promise of class consciousness, with Yank telling his shipmates to shut up so he can figure out who he is and where he belongs, and they replying that it is better to drink than to think. Insulted by a gasp of disgust inflicted by a society lady, Yank is Nietzsche's case of the "slave revolt in morality," driven by resentment against the powerful by the powerless whose identity has been destroyed by the gaze of the Other. "Yuh tink I made her sick, too, do yuh? Just lookin' at me, huh? Hairy ape, huh?"

WHY "BLASPHEMOUS SEAMEN"?

But O'Neill intended his play to speak to conditions that transcend politics. *The Hairy Ape* dealt with the theme of alienation, though not necessarily in the Marxist sense of workers being deprived of the fruits of their labor, estranged from fellow human beings, and caught up in the fetishism of commodities as they lust after consumer goods in a life of envious desperation. Instead, O'Neill's sense of alienation is more existential. Yank is a being who has no foundations in himself, a boisterous worker who thinks he knows who he is and what he is about, only to discover he is less than he is, and then feels he must be more than what he knows of himself as he sets out to find where he "belongs." In an interview given in response to the confusing interpretations of the play, O'Neill remarked:

> *The Hairy Ape* was propaganda in the sense it was a symbol of a man, who has lost his old harmony with nature, the harmony which he used to have as an animal and has not yet acquired in a spiritual way. Thus, not being able to find it on earth nor in heaven, he's in the middle, trying to make peace, taking the "woist punches from bot' of 'em.". . . Yank can't go forward, and so he tries to go back. This is what his shaking hands with the gorilla meant. But he can't go back to "belonging" either. . . . The subject here is the same ancient one that always was and always will be the one

subject for drama, and that is man and his struggle with his own fate. The struggle used to be with the gods, but is now with himself, his own past, his attempt to "belong."[23]

The existential struggle that O'Neill felt in his bones would be difficult to translate into politics for reasons he felt in his mind. The voice of Paddy in the play reminds us that the alienation of the worker is due to the industrialization of life and that under modern conditions workers would be susceptible to whatever scraps of comfort capitalism would throw at them. Whereas Marx saw industrialism as liberating life from the "idiocy of rural society," O'Neill saw it as alienating life from the harmony that could only be found in nature. Progress and technology would serve only to integrate further the worker into the class system, and the unionization of workers, rather than posing an opposition to that system, simply reinforces it. Speaking of Paddy's love for the old sailing ships, O'Neill noted in an interview:

> This feeling, by the way, does not exist so strongly now. Labor leaders have organized the seamen and have got them to think more about what is due *them* than what is due *from* them to the vessel. This new type of sailor wants his contract, all down in black and white; such and such work, so many hours, for so many dollars.
>
> Probably some abuses have been corrected by this new way of things. But under it there has been loss of the old spirit. It was more like the spirit of medieval guilds than anything that survives in this mechanistic age — the spirit of craftsmanship, of giving one's heart as well as one's hands to one's work, of doing it for the inner satisfaction of carrying out one's own ideals, not merely as obedience to orders. So far as I can see, the gain is overbalanced by the loss.[24]

While O'Neill is seldom taken seriously as a political thinker, it should be noted that in the above observation the playwright is making the same point that Max Weber did in criticizing Marx's labor theory of value. In assuming that work could continue to have the same value it had in earlier stages of history, was not Marx thinking about the handicraft economy of the Middle Ages, when labor was once honored? Marx's attributing Promethean powers to labor could scarcely be sustained in the modern age when the sailor is, as O'Neill put it, more interested in the wages he makes than in the work he does. As O'Neill and Weber saw the situation, the working class idealized by Marx that would redeem us from history had been left behind by history itself.

By no means should the impression be left that O'Neill had no use for workers. Legend has it that in the Greenwich Village era O'Neill would sneer at the helplessness of workers while John Reed would arouse them to revolutionary heights. Yet Reed returned from Russia claiming to bring the message of the Russian masses and their alleged support for the Bolshevik Revolution — quite a claim when he knew not a word of Russian. If O'Neill was more skeptical of the revolutionary potential of the workers, he was also more sympathetic to their real plight and saw nothing false about their honest attitudes toward life. "If I write often of seamen, it is because I know and like them so well," O'Neill stated in an interview. "I was once one of them." But why, the reporter asked, do you confine your writings to "blasphemous seamen"?

> Because I find more dramatic material among simple people such as these. They are more direct. In action and in utterance. Thus more dramatic. Their lives and sufferings and personalities lend themselves more readily to dramatization. They have not been steeped in the evasions and superficialities which come with social life and intercourse. Their real selves are exposed. They are crude but honest. They are not handicapped by inhibitions. In many ways they are inarticulate. They cannot write of their own problems. So they must often suffer in silence. I like to interpret for them. Dramatize them and thus bring their hardships into light. Give others a chance to see and help and understand.[25]

O'Neill's sentiments were expressed in the early twenties, a time when much of intellectual America had given up on radicalism and lost interest in politics altogether. Many of the Lost Generation went to Paris to cultivate the creative talents they thought the American environment had denied them. By fleeing to Europe, writers and artists assumed they could escape the inhibiting historical forces of Puritanism, frontier provincialism, and finance capitalism. O'Neill would also turn his mind toward Europe, not to escape America but to understand how Europe had shaped America long ago and far away, as though the country would come to be what it had been at the very moment of its discovery. The meaning of America lies in its beginnings.

4

Beginnings of American History

In the period immediately prior to the outbreak of the First World War, the period in which O'Neill wrote several one-act sea plays, American society swelled with Anglo-Saxon prejudices, at once racist, chauvinist, and nativist. Much of the Western world still felt the conceit of Rudyard Kipling's "white man's burden," and the emotions of the Boer War (1898–1902), with imperial England and Holland fighting one another in South Africa, resonate in the opening scenes of *The Iceman Cometh*. One veteran of the war calls the black character Joe "the whitest colored man I've ever knew. Proud to call you my friend." And Joe replies that he can be called anything but "Nigger." Kipling's message, conceived in the late nineteenth century, was not lost on the black characters in O'Neill's twentieth-century plays:

> Send forth the best ye breed,
> Go, bind your sons to exile,
> To serve your captive's need;
> To wait in heavy hardness,
> On fluttered folk and wild —
> Your new caught sullen people,
> Half devil and half child.

After the Spanish-American War of 1898, America looked upon the sea island cultures of Hawaii, Cuba, and the Philippines as primitive and saw itself taking on the role of "civilizing" the unenlightened heathen world.

One of the most popular plays of the era was *Bird of Paradise,* which dramatized the pagan rites of Hawaii. Featuring actress Carlotta Monterey, who years later would become O'Neill's third wife, the long-running play was adapted for a series of Hollywood films, featuring a heroine who gives up her life by leaping into a volcano to please the gods. The smug complacency with which Americans looked upon supposedly inferior cultures led the philosopher William James to feel that the nation should "puke up its soul." But in the pre–World War I years America regarded such island cultures as beyond the pale. "It is our duty toward the people living in barbarism to see that they are freed of their chains," declared President Theodore Roosevelt.[1]

Nevertheless, in O'Neill's *The Moon of the Caribbees* it is the white race that is chained to its dreams and desires. Four West Indian black women slip on to a docked freighter to sell American sailors rum, and the crew quickly deteriorates into a drunken brawl, leaving one man stabbed. The audience hears at the end of the one-act play music that also sounded at the opening — a spiritual "melancholy negro chant, faint and far off, drifts, crooning over the water." The dirge, bringing the islanders peace of mind, stirs sailors to drink themselves into oblivion, beyond the mind and its torturous memories.

History is tantamount to memory, for the question of who we are can easily turn on where we came from if the past shapes our identity. In O'Neill's most autobiographical play the mother, Mary Tyrone, sorrowfully observes, "We cannot help what life has done to us." "Done" — the past tense turns us toward history, the essence of everyone's lives, so inescapable that George Eliot could say "The happiest women, like the happiest nations, have no history." O'Neill's characters could seldom forget the past to become what Nietzsche called "unhistorical," that is, capable of living in the present alone. In *Long Day's Journey into Night* James Tyrone (O'Neill's depiction of his father) cries out to his wife. "For God's sake, forget the past!" Mary responds,

> Why? How can I? The past is the present, isn't it? It's the future, too. We all try to lie out of that but life won't let us.

Although a literary intellectual, O'Neill rarely regarded history as simply a creative act of writing, a narrative that had no bearing on factual truth. When thinking of doing a play on the French Revolution, he wrote out a list of every date and episode, from the Tennis Court Oath of June 20, 1789, to the dissolution of the Convention on October 26, 1795.[2] "I do not think you can write anything of value or understanding about the present," he remarked in an interview in 1946. "You can only write about life if it is far enough in the past. The present is too much mixed up with superficial values; you can't know which thing is important and which is not. The past which I have chosen is one I knew."[3]

Eugene O'Neill "became one of the greatest historical dramatists since Shakespeare," wrote Professor Travis Bogard, a longtime scholarly authority on the playwright.[4] As did Shakespeare, O'Neill wrote about emperors and their illusions of power, the status of women and their sexual drives, black men and their love for white women, merchants and their rapacious ways, and, lifting from the Greeks, revengeful sons returning from war to confront their households of infidelity and murder. O'Neill took American history as seriously as Shakespeare took English history, and both sought to cover a century of their respective histories.[5] Shakespeare's two tetralogies stretch from 1399 to 1485; O'Neill's unfinished historical "cycle" was intended to extend from 1755 to 1932. Both related family to political and social conditions, whether the royal family in aristocratic Europe or a rich family in democratic America or, as often the case with O'Neill, a poor family resentful of the rich. Shakespeare's histories and tragedies seldom end on an upbeat, and one has no expectation that an O'Neill play will leave us with a smile. Addressing the themes of ambition, power, and success, both playwrights saw human conduct carrying on in its expected ways regardless of the nature of the political regime, whether a monarchy or a republic. O'Neill rejected the notion that democratic America offered too mundane an environment for the setting of tragedy But when a vision of tragedy could be made manifest, it would be one akin to what Thomas Hobbes called the definition of hell: truth seen too late. As O'Neill put it in 1922:

> Suppose some day we should suddenly see with the clear eye of the soul the true valuation of all our triumphant brass band materialism; should see the cost—and the result in terms of eternal verities! What a colossal, one hundred percent American tragedy that would be. . . . Tragedy not native to our soil? Why, we are tragedy, the most appalling yet written or unwritten.[6]

Nietzsche, an admirer of the Greeks, believed that the most important thing to know about history is when to remember the past and when to ignore it. Such a choice requires the exercise of will, and few of O'Neill's characters are capable of it. The playwright sought to search with the "clear eye of the soul" for the basis of American tragedy. But unlike the Greeks and Romans, O'Neill had no hope that he could look to history to reveal the character of human excellence.

If a single historian influenced O'Neill's outlook, it may have been

Oswald Spengler and his controversial book, *The Decline of the West.* O'Neill discussed Spengler with his son Eugene Jr., who taught classics at Yale, and he defended his much-maligned book during World War II, when the author's somber views of the West were associated with Nazism. (Actually Spengler denounced anti-Semitism in 1936, shortly before he died.) In 1940 O'Neill was distressed by the fall of France and cryptically wrote in his diary, "Spengler was right!"[7] Right about what? War as the beginning of the end of civilization? History as power moving without conscience? In his attraction to Spengler, O'Neill was not simply staying abreast of the twentieth-century intellect and its preoccupation with the collapse of civilization, in contrast to earlier generations' preoccupation with civilization's origin and development. Spengler's peculiar way of writing history as morphology, with cultures analogous to plants and animal organisms, emerged in some of the playwright's stage directions, particularly in *Marco Millions,* where sacred trees and everything holy are threatened by the Western will to transform.

Spengler presents civilizations — the rise of cities, mercantilism, utilitarian philosophies, technology, the cult of the rational, the exhaustion of belief — as past their noon and on the way to decadence, the ultimate phase of a culture condemned to grow and die once it has lost its organic roots. Aside from Spengler's thesis, his observations could also appeal to O'Neill, in particular his comment that in modern tragedy there is no deliverance and that Tolstoi's hatred of property puts him "in the school of Marx, Ibsen, and Zola." Certain Spenglerian aphorisms resonated in O'Neill's plays. "The man *makes* history, the woman *is* history." In *Strange Interlude,* Nina Leeds makes nothing happen, yet history converges upon her as a domineering presence. Ultimately what perhaps attracted O'Neill to Spengler was the German philosopher extolling the Faustian spirit of restless searching, forever yearning for the unobtainable. In the concluding chapter of *The Decline of the West,* Spengler becomes almost monomaniacal about the omnipotence of money and how it has replaced the searching spirit. "What we have described as civilization, then, is the stage of culture at which tradition and personality have lost their immediate effectiveness, and every idea, to be actualized, has to be put in terms of money. At the beginning a man was wealthy because he was powerful — now he is powerful because he is wealthy. Intellect reaches the throne only when money puts it there. Democracy is the completed equating of money with political power."[8]

Both communism and Nazism could scarcely abide the thought that the power of money would become the new ruling force in the world, and liberalism assumed that democracy would bring the will of the people to bear in controlling wealth through political means. But what is the essence of money such that America is inspired to inscribe on its coins "In God We Trust"?—the U.S. Congress passed a law to seemingly sanctify money in this manner shortly after the California gold rush. One reason behind the spiritual mystique of money is suggested by the native Indian Nano in O'Neill's *The Fountain*. Having killed the God who descended to earth to teach humanity to scorn material things, and having made the point emphatic by nailing their savior to the cross, the white race, Nano remarks, expects to be feared for having defied God so that it could deify gold. O'Neill hardly needed Spengler or Nietzsche to remind him that it is easier to kill God than to obey him. But the founding of the New World, O'Neill would remind us, was based on worldly ambition and not on the self-abnegatory idealism required of true Christianity.

O'Neill approached history the same way many Greek playwrights approached story telling, as the study of the emotional depths of human nature that may tie the past to the present. After the opening of *The Hairy Ape*, a drama critic wrote about the "grim" story that jolted the expectations of the audience, which nevertheless "enthusiastically applauded when their faces were metaphorically slapped." What was the meaning of the blow? "The audiences," O'Neill replied, "sat there and listened to ideas absolutely opposed to their ordinary habits of thought—and applauded these ideas." When the critic asked him to account further for this reaction, O'Neill explained:

> They had been appealed to through their emotions, and our emotions are a better guide than our thoughts. Our emotions are instinctive. They are the result not only of our individual experiences but of the experiences of the whole human race, back through all the ages. They are the deep undercurrent, whereas our thoughts are often only the small individual surface reactions. Truth usually goes deep. So it reaches you through your emotions.[9]

O'Neill put history on the stage, where it could be reenacted as an object of contemplation and moral reflection. The playwright asks us to consider an American history that has its beginnings in two conflicting emotions: the desire to overcome alienation and achieve the salvation of the soul, and the desire to gain possession and achieve wealth, power, and status. The dualism of the spiritual and material is a conflict Americans would like to think that they have overcome. Americans see themselves, George Santayana once observed, "as idealists working on matter." But the Irish-Catholic literary imagination is haunted by the dualism between spirit and matter, often referred to as "the cross and corruption." In 1925, around the time O'Neill was working on his two historical plays dealing with the age of exploration, he remarked, in a letter to a family relative, Sister Mary Leo, "I write of the spiritually & physically disinherited whom Jesus loved," adding that although he was brought up a Catholic, "I have no faith."[10] What remained was a sense of sin, and O'Neill felt the need to write about characters with souls to save or to lose.

THE AGE OF EXPLORATION

What may be most important about the opening up of the New World was not the discovery of America but what was not discovered. Italian sailors and Spanish conquistadors set out for the New World in search of the fabled cities of Cathay and Cipangu, and the explorations often were not intended to establish settlements or even to develop a colonial empire. The men were after gold, silk, spices, and other precious resources whose value lay in their easy acquisition either through barter or plunder. Although these voyages of pillage included Jesuits and Franciscans and had the blessing of the Vatican, Christianity seldom served as a voice of conscience. Only with the later settlement of North America, especially New England, did religion play a role in guiding economic development through a strong Calvinist work ethic. Rather than simply find wealth, America would work its way to prosperity. Occasionally O'Neill remarked on this disciplined labor mentality in America, calling it "Cabotism," after the hard-working character in one of his plays. But so out of favor was the idea of Puritanism in the modern era that the product of Calvinism could only be looked upon as repressive, a religion inhibiting both freedom and pleasure. Far more significant to O'Neill was the earlier discovery of the New World that had its impulses in a covetousness without conscience.

Contemporary literary critics may be surprised to hear of O'Neill's prescience. On college campuses it is taught that conscience is little more than the "false consciousness" of idealism that serves to conceal the dark side of the white man's possessiveness. "Every western writer," insisted Edward Said in *Orientalism,* "in what he could say about the Orient, was a racist, an imperialist, and almost totally ethnocentric."[11] Professor Said started a school of thought called "post-colonial studies," which holds among its tenets that "every" Western writer misinterprets the alien "Other" as inferior, that he or she fails to appreciate that premodern societies enjoyed a "moral economy" untainted by competitive capitalism, and that all writings about the age of discovery are little more than "discourses of discovery," simply language constructions whose biases await to be deconstructed. But it so happens that long before contemporary literary theory, O'Neill, one of America's first multicultural writers, set out to deconstruct the Western imperialist mind in *Marco Millions*. "This play," O'Neill wrote in the foreword,

> is an attempt to render poetic justice to one long famous as a traveler, unjustly world-renowned as a liar, but sadly unrecognized by posterity in his true eminence as a man and a citizen — Marco Polo of Venice. The failure to appraise Polo at a fair valuation is his own fault. He dictated the book of his travels but left the traveler out. He was no author. He stuck to a recital of what he considered facts and the world called him a liar for his pains. Even in his native Venice, he was scoffingly nicknamed "the millionaire," or "Marco Millions." They could not take seriously his impressive statistics about the "millions" of this and the "millions" of that in the East. Polo, the man of brass tacks, became celebrated as an extravagant romancer and ever since has traveled down the prejudiced centuries, a prophet without honor, or even notoriety, save in false whiskers. This has moved me to an indignant crusade between the lines of his book, the bars of his prison, in order to whitewash the good soul of that maligned Venetian.

O'Neill is being ironic, for his version of Marco Polo leaves the Venetian merchant not only without a good soul but with no soul at all. Historically, the discovery of China in the reality of history and the Western imagination originates with the publication of *The Travels of Marco Polo* in 1298. The Venetian had been much maligned because his account of his seventeen years at the Chinese court seemed more fable than fact, with Polo depicting his self-importance in advising the Great Kublai Kaan and leading his soldiers to victory. With O'Neill, however, Polo becomes a symbol of the West's encounter with the East, and it is the superior moral sensibility of the Orient that stands as a reproach to the culture of Christianity.

*

In the play the Kublai Kaan has requested that Polo and his brothers return to China with a hundred wise men, selected by the Pope, to engage in a learned debate with his own sages. Yet Tedaldo, who would be anointed Pope Gregory X, scoffs that at best he might send a monk or two in order to convert a "Tartar barbarian." "But," responds Marco's brother, "he is not a barbarian. Why, every plate on his table is solid gold!" Upon hearing that it is lucre rather than learning that motivates the Polo brothers, the future Pope turns whimsical and ironic and advises that young Marco alone can "set an example of virtuous Western manhood amid all the levities of paganism, shun the frailty of poetry, have a million to his credit . . . and I will wager a million of something or other myself that the Kaan will soon be driven to seek spiritual salvation somewhere! Mark my words, Marco will be worth a million wise men — in the cause of wisdom!" Marco, the Pope exhorts, "you were born with success in your pockets." The irony is lost upon the Polo brothers, little sensing that they are being sent on a mission not to convert China but to corrupt her.

In O'Neill's play, Marco Polo travels through Persia, India, Mongolia, and China, showing great interest in the various people and their cultures. At first he is proper and virtuous, rejecting the invitations of prostitutes and restraining his delight in the splendor of grand palaces. But Polo's high seriousness turns out to be a masquerade, the pose of morality in the service of mammon. As critics commented when the play appeared, *Marco Millions* has its counterpart in Sinclair Lewis's novel *Babbitt*, its title figure a modern American businessman who combines profits and piety. The Kaan catches on to Polo's designs. "Marco's spiritual hump begins to disgust me," he says in reference to a body that claims to be more than it is. "He has not even a mortal soul, he has only an acquisitive instinct" — Polo covets everything while remaining convinced of nothing. Polo becomes the mayor of Yang-Chau, creating a courthouse that suspends free speech and raising taxes on workers while repealing them on the very rich. Governing with all the gravitas of an American politician, Polo's handsome face, as described by O'Neill in his stage directions, is "carefully arranged into the grave responsible expression of a Senator from the South of the United States of America about to propose an amendment to the Constitution restricting the migration of non-Nordic birds into Texas." Marco proudly shows the Kaan his two inventions, gunpowder and paper money, the one to conquer the world, the other to buy it, and Marco advises that arms escalation will bring security to all, for Kaan's enemies will "give in and avoid wasteful bloodshed."

O'Neill's play shifts between the comic and tragic. The young princess Kukachin falls in love with Marco after she is convinced he has an immortal soul. She observes him sighing when he hears music coming from the water and gazing at the stars as if he were at one with them. Kukachin's grandfather, the Kaan, is unimpressed, noting that like all merchants Marco memorizes everything and learns nothing. At the end of the play, Kukachin, heartbroken, understands how obsessed Marco has become with money. He tells her that he is to return to Italy to marry Donata, whose "family needs an alliance with our house." The princess explodes: "There is no soul, even in your love, which is no better than a mating of swine."

Combining missionaries with merchants, the adventures of Marco

Polo highlight the theme of the cross and corruption that runs through O'Neill's historical works. In Italy in the thirteenth and fourteenth century trade restrictions compelled Venice, Florence, and other city-states to find new outlets for commerce. Although the Renaissance republics engaged in the rituals of power and invoked the name Machiavelli and "civic virtue," the reality was something else. "The essence of its existence," the historian John Larner tells us of Venice, "was business." But O'Neill may have gone too far in his characterization of Marco Polo as a huckster on the make who readily forsakes his momentary romantic infatuations to return to the business of the day. Supposedly the embodiment of Old World avarice, historically Marco was actually more reticent than rapacious, an adventurous sojourner who opened up the West to a new culture more out of curiosity than cupidity.[12]

Marco Millions was written in 1925 and first performed in 1928. Although O'Neill had come to be recognized as one of America's leading playwrights, the production had a mixed reception. The artistic stage settings were praised, and the critic John Mason Brown believed that O'Neill went beyond Sinclair Lewis in offering "a haunting and savage beauty that lifts the play far above the mockery which is ordinarily aimed at the Kiwanians."[13] But *Marco Millions* seemed more pageantry than play, and its elaborate settings proved too expensive to stage night after night, although it would continue to be performed for years to come outside of New York. The subtleties of Taoism versus Confucianism were lost upon the audience, though not the moral lesson: the tender Kukachin died for love, the brash Marco lived for lucre. "You haven't yet proved you have an immortal soul!" the Kaan reproaches Marco, who replies, "It doesn't need proving."

But *Marco Millions* enjoyed the ultimate political irony. It was performed in the 1980s in Prague as an indictment of the totalitarian state of Czechoslovakia. What the play had associated with capitalism — soulless ambition, repression of civil liberties, and an armament race — could be turned against communism as well. O'Neill might well appreciate that Vaclav Havel, the dissident who spent six years in jail and then became the first president of democratic Czechoslovakia, was a playwright who believed, with Nietzsche, that the ruling state must die for freedom to live.

THE FOUNTAIN OF YOUTH

When O'Neill began his investigations into the age of exploration and expansion of the fifteenth century, the West, and America in particular, still looked upon itself with pride. In 1893 America held the Columbian Exposition in honor of Christopher Columbus, hailed as the discoverer of the

New World. And in school young Eugene O'Neill read about his heroic exploits worthy of celebration. Today, all this has changed. Columbus has come to be portrayed as a villain, with the Europeans rendered as brutal invaders and the native populations as virtuous, innocent, and happy until subjected to bondage and eventually exterminated by diseases carried by the white man.

In the spring of 1921, shortly after O'Neill won the Pulitzer Prize, he began studying the history of the Spanish explorers. *The Fountain,* an unsuccessful play that opened in New York City in 1925, has as its protagonist Juan Ponce de Leon with Columbus more of a secondary figure. O'Neill told critic Kenneth Macgowan that in writing the play he had found "very useful" John Fiske's *Discovery of America.* He had read other works, including James Fraser's *The Golden Bough,* but Fiske "seems to catch the spirit of the Spanish conquerors in quite wonderful fashion." O'Neill was delighted to discover that the historian's knowledge of Ponce de Leon amounted to little. "The more I ponder over this play, the more I feel that the less I know of the real Juan Ponce, the better. I want him to be my Spanish noble none other— not even his historical self. I want him a fine mixture of Columbus, Cortez, Las Casas, De Soto— in brief, the Spanish explorer of that epoch." Then O'Neill wrestled with a problem that faces the historian: how to derive meaning and understanding from factual data, especially when composing a composite character. "I am afraid too many facts might obstruct what vision I have and narrow me into an historical place of spotless integrity but no spiritual significance. Facts are facts, but the truth is beyond and outside them. And, moreover, judging from the many books I have read so far, the facts in this case seem to vary with the book. Only certain ones remain fixed and uncontroverted. So what the hell."[14]

The Fountain opens in Granada, Spain, in 1493. Juan Ponce de Leon, tall, handsome, a Spanish nobleman with a countenance at once "haughty" and "full of romantic adventureness and courage," is eager to sail with Christopher Columbus to find the western passage to Cathay. Told that the famous explorer is a madman, Juan snaps back, "Mad or not, he dreams of glory. I have heard he plans to conquer for Spain that immense realm of the Great Kaan which Marco Polo saw."

O'Neill had his facts straight. The achievements of Marco Polo were on Columbus's mind, and the Great Kaan is a key figure in his *Diario.* King Ferdinand and Queen Isabelle gave Columbus letters of credence to present to the Kaan, and when the navigator reaches the coast of Cuba he assumes that it forms part of the Chinese mainland. Columbus sends an Indian ashore to reassure the natives that the white man means no harm, but the explorer's concerns for the greater glory of God and country are far from Juan Ponce de Leon's search to recapture a lost past the better to prepare a new future.

In Granada, Maria de Cordova, an attractive woman a few years older than Juan, tries to dissuade him in "fiercely mocking" tones from embarking on the voyage, speaking of his safety only to better hide her jealousy. "It must be from love you are fleeing! (. . .) Is a woman avenging women? Tell me her name!" "Love, love, and always love!" exclaims Juan. "Can no other motive exist for you? God pity women!" Juan declares that Spain is his mistress, and his ambition for glory has no room for the personal or the material. But Spain itself, despite the authority of the monarchy and of the Church, has no coherent identity, no unified aim or motive. The officers accompanying Juan are, O'Neill writes in the stage directions, "Knights of the Cross, ignorant and despising every first principle of real Christianity," picturesque and cavalier figures, yet so greedy that they would, remarks the nobleman Luis de Alvaredo, "sack heaven and melt the moon for silver." Juan's own motives are unclear; he disdains both romantic love and material acquisition in the name of patriotic ideals, and at first he is only amused rather than obsessed by the story of the fountain of youth. Seeking to be free of all past entanglements, he sails off to the New World unsure, like so many other O'Neill characters, where he belongs or who he really is or what he ultimately seeks.

But Juan Ponce de Leon does know what he is against. "Have you no vision for the graspers of the earth?" he cries out to God, disgusted with the unmitigated avarice of his fellow sailors who think, once land is discovered, only of "the lust of loot." To O'Neill, the Western explorer experiences everything and understands nothing. To grasp is not to conceive and to know but to acquire and accumulate, not to comprehend but to take. America would be the setting for the greatest land grab in history.

What, then, did the discoverers discover? They certainly encountered a new environment, and if knowledge derives from experience and cannot go beyond it, the Spanish clearly had firsthand contact with a new world asking to be understood on its own terms. Yet O'Neill's play helps us understand that the explorers missed the meaning of America because nothing is feared more than a new experience that compels the mind to think anew. Although America's early discovery was only incidental to O'Neill's larger purpose of using the stage to probe the modern human condition, he came close to seeing America itself as almost cursed because the motive and intentions on which it was founded and settled perverted the original meaning of Christianity to serve the cause of power and exploitation. Unable to leave Europe behind, the Spanish could scarcely comprehend that they were in a "New World."

O'Neill himself avoided claiming that he was writing a straightforward history. A playwright may be less interested in getting the facts straight than in writing a dramatic narrative aiming to show that the wrongdoings of the past leave their traces in the present. Still, O'Neill believed that history could serve the purposes of morality by recapturing the "spirit" of an era that had lost its bearings. In a program note for the play he wrote:

> The idea of writing *The Fountain* came originally from my interest in the recurrence of folk-lore of the beautiful legend of a healing spring of eternal youth. The play is only incidentally concerned with the Era of Discovery in America. It has sought merely to express the emerging spirit of the period without pretending to any too-educational accuracy in the matter of dates and facts in general. The characters, with the exception of Columbus, are fictitious. Juan Ponce de Leon, in so far as I have been able to make him a human being, is wholly imaginary. I have simply filled in the bare outline of his career, as briefly reported in the Who's Who of the histories, with a conception of what could have been the truth behind his "life-sketch" if he had been the man it was romantically—and religiously—moving to me to believe he might have been! Therefore, I wish to take solemn oath right here and now, that *The Fountain* is not morbid realism.[15]

If the realism was far from morbid, it was certainly stark and theologically embarrassing to Christian faith. The story of Jesus's descending to earth to deliver the message of God scarcely makes sense to the native Indians, who think more logically and rationally than do the explorers and know the difference between spirit and matter. "Their God," remarks the Indian leader Nano, came to earth in the form of man and taught humanity to "scorn" the material world in order to "look for the spirit behind things." And how did white men respond to the miraculous messenger carrying the voice of the divine spirit? "In revenge they killed him. They tortured him as a sacrifice to their Gold Devil. They crossed two big sticks. They drove two little sticks through his hands and feet and pinned him on others."

The natives are rational enough to ask what is the significance of the crucifixion and wooden cross that the explorers bring along with their swords. The cross with the bleeding and anguished Christ can only lead them to believe that white men like to see their savior suffer and die. The cross itself becomes the symbol not of men's sin but of their strength. The explorers arrived, Nano warns, carrying "that figure of a dying God. They do this to strike fear. They command you to submit when you see how even a God who fought their evil was tortured."

The Spanish explorers are incapable of seeing that America represents the unknown future where old habits and customs need to be discarded. Hence Columbus continues to think about the Old World and, still holding on to the historical dream of Genoa's designs on Rome, aims to bring back wealth from the New World in order to resume the Crusades and have Italy take possession of the entire Mediterranean. Columbus cannot recognize that America offers a new era where there might be hope for humanity. "By living in the past," Ponce de Leon warns him, "you will consecrate your future to fanaticism." Other Europeans assume that they can force Indians to work by fear of punishment and the threat of death. But Ponce de Leon admonishes them not to repeat "the same blunder which failed on Espaniola. It means slavery. It defeats its purpose. The Indians die under the lash — and your labor dies with them."

Historically the Spanish explorers had little immediate success trying to force mezzo American Indians into doing the manual work that they themselves refused to do. Later when missions were established in Central America and in the far West, Spain instituted the *encomienda,* a system that assigned Indian groups to Spanish landholders and in exchange for work Indians were given protection and religious instruction. The American colonies, it should be noted, had no success trying to turn North American Indians into slaves, and Virginia planters eventually "solved" the labor problem by taking part in the African slave trade.

The Fountain treats both the religious and secular drives of fifteenth-century Spain, with Columbus's aspirations symbolizing the cross and Ponce de Leon's the sword. The play also offers a romance of poetic tenderness. Juan Ponce de Leon is a seeker, restless with some ultimate quest driving him but having no clear object in mind. "You will go far, soldier of iron — and dreamer," Maria says to him as he is about to leave Granada. But, she adds, "God pity if the two selves should ever clash." The clash never occurs. As the play progresses, the romantic dreamer takes over from the stern soldier, an emotional change brought on by the entrance of Beatrice, Maria's daughter, whose arrival in the New World reignites Juan's passion for love. She sings a poem that captures Juan's own earthbound desire to leap up to the stars:

> Life is a fountain
> Forever leaping
> Upward to capture the golden sunlight,
> Upward to reach the azure heaven;
> Failing, falling,
> Ever returning
> To kiss the earth that the flower may live.

O'Neill's "romantic dreamer" is caught up with thoughts of harmony and primordial unity, of the Garden of Eden, of lost paradises perhaps discoverable in the New World. A Moorish song gives the play the mood of lyrical rebirth:

> There is in some far country of the East—Cathay, Cipango, who knows— a spot that Nature has set apart from men and blessed with peace. It is a sacred grove where all things live in the old harmony they knew before man came. Beauty resides there and is articulate. Each sound is music, and every sight a vision.

Juan realizes that in the past in his relation with Maria he had only thought of Spain and glory, but in the presence of her daughter Beatrice he feels the power of true love. Yet his emotions have been aroused not so much by Beatrice as by what has been lost to age: "The Spirit of Youth, Hope, Ambition, Power to Dream and Dare." Columbus saw himself carrying out God's will; Juan subverts Christianity with the romantic imagination. "There is no God but love—no heaven but youth!" The play ends with Juan declaring, just as he is dying, that "I begin to know eternal youth. I have found my Fountain! O Fountain of Eternity, take back this drop, my soul."

Was O'Neill suggesting, with Niezsche, that existence has no meaning unless there is "eternal recurrence," that death may fulfill the desire that life continues and youth returns in all its beauty? According to Agnes Boulton, *Thus Spake Zarathustra* was "a sort of bible" to O'Neill, who kept it by his bedside and "copiously marked" up its pages.[16] Nietzsche's Zarathustra offers the eternal recurrence as an answer to Christianity, which had instilled fear of death and everlasting punishment. How to make death die away would be the parable of one of O'Neill's religious plays.

As a playwright-historian, O'Neill is no sentimentalist about alien cultures. He is hardly suggesting that goodness resides with the simple and virtuous. Nano is no "noble savage," a trusting innocent incapable of seeing evil and danger. The Chief may say of the Spanish warships that their "winged canoes are like the boats of Gods," but Nano is as skeptical as he is suspicious. The Medicine Man asks Nano how he managed to escape death if he has so defied the Spanish. "I am craftier than they," he replies. Indeed, he succeeds in deceiving the intelligent Juan Ponce de Leon, the wise warrior from Spain. Nano is no "construction" of a Western imagination that cannot comprehend a culture foreign to itself. He is a jungle Machiavel.

The Fountain does dramatize the West's fury of economic exploitation and folly of religious conversion. Juan protests the chains of slavery and criticizes the Franciscan monks: "all this baptizing of Indians, this cramming the cross down their throats has proven a ruinous error. It crushes their spirits." The European is too caught up in the past to see America for what it is, a second chance for humanity to redeem itself by changing its ways, a land not to exploit but to develop, build, and nurture:

> Adventurers lusting for loot to be had by a murder or two; nobles of Spain dreaming greedy visions of wealth to be theirs by birthright; monks itching for the rack to torture useful subjects of the Crown into slaves of the Church! And the leader to have you, Don Christopher—you who will pillage to resurrect the Crusades! Looters of the land, one and all! There is not one who will see it as an end to build upon! We will loot and loot and, weakened by the looting, be easy prey for stronger looters. God pity this land until all looters perish from the earth!

The brutal behavior of white Europe toward Central American natives was real, and the victory of the powerful over the weak was hardly due to the inability of the weak to know what was going on. Nano certainly knew, and he made it clear to his tribe that the white man had enslaved fellow Indians and raped their women. Writing about the clash of the Old World with the New, what troubled O'Neill was not the failure of cultural assimilation but the success of gluttonous imperialism.

*

Although O'Neill had an abiding interest in different cultures all over the world, he cannot readily be held up as an advocate for "multiculturalism" in the contemporary sense of the term, for the playwright hardly saw cultures so different that some might escape the original sin of avarice and the will to dominance. Distant Asia may have appeared the exception— then, if not now. Working on his Orientalist play, *Marco Millions,* provided the occasion for O'Neill to draw upon his knowledge of Eastern religions, Hinduism, Buddhism, and especially Taoism.[17] Repelled by Western materialism, O'Neill could be attracted to the mystical principles of Eastern thought, especially the need to overcome the isolation of the ego, the perils of possessiveness, and the dread of sin and punishment. But O'Neill was brought up a Catholic with a severe sense of dualism, the undeniable chasm between spirit and matter, and he was too read in Emerson and Nietzsche to conceive of life without will, desire, and struggle. Indeed, drama itself depends upon conflict, tragedy is born of opposition, and the necessity of dialogue suggests that the Western character cannot face the silence of the abyss. Becoming a transported Orientalist would have required O'Neill to give up the essence of his identity—his memory. In the 1920s, when American intellectuals subjected the world of business to satire, O'Neill used ancient China as a symbolic bastion that resisted the incursions of the commercial mentality. Today, with communist China rushing eagerly into the arms of market capitalism, it could be said that the world's most populous country has given up its history faster the playwright could give up his identity.

The economic globalization of the world would have surprised Spengler as much as it would have distressed O'Neill. The historian prophesized that the rule of money would result in Caesarism, and the playwright saw its sway as Satan holding forth at the Waldorf. But the early history of America promised a "city upon the hill" that would resist sin and the temptations of the flesh. Whereas the desire-driven Spaniards sought only to discover America in order to better appropriate its material resources and return immediately to Europe, the Puritans came to stay, and they set out to prove themselves in the eyes of God, not only by carrying out the message of Jesus Christ but that of John Locke as well. The Puritans sought not wealth but salvation through hard work and frugality, even though the doctrines of Calvinism taught that grace could only be received and not achieved. Yet the "Protestant Ethic and the Spirit of Capitalism" was short-lived in America, having died out sometime in the nineteenth century, the period of O'Neill's *Desire Under the Elms*. Thus O'Neill saw the Spaniard's lust for looting and Marco's acquisitive instinct as continuous with American history, and in the play we are about to examine, the moral significance of property is called into question as the sons make claims against the Calvinist-struck father. Property's acquisition symbolizes the urge to possess, own, and display one's holdings as a sign of status. American culture would come to worship wealth without work, and Juan Ponce de Leon's vision of the fountain of eternity would become part of the American dream, the longing for perpetual youth and unfading beauty—Tennessee Williams' Blanche DuBois, O'Neill's Nina Leeds, Arthur Miller's Marilyn Monroe. The ultimate theater of desire is democracy itself.

5

"Lust for Possession"

A scene in *The Fountain* fore tells one of the dark sides of American history. Spanish soldiers are crying for the life of the Indian Nano when Juan sees the opportunity to save him, exhorting "Speak, Nano! Tell them what you told me — of the golden cities. Speak!" Nano utters but a few words about dwellings made of gold, and the crowd cheers, drops its murderous thoughts, and rushes to set sail for the mythical Cathay in search of fortune.

The opening of *Desire Under the Elms,* a play written in 1924, two years after *The Fountain* had been composed in 1921–1922, evokes the same lusty emotion, with two characters declaring "They's gold in the West . . . fields o' gold! . . . Fortunes layin' just atop o' the ground waitin' t' be picked! Solomon's mines, they says!" Whatever the setting, a farm in nineteenth-century Protestant New England or the fifteenth-century Catholic-Spanish New World, humanity finds itself driven by the same desires. And desire is, for O'Neill, never the desirable, never what ought to be desired after reflection and deliberate consideration. O'Neill's description of the elm trees in his stage directions suggests that human emotions create the conditions of their own entrapment. The two enormous elms

> bend their trailing branches down over the roof. They appear to protect and at the same time subdue. There is a sinister maternity in their aspect, a crushing jealous absorption. They have developed from their intimate contact with the life of man in the house an appalling humanness. They brood oppressively over the house. They are like exhausted women rest-

ing their sagging breasts and hands and hair on its roof, and when it rains their tears trickle down monotonously and rot on the shingles.

Maternity, it turns out, does become sinister in the play, and the house is rotting with envy and spite, "a crushing jealous absorption."

The impression that early Native Americans had come to acquire gold without having to dig for it perplexed Spanish explorers, who could only wonder whether gold was a sign of divine favor. To possess wealth without the grind of daily labor made mockery of the "Protestant ethic," and O'Neill's *Desire Under the Elms* takes place in 1850, the year after the gold rush saw hordes of Americans heading west to strike it rich. Once again the lust for lucre caught on, this time for gold nuggets rather than dust, ingots, or coin. What Columbus failed to find in America, America itself would continue to look for — as had Islamic West Africa a century before Columbus. The California gold rush of 1849 was the ultimate expression of desire fixating on its object. The tens of thousands of men who disembarked from ships in San Francisco's harbor arrived to search, find, grab, and leave, not to settle down and build a community. Historically no one seemed to know where gold had originated, how it had come to be formed as a metal, or where to look for it — the long-held secret of the mother lode. Much of gold's hypnotic lure came from the impression that it could simply be found strewn on the ground or in a riverbed. California prospectors dipped pans into a stream and then shook them to find nuggets resting at the bottom. As Thoreau wryly observed, the whole affair was a gamble, there being no difference between rolling dice and sifting sand. Where gold came from mattered little. The same could be said of personal property; how things come to be owned is not as important as ownership itself.

In *Desire Under the Elms,* ownership of the farm represents the Christian duty to labor in an universe where "God is hard." But before long where private property comes from, who has title to it, and what it signifies become themes as burning as the love of a young man and woman for each other's minds and their lust for each other's bodies. Ephraim Cabot's farm is the object of envy, and his sons can barely wait for him to die to claim it. To Cabot the farm takes on religious meaning; its possession, he believes, comes from the sweat of the brow, God's test of character and will. Two of his sons, however, have a love-hate relation to the land, seeing their labor as not much better than the toil of dumb animals and yearning to escape to California and the rush for gold. The third son, Eben, appreciates the beauty of the land with an almost mystical sense of connection, and he believes he is the rightful heir as the son of the deceased mother who once held title to the farm. Abbie, the new young wife of Ephraim, also sees herself as the legitimate heir by virtue of marriage. The theater becomes the site of America's unsettled question: who gets what, when, how, and why? "There can be no injury," observed John Locke of seventeeth-century England, "where there is no property." In nineteenth-century America there was both.

The question of property is peculiar to modern democracy. The possessive passions that had been released under the conditions of modern society would have been less pronounced in aristocratic society, where there could be no longing for land but only for the splendor of banquets and the frivolity of fox hunts. In the Old World, property inheritance had been settled by the law of primogeniture entitling the eldest son to the farm upon the father's death. In postrevolutionary America, however, the elimination of primogeniture meant that claims to inheritance could be open to bitter rivalry, and even a woman's decision to marry could follow more from the calculation to be a proprietress than a mistress, and to marry a much older man meant that one need not be a wife for life.

The father Cabot, seventy-five years old, "tall and gaunt, with great, wiry, concentrated power, but stooped shouldered from toil," has just married thirty-five-year-old Abbie Putnam, "buxom, full of vitality" with a face that is "pretty but marred by its rather gross sensuality" (in the 1958 film version Abbie was played by the decidedly ungross Sophia Loren). Cabot wants his young bride to know and appreciate how hard he worked to build the farm while others went west and wasted themselves. His lazy sons, ridiculing his earnest life of labor, cannot see that a Calvinist God commands man to work from dawn until dusk. Cabot tells Abbie of his second wife, Eben's late mother, who was too soft and tender for farm life. Then he gives her his reasons why the farm is his and his alone:

> God's hard, not easy! God's in the stones! Build my church on a rock— out o' stones an' I'll be in them! That's what He meant t' Peter! (*He sighs heavily—a pause.*) Stones. I picked 'em up an' piled 'em into walls. Ye kin read the years o' my life in them walls, every day a hefted stone, climbin' over the hills up and down, fencin' in the fields that was mine, whar I'd make thin's grow out o' nothin'—like the will o' God, like the servant o' His hand. It wa'nt easy. It was hard an' He made me hard fur it.

But Abbie is paying no attention to what Cabot is saying. Her thoughts are on Eben and her eyes are on the wall behind which he stands in his room; his thoughts and emotions are also focused on her. Both regard each other as a threat to owning the land once Cabot dies. Abbie has taunted Cabot with the thought that he might leave the property to his son rather than his new wife — "my Rose o' Sharon," he calls her. But Cabot identifies the end of his life with the end of the land itself. "If I could, in my dyin' hour," he tells her, "I'd set it afire an' watch it burn — this house an' every ear o' corn an' every tree down t' the last blade o' hay! I'd sit an' know it was all a-dying with me an' no one else'd ever own what was mine, what I'd made out o' nothin' with my own sweat 'n' blood!" He then adds: "'Ceptin' the cows. Them I'd turn free." What about me? demands Abbie. "Ye'd be turned free, too." The exchange leads Abbie to realize that Ephraim's deepest desire is for another son and that if she can bless the aged man with such a miracle the land will be hers.

Abbie sets out to use Eben for such purposes, playing upon his love for his late mother. Before long Eben has convinced himself that by taking his father's new wife he will be avenging his mother for Cabot's cruelties to her. The seduction takes several scenes. After Abbie kisses him lightly, Eben pulls back, "I don't take t' ye, I tell ye! I hate the sight o ye!" Why, Abbie asks, did you kiss me back, "why was yer lips burnin'?" On a hot Sunday afternoon, Abbie has Eben where she wants him and tells him that the sun burns upon nature, "making thin's grow — bigger 'n' bigger — burnin' inside ye" so that he will "grow bigger — like a tree — like them elums" and that finally "Nature'll beat ye," and so it does, as "their lips meet in a fierce, bruising kiss."

These lines present one of the few scenes in all of O'Neill's plays where sex is described as more ravishing than disgusting. But even the erotics of an erection cannot subdue the deeper desires for possession. It is said that love gives itself, but rarely can O'Neill's characters give — until it is too late.

The play is a three-cornered power struggle with each antagonist locked in mental combat. Cabot seeks to rule and dominate and sees the farm as his rightful domain; Eben, wishing to see his father broken and destroyed, regards the farm as his inheritance and birthright; Abbie seeks status and sees the farm as giving her position in society as she feels confident that she can take possession of everything, including Eben, with whom she has fallen in love by the time their baby arrives less than a year later. But as in ancient Greek drama, the slightest incestuous love violates the order of nature, and instead of resolving conflict, drives it to a tragic end.

Eben finds that he resents his son for becoming part of his father's property. "I don't like lettin' on what's mine's his'n," he exclaims to Abbie. "I been doin' that all my life. I'm gettin' t' the end of b'arin' it!" Abbie reassures him that things will soon change. But later father Ephraim, boasting about the boy, tells Eben that Abbie has always despised him and wanted to have a son to make sure that the farm would go to her. Enraged, Eben attacks his father and the two go at it until Abbie rushes out to the porch to separate them. After the father leaves, Eben lashes out at Abbie and refuses to believe her desperate protests that she truly loves him. Instead, he curses the day the son was born. "I wish he'd die this minit! I wish I'd never sot eyes on him! It's him — yew havin' him — a-purpose t' steal — that's changed everthin'!" In a panic, Abbie, fearing Eben will leave her, regrets that "he'd never come up between us." "But ye hain't God, be ye?" wonders Eben. Abbie calls out, "Mebbe I kin take back one thin' God does!" Eben thinks she has cracked up. But to prove her love for him, Abbie goes upstairs and smothers to death her newborn son.

Told of the horrid deed, Eben at first thinks that it is his hated father whom she has murdered, and he delights in the idea, wondering why he had not done it first. Once he understands that it is his son who has been killed, Eben recoils, crying out "Oh, God A'mighty! A'mighty God!" He turns on Abbie, thinking that the taking of his son's life is like her old behavior in trying to steal the farm from him. With Abbie denying his accusations and professing her undying love, Eben rushes out to get the sheriff.

But Eben runs back to the house ahead of the sheriff to tell Abbie that he too must "pay for my part o' the sin" in threatening to leave to go out west. With his love for her pouring out, he pleads that they run away together, but Abbie calmly states, "I got t' take my punishment." Replies Eben: "I want t' share with ye, Abbie — prison 'r death 'r hell 'r anythin'! (*He looks into her eyes and forces a trembling smile.*) If I'm sharin' with ye, I won't feel lonesome, leastways." Abbie refuses to let him, but when the sheriff arrives Eben demands to be taken too. The couple walks hand in hand to the farm's gate, and Eben stops to point upwards:

EBEN: Sun's a-rizin'. Purty, hain't it?
ABBIE: Ay-eh (*They both stand for a moment looking up raptly in attitudes strangely aloof and devout.*)
SHERIFF: (*looking around at the farm enviously — to his companion*) It's a jim-dandy farm, no denyin'. Wished I owned it!

In the end love enables Abbie and Eben to share their guilt, to accept their punishment, even to give up their lives together. What cannot be shared is property itself.

Desire Under the Elms subverts the main currents of political philosophy. O'Neill saw property more as a passion than a principle, with people more driven to seize it than to work for it. In nineteenth-century America it was assumed that citizens needed property for their independence and capacity for self-government, and that there would always be a healthy relationship between property and virtue. O'Neill was closer to older classical thinkers in his conviction that power and wealth remain a permanent part of the human condition, and the wish to exclusive possession corrupts those who wield it to excess. The seventeenth-century philosopher James Harrington declared that power follows property just as night follows day, and that its possession is essential to liberty. O'Neill remained suspicious of such liberal formulations, believing that the craving for ownership is the curse of the human condition. It is the "creative yearning of the uncreative spirit which never achieves anything but a momentary clutch of failing fingers on the equally temporal tangible. This, in brief, is the background to the drama in *Desire*."[1]

LOVE AND PROPERTY

Some critics and viewers saw elements of Freudianism in the play. O'Neill replied in a private letter that Freud's ideas "only mean uncertain conjectures and explanations about the truths of the emotional past of mankind that every dramatist has clearly dealt with since real drama began." O'Neill acknowledged he respected Freud's work "tremendously — but I'm not an addict! Whatever of Freudianism is in *Desire* must have walked right in 'through my unconscious.'"[2]

If not Freud, one wonders what else may have been residing in O'Neill's unconscious and why the playwright deplored precisely what he himself desired. The subject of landed property was very much on his mind when writing the play. Coming into his own financially in the twenties, O'Neill was buying lots and houses and thereby following in the footsteps of his father (at least in cupidity if not in career), who also preferred real estate to stocks and bonds, and young O'Neill complained about income taxes in much the way his old man complained of electricity charges. He found himself, he wrote to critic Kenneth Macgowan, in the "snares of the 'property game' for securing spots in the sun which become spots on the sun. Property, to improve upon Proudhon," he wrote of the French anarchist Pierre-Joseph Proudhon, "is the theft of the moon from oneself."[3] The liberal theory of natural rights offered a more optimistic outlook and saw property not as theft but as the reward of labor. "In the beginning," wrote John Locke, "all the world was America" because in the New World property was so abundant it would be there for all to enjoy.

"*The things people call love* — Avarice and love: what different feeling these two terms evoke!" Thus spoke Friedrich Nietzsche. Yet the philosopher saw property and love as two sides of the same emotion and each turns on whether we value less what we have and desire more what we lack. "Our love of our neighbor — is it not a lust for new *possessions*?" asks Nietzsche. "And likewise our love of knowledge, of truth; and altogether any lust for what is new?" We become satiated with what is had and secured, with the known and familiar, and this could very well mean ourselves and our own identity. "Possessions," wrote Nietzsche, "are generally diminished by possessing. Our pleasure in ourselves tries to maintain itself by always changing something new *into ourselves*." The philanthropist and the good Samaritan depend on rescuing the suffering under the guise of love for humanity, but true association with fellow human beings is more a matter of simple friendship and fraternal sympathy than of either the romantic or the Christian notions of love. As to the "love of the sexes," Nietzsche explained why sharing becomes unthinkable as sexual love "betrays itself most clearly as a lust for possession":

> the lover desires the unconditional and sole possession of the person for whom he longs; he desires equally unconditional power over the soul and her the body of the beloved; he alone wants to be loved and desires to live and rule in the other soul as supreme and supremely desirable. If one considers that this means nothing less than *excluding* the world from a precious good, from happiness and enjoyment; if one considers that the lover aims at the impoverishment and deprivation of all other competitors, and would like to become the dragon guarding his golden hoard as the most inconsiderate and selfish of all "conquerors" and exploiters; if one considers, finally, that to the lover himself, the whole rest of the world appears indifferent, pale, and worthless, and he is prepared to make any sacrifice, to disturb any order, to subordinate all other interests — then one comes to feel genuine amazement that this wild avarice and injustice of sexual love has been glorified and deified so much in all ages — indeed that this love has furnished the concept of love as the opposite of egoism while it actually may be the most ingenuous expression of egoism.[4]

Nietzsche's outlook toward property resonates in O'Neill. It is curious how the material and ideal collapse in this analysis. Property is the passion for possession that also partakes of the ardor of romantic love, with the lover needing to exclude others from the person whom he loves and thereby denying to them the happiness he enjoys. St. Augustine, it should be noted, also likened possessiveness to the emotion of love. "To love," wrote Augustine, "is indeed to crave something for its own sake," and hence "love is a kind of craving." Hannah Arendt drew from Augustine the insight that it is in the emotion of desire that the self loses itself. "As it takes an object to determine and arouse desire, Augustine defines life itself by what it craves."[5] What, then, does America crave?

In American democracy, Tocqueville observed, the possibility of advancement and upward mobility arouses ambition. Once social barriers are removed, economic opportunity is present, and class distinctions are in flux, "there is impetuous universal movement toward those long-envied heights of power which can at last be enjoyed. In this first triumphant exaltation nothing seems impossible to anybody. Not only is there no limit to desires, but the power to satisfy them also seems almost unlimited."[6] Tocqueville believed that the "equality of conditions" in America derived from the repeal of primogeniture and entail (land descending legally through the family) in the revolutionary period. An unnamed member of the Livingston family, an old New York Hudson Valley aristocrat, told the Frenchman: "A change that partook of the magical resulted. The domains split up and passed into other hands, the family traditions, the aristocratic spirit which had distinguished the early times of the republic was replaced by an irresistible tendency toward equality, against which one can no longer have the least hope of struggling." Tocqueville may not have been entirely correct in implying that the repeal of primogeniture resulted in the disappearance of large estates, but Livingston did see the possibility of more equal access to land as related to the meaning of America. "One could not doubt that the law of inheritance was one of the principle causes of the complete triumph of 'democratic' principles," he emphasized of the law's abolition. "The Americans realize it themselves, whether they complain of it or are glad because of it. It's the inheritance law which has made us what we are, it's the foundation of our republic, such is the language we hear everyday."[7]

In *Desire Under the Elms* the law of inheritance is bitterly contested by characters whose need for land is a craving as strong as love, with both desires resulting in the loss of life itself. O'Neill tried to ennoble his story by having Abbie and Eben courageously face the consequences of their deeds. An innocent child is murdered to prove the sincerity of one person's love for another; infanticide as sacrifice is a theme in classical tragedy, and it is remarkable that O'Neill could place such a theme in an environment of liberal democracy.

It is unclear what Thomas Jefferson, who called himself an "Epicurean," had in mind when he replaced "happiness" for "property" as the well-known object of "pursuit" in the Declaration of Independence. But apparently the always in debt, slave-owning Jefferson had no qualms about the warnings of classical moralists of the ancient era. O'Neill, in contrast, comes close to the Stoics in suggesting that unhappiness is caused by becoming preoccupied with the wrong things, especially wealth and material possessions. Yet the playwright was sufficiently steeped in classical tragedy to recognize that human nature succumbs to its needs regardless of consequences. Both Abbie and Eben have a legitimate need for property: the man for his freedom, the woman for her independence. Both are right and do what they have to do, yet ultimately do wrong and bring about ruin to themselves and their child. In a rural farm in America in 1850, O'Neill gives us noble characters who can stare up into the sun and see beauty in the face of death. Tocqueville, however, anticipated that such an environment would lack nobility and tragedy:

> I think that ambitious men in democracies are less concerned than those in any other lands for the interests and judgment of posterity. The actual moment completely occupies and absorbs them. They carry through great undertakings quickly in preference to erecting long-lasting monuments. They are much more in love with success than glory. What they especially ask from men is obedience. What they most desire is power. Their manners almost always lag behind the rise in their social position. As a result, very vulgar tastes often go with their enjoyment of extraordinary prosperity, and it would seem that their only object in rising to supreme power was to gratify trivial and coarse appetites more easily.[8]

Although Tocqueville saw the equalization of access to property and wealth as energizing the passions of America, he was not altogether sure that the scrimmage of possessiveness could elevate the national character. O'Neill also recognized that an environment of equal conditions only leads the rich to suffer from fear of what they might lose and the poor to suffer from resenting what they lacked. In property one may enjoy liberty but not necessarily peace and serenity.

*

The idea of private property had its origins in English political philosophy, and thus the value of property itself became part of the American identity from the beginning of our history. Whether it was faith or fish that led the Puritans to settle in New England, land would soon become both a symbol and reality of wealth as the Massachusetts Bay Colony developed. In the southern colonies where a Calvinist fear of God had little presence, indentured servants and African-American slaves became species of property whose owners exploited their labor. The Civil War itself, the setting of O'Neill's *Mourning Becomes Electra,* was essentially a struggle over two different concepts of property: the right to keep slaves as property protected by the Constitution or the right to property as the product of one's own hard work, a Christian duty to labor as a result of original sin, as Ephraim Cabot claimed in *Desire Under the Elms.*

Land and its discontents permeate American history. Differences over concepts of land divided white settlers from Native Americans, who saw the earth as part of nature and, like the sky above and the waters below, belonging to everyone in common. By the time of the Jacksonian era, the setting for two of O'Neill's plays, the Indians' right of occupancy was challenged by those who claimed that ownership turned on labor and improvement.

The issue of property and its possession and protection ran through American history, from the colonial period to the Progressive era. O'Neill jotted down notes to write plays on Thomas Jefferson, Tom Paine, and the "Shays Rebellion" of 1786. In 1913, the year O'Neill began writing his early plays, Charles A. Beard published *An Economic Intepretation of the Constitution*, and he emphasized that the *Federalist* authors openly proclaimed that the protection of property was "the first object of government." O'Neill would agree with Beard that the state functioned to support the rich and suppress the poor, but what would the playwright have made of Jefferson, Paine, and Daniel Shays, all of whom saw government as a threat to private property? The anarchist sees the state as the antithesis to freedom, an attitude that culminates in America not in radicalism but in Reaganism.

When O'Neill was growing up in the 1890s, the historian Frederick Jackson Turner delivered a seminal address on "The Significance of the Frontier in American History." Turner insisted that the availability of "free land," the key to American democracy, had come to an end. But whether property amounted to open access or exclusive possession meant little to O'Neill, who saw the lust after land as expressing a deeper desire for dominance, with democracy the theater in which power plays its undemocratic role.

Nevertheless, there was always a touch of the romantic in O'Neill, and he concluded *Desire Under the Elms* on a note foreign to a U.S. Constitution that had forsaken any possibility of human regeneration. Having rejected the Christian idea of redemption as improbable and the romantic idea of transcendence as illusionary, the "machinery of government" had no place for the sentiment of love as the one emotion that may enable humanity to overcome its divided self. Yet O'Neill makes clear that it is only in the mutuality of loving joy that Abbie and Eben can accept responsibility for life and face death without fear. Once they are free of their lust for land, they can achieve a tragic salvation and look upward to a rising sun. American society, however, continues with its acquisitive ways — hence the last lines of the sheriff, gazing on the "jim-dandy" farm: "Wished I owned it!"

The sheriff wishing he owned the property suggests it is within his imagination that he might do so someday. Property in America, rather than being passed down through inheritance, was there to be had in a competitive environment. No longer an exclusive family possession, property did not arouse class hatred, as O'Neill's anarchist comrades — adhering to Pierre-Joseph Proudhon's adage, "Property is theft"— thought it would.

THE "CYCLE" PROJECT

Desire Under the Elms was produced in 1924. O'Neill would spend the remainder of the twenties writing prize-winning plays on a variety of subjects, including race, religion, science, labor, and sex. Yet O'Neill himself became almost obsessed with the idea of possessive desire, and in the thirties began outlining plots for a series of plays on American history that he referred to as the "Cycle" with the title "A Tale of Possessors Self-Dispossessed." O'Neill would continue to try to get across successfully what had escaped the audience of the earlier play. Many critics missed the significance of *Desire Under the Elms,* and others judged it morbid and immoral; the New York district attorney tried to have the play banned as indecent, and in Russia the audience was shocked to see infanticide depicted on the stage. But O'Neill remained convinced that America refused to look at itself to see what lies under layers of repression:

> What I think everyone missed in *Desire* is the quality in it I set most store by — the attempt to give an epic tinge to New England's inhibited life-lust, to make its inexpressiveness poetically expressive, to release it. It's just that — the poetical (in the broadest and deepest sense) vision illuminating even the most sordid and mean blind alleys of life — which I'm convinced is, and is to be, *my* concern and justification as a dramatist.[9]

O'Neill assumed he could interpret in dramatic form the meaning of America, the very subject that eluded the great historian Henry Adams. O'Neill told Americans that he sought to get at the "roots" of the country's sickness, but at best he could depict effects without dealing with causes, showing how desire manifests itself through possessiveness without necessarily explaining why the American national character remained constant over time. As with Adams, O'Neill discovered that in America power had escaped many of the constraints of authority, and desire, rather than leading to freedom, could seek its own repression. The playwright and the historian saw American history as the stage on which pride strode before the fall; both sought to awaken the people to the "most sordid and mean blind alleys of life"; each viewed democracy as succumbing to materialism, centralization, and corruption; and each had their moments of escape on the high seas and into the world of Eastern mysticism. But few readers understood what was troubling Adams, and fewer still would have grasped why O'Neill regarded the problem of America as the problem of American history.

The cycle project was "overpowering," O'Neill confided to biographer Barrett H. Clark, given the task of keeping each play a "unity in itself" while at the same time trying to make it a "vital part of the whole completion." It may be "damned interesting and worth the labor," he told Kenneth Macgowan, but still an "elephantine opus." Trying to write the cycle is "good fun," he wrote to critic John Mason Brown, "that is if one is a masochist with a fiendish sense of humor." Ultimately he asked producer Lawrence Langner to advise the Theatre Guild to "forget my Cycle entirely."[10]

*

At first the cycle was to be four plays, then seven, and eventually expanded until it reached eleven. The cycle would trace the course of American history through the story of two families, one from New England and the other Irish American, and deal with their origins and legacy, which stretched from 1775 to 1932. It was to be a story of defeated ideals and triumphant materialism, of romantic heroism and compromising resignation. Only one play was published and performed long after O'Neill's death in 1953; fragments of another survived and were reconstructed, published, and also performed (these two plays are the subject of our next chapter). When O'Neill became too ill to write, he knew he would never finish the cycle and ordered his wife to destroy the manuscripts. "It was awful," recalled Carlotta Monterey; "it was like tearing up children."[11]

Notes and papers involving the cycle have been uncovered by archivists and scholars, so we do know some of what O'Neill had in mind in addressing nothing less than the sweep of American history.[12] Significantly, what deeply concerned O'Neill also troubled a group of scholars in the late nineteenth and early twentieth century who have come to be known as "The Progressive Historians," specifically Charles A. Beard, Frederick Jackson Turner, and Vernon Louis Parrington. All three historians saw economic realities frustrating the fulfillment of political ideals. Such a scenario comes close to melodrama as greed finds its way onto the stage of history and becomes the villain that stalks the budding flower of democracy. All three historians extended their sympathies to Jeffersonianism and yeoman rural life and remained critical of Hamiltonianism, banking, and New England Calvinism. They also favored revolutionary France over conservative England. O'Neill partook of this outlook. In his work diary is an entry for a "Thomas Jefferson Play" in which the "evasive, opportunistic, cowardly" modern politician is contrasted to President Jefferson urging citizens of the new republic to exercise their rights and responsibilities as voters. Curiously, Lionel Trilling would write a severe critique of this Jeffersonian bias in his essay on Parrington in *The Liberal Imagination*. Yet Trilling would also write in praise of O'Neill because the playwright, unlike the historian, went beyond social realism to endow literature with metaphysical yearnings.

Planning a play on Maximilien Robespierre, O'Neill regarded the French Jacobin as the "savior of democracy" and "protector of the rights of man."[13] Perhaps O'Neill's Irish ancestry warped his views on history and landed him on the side of the French against the English. No doubt Robespierre's political asceticism appealed to the playwright, for the revolutionary leader so believed in the demands of civic virtue that he assumed selfishness could be purged from politics. In his notes for the play, "Robespierre: An Interpretation," O'Neill depicts the young Frenchman as affected by the early death of his mother, and describes revolutionaries as sons who, rebelling against their corrupt fathers, "drive the money changers from the temple," a redeeming generation that "will come again to judge the living and the dead."[14] These are strange musings for an anarchist. The Jacobins threw Tom Paine into jail. Can self-interest be repressed without repressing freedom itself? Oswald Spengler, the historian admired by O'Neill, predicted that democracy would put money on the throne.

At every step of the way O'Neill had difficulty with the cycle. Later he would liken the project to the story of the "American Dream" in all its deceits and disappointments. Sometimes he wondered whether he was writing history at all. In 1936 he told Lawrence Langner that he was mainly concerned only with "the spiritual and psychological history of an American family in the plays. The Cycle is primarily that, the history of a family. What larger significance I can give my people as extraordinary examples and symbols in the drama of American possessiveness and materialism is something else again. But I don't want anyone to get the idea that the Cycle is much concerned with what is usually understood by American history, for it isn't." Yet a dozen years later, in 1948, after letting the novelist Hamilton Basso know that he had destroyed most of the cycle manuscripts, he reiterated that it had been about "an American family primarily, but also intended to be the story of America."[15]

O'Neill's work on the cycle defied chronology. Although his dramatization of American history would begin in 1775, the first play he worked on, "The Calms of Capicorn," actually takes place in the mid-nineteenth century and involves clipper ships and the race for wealth and glory. O'Neill's unfinished plays deal with characters or their ancestors who will turn up in some of his later productions. But the uncompleted scripts also include some characters who would have no presence in O'Neill's performed plays. One is Leda Cade, a rare O'Neillian character who could be both acquisitive and free. She allows her body to be the prize of card-game winners and scorns the "poetic nonsense" of weak, tender men while living according to her own genuine wishes and desires. Another free spirit who did not make it to the stage is the character in "The Career of Bessie Bowen," in actual life Kate Gleason, a well-known industrialist and financier who had grown up a young tomboy in Rochester, New York, and went on to become the first woman to rise to the presidency of a national bank. In the story of America that O'Neill planned to tell, women would be prominent, especially those with a will to power, even if it meant the enfeeblement of their husbands, which confirms Nietzsche's point that whoever can command will find those who will obey.

O'Neill's "Bessie Bowen" is troubling in other respects. One of the dreams of the Greenwich Village generation, grounded in the writings of the economist Thorstein Veblen, was that the engineers would eventually prevail over business interests by virtue of superior knowledge of science and how the industrial machine operates. In the play, the exact opposite occurs as the imperious Mrs. Bowen easily overwhelms her scientist husband and makes his inventions seem frivolous in contrast to her drive to power.

Perhaps the most telling of the unproduced plays are "And Give Me Death" and "The Greed of the Meek." In the latter, the father, a parson, believes in the principle of Christian humility. One of his daughters, Abigail, would reverse the principle, not only in economics and politics but in intimate relations. "You don't love Henry?" asks her sister Susan about the man Abigail is to marry.

ABIGAIL: I don't know. Perhaps. He is very handsome. . . . But how can I tell?

SUSAN: You'd know if you did. I don't see how anyone could sleep with a man without love.

ABIGAIL: Don't you? I do. I can disassociate self from body, stand aside and observe. I have done it with Henry when he kisses me. It is easy to give the body; without the soul it is nothing to give; it cheats only the posses-sor; it does not fool the giver.

Besides, Abigail adds, "can you go to bed with a soul?"

*

Had O'Neill written at least a portion of his cycle project, it would have been the first time an intellectual with an anguished Catholic sensibility had tried to interpret the meaning of American history, where the self cannot be disassociated from society or the bodypolitik and the "black soul" is beyond redemption.[16] What O'Neill learned in prep school at Mt. Saint Vincent was the old Jansenian-Augustinian teaching that when the soul gives way to the body, all is lost to concupiscence and one goes to bed with sin. O'Neill saw humanity as condemned to losing its soul by aspir-ing to possess something outside it. The material and corporeal can be given and taken; the spiritual alone has nothing to do with exclusive plea-sure and is beyond desire. But in "The Greed of the Meek" one senses a possible reason why O'Neill may have had trouble sustaining a central theme for his cycle. Nietzsche had taught him that Christian self-denial amounted to a "slave morality" assuring the lowly station of those who give up riches in an effort to be kind and humble. At the same time an op-posite ethic of self-assertion and the will to power, which Nietzsche ad-vocated, results in the culture of possessive materialism that O'Neill saw as the sickness of America. The parson writes his sermon, "Blessed are the meek," and cannot act upon it, while his daughter mocks it. American his-tory, as O'Neill viewed it, needed both the father and the daughter, a soul that thought in compliance with Christianity and a body that willed in defiance of it.

In preparing his cycle studies, O'Neill read broadly in American history. He devoured Gustavus Meyers' *History of Great Fortunes* and Matthew Josephson's *The Robber Barons: The Great American Capitalists, 1861–1901.* From such works O'Neill sought to find data on how the rich and powerful gained control of railroads and oil pipelines. His plays also dealt with imperialism, with Admiral Dewey's visit to Manila, and with the U.S. penetration of the Far East. Unlike most American historians, however, O'Neill hardly saw the corruptions of the Gilded Age of Ameri-can big business as a departure from the virtuous ideals of the American Revolution. One character drawn for a possible play on that subject hopes that America will become the land of liberty and that the "impulse to-ward freedom will eventually lead to insight into what freedom really is." But with the possibilities of freedom come the temptations of sin and the "vanity of possession." To many historians of the American past, freedom is always in the making, rising, developing, even though retarded by economic scarcity or by a ruling elite that refuses to allow the full flowering of democracy. The playwright, perhaps more than the historian, shows us why democracy, even while offering formal freedom, breeds a deeper discontent, leaving people free of oppression yet fettered to desire, a national character, as Tocqueville put it, that "is itself dominated by its passion for dominion."[17]

6

Possessed and Self-dispossessed

Of the eleven-play cycle that O'Neill worked on in the thirties only one play survived intact to be published and performed posthumously, *A Touch of the Poet* (1957); another, *More Stately Mansions,* escaped Carlotta's fire place, and was later reconstructed and first performed in Sweden in 1962. Both plays dealt with the conviction that America and American democracy had failed its ideals, a verdict that had been arrived at by Henry Adams and other historians who also bemoaned the forces of materialism and economic determinism and the incapacity of the Constitution to prevent the Civil War. But coming from an Irish immigrant background, O'Neill was more interested in recording what the search for material satisfaction had done to a people trying to escape material deprivation. The doctrine of economic determinism depicted people as victims of forces beyond their control. O'Neill, however, recognized that the people themselves created the conditions in which they found themselves. Unlike the economic determinists, who saw little role for free will in a modern capitalist society, O'Neill sensed that people freely allowed their covetous longings to determine their actions. In a letter to producer Lawrence Langner written in the midst of the cycle project, O'Neill stated:

> I'm not giving a damn whether the dramatic event of every play has any significance in the growth of the country or not, as long as it is significant in the spiritual and psychological history of the American family in the

plays. The Cycle is primarily just that, the history of a family. What larger significance I can give my people as extraordinary examples and symbols in the drama of American possessiveness and materialism is something else again. . . . I am not much interested in economic determinism—but only in the self-determinism of which the economic is one phase and by no means the most revealing—at least, not for me.[1]

O'Neill's choice of "self-determinism" over economic determinism suggests that mind may be as important as the conditions that influence it. His emphasis on the self implies what Aristotle called "ethos," the dispositions of characters whose moral states determine their choices. In American democracy the spirit of liberty is said to prevail. But one wonders whether democracy nourishes equality or disdains it. Self-determinism would imply freedom only if the self were free of its desires and prepared to embrace democratic community.

A Touch of the Poet made its appearance in 1957, four years after O'Neill's death and a year after the premiere of *A Long Day's Journey into Night*. In the latter work the playwright bared his soul in anguish and love for his family, and the play commanded much attention from a public ready to hear a genius confess his torment and guilt. But the former work also indicates his love for and disillusionment with America, the country chosen by his immigrant ancestors. O'Neill would probably have disagreed with Jane Austen's distinction between pride and vanity. The English novelist saw pride as a healthy emotion enabling most people to feel good about themselves regardless of what others think. "A person may be proud without being vain," wrote Austen. "Pride relates more to our opinion of ourselves, vanity to what we would have others think of us."[2] The country O'Neill writes about in the two plays examined here is both proud and vain. Americans look upon themselves as free, autonomous individuals while unconsciously submitting to the "tyranny" of public opinion. What we think of ourselves may be inseparable from what others think of us.

*

A friend once chided O'Neill for always looking at himself in the mirror. This reflex was not conceit, O'Neill explained; "I just want to make sure I exist." In *A Touch of the Poet*, Major Cornelius ("Con") Melody seeks to prove more than his presence as he strikes dashing stances before a full-length mirror. Decked out in his old military uniform, he flicks a speck of lint from his sleeve, casually slings an invisible cape around his shoulders, and, striking an aristocratic pose, recites Lord Byron:

I have not loved the World, nor the World me;
I have not flattered its rank breath, nor bowed
To its idolatries a patient knee,
Nor coined my cheek to smiles, — nor cried aloud
In worship of an echo: in the crowd
They could not deem me one of such — I stood
Among them, but not of them

O'Neill's play takes place in July 1828, a crucial year in American political history when Andrew Jackson was about to defeat President John Quincy Adams, marking the demise of the old classical republic of virtue and deference and the ushering in of a mass democracy of political spleen, spittoons, and the spoils system. Henceforth, the new democracy might offer opportunity, but only at the cost of identity, for in an egalitarian society one gets ahead by adapting to the conventions of the day. Resisting this popular trend, Melody identifies with Bryon's lines, for he too feels that he is exceptional and above the crowd. In contrast to Ephraim Cabot of *Desire Under the Elms*, Melody scarcely considers work as fulfilling God's will; taken by aristocratic illusions of grandeur, he is too vain to labor and sees himself as an old military hero who deserves more recognition than American society extends to him. Tall, handsome, a womanizer, a poet and adventurer, at times a drunkard and braggart, Melody offers the last vestige of Irish romanticism as a foil to crass Yankee materialism. Like other O'Neill characters, Melody can only survive in his world of dreams, even if his self-centered illusions prevent him from knowing his own self. He keeps a beautiful thoroughbred mare as a symbol of his glorious military past, choosing to cling to what is over and gone for good.

Melody boasts of a gentry ancestry in Ireland. But his bar cronies tell us that his father was "but a thievin shebeen keeper," a tavern owner who got rich through money lending and squeezing rents from poor farmers. Once the father earned enough, he bought an estate and a pack of bloodhounds and sent his young son to college in Dublin, where Con would punch out the snobs who sneered at his modest background. Con claims to have fought with Wellington in Spain, but after the battle of Salamanca, and after being promoted to major for bravery in action, he was caught by a Spanish nobleman making love to his wife. Con killed the husband in a duel, and to hush up the scandal was forced to resign from the army. He returned to Ireland, to the castle he inherited from his father, and to Nora, the wife he left behind and with whom he had a daughter. He brought them both to America and purchased a rundown tavern on a little-used post road outside Boston. The cronies who hang out at the bar describe Nora as the salt of the earth and deny Con's claim that a priest tricked him into marrying her. He married her, we are told, out of genuine love but later distances himself from her impoverished background and regards her with contempt.

The daughter, Sara, resents the way her father treats her mother and, even more intensely, she finds his Byronic posing distasteful and his lack of ambition insulting to her own reputation in the community. Ashamed of her father, Sara sees through his rationalizations for the low status in which he finds himself in democratic America. The neighbors also resent Con, upset that he not only lords himself over other Irish immigrants but, still worse, has come out against Andrew Jackson and the Democrats and plans to vote with the Yankees and John Quincy Adams. Sara is not fooled:

> Faith, they can't see a joke, then, for it's a great joke to hear him shout against mob rule, like one of the Yankee gentry, when you know where he came from. And after the way the Yanks swindled him when he came here, getting him to buy this inn by telling him a new coach line was going to stop here. (*She laughs with bitter scorn.*) Oh, he's the easiest fool ever came to America! It's that I hold against him as much as anything, that when he came here the chance was before him to make himself all his lies pretended to be. He had education above most Yanks, and he had money enough to start him, and this is a country where you can rise as high as you like, and no one but the fools who envy you care what you rose from, once you've the money and power that goes with it. (*passionately*) Oh, if I was a man with the chance he had, there wouldn't be a dream I'd not make come true!

Sara's "chance" to fulfill her ambition to rise rests with Simon Harford, son of wealthy neighbors. Sara continually professes love for Simon, but O'Neill contrasts the almost saintly, uncritical love of Nora for her husband Con with Sara's conditional and calculated love for Simon. When Nora defends her husband's moody behavior, Sara is quick to object:

SARA: All right, Mother. You can humor his craziness, but he'll never make me pretend to him I don't know the truth.
NORA: Don't talk as if you hated him. You ought to be shamed—
SARA: I do hate him for the way he treats you. I heard him again last night, raking up the past, and blaming his ruin on his, having to marry you.
NORA: (*protests miserably*) It was the drink talkin', . . . not him.
SARA: (*exasperated*) It's you who ought to be ashamed, for not having more pride! You bear all his insults as meek as a lamb! You keep on slaving for

him when it's that has made you old before your time! (*angrily*) You can't much longer, I tell you! He's getting worse. You'll have to leave him.

NORA: (*aroused*) I'll never! Howld your prate!

SARA: You'd leave him today, if you had any pride!

NORA: I've pride in my love for him! I've loved him since the day I set eyes on him, and I'll love him till the day I die! (*with a strange superior scorn*) It's little you know of love, and you never will, for there's the same divil of pride in you that's in him, and it'll kape you from ivir givin' all of yourself, and that's what love is.

SARA: I could give all of myself if I wanted to, but—

NORA: If! Wanted to! Faix, it proves how little of love you know when you prate about if's and want-to's. It's when you don't give a thought for all the if's and want-to's in the world! It's when, if all the fires of hell was between you, you'd walk in them gladly to be with him, and sing with joy at your own burnin', if only his kiss was on your mouth! That's love, and I'm proud I've known the great sorrow and joy of it!

SARA: (*cannot help being impressed—looks at her mother with wondering respect*) You're a strange woman, Mother. (*She kisses her impulsively.*) And a grand woman! (*defiant again, with an arrogant toss of her head*) I'll love—but I'll love where it'll gain me freedom and not put me in slavery for life.

NORA: There's no slavery in it when you love!

While the mother is almost beyond desire, the daughter Sara becomes, in the play's sequel, *More Stately Mansions,* desire incarnated as power, one who equates being loved with being obeyed.

*

A Touch of the Poet stood at the center of the cycle project, whose "spiritual undertheme" was the Irish immigrant's acquisitive impulses and uncertain status. For O'Neill this theme would come to characterize American history in general, where greed and power would prevail over idealism and morality. The playwright sympathized with Nora, the unabashed peasant woman who can love for no other reason than love alone. But America itself finds its expression in Sara, who, like her father Con, is driven by pride and vanity, conceit toward the self and arrogance toward others.

Although fancying himself a poet-aristocrat, Con Melody is not above the American temptation of ambition, power, and status. Seeing the advantages of his daughter Sara marrying Simon Harford, he even suggests that she trick him into wedlock by getting pregnant with his child. She feigns being insulted by the suggestion, as though she had never thought of it. Simon's father, Henry Harford, sends his attorney to the tavern, and Con assumes there is to be a financial settlement to facilitate a forthcoming marriage. But Con soon finds out that Mr. Harford seeks to offer money only if Sara and Simon will sign a statement promising that they will never see one another again. On those conditions the attorney is prepared to offer Con three thousand dollars. Outraged to be told that "there is such a difference in station" between the two families, Con abhors the idea that he can be bought. Con seeks status and regards money groveling as the stigma of the lower classes. He threatens to beat the attorney to a pulp, then decides the honorable thing to do is to head to Harford's and challenge the rich landlord himself to a duel.

Con returns with a couple of his bar cronies, a beaten man, having been worked over by Harford's servants and by the town police. Disheveled, he looks into the mirror and begins to cite Byron only to sneer: "Be Christ, if he wasn't the joke av the world, the Major. He should have been a clown in a circus. God rest his soul in the flames av tormint! (*roughly*) But to hell wid the dead." He rushes out of the tavern, a shot is heard — but instead of taking his own life he has shot his prized mare, his last badge of honor. He reenters the tavern and begins to speak with a heavy brogue, his manners reverting to his lower-class origins. He planned to use the second bullet on himself, he confesses, but then he looked into the eyes of the dying mare, "with life ebbing out of them — wondering and sad, but still trustful, not reproaching me — with no fear in them — proud, understanding pride, loving me — she saw I was dying with her."

Sara is shocked at her father's unmasking and demands he reassume his Byronic pose and aristocratic air. But Con, realizing she has inherited his pride, accuses her of seeking to make him into what he is not, of "interferin and trying to raise the dead." In the closing scene he enters the barroom to raucous laughter, bagpipe music, the stomp of dancing feet, and a thunderous toast to the Democrat Andy Jackson, "the friend av the common men like me, God bless him!"

In O'Neill's version, Jacksonian democracy settles for a classless descent into the world of common laborers, drifters, and riffraff. Democracy rather than aristocracy would shape the future of the republic. Like Alexander Hamilton, Con Melody chooses the aristocratic resource, the duel, to defend his honor, but he is overcome by a wealthy landlord who, refusing the challenge, orders his own workers to pummel the upstart. There is "no equality before the enemy: the first presupposition of an honest duel," as Nietzsche warned. "Where one feels contempt, where one sees something beneath oneself, one has no business waging war."[3] In challenging Harford to a duel, Con demands to be respected as an equal. Proud, humiliated, defeated, he then retreats to the saloon where rounds of whiskey create the illusion that the hurts of class distinction can be laughed away.

*

In Ireland, Con rarely enjoyed the acceptance of his fellow students, and in America, reacting against his humble origins and the snobbery of the landed gentry, he is never sure of who he is or where he belongs. But after his beating he rejects all pretense of an Irish aristocratic past to find a place among those at whom he once sneered. Con Melody offers another example of desire under democracy; in this instance it expresses itself in the struggle for recognition and status in an environment without a fixed social order, where identity is not inherited but contrived out of manners, gestures, accent, looks, taste, wealth, possessions. At the basis of possession lurks power, the ability to compel others to give us what we want. The desire Melody believed he had a rightful claim to see fulfilled was position and prestige, which the individual can achieve only by commanding the recognition of others. Tocqueville offered a perfect account of Melody's predicament. Even in a democracy, Tocqueville was told, Americans are

> fond of nobility. . . . The greatest equality reigns here in the laws . . . and even customs. But I tell you the Devil loses nothing by it. And the pride which cannot come out in public finds at the very bottom of the soul a fine corner in which to instill itself. We sometimes laugh heartily to ourselves at the way some of our acquaintances affect to link themselves to the families of Europe and at the industry in which they seize upon the smallest social distinctions to which they may attain.[4]

In the setting of democracy, human beings hardly regard all others as naturally equal, as Thomas Paine and some of the Enlightenment philosophers had assumed. Often seething with resentment, people see themselves as competing with one another in the name of freedom. In the historical era that O'Neill was writing about, America was witnessing the birth of middle-class democracy. People envied what appeared to be the fulfilled desires of those above and resisted the unfulfilled demands of those below. It would be a democratic culture without political authority, in which public opinion prevails and determines what people think and how politicians behave in response to such thoughts. Although aristocracy was based on pride, on what the individual thought of himself or herself, democracy would be based on vanity, on what the masses thought others were thinking and on the effects that human beings have on each other. O'Neill's treatment of America brings together the ideas of two different thinkers, Tocqueville and Nietzsche. One saw an obsessive love for material pleasure producing anxiety and doubt, the other saw anxiety and doubt driving people toward "the petty distractions" of material gratification. Both saw the reign of desire as the "sweet despotism" of democracy. In O'Neill's sequel to *A Touch of the Poet,* democratic America comes face to face with itself.[5]

"FREE TO TAKE WHAT YOU WANT"

The sequel, *More Stately Mansions,* was never completed and was assumed to have been destroyed along with the other plays in the cycle. But the unfinished script turned up in the Beinecke Library at Yale University. Among O'Neill scholars a controversy raged about producing a work whose author wished destroyed. Yet the second play, which begins during the post-Jacksonian era, illuminates the enduring tensions of the first play and in some respects carries them to their logical conclusion. At the end of the first play Con, with "a cunning leer at Sara," says to his daughter:

> It's meself feels it me duty to give you a bit av fatherly advice, Sara darlint, while my mind is on it. I know you've great ambition, so remember it's to hell wid honor if ye want to rise in this world. Remember the blood in your veins and be your grandfather's true descendent. There was an able man for you! Be Jaysus, he nivir felt anything beneath him that could gain him something, and for lyin' tricks to swindle the bloody fools of gintry, there wasn't his match in Ireland, and he ended up wid a grand estate, and a castle, and a pile av gold in the bank.

What will succeed in America is not aristocratic poise but energy and ambition, and Con even advises his daughter to sleep with Simon Harford and then, with a great show of tears, to appeal to his honor to marry her and save both of their souls. "Be God, he'll nivir resist that, if I know him, for he's a young fool, full av decency and dreams, and looney, too, wid a touch av the poet in him." Sara is upset to be told to do what she had planned to do anyway, and she is just as upset to see her father going through a change of identity, returning to his roots. In democratic America identity can be a matter of choice rather than an inheritance from the past. In the opening scene of *More Stately Mansions,* Sara is married to Simon, and she proceeds in making him into what she wanted her father to be, not the dreamy poet but the hardheaded entrepreneur. Yet Sara, like America itself in its vast immigrant ethnic composition, is not entirely sure who she wants to be. Sara is made up of different parts, and her gender is as richly complex as her character. O'Neill offers a description of Sara, now Mrs. Harford with three children and a fourth on the way:

> Sara is twenty-five, exceedingly pretty in a typically Irish fashion, with a mass of black hair, a fair skin with rosy cheeks, and her mother's beautiful deep-blue eyes. There is a curious blending in her appearance of what are commonly considered to be aristocratic and peasant characteristics. She has a fine thoughtful forehead. Her eyes are not only beautiful but intelligent. Her nose is straight and finely modeled. She has small ears set close to her head, a well-shaped head on a slender neck. Her mouth, on the other hand, has a touch of coarse sensuality about its thick, tight lips, and her jaw is a little too long and heavy for the rest of her face, with a quality about it of masculine obstinacy and determination. . . . One gets the impression of a strong body, full breasted, full of health and vitality, and retaining its grace despite her [pregnant] condition. Its bad points are thick ankles, large feet, and big hands, broad and strong with thick, stubby fingers. Her voice is low and musical. She has rid her speech of brogue, except in moments of extreme emotion.

O'Neill was writing about a period in the American past that a historian has described as the beginning of the "feminization of American culture." The philosopher George Santayana also saw this tendency as central to "the genteel tradition." America started to divide along gender lines, with the masculine world taking to politics and business and the feminine to culture, domesticity, and the fine arts. Even in our day some feminist scholars sustain such a distinction in order to claim that women's role has always been to elevate sensibility and nurturing and thereby challenge the masculine domain of brutal profit-seeking and power. Santayana saw women becoming the custodians of culture while men went in for "aggressive enterprise."[6] O'Neill's take on American history has no hint of the feminization thesis. For Sara partakes of both peasant and aristocratic features as well as masculine and feminine traits, and it is she who is aggressive and enterprising while her husband Simon seeks solitude — nevertheless, he, too, has a masculine as well as feminine side, an instinct for business as well as an impulse for the poetic.

Simon Harford, upstairs above the tavern being nursed back to health in *A Touch of the Poet*, never makes an actual appearance in that play. In *More Stately Mansions*, he is the protagonist, and the story of his family becomes the story of a country forging its identity. Simon is described as having "a long Yankee face, with Indian resemblances," and brown eyes whose "expression [is] sharply observant and shrewd but in their depths ruminating and contemplative. A personality that impresses one incongruously as both practical and impractical." Like Sara, Simon also is made of discordant elements and is never sure what his place is in life. Gradually his impractical ideals lose out to an America with its own overflowing with a plenitude of practicality. Did Simon become what he willed himself to be or what Sara wished him to be?

To develop the character Simon, O'Neill reread the works of Henry David Thoreau, the one writer who told his fellow Americans to listen to themselves, to heed the inner voice of their own minds alone, to be true to thyself. When he was in the sanitarium in 1912, O'Neill first came upon the journals of Thoreau and Ralph Waldo Emerson. Many years later, in 1936, Van Wyck Brooks' *The Flowering of New England* was published, and O'Neill kept at his side this pathbreaking study of the Concord Transcendentalists. What O'Neill was conveying in his plays on nineteenth-century America, the Transcendentalists had already conveyed in poetry and philosophy: the vanity of Yankee materialism and the conforming servility of mass democracy. In notes to an unspecified play fragment titled "Thoreau in Simon," O'Neill jotted down ideas and made a sketch of Thoreau's cabin at Walden Pond.[7] At the opening of the play Simon is Thoreauvian; even with the responsibilities of marriage and children, he dreams of a better world for America and tries to convince his wife and mother that Rousseau was right to believe in the essential goodness of humanity. Simon himself is generous, open-minded, friendly with his black servant, a conscientious humanitarian reformer of the sort that existed among the abolitionists and utopian socialists of the 1830s. His mother, Deborah Harford, tells him that his father has had fits of "violent dyspepsia," so fearful is he about the forthcoming victory of Jacksonian democracy, which can only mean "government by the ignorant greedy mob for all future time." Simon protests:

SIMON: It's ridiculous snobbery for him to sneer at the common people. He should remember his grandfather was only a Welsh immigrant farmer. Not that I hold any brief for Andrew Jackson. His spoils system is a disgrace to the spirit of true Democracy. (*He shrugs his shoulders.*) But it is also an inevitable development of our system of government. That system was wrong from the beginning. It confused freedom with separation from England, and then mistook the right to vote for Liberty. To be truly free, we must start all over again. In a free society there must be no private property to tempt men's greed into enslaving one another. We must protect man from his stupid possessive instincts until he can be educated to outgrow them spiritually. But at the same time, we must never forget that the least government, the best government. We must renounce the idea of great centralized governments, and divide society into small, self-governing communities where all property is owned in common for the common good. In my book I will prove that this can easily be done if only men —

DEBORAH: (*cynically*) Ah, yes, if only men — and women — were not men and women!

SIMON: (*frowns, then smiles*) Now you're as cynical as Sara. . . . That is her objection, too. (*then with embarrassment*) But I'm afraid I'm boring you with my perfect society.

According to some historians, women were supposed to be the authentic reformers of a corrupt America. In O'Neill's play, mother and daughter are bored listening to how society might be improved. The only woman who understands what Simon represents is Nora, Con's devoted wife who recognizes that her daughter's husband has the pride and poetic spirit of her late husband. Her daughter Sara fears this affinity and tells her mother that if she and Simon had not been married, he would still be living alone in his cabin by the lake writing poetry and theorizing about the reformation of society. Sara boasts that she has changed his outlook. "He doesn't talk about that anymore, thank God! I've laughed it out of him!" Nora admires her daughter's effort to make a success of her life but at the same time worries that she is too determined to have her own way no matter what. Sara responds: "I am, Mother, for this is America not poverty-stricken Ireland where you're a slave! Here you're free to take what you want, if you have the power in yourself."

Democratic America had no moral authority or political institution that could have prevented Sara from taking what she wants. In the period when O'Neill's play takes place, the 1830s and 1840s, western territories became open to settlement and statehood, and some solid citizens wanted to take their slaves with them into Kansas-Nebraska. Sara, the ambitious entrepreneur — and not Simon, the at times wistful poet — represents the future of America. But Simon goes along with her ambitions and even allows them to determine his character and fate. In doing so he leaves Thoreau behind, as did America itself.

O'Neill was dramatizing what Emerson and Thoreau feared was disappearing from American life: self-reliance, the autonomy of the individual against the clutches of society, the spirit of idealism against the materialistic craving to own and possess. Sara, Deborah, and Simon each in their own way embody the alienated self unwilling to face itself. The haughty Deborah criticizes her daughter-in-law for her unrelenting acquisitiveness, but Sara justifies it. "I may have a greed in me. I've had good reason to have. There's nothing like hunger to make you greedy. But the thing you don't know is that there's great love in me too, great enough to destroy all the greed in the world." It is not at all clear that is the case, for O'Neill makes us aware that the self that is engrossed in its own desires is not free to love. Simon seems to have more self-knowledge, and tells his mother that he understands her "superior disdain for greedy traders like my father and me." Leaving Thoreau behind, the once-poetic Simon becomes "a Napoleon of finance." His mother asks him what his goal in life is. "To make the Company entirely self-sufficient," he responds. "It must attain the all-embracing security of complete self-possession—the might which is the sole right not to be a slave. Do you see?" Deborah sees only that she wants to repossess her son, even if this means returning him to infantile dependency, to "make him my little boy again." The most possessing of the three characters, Deborah is so possessed that she confesses to being a solipsist. Asked, "There is something in there [the garden] that frightens you, Deborah?" she replies, "Something? Outside me? No, nothing is there but I. My mind. . . . My life, I suppose you might call it, since I have never lived except in mind." However, the "very frightening prison" of her mind does not prevent Deborah from seeing through the illusions of others. When Simon tells his mother that the pursuit of wealth and power is only a means to the end of providing him the freedom to return to poetry and philosophy, Deborah responds: "I've found the means always becomes the end—and the end is always oneself."

O'Neill deals with a theme that not only troubled the intellectuals of the Jacksonian era but extended far back into classical thought and Christianity: the surrender of reason to passion, the bondage of will to desire, the loss of self to society. The rise of democracy was meant to free humankind from the problems that agonized ancient thinkers. Under liberal democracy in Jacksonian America, the mind was supposedly free from interference and domination, and men and women could be masters and mistresses of their own lives. Emerson, Thoreau, and Margaret Fuller knew that was not the case, and so did Eugene O'Neill.

*

The political loyalties of Sara and Simon suggest another look at American historiography.

Traditionally, it has been assumed that Jacksonian democracy represents the rise of political idealism against the acquisitive materialism of the conservative Whigs. Even historians writing about the earlier era of the postrevolutionary generation juxtaposed the egalitarian humanism of Thomas Jefferson to the elitist commercialism of Alexander Hamilton. The impression that democracy is enlightened and progressive can hardly be sustained in the play. It is the grasping Sara who supports Andrew Jackson, whom Simon describes as "an ignorant, mob-rousing, slave-dealing plantation owner," and she insists that the Union must be preserved at any price. The Thoreauvian Simon, while at first against slavery and sympathetic to the abolitionists and a reader of William Lloyd Garrison's *Liberator,* also likes John C. Calhoun and sees the doctrine of state rights as expressing the individual's claim to freedom. While one position supports a nationalism indifferent to slavery, the other promotes a sectionalism in defiant support of it. These conflicting positions suggest why O'Neill's anarchist affinities could go nowhere in America.

With Calhoun, the South would have seceded from the Union in an act of anarchist dissolution, thereby preserving slavery below the Mason-Dixon line where the North could not touch it. But the future of freedom in American, black and white, depended upon the preservation of the Union, the "last hope" for liberty in the world, as Lincoln put it. O'Neill's sympathies were with Jefferson, the thinker who left America with an unresolved contradiction between natural right and popular sovereignty, between the freedom of the individual and the will of the majority. The playwright Ibsen dealt with this contradiction in *An Enemy of the People,* where the voice of conscience battles against the corruption of the community. Earlier Tocqueville questioned the "dogma of the sovereignty of the people," and the sight of democracy in America led him to worry about the foundations of liberalism. O'Neill subscribed to neither liberalism nor conservatism, and it is hard to see him completely comfortable with anarchism, whose premise was based on the natural goodness of man.

The character Simon Harford, relatively unknown in the playwright's *oeuvre* since *More Stately Mansions* only came to public light some years after his death, and was first performed in New York in 1967, suggests why O'Neill thought self-determinism was the key to understanding human action and historical development. It is precisely because the self remains to be determined that the theater is the best vehicle in which to display a nation's history of conflicting tensions. Democracy leaves people in a state of doubt and irresolution, so much so that the philosopher of pragmatism William James would take on the responsibility of teaching Americans how to exercise "The Will to Believe." Yet Nietzsche and the Transcendentalists reminded O'Neill that even the will to power without knowledge of the self is powerless to resist the commands of others. Nietzsche called this dilemma "*malady of the will.*" It is at the heart of Simon's struggle with the two women in his life and of America's own struggle with itself.

The two women, wife Sara and mother Deborah, are polarities, one focused and almost predatory, the other aloof, effete, genteel, far removed from the sordid world of business. The more Sara wins Simon over to the market and its investment adventures, and the more Simon himself comes to enjoy the thrill of competition and mastery over his rivals, the more he is attracted to his ethereal mother and her dreams of innocent childhood. And while he sentimentally regards Deborah almost as his own fairy godmother who recites enchanting stories he recalls from boyhood, he comes to look on his own wife narrowly and more sexually, a business adviser free also to give the favors of her body as a paid mistress. "To hear you," Sara complains to Simon, "you'd think I was a wicked fancy woman you were offering to buy." Does such a proposed arrangement arouse Simon erotically or is it simply an exercise in domination? "That's a nice way to talk to a decent wife!" Sara protests. "I know," replies Simon, "you will find this game I play here in the Company as fascinating a gamble as I find it," assuring his wife that she has the talent "to demand and take what you want." She's perfect for the profession. "A fascinating game. Resembling love, I think a woman will find."

The world of business resembles the game of love in that desire only comes alive in pursuit of an object. Both involve a chase, of either wooing and courting or calculation and manipulation. The buyer may lose his money and the lover his freedom: to pursue something or somebody comes with a price. The very presence of desire indicates the desiring person feels a need in wanting what he or she lacks. Marx saw capitalist society producing a "commodity fetish" so that people desire to have and consume the things and objects made by others. Nietzsche saw desire as a positive emotion that activates the will to power and makes the individual a self-determining agent. Adam Smith even saw desire as ironic, as the productive citizen works for his own private self-interests and brings about the unintended consequences of the public good. But O'Neill's interpretation of the human condition is tragic rather than ironic. His idea of capitalism has little to do with the alienation of the worker, the production and consumption of goods, or the benevolent operations of the "invisible hand." The capitalist desires, above all, not to compete and produce but to control and possess. In his essay on "Wealth," Emerson wrote of the entrepreneurial class: "Power is what they want, not candy." O'Neill could not have agreed more.

THE DIVIDED SELF

There is no clear suggestion in *More Stately Mansions* that Simon and Sara's economic involvements produce anything satisfying that contributes to the good of society. Although they start out running a cotton mill, they are soon caught up in the cash nexus and talk about buying failing banks. All their profits, we are told, go back into specie, not the seeding of soil or the building of factories but simply into the supply of money. "The American people is, I said," observed Tocqueville, "a merchant people . . . devoured by the thirst for riches, which brings in its train many hardly honorable passions, such as cupidity, greed, and bad faith."[8] Sara has so converted her husband Simon that they both partake of such passions, having taken complete control over his deceased father's milling company, owning as well the vessels that ship cotton, the railroads that transport goods, the banks that extend credit, and the dealerships that sell products. Simon had once delved into Thoreau and lived in a hut by a pond. But at the prodding of his wife and mother, another self developed and he now identifies freedom not with autonomy and simplicity but with control and mastery. He has left Thoreau behind, forsaking self-reliance for self-assertion.

The parallel between making money and making love serves not only to equate profiteering with whoring but to bring home to Simon the depths of human rapacity. Becoming fully absorbed in business, he ridicules the romantic dreams of his youth and talks about the need for a book that will see through all pretense and self-deception. But is not freedom itself deceptive when the mind cannot think for itself? Simon likens himself to a man who keeps "on deliberately denying what he knows himself to be in fact, and encourage[s] a continual conflict in his mind, so that he lives split into opposites and divided against himself!" He is free to choose but the mind is far from free of the past and master of the future. Simon finds it remarkable that one inflicts this turmoil "all in the name of Freedom! As if Freedom could ever exist in Reality! As if at the end of every dream of liberty one did not find the slave, oneself, to whom oneself, the Master, is enslaved!"

Hearing these morbid sentiments, Sara accuses Simon of giving in to his "black loneliness." Yet Simon is articulating a post-Thoreauvian outlook and presaging where America is heading. It is an alienated outlook that brings us into the universe of Alexis de Tocqueville and Karl Marx, two disparate thinkers who could nonetheless agree that the rise of bourgeois society renders the individual self problematic. Thoreau's call to simplicity, solitude, and self-reliance had been too demanding for a country about to enjoy the comforts of bourgeois capitalism. With Thoreau, as well as with Marx and Tocqueville, O'Neill saw that at the end of the dream of liberty one becomes not free but enslaved to whatever commands our desires, and desires are arbitrary in that the mind cannot determine what it wants. Desires are also socially generated, for under the conditions of democracy people desire only objects desired by others. "Mother works in peculiar ways to steal what she desires," Simon says to

Sara, and both Sara and Deborah want Simon's soul for their own, all the more so since he is desired by the other. States Simon: "I knew Mother couldn't have entirely destroyed in you my old Sara who desired so passionately to take what she wanted from life, no matter what the cost." Responds Sara: "Destroyed me? She knows better than to try."

Sara and Deborah, establishing a tentative friendship, begin to blame Simon for his greedy, domineering ways while denying their own possessive impulses, and at the same time "tensely" convincing themselves that Simon "has taught us that whatever is in oneself is good — that whatever one desires is good, that the one evil is to deny oneself. (. . .) Again, it is not us but what he has made us be!" Simon has been listening outside the door to his mother and wife, and they gasp upon his entrance into the room, as he proceeds to give them what reads like a Nietzschean lecture on the transvaluation of values. He accuses his mother of hiding from herself, and his wife of having caught the same "cowardly habit" of rationalizing greed in the name of higher ideals. Do not be afraid of evil, Simon advises, and give up "the fool, Jean Jacques Rousseau — the stupid theory that [man] is naturally what we call virtuous and good." Such idealistic fantasies have sown the confusions in society and family, where "desires . . . are disciplined to covet what they don't want and be afraid to crave what they wish for in truth." He goes on, his face bearing "a thin tense smile": "In a nutshell, if you will pardon the seeming paradox, all one needs to remember is that good is evil, and evil, good."

*

Is O'Neill himself really suggesting that evil and good, like guilt and innocence, are simply illusions that serve only to produce the "blundering of our desires"? One wonders whether the playwright could fully endorse such a bleak conclusion. Christian values are abolished once the modern mind uncovers the forgery of their genealogy; once, that is, we understand where ideas come from historically and thereby discredit them by exposing the contingency of their origins. But good and evil may not simply be arbitrary social conventions that vary from culture to culture, constructions awaiting to be deconstructed. If they were, O'Neill would have been able to dismiss dualism as a delusion and not have a worry in the world.

Simon and Sara, however, feel deeply the dualism between matter and spirit, and they will go on to be tormented by their own selfish ways. The longing poet in Simon will never completely disappear, nor the feminine mother in Sara. O'Neill's characters are divided within themselves, and they recognize that to realize one side of one's nature is to suppress the other. To win in the world of business, Simon must deny his poetic sensibility and ethical impulses; to sustain the love of Simon, Sara must submit to his will and deny her autonomy. O'Neill's own father betrayed his creative talent to become a commercial success. Perhaps the impulse to acquire and control stems from the two selves within one self that are in a duel to possess the person. "I was trying to concentrate my thoughts on the final solution of the problem," Simon tells his wife and mother, as they mistakenly assume he is asking them to be what he wants them to be when, in fact, he is asking them to be themselves and face the dilemma of all humanity—to be possessive is to be possessed. Simon wonders whether he is about to go insane or commit suicide when he realizes that fear of enslavement verges on madness. "I have been forced to the conclusion lately that in the end, if the conflicting selves within a man are too evenly matched — if neither is strong enough to destroy the other before the man himself, of which they are halves, is exhausted by their struggle and in danger of being torn apart between them — then that man is forced at last, in self-defense, to choose one or the other."

The choice is never made in the play—O'Neill provides an easy way out of the dilemma. Injured by a fall on the head, Simon returns to his poetic fantasies as a semi-invalid, and in the last scene falls asleep with his head resting on the breast of his wife, who utters, "I'm your mother now."

More Stately Mansions concludes with Sara thinking about the future of her four sons, who appear after Simon has fallen asleep. Going forward in his cycle, O'Neill had planned to write a play about the careers of each son as a way of telling the story of American history. That O'Neill attempted to tell the story of America through generations of family history can easily lead one to conclude that the playwright had his own family in mind. To a certain extent the conclusion is valid; his brooding father, ethereal mother, and weak-willed brother are all present in his plays. Yet O'Neill's treatment of the human condition in its American setting should not be dismissed as merely the work of a tormented mind burdened by the repressed memories of his family and personal life. Even if his writings express a therapeutic need to confront his own past, they offer insights that go far beyond the personal. For much of what O'Neill wrote about America has also been observed by other writers in fields such as sociology and history.

"THE DEMOCRATIC SOUL"

American history, from the colonial revolution against English rule to the rise of Jacksonian democracy and the coming of the commercial market, clearly follows O'Neill's scenario of the dream of freedom giving way to the reality of possession. The title for the cycle, it is worth recalling, was "A Tale of Possessors Self-Dispossessed." In his *work diary,* O'Neill indicates what he means by these terms. Simon, an alien in his own family with a yearning to belong, first seeks solace in nature as a poet and then gives up solitude for the counting house. Regarding Sara, the diary notations state: "Her belonging is by possessing to be possessed—to be possessed in order to possess—her thwarting is that she can never feel she possesses all of [Simon]" since the poet resists her total absorption in him. In dialogue drafted in the diary, Simon's mother advises Sara that he is no longer a little boy and must be pushed out of the nest to "make him learn to fly and be free." Sara replies, "I don't want him free. I want him mine." She comes clean and tells her mother-in-law the truth. "I didn't want to fall in love with Simon," Sara admits. "I wanted him to fall in love with me. I wanted power over him. I'd had my own ambition to rise in the world." Her driving ambition takes over Simon himself, who seeks to obtain in the market "the all-embracing security of complete self-possession." But in the process of wanting to be what Sara calls "the King of America," even to the extent of taking over slave plantations in the South, Simon loses all in an attempt to acquire and control as much as he can, and while his wife takes over the business, he reverts to childish helplessness and eventually succumbs to a vegetative death—the possessor self-dispossessed.

One might think that O'Neill is drawing on classical thought in order to write an allegory about hubris and the excesses of "overweening ambition." But such character flaws in Aristotelian and Shakespearean themes are singular and highlight the struggle between virtue and vice. The tragedy of Simon Harford is not that he lives in pursuit of one all-consuming passion. Actually, he is divided within himself and belongs to no natural order of things. We might better appreciate what O'Neill was getting at in *A Touch of the Poet* and *More Stately Mansions* by considering Tocqueville's *Democracy in America,* also about the young, rising republic of the 1830s.

The dualistic character that O'Neill created in Simon Harford, a figure who goes back and forth between poetic withdrawal and entrepreneurial engagement, is strikingly close to "the democratic soul" that Tocqueville saw animating American history.[9] Tocqueville had been influenced by Augustine and Pascal, diagnosticians of the divided self and the restless spirit. Driven by the *angst* of endless desire, the self moves in two opposing directions: it either draws inward within itself and leaves the practical world behind to enjoy contemplation, or it extends outward into the world via hectic activities and pursuits whose ends never bring satisfaction. The self oscillates between these two extremes and is always in motion. The conflicting emotions also come between the individual and society. For Tocqueville defines individualism as "a calm and considered feeling which disposes each citizen to isolate himself from the mass of his fellows and withdraw into the circle of family and friends." A democratic culture exacerbates this tendency, so that "each man is forever thrown back on himself alone, and there is a danger that he may be shut up in the solitude of his own heart." Opposed to solitude is society, which draws the self out of itself to engage in public activities and pursue economic opportunities, leading Tocqueville to see the hope of a civic republic of citizen participation. But the rising world of capitalism also feeds on individualism, rendering people self-interested rather than public-spirited. The theoretical problem for Tocqueville was how to draw human beings out of an isolating individualism while preventing them from succumbing to a soul-devouring materialism.

Tocqueville was as worried about selfishness as O'Neill was about possessiveness. The French philosopher examined every aspect and implication of the term "interest," whether enlightened," "rational," "vicious," or "rightly understood." For Tocqueville, and earlier as well for John Locke and Adam Smith, the idea that people would conduct themselves according to their own interests and satisfactions meant that political and religious authority would no longer be needed to command obedience. And interests could well be as fickle as opinion is fashionable. "No longer do ideas, but interests only, form the links between men, and it would seem that human opinions were no more than a sort of mental dust open to the wind on every side and unable to come together and take shape."[10] Tocqueville hoped that if interest could be critically reflective and citizens made to think about the community at large, human desires could be moderated and the individual could accept restraints upon his passions and appetites. But if not, if self-interest has no capacity for self-control, then it becomes "pernicious" and its practitioners "petty" with envy and "debauched" with desire. Tocqueville's description of uninhibited self-interest captures Sara Harford's driving ambition in *More Stately Mansions.* Tocqueville's observation that American women are content to remain within the domestic sphere of life may be far from a description of Sara's continuous discontent, but O'Neill does acknowledge a nurturing maternal side along with the pernicious materialist. Significantly, in the play's very last passage Sara cannot make up her mind whether she wants her sons to follow her acquisitive ways or to lead a life of their own, the very ambivalence that her own father Con Melody expressed to her at the conclusion of *A Touch of the Poet.* It is as though the Yankee materialist and the Irish romantic still live on in unresolved tension. After Simon falls asleep in her lap and her four boys leave the garden, Sara's eyes follow them and she speaks aloud to herself, her thoughts proudly on her sons:

> Fine boys, each of them! No woman on earth has finer sons! Strong in body and with brains, too! Each with a stubborn will of his own! Leave it to them to take what they want from life, once they're men. This little scrub of a farm won't hold them long! Ethan, now, he'll own his own fleet of ships! And Wolfe will have his banks! And Johnny his railroads! And Honey be in the White House before he stops, maybe! And each of them will have wealth and power and a grand estate—(*She stops abruptly and guiltily—self-defiantly*) No! To hell with your mad dreams, Sara Melody! That's dead and done! You'll keep your hands off them if you have to cut them off to do it! You'll let them be what they want to be, if it's a tramp in rags without a penny, with no estate but a ditch by the road, so long as they're happy! You'll leave them free, do you hear, and yourself free of them! (*She looks down at Simon's sleeping face on her breast — with a brooding, possessive, tender smile*) After all, one slave is enough for any woman to be owned by! Isn't it true, my Darling? (*She laughs with a gloating, loving, proud, self-mockery — then bends and kisses him softly so as not to awaken him.*)

"So long as they're happy"! Of the American soul, Tocqueville wrote, "Whatever pains are taken to distract it from itself, it soon grows bored, restless, and anxious among the pleasures of the senses. If ever the thoughts of the great majority of mankind came to be concentrated solely in the search for material blessings, one can anticipate that there would be a colossal reaction in the souls of men." O'Neill's two plays on the post-Jacksonian era of American history reflect the "colossal reaction" of his own soul, even if American society continued in its insouciant ways.

Tocqueville, to be sure, respected religion and hoped that politics and civic duty would save America from the curse of selfish individualism. O'Neill, an agnostic and an anarchist, maintained little hope in religion or politics and saw institutions not serving to preserve liberty but standing in the way of the birth of true freedom. Nevertheless, Tocqueville's chapter on "Why the Americans Are Often So Restless in the Midst of Their Prosperity" could have been the basis for O'Neill's plays concerning the course of early American history. Both the social philosopher and the playwright saw America as a new environment that shuns the past as it dedicates itself to a future fixated on economic development, a society where older class distinctions no longer obtain, where ambition and social mobility are everywhere, where the challenge of how to rise easily leads to a culture of self-congratulation as achievement triumphs over inheritance. Sara Harford agrees completely with Tocqueville that democracy is the victory of will over birth and that America is an open field of opportunity for the ambitious. But there is a darker side to democracy that is more O'Neillian than even his characters are aware. For Tocqueville makes clear that the more equal people are, or think they are, the more they will strive to prove their worth in an insatiable longing for status and identity:

> Among democratic republics men easily obtain a certain equality, but they will never get the sort of equality they long for. That is a quality which ever retreats before them without getting quite out of sight, and as it retreats it beckons them on to pursue. Every instant they think they will catch it, and each time its slips through their fingers. They see it close enough to know its charms, but they do not get near enough to enjoy it, and they will be dead before they have fully relished its delights.[11]

Liberal, capitalist democracy makes formal, institutional freedom possible, but it also reveals the human condition in all its alienated longing. With this perspective, Alexis de Tocqueville, Eugene O'Neill, and Karl Marx are all in agreement. "No stigma attaches to the love of money in America," wrote Tocqueville in *Democracy in America,* "and provided it does not exceed the bonds imposed by public order, it is held in honor." But money seeking, Tocqueville adds, has people withdrawing into themselves and "constantly circling around in pursuit of the petty and banal pleasures with which they glut their souls."

Jotting thoughts for his projected seventh play of the cycle, titled "Twilight of Possessors-Dispossessed," O'Neill wrote a telling passage in his notebooks, which I paraphrase: A man rises from mechanic to a billionaire and loses all interest in his wife, children, family, and community. The sudden rush of wealth "bewilders, swamps, and corrupts him" as he discovers money is "beyond good and evil," making him all-powerful and God-like while leaving his six children haunted, neurotic, and depressed. He gathers a harem of kept women and gives each an annual present "the cost of the exact weight in gold her body represents." At the rear of his mansion he erects a temple, a replica of the Taj Mahal. Lonely, he sends for his former wife, who has remained unimpressed with his new life at the top of the world. Frustrated that he cannot make her feel for him or even be sorry for herself, he covers her with heavy gold jewelry and a massive crown; her heart gives out and she dies. At last he realizes he has the Midas sickness, and he tries futilely to dispossess himself of the wealth that has come to possess him. He gives it away and lavishly spends it with a frenzied irrationality. His children think he has lost his mind. But society, represented by the masked multitudes outside his gates, chants, "Billions in gold can't be mad." The man retreats to his temple, looks up at the altar of Mammon, and shouts, "you win," and shoots himself.

The idea of money as madness infused with supposedly supernatural power is precisely what Marx scrutinized in his "Economic and Philosophical Manuscripts of 1844." Far more than capitalism as an economic system, it was money itself that Marx regarded as the "alienated ability of mankind." Marx cited Shakespeare's *Timons of Athens* to indict the "yellow slave" of gold and to damn money as the "visible divinity" that transforms all human properties into their opposite and "makes brothers of impossibilities." Money is, Marx wrote, "the common whore, the common pimp of people and nations." As would O'Neill more than a century later, Marx saw money as the exchange value that commodifies all aspects of life so that rich people carry power in their pocket and purse. "Each individual possesses social power in the form of a thing," wrote Marx, and he paraphrased Goethe to explain how a thing, or anything, can be dissolved and transmuted, confounding and turning upside down all natural and human qualities. "Do not I, who thanks to money am capable of all the human heart longs for, possess all human capacities? Does not my money therefore transform all my incapacities into their contrary?" Marx, of course, was being facetious to better make the point that the more one has, the less one is.[12]

*

Many contemporary writers in the post-Jacksonian era — Orestes Brownson, William Leggett, William Gouge, James Fenimore Cooper — also saw money and its Midas touch overtaking a property-obsessed culture and stirring the passions of a "purse proud" people. American society had evolved into one without fixed social strata where wealth conferred status and power.[13] But the working classes of the era resented rich elites and made a distinction between "producers" and "parasites," those who created the wealth of the nation through labor and those who simply manipulated the money market. Such class antagonisms have led historians to regard Jacksonian workers as posing an opposition to the rising "market revolution." Those laboring in the trenches refused to believe that an ascending capitalism and free enterprise made wealth the proper reward for industry. "Contrary to liberal ideology," writes one historian critical of the liberal consensus school of thought, which saw no conflict between labor and capital, "democracy was born in tension with capitalism, and not as its natural and legitimizing expression."[14] The impression seems reinforced with Jackson's famous (or infamous) vetoing of the rechartering of the Bank of the United States. Yet the popular support for that act only indicates that the masses hated banks but loved money; or, more specifically, opposed a central, national bank and welcomed its destruction so that its specie would be relocated in local state banks where they could be better controlled by a democratic people.

In *More Stately Mansions* the Harfords are Whigs, but Sara herself is a Jacksonian Democrat, and it is Sara who delights in bank failures so that she can buy them up as she boasts to cowering competitors, "I am strong, you are weak." Sara believes the rise of American business has returned humankind to the state of nature, where men and women have a claim to anything they can seize and hold, where might determines right. Here we are in the world of natural liberty rather than civil liberty, not submission to the rule of law but the assertion of the unlimited right to everything by anyone who succeeds in acquiring and holding. In the natural state taking and seizing as the first step toward ownership requires no justification, as indeed was the case when Georgia took possession of the land of the Cherokees and America itself went to war to claim the northern lands of Mexico — just doing what comes naturally.

In dramatizing the ways of power, O'Neill's anarchism departs from both liberalism and Marxism. Simon and Sara Harford may live off the fruits of slave labor, but her greatest joy is preying not upon the poor but the rich and powerful in the competitive world of capitalism. She seeks out whoever might oppose her to better overpower rivals. In contrast to Locke and Marx, O'Neill rarely looks upon labor as the basic determinant of economic value, and when he writes of workers he is less concerned about their exploitation and more admiring of their romantic dreams and genuine solidarity and comradeship, a nostalgia for his own youth among the misfits and isolates.

In the very last utterance of *More Stately Mansions,* Sara Harford "laughs with a gloating, loving, proud, self-mockery." Did O'Neill's anarchism have an answer to Sara's ruthless impulses? Karl Marx's answer would be, of course, the social revolution that abolishes property and along with it the alienation of money — "the pimp between man's need and the object." Alexis de Tocqueville would hope that Sara Harford might give up her acquisitive ways, practice "self-interest rightly understood," and take up the public life of civic responsibility. O'Neill leaves her as we found her. But as to O'Neill's worries about the soulless, materialistic damnation of America, Tocqueville could reassure him that capitalism is as much about adventure as acquisition, more a matter of romantic challenge than pecuniary control. Commerce enjoys a "luster" in the New World in that the "American is not just working by calculation but is rather obeying an impulse of his nature." Tocqueville put his case in terms close to O'Neill's maritime heart:

> An American navigator leaves Boston to go and buy tea in China. He arrives in Canton, stays a few days there, and comes back. In less than two years he has gone around the whole globe, and only once has he seen land. Throughout the voyage of eight or ten months he has drunken brackish water and eaten salted meat; he has striven continually against the sea, disease, and boredom; but on his return he can sell tea a farthing cheaper than an English merchant can: he has attained his aim.
>
> I cannot express my thoughts better than by saying that the Americans put something heroic into their way of trading.[15]

It had been a maxim of liberal philosophy that trade and commerce would tame the passions that inflamed politics. But O'Neill's America was not about liberal natural rights, the value of labor and property, or the social contract and the consent of the governed. Like Emerson and Thoreau, O'Neill wanted Americans to see themselves as individuals and look inward to self-reliance and upward to a higher "Oversoul." But Thoreau could only teach Americans how to resist power, while Emerson went so far as to declare that "all power ceases in an act of repose."[16]

Although Marx believed the coercive authority of the patriarchal family would be surpassed in the new society of socialism, Tocqueville saw the family in democratic America as a wholesome institution because of the relative egalitarian treatment of all its members. "When the American returns from the turmoil of politics to the bosom of the family, he immediately finds a perfect picture of order and peace. There all his pleasures are simple and natural and his joys innocent and quiet, and as the regularity of life brings him happiness, he easily forms the habit of regulating his opinions as well as his tastes." Only under aristocracies, where family members are more concerned with memory and anxious to know what their ancestors thought, is the father the "political head of the family." But as aristocracy loses its power, so does parental authority. Thus Tocqueville is optimistic: "Among democratic nations every word a son addresses to his father has a tang of freedom, familiarity, and tenderness all at once, which gives an immediate impression of the new relationships prevailing in the family."[17]

Could anything be further from Eugene O'Neill's own experience with his family? With the playwright, family, memory, and history constitute an inescapable continuum. So too with his character Simon Harford, who represents American history's lack of self-consciousness, of failing to know its identity and direction. As the Transcendentalists feared, America would have a mind so divided that instead of practicing self-reliance it would seek its affirmation in the opinion of others:

SIMON: (*vaguely and drowsily*) I seem to remember I tried to find relaxation from the grinding daily slavery to the Company by engaging my mind in some study of the duality of man's nature. Did I, Sara, or is that just a dream?

SARA: (*uneasily*) Just a dream, Darling.

The equating of "grinding daily slavery" to working for a business firm is only one of several references to slavery in O'Neill's plays dealing with the Jacksonian era and the Civil War. O'Neill thought of writing a play about an abolitionist, but in the specific context of the American history he dealt with in his plays, the American people were less concerned about the institution of slavery than indifferent to it or, as Lincoln discovered in his debates with Stephen Douglas, even in support of it in the new territories. Tocqueville wrote hundreds of pages on the subject of race in America, but he remained relatively unknown outside of France, and America itself gave the subject little thought after the Civil War. The whole ugly issue of racism in America only surfaced in the early part of the twentieth century, with the establishment of the NAACP and the Greenwich Village rebellion of the pre–World War I years and the postradical era of the conservative twenties. It was in these years that O'Neill addressed directly the subject of race relations, a time when most other white writers dared not bring it up, a time when the Ku Klux Klan threatened any writer who did.

7

"Is You a Nigger, Nigger?"

THE MISSING AUTHENTIC NEGRO CHARACTER

Americans have always been uneasy about the subject of race, and historically this unspoken nervousness has included intellectuals as well as political leaders. That a playwright could deal with the subject long before most white scholars could bring themselves to investigate it is a remarkable feature of American cultural life. In recent years contemporary historians, once young radical activists from the sixties, have criticized previous generations of academics for neglecting to include in the study of American history and society the story of African Americans. No doubt guilt over the institution of slavery played a large role in repressing the story of a subjected people. Only in the world of literature, where fiction need not be determined by fact, did blacks emerge to make their presence felt. Yet writers as different as Harriet Beecher Stowe and Mark Twain wrote of their black characters, Uncle Tom and Nigger Jim, as too good to be true, so innocent of sin and sex, so purified and exempt of the foibles of the rest of the human race as to be devoid of humanity in all its deeper complexities.[1]

In the American theater around the turn of the twentieth century the tradition of using minstrelsy, white men with faces darkened by black cork, or African Americans themselves "blackening up" to accentuate their color before white audiences, continued on a stage opened to Eastern European immigrants as well as Anglo Saxons. Minstrel theater sustained the post–Civil War tradition of depicting blacks as Sambos and Mammies, happy fieldhands with banjos on their knees, or folk heroes of ballads like the legendary strongman John Henry. White America could be assured that blacks needed to be cared for as improvident children. Even as the minstrel show faded away in the early decades of the century, the stage continued the same treatment of blacks, most notably in Thomas Dixon's *The Clansman,* subsequently turned by D. W. Griffith into the popular film *Birth of a Nation* (1915), which cast the Ku Klux Klan as valiant redeemers rescuing the South from the evils of northern Reconstruction.

In recent years, the minstrel stage has been interpreted not only as a performance allowing whites to fantasize about blacks but also as an opportunity for blacks, through subtle gestures and jokes, to define themselves in opposition to whites. But in O'Neill's era such subtleties were lost upon the audience, and O'Neill himself perceived blacks struggling with the same human condition as whites, the same tormenting desires. At the time, however, white culture found on the stage its own prejudices. When not regarded as a threat to white womanhood, the African-American male was seen as kind, good-natured, naturally obedient, as loyal to his employer as a dog to his master. Of the cultural image of blacks in the early twentieth century, the literary critic Kenneth Burke wrote, facetiously, that "one could safely bestow one's love upon such essentially ineffectual foibles and imaginings. They had the lovableness of the incompetent. Americans, driven by some deep competitive fear, seem to open their hearts most easily to such symbols of 'contented indigence.'"[2] An early enthusiast of O'Neill, drama critic George Jean Nathan, wrote in the *American Mercury* a statement summarizing the deplorable status of blacks on the American stage, a statement quoted approvingly in *Opportunity,* the magazine of the National Association for the Advancement of Colored People. "Up until eight or nine years ago," Nathan wrote in 1924,

> it is doubtful if in the entire range of the American drama there was to be found a single authentic Negro character. The Negro of drama was then either of the white wool wig and kidney pain species, given to excessive hobbling, many a "yas, yas, massa, I'se a-comin," and a comic line on his every exit, or of the species that was essentially a mere blacked-up Caucasian minstrel end man, in a cutaway coat three sizes too large for him and a snowy toupee, who was rather dubiously transformed into a dramatic character by giving him one scene in which he taught little Frieda and Otto how to say their prayers and another in which he apologetically shuffled into his master's library when the mortgage on the latter's old southern estate was about to be foreclosed by the northern villain and,

with tears in his eyes and a quaver in his voice, informed him that, come what might, he would stick to him until he was daid.[3]

When O'Neill arrived on the scene of the American theater in the early part of the century, the American cultural imagination still remained in a state of denial about the African American. O'Neill's interest in blacks and black history has generally been interpreted as expressing his own experience of deprivation and discrimination as a descendent of Irish immigrants. True, both blacks and Irish had been denied political freedoms in their native countries, and both arrived in America as slaves to be sold or as laborers and servants in flight from famine and penal laws. And young O'Neill could never forget the snubbing of his Irish family by Yankee New Londoners.

Yet despite these affinities, it was unusual for the Irish to identify with blacks. Before the Civil War in various eastern cities, Irish dockworkers assaulted blacks as potential strikebreakers. In 1863, during the Civil War, draft riots broke out in New York City, taking the lives of 105 people, including police officers, immigrants, and many blacks, some chased down and beaten to death by Irish hooligans. Class as well as race inflamed the riots. The Conscription Act of 1863 allowed those who could afford $300 to be exempted from the draft; at the time of the Emancipation Proclamation it seemed that the wealthy classes had arranged a poor man's war. Lower-class whites, many Irish, viciously took out their hostility on blacks with lynchings, drownings, burning of dwellings, and sexual mutilations. Later in the nineteenth century Tammany Hall, the powerful Irish political ring, closed itself off to the postemancipation presence of black Americans.[4]

Eugene O'Neill's compassionate treatment of African Americans may tell us more about the need of a writer to transcend his background than to express it. The budding playwright came to know several blacks when hanging out in New York taverns, at least one of whom would provide the life story of characters in two future plays. O'Neill himself jotted down notes for a play about the Civil War draft riots, and he planned another play about a runaway slave. Against the conventional Sambo image of the black slave, O'Neill wrote of the black man's dignity and intelligence, his strength and endurance, even his capacity for autonomy within the confines of slavery. In notes for a "Negro Play" about a "Bantu Boy," O'Neill sketched the first part of his plot:

Negro play of the Negro's whole experience in modern times, especially with regard to America—Bantu chief and his krall—tricked, his honor played upon, drugged and he and his wives captured—slave ship—America, sold into slavery—proud, sure of his integrity, he baffles his different owners who chain and beat him—finally property of exceptional planter who appreciates his quality—offers to free him. "Freedom is God's, white man. You cannot set me free. I am free."[5]

Does O'Neill overcompensate for the conventional view of the slave, at once happy and helpless, by idealizing him as a paragon of virtue? Whatever the answer, the playwright seems to have presaged a fierce debate that has been taking place in historiography, one that first had its point of departure in the controversial Moynihan Report in the 1960s. The brief document was written by the late New York senator, Daniel Patrick Moynihan, in an effort to provide a grimly realistic portrait of the conditions of African-American life in contemporary America. Moynihan, who himself had come from a broken home with a father who spent more time at the local bar than at the family table, was troubled by the absence of male authority in the African-American household. The debate has gone through three phases.

The historical scholarship of the fifties provided a severe view of slavery. The institution reportedly devastated blacks, who had lost all sense of family and identity and were denied the possibility of education and the development of healthy work habits. This "damage" argument was challenged in subsequent decades by what came to be called the "resistance" school of thought, which describes blacks as opposing the degradations of slavery, negotiating certain conditions of work, abiding by religion and family values, and sustaining mechanisms of stability. In more recent years this favorable portrait has been challenged by black scholars who view slavery as nothing less than a form of "social death" that left many of their ancestors doomed to deprivation.[6]

*

O'Neill used black characters in early one-act works, but such efforts aimed only to give a multicultural backdrop to stories that unfolded in the West Indies. It was in *The Dreamy Kid* that O'Neill first addressed the situation of the black ghetto in New York City. The play was produced in 1919, a time when America was seething with racial violence. Between 1915 and 1920, thousands of blacks had moved from the rural South to northern urban cities to take advantage of job opportunities made possible during the World War I years. Having left behind the resigned passivity of life on isolated country farms, migrating young black males had high expectations of better things to come. But with the end of the war in 1919, race riots erupted in industrial cities where blacks also experienced job discrimination and housing restrictions. In New York City several black men were killed in fights and shoot-outs. It was during this tense period that O'Neill learned from his close friend, the black gambler Joe Smith, of a young, streetwise, small-time gangster named "Dreamy," the prototype for the character in the one-act play.

The play takes place in a rundown bedroom in a black neighborhood in New York City. The ninety-year-old grandmother Mammy is on her deathbed surrounded by medicine bottles. Her last wish is to see her grandson Abe, nicknamed Dreamy, the apple of her eye. His sister Ceely makes every effort to prevent the grandmother from knowing that Dreamy has fallen into the wrong crowd and is no longer "de mos' innercent young lamb in de worl'." He tiptoes into the room in a crouched position, checking back to see if he is being tailed. "His eyes," O'Neill describes, "are shifty and hard, their expression one of tough, scornful defiance." The sister questions why he is sneaking around. "I croaked a guy, dat's what!" he replies proudly of a white man who had threatened to kill him first. The grandmother hears his voice and is joyous. As she reminisces about her grandchild as the budding flower of hope, Dreamy notices plainclothesmen outside surrounding the house. He can make a run for it out the back door, as his girlfriend urges, but he returns to the bedroom where Mammy asks her grandson to kneel down and pray for her. She clutches his left hand while his right holds a revolver. With his grandmother seconds away from certain death, he vows not to be taken alive, "Lawd Jesus, no suh!" Then the curtain descends, with Dreamy holding the gun he will never use, and Mammy, mistakenly thinking her grandson's last utterance expresses piety, whispers falteringly, "Dat's right—yo' pray—Lawd Jesus—Lawd Jesus."

In Dreamy O'Neill presents a hardened black man rising to individual responsibility and moral choice, an authentic Negro character capable of sensing the conflict of values that is at the heart of tragedy, a character divided against himself, torn between the warnings of his gang to stay away and the memories of his grandmother that compel him to return. Had Dreamy thought only of his own survival, he would have never come back to be by the person who had raised and cared for him. He comes to his grandmother, of course, to avoid a superstitious curse that would otherwise befall him for forsaking a parent in time of need. But he knows that the luck he had expected has run out, and still he stays at the bedside. With one hand holding a revolver and the other placed in the grandmother's death grip, Dreamy shows himself to be capable of both protection and contrition. The African-American family, broken as it may be and marred by the violence of the streets, could be less the "tangle of pathology" described by later scholars than the site of tragic struggle, possible self-sacrifice, and even hopeful redemption.

THE HARLEM RENAISSANCE
AND *THE EMPEROR JONES*

The Dreamy Kid, written in the year of the 1919 riots, intimates what would become more explicit in O'Neill's future plays: that American culture could well have eroded any ties that may have sustained the core values of the black family.[7] O'Neill presages the fate of future ghetto youths coming of age amid the dissolution of the family as an institution. Abe's grandmother represents the older forces of maternal authority and religious guidance that would no longer be viable. The sister Ceely remains the last caretaker, horrified to discover that her brother has grown from innocent child to cynical killer. Abe, aka "The Dreamy Kid," shirks the nurturing spiritual values of the grandmother to become a gang leader, and in doing so he abandons an African culture of community and succor for an American culture of individualism and strife.

The crisis of the black American is the crisis of recognition. No thinker was more attuned to this issue than W. E. B. DuBois, the black historian who had the good fortune to study under the philosopher William James at Harvard and also at Heidelberg University where the influence of G. W. L. Hegel's philosophy was still felt. Scholars today debate whether Du Bois' thesis on the "dual consciousness" is authentically a black formulation since James, Henry Adams, Ralph Waldo Emerson, and other white intellectuals had also written about the divided self.[8] O'Neill's view on this matter may well suggest that there can be no authentic black essence apart from the vicissitudes of experience in the larger society. If humankind's deepest need is to be recognized by others, then the self is bound to look outward rather than inward. Du Bois comes close to recognizing the dilemma when he reflects on the black's "double consciousness" and its implications:

> It is a peculiar sensation, this double consciousness, this sense of always looking at one's self through the eyes of others, of measuring one's soul by the tape of a world that looks on in amused contempt and pity. One ever feels his twoness — an American, a Negro; two souls, two thoughts, two unreconciled strivings; two warring ideals in one dark body, whose dogged strength alone keeps it from being torn asunder.
>
> The history of the American Negro is the history of this strife — this

longing to attain self-conscious manhood, to merge his double-self into a better and truer self. . . . He simply wishes to make it possible for man to be both a Negro and an American, without being cursed and spit upon by his fellows, without having the doors of Opportunity closed roughly in his face.[9]

What Du Bois described as peculiar to the Negro, O'Neill might have defined as part of the human condition: a self lacking the capacity for inwardness and thus allowing itself to be shaped by the gaze of others. Du Bois' worry about "always looking at one's self through the eyes of others" is an example of desire as constituted by social pressures, the need for recognition and self-esteem. Emerson and Thoreau saw the American character as subjecting itself to the eyes of others as the self is strangled by society in the white America of the Jacksonian era. O'Neill's Con Melody continually looks at the mirror as he imagines how society sees him. The idea of a "double consciousness" may be part of the human condition, though perhaps more acute among blacks and ethnic minorities.

Du Bois' idea that the Negro could redefine himself became the idea *elan* of the Harlem Renaissance that emerged in the post–World War I years and flowered throughout the twenties. In this period of hope, few wrote about the condition of the black family and the coming alienation and disorientation of its youth. Cut off from avenues of opportunity by means of office holding and electoral politics, excluded from most of the trade unions, shunned by white society, blacks took to culture with creative vengeance.

In Van Wyck Brooks' seminal *The Confident Years* (1952), he devotes a chapter to black intellectual life titled "Eugene O'Neill: Harlem." Brooks understood that the great questions that preoccupied black intellectuals like Du Bois had also gained the attention of O'Neill, and both saw Harlem as the "cultural capital of the Pan-African cause." Marcus Garvey tried to turn that cause into a political and economic venture with his steamship lines and other entrepreneurial ventures. Yet it was Alain Locke who gave cultural articulation to the cause in his anthology, *The New Negro* (1925). American black art had been spontaneous in its exuberance and sentimentality, Locke pointed out, but music as well as literature and philosophy now required discipline and sophistication. The philosophy of pragmatism that Locke studied at Harvard appealed to him, since it could inspire black Americans to turn their faces toward the future and experience life in all its endless possibilities — a fitting message for a people who could only look back to slavery.

A leading light of the black literati was Claude McKay, the West Indian poet who dropped into the Village bars frequented by O'Neill and wrote the poignant novel *Home to Harlem* (1924). One of the most discussed works of the period was Jean Toomer's *Cane* (1923), a collections of stories, poems, and plays that dealt with the joys and sorrows of black life in America where striving after identity remained a challenge without a conclusion. Toomer and other black writers were also working out methods with which O'Neill had experimented, particularly expressing character through dialogue and even interior monologue, which makes every character a thinker as well as actor. O'Neill himself had been working on a play that left the black man alone with himself, removed from white society yet still not far away from a past that returns to haunt him unto death. With the burden of history tracking him down like a bloodhound, his life is hardly his own. He is trying to run away from what he carries within, a self-hatred that leaves him with no trace of his innermost self. History forbids him what might have fulfilled him.

O'Neill's *The Emperor Jones* was an instant success. Immediately it moved from the Provincetown Playhouse in the Village to Broadway. Two days after Christmas, on December 27, 1920, the cultural world witnessed a milestone — for the first time in American history a serious play presented a black man as the overriding presence and towering protagonist. The role was played by Charles Gilpin, a part-time Harlem actor whom the Provincetown officials had found working as an elevator man at Macy's. Despite achieving recognition, Gilpin would complain that the American theater had yet to open itself to his career and that of other blacks, and O'Neill and Gilpin would have a falling out when the actor tampered with the author's carefully wrought dialogue. When, however, the Drama League invited Gilpin as a guest of honor to its annual dinner, and some members withdrew the invitation, an outraged O'Neill sought out other actors to let them know what happened and urged them to decline their invitations. As a result of O'Neill's efforts, Gilpin was reinvited to an occasion that turned out to be a cultural success. Years later when *The Emperor Jones* was revived, the role went to the exciting new black actor, Paul Robeson.[10]

The play is set somewhere in the West Indies in an emperor's palace with high ceilings, whitewashed walls, white tiled floors, and a throne "painted a dazzling, eye-smiting scarlet." The idea for the play, O'Neill later remarked, came from a friend who told him about the late Guillaume Sam, president of Haiti, who boasted that no one could kill him with regular bullets and that only he could kill himself with a silver bullet. The island political leader Henri Christophe may have also been an influence, as were the photos of African sculpture by Charles Sheeler. O'Neill had learned about religious feasts in the Congo, and having himself experienced the incessant pulse of blood in his eardrums when struck with malaria in Honduras, came up with the idea of a drumbeat beginning slowly and building up in volume and tempo to dramatize the heart's desperate thumping when the mind is overcome with fear.

Brutus Jones enters the stage a middle-aged, powerfully built man, with a face displaying "an underlying strength of will, a hardy self-reliant confidence in himself that inspires respect. His eyes are alive with a keen, cunning intelligence. In manner he is shrewd, suspicious, evasive." He sports an outlandish uniform dazzling with brass buttons, gold braids and epaulets, leather patent boots, and a pearl-handled revolver. "Yet there is something not altogether ridiculous about his grandeur," O'Neill explains. "He has a way of carrying it off."

Jones, a former Pullman porter, has escaped from America, fleeing two murders, one of a fellow black gambler, the other of a white guard of a chain gang, whose skull he smashed with a shovel in retaliation for having been beaten by him. On the island, Jones has easily established himself as the emperor and seems to rule almost effortlessly, to the surprise of the only white character, the sniveling, conniving Smithers. The stoop-shouldered Smithers is a rum-soaked creature of forty, whose "washy blue eyes are red-rimmed and dart about him like a ferret's. His expression is one of unscrupulous meanness, cowardly and dangerous." Smithers cannot figure out how Jones has been able to get away with his pretense of being an emperor, how he can exploit the people with exorbitant taxes and stash away the money.

Jones has no standing army, no palace guard, not even a corps of officers who back his regime. The source of Jones's power is fraud, fear, and pride in his own superior instincts. He plays upon the island's local superstitions, manipulating stories about his death-defying conquests and threatening to shoot down any would-be rivals. Jones is a machiavel, an "emperor" better feared than loved whose politics turns on what is seen rather than known. But there is no trace of Machiavellian civic virtue in Jones, not the slightest hint that a life of politics aspires to higher principles than brute survival and success. Yet he has ambition and determination, and dismisses Smithers as "shiftless" white trash. Smithers cannot believe that Jones can succeed in his politics of fraud and fear, convinced that his attempt to show himself as greater than he actually is will soon be discovered. Jones tells Smithers that he has the "woods' niggers right where I wanted dem" and boasts that he has gone from stowaway to emperor in two years. Smithers thinks he can upset Jones by accusing him of salting away the people's money in a safe place, but Jones responds "with satisfaction":

I sho' has! And it's in a foreign bank where no pusson don't ever git it out but me no matter what come. You didn't s'pose I was holdin' down dis Emperor job for de glory in it, did you? Sho'! De fuss and glory part of it, dat's only to turn de heads o'de low-flung, bush niggers, dat's here. Dey wants de big circus show for deir money. I gives it to 'em an' I gits de money. (*with a grin*) De long green, dat's me every time!

O'Neill's Emperor Jones, contemptuous of glory, moved more by greed than greatness, presages by more than a half-century what social scientists of comparative culture would call "kleptocracy," the tendency of leaders of Third World countries, particularly captivating personalities, to grab the money and run. When political theorists wrote of the usurpation of power and tyranny and the loss of liberty, it was more the bankers than the politicians in American history they accused of plundering the national wealth and looting people of their hard-earned money. But Jones, with his fixation on "de long green," also knows something that political philosophers could well ponder: that all power, however absolute, is impermanent. "I ain't no fool. I knows dis Emperor's time is sho't." Thus, when Smithers tells Jones that a rebellion against his regime is underway, Jones is fully prepared to escape into the jungle, where he has stashed his treasure as well as supplies of food, and head to the coast where a French gunboat is anchored.

The swaggering emperor can run away from everything but himself. The successive scenes of Jones in the jungle confront him with his previously suppressed fears. Jones conjures up memories of his people confined to the hold of a slave ship crossing the Atlantic, imagines himself on the auction block being sold in a slave market, relives his murder of the prison guard and the dice-shooting Pullman porter he knifed to death, and encounters a Congo witch doctor who tries to lure him to death in a river where a crocodile god awaits. As he crawls toward the open jaws in a penitential panic, Jones uses his last silver bullet firing at the phantoms of his imagination. In each scene he discards pieces of his clothes and all the trappings of white society as the atmosphere quickens with the ever-louder beat of the tom-tom. In his twisted mind Jones ends up in Africa, having to face the black identity and heritage he once scorned with nothing left but his fears and superstitions. "Mercy, Lawd! Mercy!" he cries. Rebel soldiers finally track him down and kill Jones with their own silver bullets.

*

The Emperor Jones is a complicated play that remains to this day susceptible to numerous interpretations. It was as though O'Neill took the conventional Sambo image of the black male, humble and loyal, and presented an extreme counterimage of arrogance and pride, particularly the
Christian pride that goeth before the fall. Because Jones comes to admit
he is a sinner and capitulates to guilt, and because he tries to kill the crocodile, a possible projection of his own evil self, and looks up to the skies to
cry for mercy, some scholars have regarded the play as a redemption story
with Jones praying for his salvation.[11] Others are disturbed by the racial
atavism, the sight of a black man supposedly succumbing to primordial
darkness. A leading O'Neill scholar, Travis Bogard, believes that O'Neill
committed an act of political incorrectness in having Brutus Jones reduced to a creature groveling like an animal in the jungle. "Although he has
evidently read Conrad's *The Heart of Darkness,*" Bogard writes, "O'Neill
makes no generalization such as Conrad does that there is savagery in the
hearts of all men. Instead, it is the Negro who is essentially uncivilized,
wearing contemporary sophistications as a loosely fitting mask over an
incorrigibly savage countenance." Such an approach may have been acceptable in the twenties, "but today, the ethnic and social implications of
the play can no longer command respectful attention."[12]

Whether or not there be savagery in the hearts of all men and women,
O'Neill saw something just as universal and damnable: greed and possessiveness. In his personification of African-American history O'Neill
makes us aware of what white society has done to black culture. Capitalism once grew out of a Calvinist conscience tormented by doubts about
the state of one's soul, doubts that led to efforts at honest work, frugality,
and simplicity. Jones reverses the formulation: "I'se after de coin, an' I lays
my Jesus on de shelf for de time bein'." Jones has taken on all the pecuniary
values of America's materialistic culture. "Dere's little stealin' like you
does," he advises Smithers, "and dere's big stealin' like I does. For de little
stealin' dey gets you in jail soon or late. For de big stealin' dey makes you
Emperor and puts you in de Hall o' Fame when you croaks. (*reminiscently*)
If dey's one thing I learns in ten years on de Pullman ca's listenin' to white
quality talk, it's dat same fact."

Listening to the dominant white class talk, Jones allows the rich and
famous to impose their way of life on him. He learns that people can be
fooled by appearances and awed by the trappings of wealth and power.
Having observed the ways of white society, and knowing how the plantation master treated the slave, he has no compunctions about abusing and
exploiting "bush niggers." O'Neill's Brutus Jones offers a portrait of the
black race with white habits. The play may be less a study in racial atavism
or in religious salvation than in social emulation, with Jones aping the

worst aspects of the leisure class by assuming that money alone symbolizes that which is the highest and the best. Ironically, the slave owner Thomas Jefferson had a premonition of such behavior when he saw how classes and races, like children, imitate one another's "odious peculiarities." In *Notes on the State of Virginia* (1784), Jefferson warned America:

> There must doubtless be an unhappy influence on the manners of our people produced by the existence of slavery among us. The whole commerce between master and slave is a perpetual exercise of the most boisterous passions, the most unremitting despotism on the one part, and degrading submissions on the other. Our children see this, and learn to imitate it; for man is an imitative animal. From his cradle to his grave he is learning to do what he sees others do. If a parent could find no motive either in his philanthropy or his self-love, for restraining the intemperance of passion toward his slave, it should always be a sufficient one that his child is present. But generally it is not sufficient. The parent storms, the child looks on, catches the lineaments of wrath, puts on the same airs in the circle of smaller slaves, gives loose to the worst of passions, and thus nursed, educated, and daily exercised in tyranny, cannot but be stamped by it with odious peculiarities.[13]

As an anarchist, O'Neill admired Jefferson's libertarian distrust of the state and his defense of the natural rights of man. But Brutus Jones is a child of Jefferson, a product of the very psychological consequences of slavery that Jefferson warned against and yet did little to alleviate. Brutus Jones is emulating such "odious peculiarities" when he shows disdain for his own people and envy for the white race. Like the white master class in the old plantation South, he believes wealth can be had without work. Superiority presupposes leisure rather than labor. O'Neill took the old anarchist dictum, formulated by Pierre-Joseph Proudhon, that "property is theft," and applied it to his protagonist, whose condition exemplifies a theory intended as an indictment. Brutus Jones learns the lessons of life by "listenin' to white quality talk," and what he learns is that slavery is property and that power rules and wealth steals.

PRIDE, PREJUDICE, LOVE

The African American who takes the stage in the plays of Eugene O'Neill has no predictable script, no singular image, no one defining identity, no plaster casts of stereotypes. His black protagonists, women as well as men, can speak in different voices and express conflicting values that are not necessarily determined by either role or race.

While Abe, "The Dreamy Kid," represented the young ghetto hood who accepts his fate, and Brutus Jones the haughty ruler who panics in the face of his racial past, Jim Harris, of *All God's Chillun Got Wings,* has every solid virtue only to be defeated by one single flaw — love. Jones absorbed the worst aspects of an American materialism that prized wealth and disdained work; Harris aspires to the best aspects of an American idealism that supposedly rewards ambition, industry, and honesty. While *Jones* could well suggest that behind the chauvinism of black bravado lies a fearful void, *All God's Chillun* offers a black male with a depth of feeling that is noble in its unswerving loyalty. Yet *All God's Chillun* displeased as many blacks as it upset whites.

The play deals with the delicate topic of miscegenation. Interracial marriage had always been an outrage in American history, and even Abraham Lincoln was forced to deny that he wanted a black woman for a wife. Sexual relations with the opposite race have been in such a state of denial that to this day the white descendents of Thomas Jefferson have had a hard time accepting that one of our Founding Fathers sired children by Sally Hemings, his teenage black house slave. Prospects of miscegenation grew more controversial when culture became less inhibited with the Greenwich Village rebellion of the pre–World War I years. During that period people of both races thought it scandalous that the great black heavyweight boxer Jack Johnson would marry a white woman. A few public officials, like the explorer Clarance King, kept marriage to a black woman a secret. In various states throughout the country interracial marriage was illegal. Although Greenwich Village intellectuals like Randolph Bourne called for a cosmopolitan "trans-nationalism," he dared not bring up the subject of racial assimilation between whites and blacks. Nor did many black leaders of the Harlem Renassiance, who were searching for the roots of African culture in white America.

Even before O'Neill's play opened in New York in 1924, the media was abuzz about what the audience might expect. The most upsetting scene had a white woman kissing the hand of a black man, and the play's opening scene showed black and white children playing together in a tenement district of New York, with their street corner an environment of innocent integration despite the apartment house dwellers being distinctly segregated. Given such daring settings, O'Neill would open his mail to find letters from the K.K.K. and other hate groups, one threatening the life of his son. O'Neill let the press know what the Klan, in the twenties a force to be reckoned with, could do with their threat. As opening night approached, rumors of race riots spread through New York City, and the police received warnings of bomb threats. O'Neill released a statement to the press assuring the public that the play was not meant to stir up racial animosity but was intended instead to promote "a more sympathetic understanding between the races, through the sense of mutual tragedy involved." In an effort to prevent black and white actors from sharing a stage, the New York police tried to stop the play from being performed on a technicality. But O'Neill agreed not to have the play open with the white children at play with black children, and their dialogue was read to the audience as the play proceeded without incident. "It is no risk at all to say that *All God's Chillun,*" wrote Arthur and Barbara Gelb, "received more negative publicity before production than any play in the history of the theatre, possibly of the world."[14]

*

O'Neill deals with the interrelated theme of white prejudice and black pride, and he seeks to show how love, an emotion that is as much Christian as romantic in the play, fails to overcome racial difference. The white character Ella harbors all the traits of prejudice, her black husband Jim the deep, unswerving sentiment of love, and his sister Hattie the confidence of racial pride. The audience soon knows how white prejudice expresses itself, but where does it come from?

Today scholars tell us that "whiteness" is a constructed phenomenon. Not the color of one's skin but attitudes toward one's racial identity have been devised so that in moments of historical conflict whites can see themselves in safe opposition to others. Only in two scenes in the play does the meanness of racial difference erase itself: the opening when Ella and Jim are children playing together and the closing scene when the two are reduced to the chatter of infantile regression. Both scenes suggest that the racist mind is not born but made, not an innate instinct but a social convention. O'Neill's character Ella conjures up a counterimage to her husband in order to maintain her sense of superiority. On the other hand, Hattie has a firm identity that no one but herself has shaped, and her brother Jim wants to make it in white society and courageously confronts every challenge it offers. He refuses to accept his place, an attitude that generates more resentment among blacks than whites.

The play, in its script version, opens with Ella and Jim at the age of eight, playing marbles with other children, all aware of their color difference but with no suggestion of superiority or inferiority. They tease one another about daubing their faces with paint to take on each other's shade of skin. They are deeply fond of one another. "You mustn't never be scared when I'm hanging around, Painty Face," Jim says to Ella protectively. "Don't call me that, Jim — please!" protests Ella of the reference to her pinkish white skin. "I didn't mean nuffin'. I didn't know you'd mind," Jim replies. "I do—more'n anything," Ella responds. "You oughtn't to mind," Jim advises. "Dey's jealous, dat's what." Pointing to her face, he states, "Of dat. Red 'n' white. It's purty." But Ella objects. "I hate it! . . . I hate it. I wish I was black like you."

Nine years later the early affection for one another is gone. It is graduation day, and Ella, now a confident seventeen, is involved with Mickey, a rising young white prizefighter who boasts of his erotic conquests. Jim tries to tell Mickey that Ella is not like the rest of his female admirers. "I'm still her friend always—even if she don't like colored people," explains Jim. "*Coons,* why don't yuh say it right!" explodes Mickey, who accuses him of "gittin' stuck up" and trying to "buy white" with the money his father has earned. Heated words are exchanged; then Ella shows up, barely acknowledges Jim, and leaves arm in arm with Mickey.

Joe, a black street-gang leader, is furious seeing Jim humbling himself before a white woman and aspiring to be white himself by studying hard in order to graduate, perhaps even to go to college and law school. "Listen to me, nigger," he shouts at Jim. "I got a heap to whisper in yo' ear! Who is you, anyhow? Who does you think you is? Don't yo' old man and mine work on de docks togider befo' yo' old man gits his own truckin' business?" The only differences between their old men is one went into business and the other blew his money on beer. "Don't you 'n' me drag up togidder?"

JIM: (*dully*) I'm your friend, Joe.
JOE: No, you isn't! I ain't no fren o' yourn! I don't even know who you is! What's all dis schoolin' you doin'? What's all dis dressin' up and graduatin' and sayin' you gwine study to be a lawyer? What's all dis fakin' and pretendin' an' swellin' out grand an' talkin' soft and perlite? What's all dis denyin' you's a nigger—an' wid de white boys listenin' to you say it! Is you aimin' to buy white wid yo' ol' man's dough like Mickey say? What is you? (*in a rage at the other's silence*) You don't talk? Den I takes it out o' yo' hide! (*He grabs Jim by the throat with one hand and draws the other fist back.*) Tell me befo' I wrecks yo' face in! Is you a nigger or isn't you? (*shaking him*) Is you a nigger, Nigger? Nigger, is you a nigger?
JIM: (*looking into his eyes—quietly*) Yes, I'm a nigger. We're both niggers.

Upon hearing these simple words, Joe's rage subsides and he offers Jim a cigarette, which he lights for him. Then, as if all misunderstandings have lifted, Joe asks: "Man, why didn't you 'splain dat in de fust place?" Now that Joe thinks Jim is secure in his identity, he even says, referring to the ceremony about to start at the high school, "Time you was graduatin', ain't it?"

O'Neill leaves it unclear whether Jim's desire to become a lawyer stems from his need to escape his black roots, his hope of winning over Ella by proving his competence, or simply his desire to make something of himself. Must the fulfillment of a worthy aspiration signify a betrayal of one's self? Du Bois' idea of the black man's "double consciousness" haunts O'Neill's play, but in this instance it takes on a triple meaning, for Jim knows he is a Negro, aspires to the values of white society, and feels even more deeply the love for a woman who cannot return it.

Five years pass and Ella, thrown over by Mickey after their child has died, is weary and ready to accept Jim as a provider and protector. Deeply ambivalent, she loves Jim for what he is but despises him for what he wants to be. While Jim prepares to take the bar exam that he once failed, Ella resents his ambition and secretly dreads that he might pass and prove he is her equal. After postponing the exam and spending time in Europe where miscegenation is more acceptable, they return and Jim brings her to a house that his mother bought them as a wedding present. There she sees a portrait of Jim's father (resembling the black nationalist entrepreneur Marcus Garvey) and a huge black Congo mask that Jim's sister Hattie has given him as a gift. Ella loathes the mask, a symbol of the continent that nurtures the racial pride and identity of African Americans. Ella cannot bear the thought that Jim might have the strength to rise from his primitive roots to enter the world of the white professional. The following exchange between Ella and Hattie exemplifies the rift between white prejudice and black pride. After introducing Ella to Hattie, Jim asks his sister if she remembers once playing marbles with his wife when they were children.

HATTIE: (*coming forward with a forced smile*) It was a long time ago — but I remember Ella. (*She holds out her hand.*)

ELLA: (*taking it — looking at Hattie with . . . queer defiance*) I remember. But you've changed so much.

HATTIE: (*stirred to hostility by Ella's manner — condescendingly*) Yes, I've grown older, naturally. (*then in a tone which, as if in spite of herself, becomes bragging*) I've worked so hard. First I went away to college, you know — then I took up post-graduate study — when suddenly I decided I'd accomplish more good if I gave up learning and took up teaching. (*She suddenly checks herself, ashamed, and stung by Ella's indifference.*) But this sounds like stupid boasting. I don't mean that. I was only explaining —

ELLA: (*indifferently*) I didn't know you'd been to school so long. (*a pause*) Where are you teaching? In a colored school, I suppose. (*There is an indifferent superiority in her words that is maddening to Hattie.*)

HATTIE: (*controlling herself*) Yes. A private school endowed by some wealthy members of our race.

ELLA: (*suddenly — even eagerly*) Then you must have taken lots of examinations and managed to pass them, didn't you?

HATTIE: (*biting her lips*) I always passed with honors!

ELLA: Yes, we both graduated from the same High School, didn't we? That was dead easy for me. Why I hardly even looked at a book. But Jim says it was awfully hard for him. He failed one year, remember? (*She turns around and smiles at Jim — a tolerant, superior smile but one full of genuine love. Hattie is outraged, but Jim smiles.*)

JIM: Yes, it was hard for me, Honey.

ELLA: And the law school examinations Jim hardly ever could pass at all. Could you? (*She laughs lovingly.*)

HATTIE: (*harshly*) Yes, he could! He can! He'll pass them now — if you'll give him a chance!

JIM: (*angrily*) Hattie!

The only answer to white bigotry is black boastfulness, and Hattie hates herself for having to resort to it. But love as well as hate turns ironic in the play. The play would have us believe that Ella has grown to love Jim sincerely, but only to the extent he remains a humble failure without ambition, a provider rather than an achiever. His possible success endangers her fragile sense of superiority, and the possibility of his passing the bar exam means he can pass as white.

O'Neill's play was performed at a time in American history when segregation was almost universal and blacks had to cope with an inferior place in a society that had no welfare state and little private charity. Although the father of Jim and Hattie has died, the absence of male authority in the household has no bearing on the story. Both Jim and Hattie are educated and highly motivated; neither sees themselves as victims of racism. Unlike subsequent sociologists, O'Neill focuses the spotlight on white society and its barely concealed maladies.

Ella's hopelessly divided feelings toward Jim torment her to the point of bringing on a nervous breakdown, and trying to cope with his insane, bedridden wife and his law studies almost causes Jim to collapse. Hattie visits her brother and advises him to commit Ella to an institution. When Hattie tells Jim that Ella has called her "a dirty nigger," Jim replies, even though he knows that his wife has hurled the same slur at him, that Ella is too ill to be responsible for what she is saying. "I know she isn't — yet she is just the same," answers Hattie. "It's deep down in her or it wouldn't come out." Jim responds: "Deep down in her people — not deep in her."

Ella charges her brother with being too soft and weak to understand that Ella could both love and hate him at the same time. She has come to the house to speak to him in order to try to turn his head around "for your own good." "I have no own good," answers Jim. "I only got a good together with her. I'm all she's got in the world! Let her call me nigger! Let her call me the whitest of the white! I'm all she's got in the world, ain't I? She's all I've got! You with your fool talk of the black race and the white race! Where does the human race get a chance to come in?"

The question remains unanswered. In the final scene Ella is wielding a knife, a weapon she had earlier held up to her husband's back, and with murderous thoughts is now threatening to slash apart the Congo mask. She remembers that Jim has gone to the mailbox downstairs to collect a letter with the results of the bar exam. The demented Ella desperately wonders whether her husband has passed, and learning that he has failed again, she cries out joyously and pushes all the law books crashing to the floor—"then with childish happiness," the stage directions read, "she grabs Jim by both hands and dances [him] up and down." She grabs the Congo mask and plunges the knife through it. Jim, his eyes bulging in anger, calls Ella a "white devil woman" and raises his fist above her head. But she assures him that the devil that caused her to take up the murderous knife is gone and that she herself may not have much time to live. Jim cannot imagine a life without her, and he lashes out at God, questioning how He could forgive Himself for creating such twisted lives on earth. But when Ella tells of her deep love for him and "kisses his hand as a child might, tenderly and gratefully," Jim breaks down crying and asks for God's forgiveness, imploring Him to cleanse Jim of "selfishness" and to make him "worthy of the child You send me for the woman You take away!" Ella pleads with him to get up off his knees and come out to play with her as the children they once were. An exalted Jim exclaims: "Honey, Honey, I'll play right up to the gates of Heaven with you!"

*

The poet T. S. Eliot praised *All God's Chillun* as an exemplary treatment of an important, unexplored subject in literature. O'Neill "not only understands one aspect of the 'negro problem,'" wrote Eliot without explaining what that aspect was, "but he succeeds in giving this problem universality, in implying a wider application. In *this* respect, he is more successful than the author of *Othello*, in implying something more universal than the problem of race—in implying, in fact, the universal problem of differences which create a mixture of admiration, love, and contempt, with the consequent tension. At the same time, he has never deviated from the exact portrayal of a possible negro, and the close is magnificent."[15]

Others judged the conclusion deplorable, and some black critics thought O'Neill was writing about a culture he did not understand and blamed him for dramatizing interracial marriage when what blacks really wanted was to sustain their own self-respect. Why would a black man fall in love with a white woman who lacked the strength to overcome the prejudices of her own white society? Years later, academic critics writing from a classical perspective faulted the ending for offering no tragic recognition, no understanding on Jim's part of what was happening. "It is rather a travesty of the resurrection implied in true tragedy," observed the O'Neill scholar Doris Falk, that Jim would settle for "a groveling, masochistic humility from which he will never be forced to rise again."[16] One angry black writer wondered how "a slim, depraved and silly white woman" could enslave "a big, respectable and cultured" black man.[17] However Paul Robeson, who was praised for his superb performance as Jim, defended the play. Robeson explained his acceptance of the role, claiming that it "accentuated . . . the almost Christ-like spiritual force" of Jim and reaffirmed what O'Neill termed the "oneness" of mankind.[18]

The play's closing scene left most Americans, white and black, confused and troubled. One does not look to O'Neill to give us a story of liberation arising from the conditions of oppression. Yet the character of Jim emerges as a cruel abasement not only of masculinity but of identity itself, the failure of consciousness to rise to self-knowledge. He seems completely unaware that his wife is a neurotic racist and wants him only as a childish playmate. O'Neill shows Jim accepting the comforting illusions of Christianity at the same time that he is deceived by the wiles of a woman. Was the play then a Nietzschean morality tale of self-deception? O'Neill's own Nietzschean proclivities could well be responsive to that wicked theme. *All God's Chillun* demonstrates not only the trauma of race relations but of the human condition in general. Whether or not Jim's plight is emblematic of the African American, and whether the forces of racism may reduce one black male to childhood dependency, the play certainly dramatizes a familiar predicament discerned by Emerson as well as Nietzsche. Jim wants to become someone other than who he is, and both his black friends and his white wife try to shame him into staying who he is, foiling his desires and frustrating his determination. Become who you are, or be dominated!

*

Some of O'Neill's women characters seemed to have intuitively understood such advice. If one or two of them were noble souls, many more were almost natural Nietzscheans with an unrelenting will to power. Turning to the subject of women, a question arises. Does desire take on a different meaning when it speaks with a different voice?

8

"The Merest Sham": Women and Marriage

WOMEN: "GOD'S SECOND MISTAKE"

To turn to a male writer to understand women is asking for trouble. The challenge of comprehending "the Other" has become the intellectual war cry in the contemporary academy. But the inability to think openly and freely about that which is unfamiliar, to know the Other as really other, has long been a problem. "He who knows woman only through man," wrote Henry Adams, "knows her wrong." Simone de Beauvoir, author of *The Second Sex,* agreed that men are more content to conquer women than to comprehend them. "All that has been written about women by men should be suspect." On this note even a crotchety American conservative would agree. "There is no book on woman by a man," wrote H. L. Mencken, "that is not a stupendous compendium of posturings and imbecilities."[1]

The philosophers and playwrights of O'Neill's era contributed significantly to the misperceptions of women, whom Nietzsche regarded as "God's second mistake." Schopenhauer depicted them as lacking in compassion and a sense of justice; Strindberg, as neurotic and vindictive; Ibsen, as succumbing to the security of respectability; Shaw, as living with hypocrisy rather than facing ostracism. Wilde wryly observed, half in jest in *A Woman of No Importance,* that "the history of women is the history of the worst form of tyranny the world has known. The tyranny of the weak over the strong. It is the only tyranny that lasts."[2]

At the time of such remarks the women's movement was gathering force in America as well as in Europe, and the misogynistic utterances unwittingly reveal how male egotism can warp male perceptions. Nietzsche was fond of remarking that women and truth have one thing in common: both are beyond man's grasp. H. L. Mencken, close collaborator of the O'Neill enthusiast George Jean Nathan, wrote *In Defense of Women* (1922) to drive home the point that women for the first time in history had, by virtue of birth control, new economic opportunities, and changing cultural conventions, the freedom to choose the life they sought for themselves and themselves alone.

O'Neill arrived on the scene of the American theater when many women, particularly in New York, Chicago, and San Francisco, were feeling the first stirrings of feminism. In the years of the First World War, suffragettes were on the march, and Greenwich Village was abuzz with new experiments in sexual relations as well as poetic expression. Mabel Dodge's salon welcomed the voices of anyone who had a plan to remake the world: "Socialists, Trade-Unionists, Anarchists, Suffragists, Poets, Relations, Lawyers, Murderers, 'Old Friends,' Psychoanalysts, I.W.W.'s, Single Taxers, Birth-Controlists, Newspapermen, Artists, Modern-Artists, Clubwomen, Women's-Place-is-in-the Home Women, Clergymen, and just plain men all met there." In this setting "barriers went down and people reached each other who had never been in touch before."[3]

O'Neill experienced the Village in ways that had little in common with the lyrical rebels and their boundless optimism and joys about the possibilities of a brave new world. It was during the Village years that O'Neill drank heavily, came down with tuberculosis, and attempted suicide. In the following decade, the twenties, when feminism and radical politics had all but disappeared from American life, O'Neill would write numerous plays dealing with women, marriage, and sexual relations. His contemporaries among the writers of the Lost Generation similarly dealt with women, as the object of lust (Eliot), as the elusive adored (Fitzgerald), or as "the happiness of the Garden that a man must lose" (Hemingway).

It has been said that romance depends upon obstacles, and O'Neill understood that it also depends on illusions driven by needs. With the end of World War I came the "end of American innocence" and supposedly the end of all illusions. Did, then, the idea of romantic love die as well? Such was the verdict offered in *The Modern Temper,* a poignant treatise written by O'Neill's friend and admirer, Joseph Wood Krutch.

LOVE: AN "OBSCENE JOKE"

Krutch saw a fundamental paradox between the human and the natural world, with one sphere aspiring to consciousness and to the things that make life worth living, and the other simply existing on the basis of biological impulses. In a chapter titled "Love — or the Life and Death of a Value," Krutch observed how scientific knowledge rendered the hitherto unknowable comprehensible and thereby deprived life of mystery and meaning. Now that the phenomenon of romantic love had come to be understood biologically and psychologically, a matter of genetic affinity or mental neurosis, it had lost its value: "If love has come to be less often a sin it has come also to be less often a supreme privilege." Writers like Ernest Hemingway and T. S. Eliot, Krutch observed, give us "tragic farces" with their characters pursuing the love of another person. The desire to possess is reduced to "a mere bathos," and the only response to uninhibited satisfaction summed up as "Well, what of it?" With some writers love becomes "at times only a sort of obscene joke." The sweating, mooning, and heavy-breathing passions subside, and "a great and gratifying illusion has passed away, leaving the need for it still there." In our "generally devalued world" of the senses, Krutch concluded, men and women cannot "transmute that simple animal pleasure into anything else," and "they themselves not infrequently share the contempt with which their creator regards them, and nothing could be less seductive, because nothing could be less glamorous, than the description of the debaucheries born of nothing except a sense of the emptiness of life."[4]

Throughout three decades, from the early twenties to the early fifties, Joseph Wood Krutch remained Eugene O'Neill's most admiring critic, and when O'Neill died in 1953, his widow Carlotta asked Krutch to be the playwright's biographer. Years earlier O'Neill, grateful for Krutch's introduction to a collection of plays that Modern House Library published in 1932, sent a copy of the manuscript of *Strange Interlude* to Krutch for comment. O'Neill had regarded the text that Krutch read as his one concentrated effort at writing "a woman play," and the feminine protagonist in the story is clearly searching for sexual fulfillment in order to compensate for "a sense of the emptiness of life," as Krutch put it. But did O'Neill himself regard love as, in Krutch's terms, a "wry joke played by the senses and the imagination upon the intellect"? Some romantics regard love as an impossible ideal born of emotional need that can break the heart, whereas the naturalist Krutch discerned in it one of life's precious enchantments whose value is destroyed in the process of understanding it. The poet tells us that it is better to have loved and suffered than not to have loved at all. O'Neill could accept Nietzsche's dictum that pain and the discipline of sorrow intensify and heighten human life. But could he also agree that, when it comes to love, "life needs illusions, that is to say, untruths that are taken for truths"?[5] In his two masterpieces, *The Iceman Cometh* and *A Long Day's Journey into Night,* love is a missing passion as each character is left alone in an illusory world, yet the thought of love was too real to be easily dismissed by O'Neill. The philosopher may examine ideas to discern what is true and what is false; the playwright knows that emotions can be confused but they cannot be untrue.

In a letter to the critic Kenneth Macgowan, written in 1928, the year in which *Strange Interlude* opened, O'Neill confessed: "I really feel as if I have never been in love before. Even in the matter of sex where I have had, God knows, sufficient experience hither and yon in the past, I have come to the conclusion that I never even dreamed what it could be in the way of a physical and spiritual expression before. This is a revelation to me." The revelation grew out of his relationship with the newly found Carlotta Monterey, believing it unlike any he had ever before enjoyed. "To say that Carlotta and I are in love in the sense of any love I have ever experienced before is weak and inadequate. This is a brand new emotion and I could beat my brains out on the threshold of any temple of Aphrodite out of pure gratitude for the revelation. It is so damn right in every way. We 'belong' to each other. We fulfill each other!" Curiously, O'Neill puts the expression *belong* in quotations, as though love might entail possessiveness, his nemesis. But he proudly announced his new emotional state: "I'm in love," he wrote to the radical Michael Gold, "and that's always something."[6] As for Carlotta, she was a little less effusive, often not altogether sure that O'Neill was deeply in love with her, eventually resigning herself to serving as his secretary as well as companion while fervently committing herself to her husband's art.

For an anarchist, a relationship of more than one can be one too many. O'Neill, however, felt he knew enough about women and marriage to base many of his plays on such problematic subjects. His friend George Jean Nathan recalled a rather upsetting scene. "Once, he let me read the manuscript of his play, *Welded,* in which he had great faith. When I reported to him that all I could discern in it was some very third-rate Strindberg, he sharply observed that I couldn't conceivably understand any such play as I had never been married, put on his hat and walked out and didn't let me hear from him for two months afterward."[7]

The play Nathan disliked actually derived from O'Neill's own experience in his marriage to Agnes Boulton. As with many rebels of the Greenwich Village generation, O'Neill could be sincere about love and cynical about marriage. He kept a file of quotes by Nietzsche, many on the institution of marriage: "The will to create that which is more than they create," the philosopher warned of asking more than is there in another person. "Oh, ye sentimental dissemblers, ye La Lascivious! Ye lack innocence in desire, and therefore backbite desire."[8] The German philosopher as marriage counselor!

Although raised a Catholic, O'Neill was no altar boy. In his rambunctious youth he flirted with girls, dallied with tarts, had one revolting experience with a prostitute, and got Kathleen Jenkins pregnant and left her with a son he never saw until a decade later. But women remained a powerful presence in his life.

As a teenager he had a crush on a soft, demure eighteen-year-old, Marion Welch, whom he met in Connecticut in the summer of 1905. O'Neill had been studying French and his letters to her open with "*Ma Cher Boutade*," that is my dear fancy or witty one. Marion would later figure in a play O'Neill wrote thirty years later, *Ah, Wilderness!* The first young woman O'Neill took seriously as a companion was Maibelle Scott, an elegant, slender, "golden"-haired blonde whom he met while working as a reporter for the New London *Telegraph*. Maibelle had heard about O'Neill's drinking escapades, but he would straighten out for her and offer her advice on books and authors, even introducing her to the complexities of Nietzsche's *Zarathustra*. But O'Neill's father strongly opposed any thought of his son marrying before he had established a career. Depressed by this, O'Neill wrote Maibelle a painful poem: "Have I not known enough of doubt and death / O God, great God, that Thou shouldn't sternly place / A wall between my lips and her fair face / And make me taste of Hell while still on earth?"[9]

Fragile and weak, O'Neill seemed not to care whether he lived or died when he was diagnosed with tuberculosis (then often a lethal disease), and in December 1912 he entered a sanitarium. O'Neill would forever attribute this illness, and, many years later, his shaking, palsied hands, to the derelict years of his wayward youth. He used his half-year in the sanitarium as material for a play, *The Straw*, in which the male character, a writer obviously based on O'Neill, grows close to the ill Eileen Carmody (in real life Catherine Mackay); when he discovers her illness is incurable, love is born of grief as he offers to marry her to fight off the despair they both feel. Had O'Neill been callous with women, he would have felt little guilt in leaving them and no need to talk about them with subsequent women in his life. But Agnes and Carlotta, his second and third wives, would hear his remorseful recollections, and some of his plays dealing with earlier relations are efforts at atonement.

O'Neill left Gaylord Sanitarium in June 1913; his health was fully restored and he had regained confidence in the future. The following year he enrolled in English 47, the famous drama course at Harvard University taught by Professor George Pierce Baker. During this period O'Neill wrote several one-act plays dealing mainly with marriage and ship-wrecks — in one a character quotes Nietzsche on marriage: "Ah, the pov-erty of the soul in the twain." Yet it was at the very time that O'Neill was writing cynically about marriage that he tumbled head over heels in love with Beatrice Ashe. Tall, slender, with pale white skin and arrestingly dark hair, eyes flecked with shades of green and gray, Beatrice captivated O'Neill in more ways than one. The outpouring of love he felt for her not only seems, at least at first, to belie O'Neill's later testimony that he had never been in love and had no knowledge of its emotional depths; it also seems puzzling coming from a writer under the spell of Nietzsche and the doctrines of anarchism. Many anarchists valued independence above all else, and they would probably agree with Henry D. Thoreau's dictum that the more a man and woman love one another, the less they need each other. But passion for autonomy becomes the first casualty of the play-wright who allows himself to "fall" in love.

The sixty letters that O'Neill wrote to Beatrice from 1914 to 1916 vac-illate between ecstasy and desperation.[10] O'Neill tells her of how "sweet" she is and how "glorious" has been the time spent together, only to express a longing for her that comes close to panic. "I want you! I want you! I want you!" Occasionally O'Neill turns to other subjects, like his course at Har-vard or the world's political developments, but always he returns to the void within himself that can only be filled by her presence. He opens his letters with the salutation "My own" and "My own little wife" and closes in a fit of despondency: "God, God, I could cry — I am so lonely."

Beatrice appeared untroubled by the diminutive "little," the posses-sive "own," and the presumptious "wife." But she sensed the desperation in the letters and apparently told O'Neill that he might be searching for a surrogate mother and that she herself was responding accordingly rather than romantically. O'Neill replies: "I say *I love you!* Am I a liar, then? Why should you think I am? I don't understand. I don't understand some parts of your letter — your invocation of God, par example. Your mother-love, for another thing. Of course, a great part of every woman's love for a man is mother-love. Why not? Am I not a child, in great part, and every other man also? What is strange in that?"

O'Neill, age twenty-seven when he wrote this letter, was far from childhood, even if the child is father to the man. O'Neill was asking from Beatrice what he could never obtain from his own mother: forgiveness, understanding, absolution — the very acts of grace and mercy that lead Catholics to turn to the Virgin Mary. His own mother Ella was not there for young O'Neill, and his wasted life may have been a way of protesting her absence. But with Beatrice, O'Neill's wanting and demanding take on the tone of an epiphany. "My wanting is holy," O'Neill assures Beatrice,

"O soul of my soul." In the clean, unspoiled character of Beatrice, O'Neill sees a chance of realizing his hope for expiation. "All the sordid values the world has rubbed into me lose their cruel validity before your love," he wrote to Beatrice. "When I look into your eyes I feel a sense of deep shame; I want to cry out and ask your forgiveness for being what I have been, to crave your indulgence for the grimy smears on my life, to pray your pity for the tattered wings of my spirit stained with the muck of the long road." O'Neill could turn neither to his mother nor to the Catholic confession to attain the spiritual rehabilitation that he felt he had been receiving from Beatrice. "Beneath all this depression is a feeling of pride," O'Neill wrote to her, "pride in myself, in you, in Us. . . . Now indeed do you possess all my soul. You have routed the Gene O'Neill of the Past. I am born again—your very own child. Your influence in my life has ever been of the sweetest and finest. You have inspired my manhood with a great desire to be clean, and faithful to your trust in me. Your clear girlhood or womanhood has put my unwholesome cynicism to shame, has called out all the best that is in me. When I think of all the wonder which is you a sense of my own unworthiness saddens me—*but I do love you so!* At least my love is worthy."

Could it be that O'Neill was equating his love for another human being with a deeper need to purge his soul of sin? He is asking of Beatrice what he cannot do for himself: let go of the past and forgive his transgressions. Significantly, his ardent feelings for Beatrice would fade away, and within a year he was involved in a relationship with Louise Bryant, soon to be the wife of the journalist John Reed.

The O'Neill-Bryant affair, which has been dramatized in the film *Reds,* has seemed merely another of the brief flings that the Greenwich Village rebels were in and out of during the World War I years. Yet the recent discovery of O'Neill's poems and love letters to Louise tells another story, and they are especially revealing since they were written while he was married to Agnes Boulton.

O'Neill referred to Louise as "Blue Eyes" and described her having a mouth that smiles radiantly but never speaks. Such poetic flights could not hide the anguish; Louise broke O'Neill's heart when she followed Reed to Russia. But Louise has heard that he has been with other women, and he tries to reassure her that his relapses have been few and "the result of drunkenness and a dead soul." O'Neill keeps no secrets from Agnes, he informs Louise, and has told his wife of their past love affair. He has also told her that he doubted he would still be in love with Louise when she returned from Russia, most likely a different woman. Agnes had done much for him and accepted him unconditionally, O'Neill writes to Louise, and he "would not hurt her for the world." Curiously, O'Neill's own mother had a hard time accepting her son as he was, and he in turn had a hard time facing his mother as she was. Each had addictions they knew they could easily succumb to and suffered the guilt. Agnes is not the problem, O'Neill insists — Louise is:

> You needn't damn Agnes to Hell for letting me drink. She knew she couldn't have stopped me or anyone else but myself; but she pulled me together until I realized what I was wasting of myself and felt a longing to be clean and do clean work again. She accepted me as I was — at my worst — and didn't love me for what she thought I ought to be. She knew I could be led but not pushed. She helped understandingly, in every way she knew how, and I owe a lot to her. Whether I love her in a deep sense or not, I do not yet know. For the past half-year "love" has seemed like some word in a foreign language of which I know nothing. It dazes me. It is more than probable that you have burned yourself so deep into my soul that the wound will never heal and I stand condemned to love you for-ever — and hate you for what you have done to my life.

Apparently Louise wrote letters telling O'Neill that his own unstable behavior was responsible for her deciding to leave him. Your letters, O'Neill replies, "are characteristically unjust. You ignore my side of the question entirely. You are blameless — although you have done more to ruin my life than any other person in the world, not even excepting my-self — and you cannot, or will not, see wherein you are responsible for all this." The failure of their love, O'Neill persists, lies not in the stars but in Louise's own malignant heart:

> Does it cause you pain to know I have been living with another wo-man? Then you know now how I suffered for five hundred days — and still suffer. You will immediately say the circumstances are different. You are wrong. In my eyes they were not. I suffered as you suffer. The cases are the same. For a year and a half — perhaps for the rest of my life, too — my love for you kept me in Hell. I lived only in that love, in the hope of those fleeting bits of Paradise you tossed me once in a while — only to turn back to the other man the next moment. Spiritually you tortured me as if, in-stead of love, a devil of hatred possessed you. You knew my agony. You must have known.[11]

O'Neill's blaming Louise Bryant for the breakup of their relation be-speaks a desperation as well as discernment. He always believed that the human condition implanted a tendency toward self-destruction in all living beings, but when it came to his first maddening romantic affair he blamed its failure not on his own behavior but on the one he had loved and now came to hate. In his subsequent plays, he would depict his characters as rationalizing creatures, always citing reasons for how they ended up, and the reasons are more excuses than explanations.

The loss of his first loves crushed O'Neill. Whether he thought of his mother Ella, Beatrice Ashe, Agnes Boulton, or Louise Bryant, O'Neill could rarely write about women as objects of sensual pleasure, intellectual companions, or as hopes of spiritual deliverance. Instead he would write plays satirizing marriage, parenting, free love, and the search for sexual fulfillment. Unlike Reed, Max Eastman, and some other Greenwich Village rebels, who could tolerate their wives' involvement with other men (Eastman shared the actress Florence Deshon with O'Neill's future son-in-law, Charlie Chaplin), O'Neill looked to women for loyalty as much as love. But whether love was a permanent commitment or a momentary infatuation, for O'Neill it was also bound up with the question of power. His own outlook toward marriage and gender relations had been influenced by Ibsen and Strindberg, in whose plays relationships between men and women become a struggle between mastery and servitude.

SERVITUDE IN LOVE,
LOVE IN SERVITUDE

The anarchist O'Neill understood Emma Goldman's distrust of mass democracy, political parties, and large union organizations. "The right to vote, or equal civil rights," exhorted Goldman, "may be good demands, but true emancipation begins neither at the polls or in the courts. It begins in women's soul. History tells us that every oppressed class gained true liberty from its masters through its own efforts. It is necessary that woman learn that lesson, that she realizes that her freedom will reach as far as her power to achieve her freedom reaches." Goldman also taught Americans that love had nothing to do with marriage and that marriage had everything to do with woman's subordination, condemning the wife to "life long dependency, to parasitism, to complete uselessness."[12]

Mary Tyrone, O'Neill's portrait of his own mother in *Long Day's Journey into Night,* comes close to sharing such sentiments. She tells her husband and sons that they, as well as herself, are objects instead of subjects, people to whom things happen. But O'Neill is as much interested in what we do with what life has done to us, with the possibilities of freedom as much as the predicament of fate. What, then, did O'Neill's women do with their lives? The question contains no easy answer, for when the playwright put women on the stage of history almost a century ago, he had them acting out roles so various as to defy generalization.

Did O'Neill's tormented thoughts about his mother determine his outlook toward women in general? No doubt he never got over memories of the effect that his painful birth had on his mother. It was as though life enters the world as a curse to be borne by mother and son, with each succumbing to their own addictions. "Men are what their mothers made them," wrote Emerson in "Fate"; "when each comes forth from his mother's womb, the gate of gifts closes behind him."[13]

Beatrice Ashe believed that when O'Neill was fervently courting her he really had his own mother in mind. When O'Neill wrote about women in his plays, however, they came in all types and with such subtle nuances as to escape easy classification: wife, lover, nurse, patient, prostitute, capitalist, and radical activist. Perhaps the most interesting aspect of O'Neill's treatment of women is that the author remained unsure of what he would like to see women be. In some of his plays women are so controlling that their demands for domesticity and responsibility leave men thwarted and depressed. With O'Neill women can be courageous or they can be conniving; they can barely cope with their own emotions that leave them weak, or they can be unaware of their own will to power and domination that leaves man wallowing. In one play the woman protagonist embodies love, in another power. O'Neill wrote about women at a time in American history when feminists were making demands for divorce, education, and the ballot. To be truly free and self-reliant, women, just as is true for men, may need more than political emancipation. And to see women simply as victims is to settle for the symbol of Ophelia's fate — get thee to a nunnery or the graveyard.[14]

O'Neill saw Henrik Ibsen's *Hedda Gabler* in 1907, the first modern European play he attended, and he would return to see it night after night. With *A Doll's House* Ibsen had gained the reputation of a feminist who would lead the fight for women's freedom. In O'Neill's three-act play *Servitude* (1914) the character David Roylston is a writer with an Ibsen-like reputation, but this rendering is more ambiguous than didactic. Ethel Frasier, seeking advice on her own troubled marriage, visits Roylston, known for championing women's independence and autonomy. She tells Roylston that after reading him she agrees that marriage is "the merest sham." She further discovers, after talking to Roylston's wife Alice, that the writer is an egotist who uses women and treats his wife as a piece of property. Yet Ethel is moved by the wife's stories of sacrifice and devotion and, having convinced herself that love lies in servitude, resolves to return to her husband and marriage, "to the chains which have suddenly become dear to me." Ironically, Roylston's wife, thinking he has had an affair with Ethel, slams out the door in an Ibsenian gesture of liberation — only to return to resume once again her submissive role.

"Nora wasn't the only woman who walked out of the Doll's house," F. Scott Fitzgerald wrote to his daughter; "all the women in Gene O'Neill walked out too. Only they wore fancier clothes."[15] The predicament of marriage preoccupied O'Neill in 1916, and the fancy clothes of his female characters were not as important as their fanciful convictions. In that year O'Neill had been involved with the vivacious but flighty Louise Bryant, an affair that went on even after her marriage to John Reed. In Greenwich Village, rebellious spirits had debated one another about free love versus the institution of marriage, the cultural plot-motif of O'Neill's *Now I Ask You* (1916). "An intelligent, healthy American girl suffering from an overdose of undigested reading," an implacable spirit described in the stage directions as having "mistaken herself for a heroine of a Russian novel," defiantly calls off her wedding, declaring that marriage "would be the meanest form of slavery." But her progressive mother persuades her into going through with an "open" marriage that allows each partner to take on a lover. O'Neill intended the play to be a "farce comedy," an apt expression for his views on marriage, which, in his early plays, is treated either harshly or satirically, the scene of the battle of the sexes, of family conflict, sons struggling against the brute authority of the father, weddings rushed into because of pregnancy, liberating "open" arrangements arousing petty jealously, or demanding wives driving their husbands to desperation.

In *Before Breakfast* the curtain rises to a scene in a drab kitchen in which sits a rumpled wife berating her hapless husband, a failed writer whose only appearance is his hand reaching out from the bathroom requesting a towel. After forty minutes of listening to verbal abuse, the audience hears the husband let out a shriek and assumes that he has taken a razor blade to his throat.

O'Neill's mockery of marriage is only one of his many approaches to gender relations, His treatment of love could partake as much of the tragic as the comic. *Diff'rent* takes place in a New England seaport town beginning in the year 1890. The "romantic dreaminess" of the young Emma Crosby, age twenty, triumphs over the repression of Calvinism when she allows herself to fall in love with the sea captain Caleb Williams. She endures his absence in her dreary household only by fantasizing that her fiancé is unlike other lusty seamen. Later she is shattered when she discovers that he is so, or believes him to be, based upon a story her brother tells. When their ship was docked at a South Seas island, the crew told a native "brown girl" that the captain had wanted her in his cabin, and when the ship set sail the native girl was "howlin' and screamin'"on the beach and then plunged into the water to swim out to the vessel, only to be forced back by gunfire. Hearing the story later, the bitterly disillusioned

Emma refuses to accept her mother's advice to forgive Caleb this one indiscretion. To do so would mean her fiancé is like the rest. "I ain't got any hard feelings against you, Caleb," she explains. "It ain't plain jealousy. . . . It ain't even that I think you've done nothing terrible wrong. . . . I know that most any man would do the same, and I guess all of 'em I ever met has done it. . . . I guess I've always had the idea that you was — diff'rent. . . . And that was why I loved you. And now you've proved you ain't. And so how can I love you any more? I don't, Caleb. . . . You've busted something way down inside me — and I can't love you no more."

The crushed Caleb promises to wait indefinitely for a change of heart, but the audience sees the aged Emma, thirty years later, infatuated with Caleb's much younger cousin, showering him with money as well as affection. When the youth tells his uncle that he is to marry Emma (not for love but financial opportunity), Caleb hangs himself in his barn, and Emma, finding out that her lover would have accepted money from Caleb as a bribe not to marry her, and that the youth had only been leading her on, rushes out to her own barn to follow Caleb's fate.

O'Neill's characterization of Emma as a product of a rigid Puritanical moral code could mislead us into seeing her as a victim of New England's conventions. Actually, a true Puritan would hardly regard a single individual as "diff'rent" and immune to the ways of the flesh and beyond the forgiveness of sin. If O'Neill may have taken liberties with American intellectual history, women believed that his play set back the cause of women by a century.

"*Diff'rent* seems to have aroused the ire of all the feminists against me," O'Neill wrote to the journalist Louis Kanter in 1921. O'Neill objected that the same theme "could have been woven with equal truth about a man, with a different reaction, of course."[16] In an interview in the *New York Tribune,* O'Neill described the play as "merely a tale of the eternal, romantic idealist who is in all of us — the eternally defeated one." Responding to the charge that his play was too gloomy and devoid of deeper human emotions, O'Neill lashed out: "damn the optimists," those who cannot cope with defeat and failure as the price for aiming at the highest aspirations. "To me, the tragic alone has that significant beauty which is truth." The play is life incarnated on the stage, "the lives of the people in it as I see them and know them." Does O'Neill truly know women? Or should we turn to the psychoanalysts? Emma represents a life that "swallows all formulas," O'Neill replied in reference to the formulas of Freud and Jung:

Some critics have said that Emma would not do this thing, would undoubtedly do that other. By Emma they must mean "a woman." But Emma is Emma. She is a whaling captain's daughter in a small New England seacoast town — surely no feminist. She is universal only in the sense that she reacts definitely to a definite sex-suppression, as every woman might. The form her reaction takes is absolutely governed by her environment and her own character. Let the captious be sure they know their Emmas as well as I do before they tell me how she would act.[17]

Feminists and their supporters once regarded marriage as man's requirement and woman's predicament. In the Ibsenean formula, man upholds the sanctity of marriage while woman embodies the spirit of freedom. Around the turn of the twentieth century emerged the expression *la femme incomprise,* suggesting a superior woman misunderstood and unappreciated. O'Neill's domestic plays could well offer *l'homme incomprise,* suggesting that man's dedication to his vocation could go unappreciated, the theme of *The First Man,* where the husband puts scientific inquiry ahead of family responsibility.

In his marriage to Agnes Boulton, O'Neill felt the conflict between the dedicated writer and the dutiful husband, and in *Welded* the audience watches a playwright and his actress wife circle about a living room, two egos out to overcome one another — he jealous of her past popularity, she resentful that her only successes came in his plays. Agnes was actually a writer, but O'Neill depicts her as an actress in this play in order better to put down her profession: "Good God, how dare you criticize creative work, you actress!" thunders the "furious" husband. It is a banal play, but what is interesting is Michael Cape's resemblance to O'Neill: a conflicted, dreamy idealist, a self-indulgent sensualist, one who believes in autonomy but finds himself in situations of dependency. "There is," note the stage directions, "something tortured about him — a passionate tension, a self-protecting, arrogant defiance of life and his own weakness, a deep need for love as a faith in which to relax." The wife Eleanor is also torn between love and freedom, and she insists that her love is hers to give or withdraw, while Michael accuses her of escaping the conditions of wedlock — as the play's title likens marriage to a "welded" entrapment. "At every turn you feel your individuality invaded," Michael shouts at her, "while at the same time, you're jealous of any separateness in me. You demand more and more while you give less and less. And I have to acquiesce. Have to? Yes, because I can't live without you! You realize that! You take advantage of it while you despise me for my helplessness!"

Welded was the script that George Jean Nathan dismissed as "third-rate Strindberg," and indeed the production failed on Broadway in 1924. Yet the play not only tells us a good deal about O'Neill's own ambivalent feelings toward marriage but also depicts scenes that foreshadow the new feminist movement of the 1970s and after. What O'Neill explored has become all too familiar: marriage as the site of contestation between two career-driven professionals, each subverting love in the very effort to preserve it.

Eleanor Cape, an actress who fears losing her identity to her husband, is the only major female character in O'Neill's plays who has an occupation. All other women in the vast corpus of his writings have no careers and no serious thoughts about a vocation, although Sara Harford of *More Stately Mansions* dabbles in investments. Except for a few minor characters, women function biologically rather than professionally—as wives, mothers, daughters, lovers. O'Neill's depiction of women without a professional life scarcely reflects American society of the teens and twenties. In Susan Glaspell's plays of the period, women's ambitions are in the forefront, and feminists of the era demanded entry into the professional work force while protesting the image of the mother-in-the-home. But O'Neill sets his female characters firmly within the home, where they prove as problematic as the playwright himself. Women, no less than men, do to others what they do to themselves as they allow their desires to destroy the objects of their dreams. To desire or not to desire, that is the question of love.

AN AMERICAN TRAGEDY

To our contemporary moralists who tell us that at one time in American history values were born on the farm and sustained in the family, an encounter with O'Neill's *Beyond the Horizon* comes as a shock. In the urban settings of his plays, male-female interactions amount to a struggle to establish some rough equitable grounds for a relationship, and marriage is the setting where love has the possibility of being a unifying force. In the rural environment of *Beyond the Horizon,* however, marriage is the graveyard of love.

The play, written in 1918 and produced in 1920, won O'Neill the first of his four Pulitzers. Americans saw the play in the aftermath of the tragic consequences of World War I, and that experience may have prepared the audience to appreciate the ways in which the ideals of youth are destined to frustration and failure. The political decisions made by the American government and the personal decisions made by O'Neill's characters both produced ironic results. The world could no more be made safe for democracy than life could be made safe for domesticity. What begins in sentimental idealism ends in tragic realism.

Two sons, Robert Mayo, a bookish dreamer who yearns to ship out and explore the horizons, and Andrew, a practical farmer who is happy laboring on the land, make fatal decisions. O'Neill sides with the poet rather than the ploughman, with freedom instead of the farm. Andrew is expected to marry the neighbor's daughter, Ruth Atkins, whom Robert secretly loves but assumes has no chance with her. Hence when Robert discovers that she loves him, and not his brother, he changes his mind about going on a three-year voyage with his sea captain uncle. Robert allows himself to believe that getting married will ward off second thoughts about his sudden decision not to go to sea and all gnawing doubts about the future, and thus his dreams of freedom succumb to his desire for love. But by the second act, after three years have passed, Ruth resents Robert's dreamy escapism and inattention to the farm, and she sets out to crush his independent spirit. Five years later Andrew, who took his brother's place shipping out so as to be away from the Ruth he loved, returns to find Robert sick and depressed, despondent over the death of his daughter, and his wife embittered and desperate to switch her affections to himself. But Andrew, who has speculated in grain shares, is broke and in no mood for romance as he thinks only of trying to restore his brother's health and to save the farm from bankruptcy. Robert, knowing he is dying, asks Andrew to marry Ruth and take care of her after he is gone and help relieve her suffering. In the last scene Robert is found lying on the road on which the play opened. As life runs out, he tells his wife and brother not to feel sorry for him since at last he is free to "wander on and on — eternally. . . . I've won my trip — the right of release — beyond the horizon."

O'Neill remained suspicious of the feminine instinct of nesting and nurturing, often seeing behind it the will to control and dominate. Ruth cannot allow Robert to be himself; she must transform him into an extension of herself. Hence the emotion of love fails to be self-sustaining and turns into jealousy and possessiveness. For his part Robert cannot remain loyal to his deeper instincts to be independent and free; instead he has allowed himself to assume that love can be more than a sudden rush, when, in reality, marriage may only be a futile attempt to institutionalize a mysterious moment.

O'Neill spent considerable time out at sea and in barrooms, and being around men he perceived the problem of marriage as the problem of settling down, of forsaking the call of the wild and free for the comforts of the familiar. This lost wanderlust theme would run through many of O'Neill's plays as though he sensed a crisis of masculinity. Revealingly, two months after *Beyond the Horizon* opened, O'Neill wrote a letter to the *New York Times* that suggests what he had on his mind when writing the play. On his trip to Buenos Aires in 1910, O'Neill became friends with a Norwegian sailor who longed to be back on his family farm and regretted going to sea. While thinking about a new theme for a play, O'Neill recalled the sailor and asked himself:

"What if he had stayed on the farm, with his instincts. What would have happened?" But I realized at once he never would have stayed. . . . It amused him to pretend he craved the farm. He was too harmonious a creature of the God of Things as They Are. . . . I started to think of a more intellectual, civilized type from the standpoint of the above-mentioned God—a man who would have my Norwegian's inborn craving for the sea's unrest, only in him it would be conscious, too conscious, intellectually diluted into a vague, intangible wanderlust. His powers of resistance, both moral and physical, would also probably be correspondingly watered. He would throw away his instinctive dream and then accept the thralldom of the farm for—why, for almost any nice little poetical craving—the romance of sex, say. And so Robert Mayo was born. . . .[18]

Andrew, with farm life bred in his bones, goes to sea; Robert, with his imagination roaming the world, remains on the farm. O'Neill is hardly suggesting that we poor mortals are victims of the road not taken. The decision as to what to do with one's life can never be unambiguous when the primal instincts cannot resist opposing appeals, when human nature is so divided within itself that there can be no harmonious resolution. In other O'Neill plays male characters long for wife and farm only to stay as far away as possible. It is not simply that absence makes the heart grow fonder. To long for, and the desire to belong to, are sharply opposing emotions, and O'Neill feared that settling down would be the end of life's questing challenge. It would be, as Melville put it, to hug the harbor.

Beyond the Horizon has been praised as the first successful classical tragedy in the American theater. The play does deal with sorrow and suffering, and the protagonist Robert Mayo makes a fateful decision that seals his unintended destiny. The audience watches the waning of love and romance, the disillusionment with decisions gone sour, the wife growing drab and the husband numb, and the last scene with Robert crawling out of a dreary house to die on the road that once promised escape to freedom.

Beyond the Horizon may follow some of the ideas in classical tragedy, but in the male-female relationships of O'Neill's plays the characters have no access to classical knowledge. The Greeks believed that it could be possible to come to know who we are and identify with our essential nature and proceed through life as coherent, unified beings. O'Neill's characters either resist trying to know who they are and refuse their destiny or, what is more chilling, sense there is no self to be known, no original nature, no essence that enables us to know what we want because we know who we are—hence love is experienced as a neediness born of the incompleteness of being. "The moderns, men and women of passion," writes Denis de

Rougemont, "expect irresistible love to produce some revelation either regarding themselves or about life at large."[19] In O'Neill love obscures more than it reveals, and marriage can barely survive the second act.

A Strindbergian influence may be seen in *Beyond the Horizon*, where the high hopes for love give way to the tiresome trivialities of life. Often O'Neill's plays about marriage take place over the course of many years to suggest that time is the enemy of happiness. In the character Robert Mayo resides a great deal of O'Neill, who could never decide whether a woman in his life could be a fulfillment or a fantasy, a true passion or a "nice little poetical craving."

WOMEN IN LOVE, WOMEN IN CONTROL

The first play O'Neill wrote that would give prominence to the female character was *Anna Christie*. The work, written between 1918 and 1920 and produced in 1922, went through several versions. In the earliest drafts, the primary focus was the character of Anna's father, Chris Christopherson, modeled on a sailor and drinking companion of O'Neill's. Eventually Anna displaces him as the central protagonist, and O'Neill tries his best to create a heroine out of a fallen woman. The subject itself was familiar. Between 1890 and 1920 American theatergoers saw roughly fifty plays about brothels and prostitutes, and the motif of "the repentant courtesan" became well known. But O'Neill's play offered a new twist, an unrepentant heroine capable of recovering from a wayward life.

In *Anna Christie* O'Neill restates a theme present in *Beyond the Horizon* and continuing in subsequent plays — rural America as sick with sin and repression. In America's political culture the countryside had been seen as far removed from the corruptions of the city. Jacksonian America was supposedly born of the egalitarian West, and the Jeffersonian ethos exalted the tillers of the soil as "God's chosen people." In O'Neill's plays, however, people in the country are given more to vice than to virtue, usually greed, envy, spite, and lust. In *Anna Christie* the heroine has been raped on a Minnesota farm. Anna describes "men on the farm ordering and beating me," and recalls that one of them, the youngest son, "started me — when I was sixteen." In the Irish-American mentality, memories of having been driven off the land in the old country left a bitterness about rural life. America's Jeffersonian idolization of the farm never convinced O'Neill, and his character Anna regains her strength on a barge in a city harbor.

Anna arrives at a New York waterfront saloon to meet her father, a Swedish coal barge captain who had sent his daughter to be raised by relatives in Minnesota after her mother died. Anna's first line upon entering the saloon establishes her hardened, brazen character: "Gimme a whiskey — ginger ale on the side. And don't be stingy, baby." Befriending a female barmate, Anna tells her story of brutal life in Minnesota. After being raped by her cousin, she was forced to find work in a "house" in St. Paul, only to be sent to a prison hospital after it was raided by the police. Even later while working as a nurse, men abused her. "Gawd, I hate 'em all, every mother's son of 'em!"

Anna's protective hardness begins to melt away while she is on her father's barge and is lifted by the mystical force of the fog-drenched ocean. What her father sees as perilous, "dat ole davil sea," she experiences as a purgation. Then enters Mat Burke, the hulking, handsome sailor, stripped to the waist, his body glistening with dripping water, who plops onto the barge after his freighter has been wrecked. Even though her father has warned her to stay away from all sailors, Anna finds herself powerfully drawn toward Mat. He tells her of his loneliness, his longing to return to Ireland and leave behind the hustlers he has met in seaports all over the world, and his desire to find a wife like Anna, "a fine, dacent girl the like of yourself." In love with Mat, Anna feels unworthy of him. But Mat thinks it is the will of God that has brought them together. Determined to marry Anna, Mat faces her father's fierce objections. As the two men quarrel, Anna, fed up with others deciding her life, comes clean about her sordid past. "I was in a house, that's what! — yes, that kind of house — the kind sailors like you and Mat goes to in port." The father breaks down in tears; Mat is furious. Then in the play's most poignant passage, Anna pleads to Mat to consider that she could not bring herself to deceive him, that the mystic power of the sea has changed her, and that loving him had made her clean and honest. "God's curse on you," shouts Mat. "Clane, is it? You slut, you, I'll be killing you now!" Mat raises a chair over his shoulder, the father rushes to stop him, but Anna urges him to go ahead and kill her since she is "sick of the whole game." Mat cannot go through with it, throws down the chair, and heads to the nearest saloon to get crocked.

Two days later, Mat returns, hung over and bedraggled, and pleads with Anna to tell him that she was lying about her past. But the past cannot be changed, Anna replies, and assures Mat that she hated all the men she has had and only loves him and him alone. Mat wants her to swear an oath that she means what she says and takes from his pocket a small crucifix given to him by his mother. As Anna is so swearing and promises never to revert to her old ways, a thought suddenly hits Mat. "Is it Catholic ye are?" Her honest reply of no throws him into confusion, but with a burst of passion he clasps her: "I'd go mad if I'd not have you!" They are to be married the following morning.

Some critics regarded the conclusion as a failure of nerve. George Jean Nathan judged it banal, a conventional happy ending that gave the audience what it wanted. Anna's conversion from slut to saint also seemed unconvincing. But O'Neill told Nathan that sometimes melodrama can be true to life and that as he worked on the play he saw that it would be dominated by "the woman's psychology," by Anna's emotional state:

> I have a conviction that with dumb people of her sort, unable to voice strong, strange feelings, the emotions can find an outlet only through the language and gestures of the heroics in the novels and movies they are familiar with — that is, in moments of great stress life copies melodrama. Anna forced herself upon me. . . . In real life I felt she would unconsciously be compelled, through a sheer act of inarticulateness, to the usual "big scene," and wait hopefully for her happy ending. And as she is the only one of the three who knows exactly what she wants, she would get it.[20]

Travis Bogard observed that of all of O'Neill's characters, only Anna and Mat know what they want and willingly follow the instincts of their inner being. Neither will allow reputation or convention to stand in the way of their deepest emotions. Other O'Neill characters rebel against their own instincts and passions. "But for Mat and Anna trust is enough. To belong to one another is to belong to the sea, and in that, although he fought the conclusion through three versions, O'Neill, in the first phase of his career, could not finally deny that there is happiness."[21]

Perhaps. But in recent years women critics of the play have bristled at so masculine a conclusion. Marriage or no, Mat intends to sail out and join up with her father immediately following the wedding. And Anna's fate seems at odds with her exclamation, when she finds herself the bone of contention between two grasping men, "Nobody owns me, see!" Anna may have "forced herself" upon O'Neill, but why did he allow her to acquiesce to the men's demands that she be domesticated while they retain their freedom as buddies on the go?

If one man is enough for Anna Christie, for the heroine of *Strange Interlude* even five men are not enough and marriage but a convenience and bearing a child a deceit. Anna loves Mat, an emotion as novel as it is powerful that it completes her being. In *Strange Interlude* Nina Leeds manages to inspire the love of three men while seeking to dominate her father and son, yet remains as unfulfilled at the end of the play as she is frustrated at its beginning.

Strange Interlude opened on Broadway in 1928. Perhaps because its themes reflected trends within American society in the twenties, it became O'Neill's most successful play, winning him his third Pulitzer and earning several hundred thousand dollars that set him up for life. It was his most experimental production, a long nine-act play that took five hours to perform, with actors using interior monologues to convey unsayable thoughts. O'Neill actually thought of having the entire play carried by voices heard only by the audience. "Thinking aloud is more important than actual talking, or speech breaking through thought as a random process of concealment," he wrote in his notes.[22] With the devices of asides and soliloquies, the audience could hear a woman talking to herself and could hear what the men in her life are thinking as the latter try to imagine what she is thinking about both herself and them. The asides render the audience omniscient while keeping the characters guessing. With such devices speech can no longer hide thought, and there are no secrets between men and women that are withheld from the audience.

Strange Interlude raises a question. In *The Second Sex* Simone de Beauvoir insisted that women are not born but made, that is, they do not come into the world with an innate essence but are shaped by society's conventions—a "social construction," to use today's academic jargon. Is Nina Leeds such a construction? At the opening of the play we are led to believe she was so at one time since she accepted all of society's conventions about virginity and obedience to one's father. But having been submissive, she becomes assertive. Nina is the dominant presence in the play, and almost every scene turns on her moods and decisions. She sees herself only in terms of the men in her life, whose affections and desires she seeks to command. Rather than a character formed out of social conventions, Nina is an unprecedented natural force, with the audience feeling "the charged atmosphere she gives off," and the men in the play with no lives of their own other than what is bound up with hers. Nina Leeds defies gender.

So powerful is her hold over men that even her father refused to give her up to her fiancé—Professor Leeds warned Nina against consummating her relation with her lover, Gordon Shaw. The handsome, all-American athlete and aviator joins the Lafayette Escadrille and is killed when his plane crashes in flames two days before the armistice. Nina is left mourning but also defiant.

Nina knows love and death as a result of the First World War, one reason to consider *Strange Interlude* as a "Lost Generation" text.[23] Gordon, the embodiment of America's youthful democratic ideals, is shot down, leaving Nina's lover a mess of "charred bones in a cage of twisted steel." Many American writers emerged from the war with psychic wounds and a loss of innocence, and Nina's mourning for Gordon echoes the twenties' lament for the promises of an old world that no longer exists. Like characters in the novels of Fitzgerald and Hemingway, Nina knows that the past cannot be undone and yet she is condemned to remember it.

Strange Interlude also offers observations on the nature of American society in the twenties, particularly the occupations that constitute a cross-section of the country during the "roaring" prosperous times: the professor who buries himself in the ancient classics as a means of escaping reality; the scientist who thinks that detached analysis will break things down as though truth is found in the parts and not the whole; the businessman less interested in making goods than in making money by "making it up" writing advertising copy. The idle rich make their presence felt, with their yachts, airplanes, and country estates. The sexual revolution of the twenties also intrudes in the flapper life style, affairs real and rumored, abortion and adultery, the many Freudian allusions to the Oedipal and the carnal, and Nina's shocking promiscuity. Nina works in a hospital and gives herself to wounded soldiers to compensate for having withheld herself from Gordon Shaw. But sex is far from a life force for Nina, nor is it for O'Neill himself.

If young men's lives are about, among other things, "getting laid," one might expect that O'Neill would have given us a scene or two of this sort to remember, at the very least a provocative fade-out. But when O'Neill hints about sex it is almost always with revulsion, and his male characters, having argued with their wives, stomp out of the house to take up with a prostitute, who often turns out to be a kind soul with no aroma of the erotic. It is well known that O'Neill's older brother introduced him to sex by taking him to a brothel. The playwright never acknowledged explicitly what it was like in any of his letters. But the experience spills into *Strange Interlude* in a passage whose emotions are more recalled than invented. Wondering why he has never fallen completely in love with Nina, and fearful that his mother would be jealous if he did so, the novelist Charles Marsden thinks of Nina erotically, and then, grinning "torturedly," says to himself:

Why? . . . oh, this diggin in gets nowhere . . . to the devil with sex! . . . our impotent pose of today to beat the loud drum on fornication! . . . boasters . . . eunuchs parading with the phallus! . . . giving themselves away . . . whom do they fool? . . . not even themselves! . . .

(*his face suddenly full of an intensive pain and disgust*)
Ugh! . . . always that memory! . . . why can't I ever forget? . . . as sicken-

ingly clear as if it were yesterday . . . prep school . . . Easter vacation . . . Fatty Boggs and Jack Frazer . . . that house of cheap vice . . . one dollar! . . . why did I go? . . . Jack, the dead game sport . . . how I admired him! . . . afraid of his taunts . . . he pointed to the Italian girl . . ."Take her!". . . daring me . . . I went . . . miserably frightened . . . what a pig she was! . . . pretty vicious face under caked powder and rouge . . . surly and contemptuous . . . lumpy body . . . short legs and thick ankles . . . slums of Naples. . ."What you gawkin' about? Git a move on, kid". . . kid! . . . I was only a kid! . . . sixteen . . . test of manhood . . . ashamed to face Jack again unless . . . fool! . . . I might have lied to him! . . . but I honestly thought that wench would feel humiliated if I . . . oh, stupid kid! . . . back at the hotel I waited till they were asleep . . . then sobbed . . . thinking of Mother . . . feeling I had defiled her . . . and myself . . . forever! . . .

Sex is a missing theme in O'Neill's plays, except for a single scene in *Desire Under the Elms*. In his works the relationship of man and woman is moved more often by the calculations of possession than by the irrationalities of passion. Nina Leeds is all calculation. After once accepting the advice of her father to postpone sleeping with Gordon, she never again listens to men but instead bends them to her will. In Nina, O'Neill gave America a portrait of a woman determined to prevail and not yield, as did Anna Christie. O'Neill's mother, as presented in *Long Day's Journey into Night,* was forever lamenting "what life has done to us," as she drugged herself into a state of victimhood. Nina is resolved to take what life has done to her and overcome the loss of her lover, persevering by force of conviction until the willing of power triumphs and desire seeks its fulfillment — if it ever can!

When the play opens Nina is twenty, tall, athletic, tanned, beautiful, and smartly dressed. The "strange interlude" refers to the period between the death of her lover, Gordon Shaw, and her resigning herself to marry the writer Charles Marsden, a forty-year journey that takes her from heightened romance with Gordon to compensatory sexual adventures, then from an early marriage to the decent Sam Evans to, in old age after her husband has died, the arms of Marsden, the secure father figure. While pregnant, Nina is told of insanity in the Evans' family and, on her own, decides on an abortion and then secretly has a baby with the scientist, Ned Darrell. After the baby's arrival, Darrell tries to talk Nina into running off with him. But she wants him only for a romantic rendezvous and delights in raising his child who reminds her of her dead Gordon. Charles, Sam, and Ned are all in love with Nina, yet she is in love not with them but with their love for her, not with the persons but with their passions. Triumphantly, Nina lets the audience know what she is thinking in an aside:

> My three men! . . . I feel their desires converge in me! . . . to form one complete beautiful male desire which I absorb . . . and am whole . . . they dissolve in me, their life is my life . . . I am pregnant with the three!. . . husband! . . . lover! . . . father! . . . and the fourth man! . . . little man! . . . little Gordon! . . . he is mine too! . . . that makes it perfect!

Nina speaks of an arrangement rather than a realization, one that quickly fades in the last scenes as she ages and loses Darrell to his laboratory and her son Gordon to his fiancée. Gordon and Madeline take off in a private plane and circle over the estate, and Nina looks up to the sky and declares:

> My having a son was a failure, wasn't it? He couldn't give me happiness. Sons are always their fathers. They pass through the mother to become their father again. The Sons of the Fathers have all been failures! Failing they died for us, they flew away to other lives, they could not stay with us, they could not give us happiness!

The inconstancy of desire is such that we fear losing what we desire to have. In *Strange Interlude* the craving of love that gives way to the dread of losing is present in men as well as women. Charles expresses nervousness around Nina, and she asks him, "Why are you always afraid? What are you afraid of?" Charles, thinking in a panic, replies timidly, "I'm afraid of—of life, Nina." But Nina is more angry than afraid, outraged that she is of woman born and has known loss as well as life, as though death and birth go together:

> The mistake began when God was created in a male image. Of course, women would see Him that way, but men should have been gentlemen enough, remembering their mothers, to make God a woman! But the God of Gods — the Boss — has always been a man. That makes life so perverted, and death so unnatural. We should have imagined life as created in the birth-pain of God the Mother. Then we would understand why we, Her children, have inherited pain, for we would know that our life's rhythm beats from Her great heart, torn with the agony of love and birth. And we would feel that death meant reunion with Her, a passing back into Her substance, blood of Her blood again, peace of Her peace! (*Marsden has been listening to her fascinatedly. She gives a strange little laugh.*) Now

wouldn't that be more logical and satisfying than having God a male whose chest thunders with egotism and is too hard for tired heads and thoroughly comfortless? . . . Oh, God, Charles, I want to believe in something! I want to believe so I can feel!

In Nina's vivid recollection of the traumas of birthing, O'Neill is no doubt drawing on his own impressions of his mother's ordeal. But blaming the loss of love on a bungling deity is a theme that recurs in the literature of the Lost Generation. Even though he was haunted by his own mother's pain and suffering, O'Neill recognized that it was too easy to blame her for his troubles. And his creation Nina, the opposite of the yielding Anna and O'Neill's crippled mother, is problematic for other reasons. Domineering, meddling in the life of others as though nothing can be left to chance, she is accused of playing God.

Characteristic of upper-class women of the twenties, Nina Leeds has no interest in politics and no professional ambitions. O'Neill never bothers to hint from where her income is derived (perhaps inherited from her father), for women's economic dependence on men seems of little concern in his plays. O'Neill created a heroine who could stand on her own, but one as complex as his attitudes toward women were ambivalent. Both author and subject try to identify with the mysterious force from which life takes its meaning; neither allows convention to stand in the way of their search for fulfillment; and the playwright and his creation can long for love better than they can receive it. When Nina decides to marry the asexual Marsden, it is out of the need to rest in the arms of her old father: "God bless dear old Charlie . . . who passed beyond desire." The words are Marsden's, who is voicing his thoughts about what he thinks Nina is feeling—that she has settled upon him because he has long gone beyond desire and she has never, after falling in love with Gordon Shaw, allowed it to determine her life. To submit to what is beyond one's capacity to control is no longer to be free, and Charles is beyond desire, without a determining will, what Nietzsche called "castrated." Nina Leeds does only what she wants to do. O'Neill's strongest female creation is a study in power, not love. Yet even Nina cannot control her own creation, her son Gordon, who has been born not to his legitimate father but to Darrell in a secret arrangement. To Nina's despair, young Gordon takes an instinctive hatred to his real father, as though the sin of adultery will not go unpunished.

America looked nervously upon O'Neill's daring creation, or at least New England Victorian society did so and no doubt other parts of America as well. After *Strange Interlude*'s success in New York City, the play was banned in Boston. In the twenties Boston and much of the Midwest remained the last holdouts of the older morality that was being challenged by the Lost Generation. Propriety, reticence, discipline, conscience, responsibility, decorum, duty, modesty, gentility—such were the virtues that Nina seems to be flouting in her search for sexual gratification without fear of pregnancy and personal fulfillment without fear of reputation. Boston officials judged O'Neill's play, which treated abortion and adultery casually, as "salacious and indecent" and "a menace to the moral community." Nina was the "new woman," at once defiant and notorious, an indomitable spirit who took more than she gave and seemingly drew strength from sin. She may not have been what the feminists had in mind but no one could doubt that she knew the meaning of power and had men at her beck and call. The American stage, declared a Protestant minister, had no place for O'Neill's "psychological surgery on decaying souls."[24]

The minister was right, though perhaps for the wrong reason. A decaying soul results as much from the loss of faith as from the lust of flesh. "I want to believe in something!" cries Nina. "I want to believe so I can feel!" O'Neill also felt the need to believe and feel, especially in matters of religion. Some devout Christians believe that it is better to love God than to know Him. If O'Neill could do so, he and his characters could begin to try to overcome the sin of desire.

*

O'Neill's plays registered the ferment of feminism that was in the air in the World War I era. But the playwright's observations do more to complicate than clarify woman's predicament in man's society. In *Servitude* and other plays O'Neill indicates the extent to which women still saw themselves as renouncing their own desire for freedom to fulfill their husbands' expectations. Then again, if women are neurotically controlling, as in *Strange Interlude,* men are weak and needy. *Welded* examines the institution of marriage, with the husband the romantic idealist who demands total commitment and the wife capable of having casual affairs to feel she is not being "crushed." The anarchist-leaning O'Neill sometimes treated the emotion of love with the same suspicion that he treated religion: faith in either meant loss of freedom and self-control. "He saw," says the character John Loving in *Days Without End,* "that underneath all his hypocritical pretense he really hated love. He wanted to deliver himself from its power and be free again." What biology had torn asunder, humanity cannot put back together. It was a half a hundred millions years ago, exclaims Michael in *Welded,* that the cell of male and female split in half, dividing "you and me, leaving an eternal yearning to become one life again."

"Man is born broken," exclaims a character in *The Great God Brown*. "He lives by mending. The grace of God is glue!" "What?" asked Nietzsche in *Twilight of the Idols*. "Is man merely a mistake of God's? Or God merely a mistake of man's?" Born and raised a Catholic, O'Neill quickly left that faith though it never really left him, or perhaps it left him wondering: who mistook whom, God or man?

9

Religion and the Death of Death

"BELIEF IS DENIED TO ME"

One morning in the summer of 1903, Eugene O'Neill and his father James were descending the stairs of their New London home on the way to Sunday mass. Suddenly young O'Neill pulled away and announced he was not going. The father tried to drag him along forcefully, and the two struggled going down the stairs. After a scuffle the father gave up and glared furiously at his son, standing with his shirt torn. But Eugene got his way and, indeed, would never again enter the Church that had been the spiritual home of his parents and centuries of Irish ancestry.[1]

The scene of the scuffle on the stairs has all the symptoms of the Irish-Catholic temperament struggling against authority. It used to be a dictum of Jesuit teachers that they had only to teach a youth until the age of seven, supposedly the "age of reason" when the mind becomes responsible for its thoughts and acts. Thereafter a Catholic would always be haunted by what the priests and nuns had taught: this life is nothing, the afterlife everything. But O'Neill was fourteen, long past the age of seven, when he broke from his father and the Church, and his answer to Catholicism would be, in his later life as a playwright, not fear and trembling but scorn and laughter.

Like other Irish-Catholic youths, O'Neill attended mass and took the sacraments along with his fellow students. But although he apparently never became acutely absorbed in the teachings of the Church, he later experienced a lingering crisis of inability to believe in a just God. From the time he was in a Catholic boarding school he found religious instruction cold and boring, and he talked his father into allowing him to transfer to a secular school. But in the years 1902–1903, he noticed that his mother was suffering some kind of illness and behaving erratically. At the time he seemingly was unaware of the mother's morphine addiction. Then, one evening in the summer of 1903, his mother, desperate without her morphine, tried to drown herself in the Connecticut Sound, and his father James and brother Jamie decided it was time that Eugene knew the truth about her illness. It was the following Sunday that the son nearly came to blows with his father. If he ever once believed in a divine Creator or tried to pray to Him, the awareness of the affliction suffered by his mother cast into doubt a God of mercy. O'Neill had no trouble with the gentle teachings of Jesus but not with the harsh dogmas of the Church.

The liberal philosopher John Stuart Mill regarded the essence of religion as the elevation of our minds to an ideal state beyond the selfish objects of desire. The anarchist philosopher Friedrich Nietzsche, in contrast, believed that religion frustrated the realization of desire by filling the mind with guilt, leaving humankind to see itself as the cause of its own suffering. Many American intellectuals of O'Neill's early period were influenced by Darwinism and the philosophy of pragmatism, and some experienced a trauma upon discovering that religion could not easily be reconciled with modern science. Eugene O'Neill's encounter with religion was as much personal as philosophical, and it is understandable that he would be attracted to Nietzsche and think that he could regard the once-shocking saying "God is dead" as a celebration. But could he? "Most modern plays are concerned with the relation between man and man, but that doesn't interest me at all," O'Neill remarked to Joseph Wood Krutch. "I am interested only in the relation between man and God."[2] In *The Modern Temper,* Krutch observed that even when all evidence of religion is lost to philosophical analysis and scientific inquiry, the psychological need for some form of faith still remains. O'Neill always believed that the emotions reveal the depths of the human condition far better than reason, and an exchange from *Days Without End* indicates why the power of religion lingers on even after it has lost its credibility:

ELIOT: God, John, how you've changed! What hymns of hate you used to emit against poor old Christianity! Why, I remember one article where you actually tried to prove that no such figure as Christ had ever existed.
JOHN: I still feel the same on the subject.
ELIOT: Feel? Can't understand any one having feelings any more on such a dead issue as religion.

A friend of O'Neill's father had known Eugene as a youth in New London. "Always the gloomy one," the friend observed, "always the tragedian, always thinkin.' My God, when he looked at you he seemed to be lookin' right through you, right into you soul. He never said much and then spoke softly when he did speak. Brilliant he was too, always readin' books. We're all Irish around here and knew the type. He was a real Black Irishman."[3]

The expression "Black Irishman" has perplexed some O'Neill scholars who wonder where it came from or whether there is such a creature. But the term has less to do with ethnicity than psychology, and O'Neill himself often referred to humankind's fallen, "black soul." A Black Irishman, the family friend went on to explain, is one who had believed in the Catholic religion and then lost his faith and spends the rest of his days searching for life's meaning in a world without God. O'Neill's wives Agnes Boulton and Carlotta Monterey questioned such a description, convinced that their husband had little interest in religion and remained untroubled by the thought of God. The activist Dorothy Day, however, had a different recollection, and one based on evenings spent with O'Neill discussing Baudelaire and Strindberg as well as religion. "Gene's relations with his God was a warfare in itself," she wrote. "He fought with God to the end of his days. He rebelled against man's fate."[4] Day's observations remind us of Herman Melville, who also had a lifelong "quarrel with God" along with a mystical streak. At the age of forty, O'Neill wrote to his friend Sister Mary Leo Tierney:

> There is nothing I would not give to have your faith — the faith in which I was born and brought up (as a good O'Neill should be) — but since I may not know it, since belief is denied to me in spite of the fact that my whole adult spiritual life is that search for a faith which my work expresses in symbols, why then my thwarted search must have its meaning and use, don't you think, for whatever God may be? Perhaps they also serve who only search in vain! That they search — and not without knowing at times a black despair that believers never know — that is their justification and pride as they stare blindly at the sky! The Jesus who said, "Why has Thou forsaken me?" must surely understand them — and love them a little, and forgive them if no Savior comes today to make these blind to see who may not cure themselves.[5]

Most believers never know "black despair" since their belief is not denied to a mind more accepting than questioning. Upon what, then, do beliefs depend? In William James's classic essay, "The Will to Believe," the philosopher sees belief as a matter of overcoming doubt, hesitation, and uncertainty through the force of resolution and will power. Human beings have a right to believe in religion when belief proves to be useful and satisfying, even if belief in God amounts to a "leap of faith."[6]

James's philosophy of pragmatism had little attraction for a "Black Irishman" like O'Neill. An Irish Catholic, even an ex-Catholic, has difficulty believing in a doctrine or proposition simply because it is useful. Genuine ideas and principles require the authority of some transcendent truth, wherever it may be found. America's culture may identify truth with practical results, but O'Neill insisted that the American audience needed more than immediate gratification. "Success is still our only real living religion," he wrote despairingly, knowing full well that Christianity is about suffering and sacrifice.[7]

A Catholic is brought up to accept such doctrines as the Immaculate Conception, the assumption of Mary, atonement, and, the unimpeachable belief, papal infallibility. The anarchism to which O'Neill was later drawn asks the mind to accept nothing and doubt everything. Yet a certain religiosity remained with O'Neill, and the attitudes toward religion that dwell in his plays are far from personal. Not everything that troubled the playwright can be reduced to the tensions within his family.

O'Neill felt deeply the dualisms of philosophy, particularly between matter and spirit, experience and meaning, and the individual and society. Much of modern philosophy promised to overcome such dualisms and even claimed that there existed no deep conflict between science and religion. O'Neill's great admirer, Joseph Wood Krutch, knew exactly what the playwright was getting at when he stated that his primary interest was man's relation to God. In *The Modern Temper* Krutch articulated what O'Neill dramatized: our need for a relation to something majestically mysterious beyond ourselves, a need for that which may not be there. The same year that Krutch's book appeared, 1929, also saw the publication of Walter Lippmann's *A Preface to Morals*. Lippmann, America's leading political philosopher, and Krutch, one of its leading drama critics, arrived at the same conclusion about the intellectual costs of modernity to religion and about the failure of modern science to serve as a surrogate. O'Neill was not alone in his quarrel with God.

THE MODERN TEMPER AND THE PROBLEM OF UNBELIEF

By the end of the 1920s the "Lost Generation" was lost in more ways than one. The year 1929 saw not only an O'Neill play on religion and science and the books by Krutch and Lippmann but puzzled discussions over new outlooks in philosophy and physics that questioned truth and objectivity. While the intellectual felt the loss of truth, many of O'Neill's characters seemed unable to face truth even if they could find it. After describing the

features of a friend who behaved with the obstinacy of the reformed reformer, an O'Neill character observes: "I wondered what Jimmy would do
if he ever saw that face in the clear, cruel mirror of Truth. Straggle on in
the same lost way, no doubt, and cease to have faith in mirrors."[8]

In a later one-act play, *Hughie,* the character Erie cannot turn his face
toward the mirror. The death of the night clerk Hughie reminds Erie of
his own finitude, and he cannot stop talking to the replacement clerk out
of fear of solitude and the thought that he could go upstairs to his room
and jump out the window. Talking is as desperate as praying, and the words
spill out at random. After Erie relates another of his long stories, the hotel
night clerk fails to follow the narrative:

NIGHT CLERK: (*His glassy eyes stare through Erie's face. He stammers deferen-
    tially*) Truth? I'm afraid I didn't get—What's the truth?
ERIE: (*hopelessly*) Nothing, Pal. Not a thing.

Young Eugene O'Neill may have successfully resisted his father's efforts to keep him within the folds of Mother Church, but as an adult the
playwright sensed a spiritual vacancy in his life that was as acute as the
moral emptiness that other writers saw in American society itself. Unlike
T. S. Eliot, however, O'Neill was too much the anarchist to envision order,
tradition, and hierarchy as an answer to modernity's religious void. Some
thinkers can leave behind the religion with which they have been raised.
Not O'Neill, who knew the yearning to be at one with nature and spirit.
In *Long Day's Journey into Night,* life without God leaves us staring into
the void. Edmund imagines himself to be a seagull or dolphin, flying and
swimming in mindless reverie, or lying on a ship's bowsprit, purified by
the salty ocean spray. His older brother Jamie ridicules Edmund's escapism and announces there are no cures for the hurts of life. Edmund protests that his brother sees everything as fixed and cries out, "Christ, if I
felt the way you do—!"

JAMIE: (*stung for a moment—then shrugging his shoulders, dryly*) I thought you
    did. Your poetry isn't very cheery. Nor the stuff you read and claim you
    admire. (*He indicates the small bookcase at rear.*) Your pet with the unpro-
    nounceable name, for example.
EDMUND: Nietzsche. You don't know what you're talking about. You
    haven't read him.
JAMIE: Enough to know its's a lot of bunk!
TYRONE [the father]: Shut up, both of you! There's little choice between
    the philosophy you learned from Broadway loafers, and the one Edmund

got from his books. They're both rotten to the core. You both flouted the faith you were born and brought up in — the one true faith of the Catholic Church — and your denial has brought nothing but self-destruction! (*His two sons stare at him contemptuously. They forget their quarrel and are as one against him on this issue.*)

EDMUND: That's the bunk, Papa!

JAMIE: We don't pretend, at any rate. (*caustically*) I don't notice you've worn any holes in the knees of your pants going to Mass.

TYRONE: It's true I'm a bad Catholic in the observance, God forgive me. But I believe! (*angrily*) And you're a liar! I may not go to church but every night and morning of my life I get on my knees and pray!

EDMUND: (*bitingly*) Did you pray for Mama?

TYRONE: I did. I've prayed to God these many years for her.

EDMUND: Then Nietzsche must be right. (*He quotes from Thus Spake Zarathustra.*) "God is dead: of His pity for man hath God died."

Why would O'Neill have Edmund declare that "Nietzsche must be right" after hearing how his father desperately prayed for so many years? God's "pity for man" is a curious formulation. The German expression, *Mitleid,* can be rendered as compassion or empathy, meaning to "suffer with," which would imply that God chose to die rather than suffer along with his own creations. But the text *Zarathustra* warns against pity as the folly of unwarranted mourning. If you did me wrong, "then say," advises Zarathustra, "'I forgive you what you did to me; but that you have done to *yourself*—how could I forgive that?' Thus speaks all great love: it overcomes even forgiveness and pity." O'Neill cannot forgive his father for what he had done to himself, and thus speaks his love for him.

Friedrich Nietzsche's reputation in America, always controversial, received another blow with the publication of Allan Bloom's *The Closing of the American Mind* (1988), a surprisingly best-selling book by an academic steeped in the classics. Bloom holds the "German disease" in modern philosophy, supposedly derived from Nietzsche, responsible for relativism, nihilism, totalitarianism, the assaults on democracy, and the crisis of Western culture in general. But if Nietzsche could be regarded as a destroyer of civilization, O'Neill saw him as its liberator from cant and mendacity.

Nietzsche's proclamation that "God died" for reasons of pity is a little playful, for what passes out of existence must have at one time existed. Like O'Neill, Nietzsche preferred to interrogate God rather than to bury Him. But the real quarrel was not so much with a Supreme Being as with the doctrines of Christianity, whose tenets of obedience and submission were anathema to the anarchist. Nietzsche argued that Christian morality was born of resentment, leading the poor and powerless to rationalize their envy by believing they possess a virtue superior to that of the rich and mighty and hence would find the gates of heaven open to them. Nietzsche's genealogy of Christianity, his study of how it was first received and developed historically, convinced him that God is the expression of the spirit of life fighting against the dwindling of time and the approach of death. Thus religion compels humanity to await its salvation from an exterior cause, rendering the mind without will or its own purposes. The characters in *The Iceman Cometh*, in Harry Hope's bar, live out a "hopeless hope," itself a longing for what is absent and a desire to wait for the expected.

References to religious ideas run through both Nietzsche's works and O'Neill's plays. Religion was supposed to be a force for good that brings people together in spiritual solidarity. But the idea of sin, Nietzsche pointed out, leaves people with a bad conscience, and "the bite of conscience teaches men to bite." The family members in *Long Day's Journey* each have their own bad conscience, and while snapping at one another, they can do little to ease each other's suffering.

Nietzsche's father was a Lutheran minister who conducted prayers in the home, and O'Neill's a Catholic actor who felt guilty for not attending church daily. The philosopher provoked a family crisis when he dropped his theological studies and refused to become a parson; the playwright provoked his father's wrath when he came to doubt a merciful God and refused to go to mass. The renunciation of Christianity is only one of many affinities between the two thinkers. Neither Nietzsche nor O'Neill would deny that although one wrote philosophy and the other drama, each was writing about himself as much as the world. Each knew the Bible and would quote from it in their works, each knew that religion entered the mind at the moment of solitude, and each turned to Schopenhauer to understand why people need religion even if it left them in a state of ceaseless striving, suffering, hope, and pity.

Young O'Neill's early education took place in a Catholic convent run by the Sisters of the Ursuline Order, and there he learned the Baltimore Catechism:

> Who made the world?
> God made the world.
> Who is God?
> God is the Creator of Heaven and earth, and of all things.
> What is man?
> Man is a creature composed of body and soul, and made to
> the image and likeness of God.

Such a simplistic formulation could do little to relieve O'Neill's disillusionment with God in the face of his mother's affliction. Many other thinkers disillusioned with religion turned to science, but O'Neill could not readily embrace empiricism and see the mind as an instrument of intelligence, reflection, and adaptation; instead he saw it as an agency of dissolution and self-interrogation. While his mind's inner vacuum may have longed for religious fulfillment, faith ended once Nietzsche showed it to be a fiction based on need. As Joseph Wood Krutch noted, historical faiths once "served to guide and control many rebellious generations, but they could do so only because they were not known to be fictions, and they lose their power as soon as we know them to be such."[9]

Many modern "isms"—Marxism, positivism, pragmatism, Freudianism, and, more recently, structuralism and poststructuralism—have tried, each in its own way, to extirpate religion as an illusion born of the desperate need to believe in the afterlife. The attempt to purge life of illusions is a dominant theme in *The Iceman Cometh,* which has been interpreted as a religious play. The setting is not only a "hell-hole" of sin and suffering but arguably recreates parts of the Last Supper.[10] The play does have its twelve disciples, three women (the number of women in the Easter morning narrative), and Parritt as the Judas figure who betrays Christ-as-mother. But in the play Hickey is no Christ figure who invokes the authority of Father-the-God to convert the bums from their fallen ways. He is a salesman who tries to persuade the barflies that they need no savior since they have the potential of saving themselves—by facing the world as it is. Hickey carries the message not of Christianity but of its antagonist, secular humanism, which views the mind on its own, in no need of spiritual salvation since there is scientific progress. But the characters in the play, and particularly Harry Hope, fear to go out into the modern world of science, where streets clang with the noise of speed and traffic and no longer the quiet clopping of horse and buggy. Hickey is a nihilist who would strip humanity of its illusions. But O'Neill, like Nietzsche, wonders how science will come to terms with the needs that created those illusions. And in one of O'Neill's religious plays, science itself is not without its own illusions.

DYNAMO AND THE GREAT GOD BROWN

The conflict between science and religion divides two families in O'Neill's *Dynamo,* which opened in 1929, the same year that saw the publication of the Krutch and Lippmann books registering the crisis of faith and a few years after America followed the Scopes trial over the teaching of Darwin in a Tennessee high school. Hutchins Light is a Protestant minister with a stubborn wife Amelia and a son Reuben, seventeen and unsure of himself. The neighboring family consists of Ramsey Fife, superintendent of a hydroelectric plant and a fierce atheist, his dreary wife May, and their flippant daughter Ada. Fife would like to debate the topic of science versus religion with the minister, but Light, refuses, claiming it is beneath his dignity. Ada, hearing her father snorting in disgust about something in the paper, teases him: "What's the bad news, Pop? Has another Fundamentalist been denying Darwin?"

Ada and Reuben have fallen in love but each set of parents resents the possibility of losing their only child to a family of opposite minds. A test of character and religious conviction takes place when Fife tells Reuben a story (which he actually picked up in the press) of a man who kills a rival in a fight over a girl, who then helps the man escape and later marries him. They settle down, have a daughter, and the man becomes a respectable citizen. Years later, just before the daughter is to marry, Fife tells Reuben, the father lets his daughter's fiancé know of his crime and asks him to keep it secret. But instead he repudiates his bride-to-be and hurries away to inform the police. Fife then spills out "the secret of the family," confessing (falsely) that he is actually the man he has been talking about and asks Reuben to give him his "word of honor" that he will keep his revelation secret. Horrified, Rueben starts for the door, with Fife feigning to be sorry for having put "such a load on your conscience." Reassuring Fife and his wife and daughter that they need not be afraid he will reveal their secret, Rueben advises Fife to turn himself in since he is guilty in God's eyes. "Do you want to burn forever in hell?" he asks. But Fife scoffs that hell means nothing to him as Reuben stumbles from the room.

Walking outside his house, Reuben wonders about a God who allows murder to go unpunished. When a crash of thunder lights the night, Reuben cries "Mother! Mother!" and rushes into his house. Amelia has overheard her son proposing to Ada, and in a fit of jealousy tells her husband. Reuben finds his mother in the bedroom unaware that his father is standing behind a closet door, and Amelia demands to be told what is upsetting him. Reuben repeats the story of the crime, and sinks into remorse for having broken his pledge and moans that Ada will hate him. "So you want to marry that little harlot, do you?" snaps the mother. Mr. Light steps from the closet with a strap and begins to beat Reuben, who is stunned that for the first time his mother refuses to intercede and even seems to be taking pleasure in the thrashing. Light gives up when he cannot make Reuben cry, and goes off to report his neighbor to the police, only to return in a few minutes feeling like a "stupid dolt" for falling for the story. Reuben denounces his mother as weak and cowardly for having betrayed him in not letting him know of the father's presence. The father takes up the strap again and Reuben, emboldened, shouts he is no longer scared of him or his "fool God." While the father stands shaken and the mother begins to weep, Reuben dares God to strike him dead. "There! Didn't I tell you! There is no God! No God but electricity! I'll never be scared again! I'm through with the lot of you!"

O'Neill's play departs from Catholicism, where the father usually stands for judgment and punishment, the mother for mercy and forgiveness. In *Dynamo* the mother is as possessive and vindictive as any male. When Reuben returns more than a year later, he is cold and aggressive, and with his mother passed away, he desperately looks to electricity as a divine force and the dynamo, the generator of power, as a "great dark mother," a surrogate for the maternal security he once enjoyed. The dynamo becomes an electrical God with its metallic purr suggesting nature alive with spirit.

Ada's mother is also drawn to the dynamo, and in the last scene she is on the observation balcony of the electrohydraulic plant and her daughter stands in the gallery trying to get close to Reuben. He rebuffs her when she tries to embrace him and express her deep love. Reuben remembers his mother had called Ada a "harlot," and he sees her as a barrier to his receiving a revelation from the dynamo. Taking a gun from a drawer, he shoots Ada and rushes to the dynamo, seizing the carbon brushes until the current short-circuits through his body, immolating him in a flash of blue light.

Dynamo received only mild praise on Broadway. Coming after the commercially successful and Pulitzer prize-winning *Strange Interlude,* the play disappointed O'Neill as much as the audience. The juxtaposition of the dynamo to the Bible, of the confident atheist Ramsey Fife to the arrogant theist Hutchins Light, seemed dramatically inconsequential. So, too, the painful presence of the mother. "She cheated me!" Reuben exclaims of Amelia, "when I trusted her! . . . when I loved her better than anyone in the world!" The kindness and mercy promised by religion, and once felt in his mother, desert Reuben, who turns in frantic hope to the dynamo, the visible material reality of electrical power that must fulfill the place of the old religion. But the "disenchantment with the world" cannot undergo the miracle of a reenchantment, and Reuben's over-belief that he can see the face of God and feel the presence of his redeeming mother in the dynamo leads to his death in the grip of its electrical volts.

The confusing negative reception the play drew led O'Neill to think about redoing it. He wrote a letter to George Jean Nathan to suggest what he had in mind as the play's philosophical, or theological, message:

The playwright today must dig at the roots of the sickness of today as he feels it—the death of the Old God and the failure of science and materialism to give any satisfying new One for the surviving primitive religious instinct to find a meaning for life in, and to comfort its fears of death with. It seems to me that anyone trying to do big work nowadays must have this big subject behind all the little subjects of his plays or novels, or he is simply scribbling around on the surface of things and has no more real status than a parlour entertainer.[11]

O'Neill's play has been compared to Henry Adams's chapter on "The Dynamo and the Virgin" in *The Education of Henry Adams*.[12] But the contrasts are more telling. While O'Neill and Nietzsche saw religion as crippling, Adams depicted the Virgin as a rebel who flouted Christian orthodoxy in order to bestow "love," "charity," "pity," "mercy," and, above all, "forgiveness" on suffering humanity. In *Dynamo* there is little suggestion that the feminine stands for mercy and compassion. But Adams called himself a "Conservative, Christian, Anarchist" and O'Neill called himself a "philosophical anarchist," and both depicted the modern world worshipping at the altar of science. O'Neill's character Reuben Light leaves behind his fundamentalism to embrace atheism, and looks to the dynamo for spiritual deliverance. Having read Adams, O'Neill must have been familiar with the following exclamation from his book: "O Dynamo, God of Electricity, which gives life to all things; hear my prayer! Receive me into the Great Current of your Eternal Life. Bless me with Your secret so that I can save men from sin and sorrow and death! Grant me the miracle of Your love!"

The possibility of a dynamo responsive to prayer would indeed be a miracle. The very current Adams asks to receive as the bringer of light is, in O'Neill's play, the voltage of death. Whether it be religion or science, the playwright had no wish to see the mind yielding to an alien force. To the anarchist science can be as paralyzing as religion since both depend on a world of laws and rules. Indeed, religion and science stand together against the irrational, arbitrary nature of freedom and desire, the will to follow one's own instincts regardless of society's rules and regulations.

Three years after *Dynamo* appeared on Broadway, O'Neill was still revising it, apparently convinced that its message, admittedly murky, had been lost on the audience. He felt deeply about the play, no doubt because it dealt with his own life experience: a youth is betrayed by his mother and his religious beliefs shatter. In a letter to Saxe Commins, O'Neill confesses his struggles:

I'm doing all this labor on *Dynamo* not because of any of the boob critics outcry of bunk, as you well know, and not because of its failure as a
production, but simply because, ever since I read it over after my return
from Europe . . . I've felt extremely dissatisfied with it. One of my main
ideas in the play — what the treachery of his mother does to him in taking his father's (and his father's God's) side against him, his obscure
concealed from himself longing for her and what the news of her death
does to him, and finally how he finds her again in the *Dynamo* — the God
Mother—who demands the sacrifice of the girl's life because he has
been untrue to Her— all this got completely lost in the obvious religious
struggle in the latter portion of the play and left it dehumanized and unconvincing to me. . . . I want it to be above everything the story of that
human boy and the psychological mess he gets into and his mad solution
via a combination of his deep yearnings, his Fundamentalist upbringing,
and the popular science books.[13]

O'Neill had taken another stab at a religious play in a work produced
three years earlier than *Dynamo*. One of O'Neill's favorite plays, *The Great
God Brown*, proved too ambiguous and confusing for the audience when
it opened in 1926. A demanding play, it had many shifting of scenes and
much donning of masks, which seemed to strive toward symbolic effect at
the expense of clarity. O'Neill explained his use of masks as an effort to
contrast the outward social conduct of life with the inner, hidden "drama
of souls."

The materialist businessman William Brown and the sensitive artist
Dion Anthony are the play's alter egos. In his work diary O'Neill recorded
the texts he had been reading while developing the play: Nietzsche's *Birth
of Tragedy,* Goethe's *Faust,* Anatole France's *Revolt of Angels,* and Thomas à
Kempis's *Imitation of Christ.* Dion wears the mask of Pan, the god of fer-
tility that insulates its wearer from the realities of the world, and O'Neill
tells us that in this figure he intended a combination of Dionysius and
Saint Anthony, the wildness of the pagan Greek spirit and the life-denying
prohibitions of Christianity.

The successful architect Brown does what he is told; the searching
Dion hides his spiritual restlessness behind his mask. When his wife Margaret sees Dion without the mask, she demands "Who are you?" preferring the outward facade to the real husband. During the dozen or so years
covered by the play, Margaret never tries to understand Dion's true self
and instead persuades Brown to hire her husband as an assistant in his
architecture firm. In a scene with a prostitute, Dion removes his mask
and bares his soul to Cybel, who senses that he suffers as Christ had suffered for our sins and that his inner life is superior to that of other mortal

human beings, including Brown, who has taken her as a mistress. The self-controlled Brown comes to depend upon the daring and creative Dion for his building plans. "I've been the brains! I've been the design!" cries Dion. "But Mr. Brown, the Great Brown, has no faith! He couldn't design a cathedral without it looking like the First Supernatural Bank!"

The dying Dion plans to leave his mask to Brown so that he will "become me" and his wife and children will continue to love him after he is gone. Just before he dies Dion's mask falls off, and in his final words he utters, "Our father who art in Heaven," and cries out for Brown to forgive and forget him for the sake of his own happiness. Instead, Brown puts on Dion's mask and starts to live two lives so convincingly that Margaret is not even aware that her husband Dion is dead. But wearing Dion's mask is too much for Brown, who lacks the inner spiritual resources of his deceased partner. The police, suspecting that the new Dion has murdered the missing Brown, wound him with a pistol shot, and as he lies dying, Brown can only utter "Our Father Who Art," repeating in desperate ecstasy "Who art! Who art!" He cannot locate a God in Heaven and instead sees life not as a spiritual culmination but as a biological cycle of birth, suffering, and death.

Brown dies in peace not knowing God but sensing he is part of the cycle of eternal return. O'Neill assigns to the prostitute Cybel the mind of the philosopher, affirming naturalism and the everlasting birth of life rather than honoring any of the canons of Christianity. To be raised as a Catholic is to be told that God grants a person only one life; with Nietzsche there is the promise, though rather whimsical, of the cyclical repetition of all things, the reenactment of life's stages not only once "but again and again, through all eternity."[14] It is difficult to know how seriously O'Neill took Nietzsche's philosophy as an answer to Christian theology; after all, both promise eternity in the face of life's death and annihilation. But just as the play comes to an end affirming that "always spring comes again bearing life! Always again! Always, always forever again!" the concluding lines mock the message. The police captain, reasoning that the living Dion has killed the dead Dion, returns to the room to question Cybel:

CAPTAIN: Well, what's his name?
CYBEL: Man!
CAPTAIN: (taking a grimy notebook and an inch-long pencil from his pocket) How d'yuh spell it? (Curtain)

The Great God Brown lost its audience with all the bewildering changes of masks. The use of such devices may have shown how personalities can be transferred from one character to another but whether the soul can be known to be in touch with its Creator is unclear. "Our father who art in Heaven" may very well not be there.

HORROR OF DEATH, DREAD OF LIFE

What makes O'Neill a religious thinker is not his continual belief in God but the force of memory that reminded him what it was like to once have believed in a Superior Being. With other Catholics he had no trouble living in a world of mystery, and with modernists like Darwin, Marx, Nietzsche, and Freud he no longer saw man at the center of a benevolent universe whose energies could be brought under control. At the same time, to accept a godless world is to live without meaning and significance, and even though he came to deny the existence of God, the very act of doubting can reveal a deeper need for believing.

The need derived from pain. It has been said, by Max Weber among others, that historic religions have endured because they provide answers to the meaningless suffering in the world. Oswald Spengler observed that religion captures the imagination of the child who has seen death and realizes his immense loneliness, and senses, as Mencken put it in *Treatise on the Gods,* that there is nothing beyond the grave despite what the nuns have taught. But to be good and obey the commandments is to be set free of fear, and O'Neill the anarchist sought to overcome fear without obeying. Some Catholic writers, such as the poet Charles Peguy, concluded that it was the experience of suffering that brought him into communion with the Church. O'Neill's memories of the suffering of his mother, however, had no such effect as the playwright kept his distance from the Catholicism of his youth. Here he was closer to the historian Henry Adams who, after watching his sister die an agonizing death, concluded that God could not be a person but merely a "thing" without feeling or conscience. Adams spent years exploring the teachings of Catholicism, knowing full well that it required not the exercise of reason but the surrender of intellect. The subject of religion was for O'Neill more personal than theological. The Catholic imagination is haunted by the thoughts of sin, damnation, and suffering, and their connection with personal experience renders the burden of the cross indelible on the memory. As Conor Cruise O'Brien put it in discussing Catholic writers: "Man remains nailed to the mother. When he seeks to break loose, to find 'paradise' in loving another woman, he becomes aware of the crucifixion."[15]

O'Neill knew by heart Francis Thompson's "The Hound of Heaven," in which the poet, pursued by the great hound of God, runs in fear from his salvation and judgment day. The words suggest that O'Neill, too, saw himself as a fugitive from faith:

> I fled Him, down the nights and down the days;
>   I fled Him, down the arches of the years;
> I fled Him, down the labyrinthine ways
>   Of my own mind; and in the mist of tears
> I hid from Him, and under running laughter.
>   Up vistaed hopes I sped;
>   And shot, precipitated,
> Adown Titanic glooms of chasmed fears,
>   From those strong Feet that followed, followed after.
>   But with unhurrying chase,
>   And unperturbed pace,
> Deliberate speed, majestic instancy,
>   They beat—and a Voice beat
>   More instant than the Feet—
> All things betray thee, who betrayest Me.

Catholicism chases the soul that had been brought up on it, pursued by the specter of death and everlasting damnation. But O'Neill stopped running, turned around, and faced "the hound" head on with *Lazarus Laughed.* Again O'Neill composed a play that was as much personal as philosophical.

*

During the years immediately preceding *Lazarus Laughed* and *The Great God Brown,* O'Neill was confronted by sickness and death. In 1920, the year the author achieved fame with *Beyond the Horizon,* his father was struck by an automobile, suffered a stroke, was discovered to have intestinal cancer, slipped into a coma, and died in August. In 1922 O'Neill's mother died after a series of strokes. During this period his brother Jamie relapsed into alcoholism and, after an acute breakdown, was committed to a sanitarium where he died in November 1923. Within the brief span of three years O'Neill lost his entire family. Stephen Black has shown how this experience of loss weighted his plays with the gloom of grief and mourning, yet such painful experiences can lead a sensitive mind to philosophical speculation as well as personal sorrow. Consider Saint Augustine. When his closest friend died, Augustine said that he became a "great riddle" to himself, questioning his own identity and fate. Religion was of little help, and hope in God was useless, "because the dearest friend my soul had lost was an actual man, both truer and better than the imagined deity" in which we are ordered to place our hopes.[16]

In one of the most moving passages in *The Great God Brown,* Dion recalls his dead father and mother:

> What aliens we are to each other! When he lay dead, his face looked so familiar that I wondered where I had met that man before. Only at the second of my conception. After that, we grew hostile with concealed shame. And my mother? I remember a sweet, strange girl, with affectionate, bewildered eyes as if God had locked her in a dark closet without any explanation. I was the sole doll our ogre, her husband, allowed her and she played mother and child with me for many years in that house until at last through two years I watched her die with the shy pride of one who has lengthened her dress and put up her hair.

Death is a meditative dread to O'Neill during the writing of *Lazarus Laughed* in 1925–1926, and a possible answer to facing death becomes the central theme. The play was designed as an extravagant religious pageant, with a dozen characters in masks and semi-masks along with crowd scenes and choruses conveying Rome at the time of Christ and the crucifixion. O'Neill drew on the biblical account of Jesus learning of Lazarus arising alive after being laid to rest in the tomb.

The opening setting is in Bethany outside of Lazarus's home. Amid the many guests Lazarus is the only character without a mask since he alone is at one with himself and freed from the fear of death. Asked what there is after life, Lazarus simply laughs, making the crowd all the more curious about the nature of the "beyond." Finally Lazarus replies: "There is only life! I heard the heart of Jesus laughing in my heart; 'There is Eternal Life in No,' it said, 'and there is the same Eternal Life in Yes! Death is the fear between!' And my heart reborn to love of life cried 'Yes!' and I laughed in the laughter of God!" The crowd, moved to see a mind so transparently devoid of all consciousness of fear, begins to laugh with Lazarus. The lifting gaiety spreads contagiously wherever Lazarus appears.

Such a message is more threatening to political power and social order than Christianity itself, which would have its followers embrace submission and obedience in the hope of eternal reward. The Protestant work ethic was said to have been founded on anxiety about the state of the soul. O'Neill's play indicates what happens when the anxiety disappears. Overcome by laughter, the young leave the farm to dance and sing, and when the elders, fearing starvation, tell the youths that they will be paid to return to work, neither labor nor lucre has any meaning. "How can we compete with labor for laughter?" asks an orthodox Jew. The chief priests and Pharisees are determined to see Lazarus killed. But why should Lazarus, who grows younger in every scene, be afraid of something so familiar as dying? Even when Roman soldiers kill members of his family and he hears of Jesus's death, Lazarus first shows no emotion and then begins to smile and laugh, and everyone, including the soldiers, laughs with him.

But Tiberius and his heir Caligula are not laughing. The threatened rulers believe they can call Lazarus's bluff, expose as false his conviction that the worm of worry ceases when "death is dead." They make him witness the suicide of his own wife, the aging Miriam. Upon her death Lazarus for once cannot laugh and expresses his loneliness. The Romans are about to set upon him when Miriam's body stirs and she announces "in a voice of unearthly sweetness," "Yes! There is only life! Lazarus, be not lonely!" Lazarus exults in ecstasy.

O'Neill's play had political as well as religious implications. In the seventeenth century the English philosopher Thomas Hobbes made fear of death the basis of political order. In his view, people need to be persuaded to surrender some of their freedoms and submit to political sovereignty for the sake of self-preservation. In the state of nature prior to the origins of government, life is "solitary, poor, nasty, brutish, and short." The liberal social contract guarantees life and property in a world threatened by murder and starvation. In O'Neill's play, Nietzsche takes the place of Hobbes, and life is guaranteed for other reasons.

Lazarus tries to convert the groveling Caligula, advising him not to delight in cruelty and take pride in evil but rather remember that fear cannot be conquered by terrifying others. Instead, Caligula kills both Tiberius and Lazarus, and proclaims himself the new Caesar who will never again succumb to anxiety. Yet the specter of death continues to haunt him as he asks Lazarus, again arising from the dead, for forgiveness. Earlier Lazarus had observed Caligula looking into a mirror and making horrible facial contortions in an effort to look menacing and shouting threats to an empty room. Lazarus tells the pathetic ruler to accept his insignificance and let himself be reborn into the everlasting cosmos, counseling "then perhaps you may be brave enough to love even your fellow men without fear of their vengeance!"

CALIGULA: (*dully*) I cannot understand. I hate men. I am afraid of their poison and their swords and the cringing envy in their eyes that only yields to fear!

LAZARUS: (*gaily mocking*) Tragic is the plight of the tragedian whose only audience is himself! Life is for each man a solitary cell whose walls are mirrors.

Lazarus Laughed is a meditation on death and the self-delusions of those who think they can rule by fighting fear with fear. The play may be interpreted personally as well as politically, as several scholars have noted. In Lazarus's wife O'Neill evokes his own mother, and the Hebrew name Miriam may stand for Mary Ellen O'Neill, who dies awaiting reunion with O'Neill's dead father James. O'Neill needed to obtain from his mother what Lazarus desperately sought from his wife Miriam, solace from suffering. The confession "I am lonely!" could only be overcome with his mother's reassurance that life continues after death.[17]

Yet to O'Neill the meaning of the play was as much universal as personal. "I am certain that 'Lazarus' fills a long felt spiritual want that everyone today is suffering from — want of faith in life," he wrote two years after the play had been performed to lukewarm reviews at the Pasadena Playhouse in California.[18] To restore faith in life O'Neill had to ease fear of death. The Hebraic God of punishment and judgment had to be purged. O'Neill drew upon Nietzsche to teach us that we must remember what we have forgotten, that fear of death and the dreadful emotions invoked by the thought of annihilation are the products of a religious upbringing. We must, Nietzsche insisted in *Twilight of the Idols,* resist "the wretched and revolting comedy that Christianity has made out of the hour of death." O'Neill added in his play: "All death is men's invention! So laugh!" And "the greatness of Man is that no god can save him — until he becomes a god!" O'Neill presages our own contemporary school of post-structuralism with his Nietzschean conviction that what passes for the natural and spiritual is simply a construction of human artifice. Cries one Roman, "We will build you a temple, Lazarus, and make you a god!" Lazarus replies: "When men make gods, there is no God!" When truth is made instead of being found as an act of discovery, when it can be seen as an invented construction, religion awaits its deconstruction and the shadow of death becomes a revolting comedy.

In a letter to Arthur Hobson Quinn in 1927, O'Neill told the drama critic what he had in mind when writing *Lazarus Laughed:*

> The fear of death is the root of all evil, the cause of all man's blundering unhappiness. Lazarus knows there is no death, there is only change. He is reborn without that fear. Therefore, he is the first and only man who is able to laugh affirmatively. His laughter is a triumphant Yes to life in its entirety and its eternity. *His laughter affirms God,* it is too noble to desire personal immortality. . . . His laughter is the direct expression of joy in the Dionysian sense, the joy of the celebrant who is at the same time a sacrifice in the eternal process of change and growth and transmutation which is life of which his life is an insignificant manifestation,

soon to be reabsorbed. And life itself is the Self-affirmative joyous laughter of God.[19]

To mock the nothingness of existence is to deny that death contradicts life. Nietzsche's conviction, borrowed from Schopenauer, that the will to life will endure no matter what, enables Lazarus to indulge in an ecstatic affirmation of life in the face of death. But one wonders whether O'Neill himself could overcome the horror of mortality that haunted him in his own life. O'Neill was too much the tragic dramatist to deny that the most important things in life are fated, too much the Catholic to affirm that laughter alone can conquer death, "the king of terror." Travis Bogard suggested that in *Lazarus Laughed* O'Neill simplified both Nietzsche and Christianity. "The death of God, because He has pitied men, is no part of Lazarus's doctrine. Jesus wept and Lazarus laughed for the same reason: that God is life . . . and [men] have no reason to fear a return to their elemental essence."[20]

It makes all the difference if one had been taught to believe that that "elemental essence" had been stained by original sin. To laugh with Lazarus is to leave behind the sufferings of the soul, to abolish the very dualism of flesh and spirit that haunted O'Neill. The playwright as a youth had witnessed his own mother's sufferings; her death drove O'Neill to despair and his emotional response to the loss of family members became a source of power in his drama. O'Neill sensed what Christian existential theologians recognized: that death, instead of being accepted as a long, deep sleep, or a door into another existence, or even deserving of a laughter perhaps more forced than felt, becomes fear of the ultimate finality, the fate of the soul after the flesh has rotted away. "Nothing expresses the insecurity and anxiety of human existence more profoundly than the fact that the fear of extinction and the fear of judgment are compounded in the fear of death," wrote Reinhold Niebuhr. "The fear of extinction is the fear of meaninglessness. When life is 'cut off' before any obvious completion; when *finis* so capriciously frustrates the possibility of achieving *telos,* the very meaning of life is called into question."[21]

Lazarus Laughed called into question the very meaninglessness of death and thus hoped to subvert religion and its inhibiting terrors. People allow themselves to be indoctrinated by the ruling elites, made to feel morally superior to those above them as they listen to the promises that the "poor shall inherit the earth" and that the "last shall come first." As the Niezschean O'Neill was aware, Marxism carries on this eschatological messianism, looking to the proletariat as the class that would, even before the end of the world, redeem the world from its wayward ways. Nietzsche suggested that the awakening of consciousness to atheism may spark in the people a "second innocence" relieving them from guilt and resentment. But conservative religion and radical politics both play upon the weak with promises of otherworldly salvation and the overcoming of worldly alienation.

Curiously, Eugene O'Neill wrote *Lazarus Laughed* around the same time Martin Heidegger was writing *Sein und Zeit* (*Being and Time*). Both texts attempt to escape the dread of death, one through comedy, the other through philosophy. As Heidegger observed, in some respects one need not worry about one's own death, for it will never be a fact in one's life. We will never know ourselves to have died; it is impossible for consciousness to experience that it is no longer conscious when life ceases to exist. But the experience of the death of others is the terror, for no one can relieve another from dying. If *Lazarus Laughed* would have the audience believe that "death is dead," O'Neill himself could never get over the helplessness he felt in watching his father, mother, and brother die. The playwright's genius may have sprung from emotional turmoils involving his family, but his quarrel was with God. The philosopher tried to demonstrate that death is no problem since it is not an event in our life. The playwright's response is that the problem is not death but dying.

"A SEARCH AND A CRY IN THE WILDERNESS"

O'Neill made his last effort at treating religion on the stage in *Days Without End,* a play that opened in January 1934 to disappointing reviews and closed six months later in New York. O'Neill himself acknowledged that he was not exactly sure what he intended in writing the play, the third of his "God trilogy" after *Dynamo* and *Lazarus Laughed.* It reads as though he somehow wanted to return to Catholicism, and no doubt the Church would have welcomed the apostate with open arms. But he may have had more than religion in mind at the time. The play was written after his second marriage had floundered, and the loss of love and the loss of faith both took its toll on what Krutch called the "Modern Temper."

Performed in the midst of the Great Depression, it is hard to imagine how *Days Without End* would be appreciated by an audience worried about jobs, money, and the desperate state of the nation. The successful plays and musicals of the era offered either easy political solutions (*Waiting for Lefty*) or escapist fantasies (*You're in the Money*). O'Neill's play asked the audience to forget the political and social and to think about one's most private anxiety, the inexorable sentence of death that calls into question life's meaning.

The play features two characters in the person of John Loving. John is a handsome businessman with the free time during the Depression to be working on a novel. Loving, his alter ego, has identical features but wears a death mask indicating he is the part of John who has passed away and remains unseen, a cynical Mephistophelian "with a sneer of scornful mockery on his lips." John is trying to work out in his novel what he has worked himself into in his life. He has been having an affair with Lucy, the best friend of his loving wife Elsa. The novel's purpose is "to try to explain to myself, as well as to her . . . to get at the real truth and understand what was behind—what evil spirit possessed me." The sardonic Loving suggests to John that, rather than have his character reveal his marital infidelity, he should simply have the wife die and end the novel on that note. John's real wife happens to be sick with the flu, and the thought of death is as painful as the thought of the truth that might have to be revealed.

A surprise visit by John's uncle, Father Baird, whom he has not seen since childhood, occasions discussion of religion, and we learn from letters sent by the nephew to the priest that in his young years John had been a seeker, "running away from truth in order to find it." The priest recalls John's search:

> First it was Atheism unadorned. Then it was Atheism wedded to Socialism. But Socialism proved too weak-kneed a mate, and the next I heard Atheism was living in free love with Anarchism, with a curse by Nietzsche to bless the union. And then came the Bolshevik dawn, and he greeted that with unholy howls of glee and . . . he'd found a congenial home at last in the bosom of Karl Marx. . . . I knew Communism wouldn't hold him long. . . . Soon his letters became full of pessimism, and disgust will all sociological nostrums. . . . And what do you think was his next hiding place? Religion, no less — but as far away as he could run from home — in the defeatist mysticism of the East. First it was China and Lao Tze that fascinated him, but afterwards he ran on to Buddha. . . . But the next I knew, he was through with the East. It was not for the Western soul, he decided, and he was running through Greek philosophy and found a brief shelter in Pythagoras and numerology.

Sex and religion come together as John explains to Father Baird and his wife his novel's plot. The protagonist has been in his youth so devout a believer he served as an altar boy and dreamed of becoming a priest. Then he learned in Catholic school of the God of Punishment and, with the death of his parents, turned against religion and became a militant atheist, "a damned soul." Later in life he finds the truth of life in love itself, but he also worries that, as with his parents, his beloved wife might die too. Whether it was that fear that led the novel's character into an affair is unclear, but as John describes the details of the infidelity in terms familiar to Elsa, she senses that her husband has been describing himself and that Lucy has been sleeping with him. Elsa, ill with the flu, leaves the room and, unknown to the others, goes out into a rainy night. In a closing scene she is hovering between life and death with a doctor and the priest at her bedside. Her will to live could return if she would only forgive her husband, and Father Baird urges John to pray to God.

In the final scene John is in a church kneeling before a cross uttering religious incantations about the mystical body of Christ, then rising and stretching out his arms while Loving, the Nietzschean-like cynic who denies God's existence, collapses dead at the foot of the cross, "like a cured cripple's testimonial offering in a shrine." Father Baird rushes in to announce that Elsa will live:

JOHN LOVING: (*exaltedly*) I know! Love lives forever! Death is dead! Ssshh! Listen! Do you hear?
FATHER BAIRD: Hear what, Jack?
JOHN LOVING: Life laughs with God's love again! Life laughs with love!

Although melodramatic, much is autobiographical in *Days Without End*. The playwright lost faith in God with his mother's seemingly incurable illness and had to live with his "damned soul" after the death of all the members of his family, and it is the woman as wife who offers the forgiveness of sin. Catholic scholars are pleased to cite O'Neill's edifying premise: "In all my plays, sin is punished and redemption takes place." Edward L. Shaughnessy has shown how O'Neill's Catholicism endowed him with a sensibility toward humanity's fallen condition, leaving the playwright to wonder about the world's suffering and to question whether sin and evil were real or whether, as Nietzsche insisted, feelings of guilt and inadequacy derived from the very religion that promises our salvation at the price of unquestioning obedience.[22] But the play has little to do with the temptations of sin and its punishments, and the final scene, so dripping with bathos and lacking in what Nietzsche called the "pathos of distance," the need to get beyond one's own emotions, undermines any possible philosophical message. "Has any other major playwright ever written a play so awkwardly contrived or with such a feeble epiphany?" asked biographer Louis Schaeffer.[23] Perhaps not. But O'Neill came closer than any other playwright in dramatizing on the stage T. S. Eliot's lament that nearness to death does not bring us nearer to God.

After *Days Without End* O'Neill was asked if he had rejoined the Catholic Church and accepted its doctrines. "I'm afraid not," he replied. Was he, then, sincere about the conclusion to *Days Without End*? "I was," he wrote in a private letter, "as sincere about John Loving's solution as I have been in all my other plays." But O'Neill added that his life was not Loving's any more than Dion's. "I don't pretend to know or prove any *the* Truth. I sense truths about the conflicts in the souls of men and women and I am driven to express them in dramatic form — that is all." As to Loving's truth: "In the end it may prove to be my truth . . . or it might not. I seek — but who knows what shall I find, if anything." In another letter pertaining to the play, O'Neill comes close to offering a credo. "As to your question . . . I do believe absolutely that faith must come to us if we are ever again to have an End for our days and know that our lives have meaning. All of my best plays, even when most materialistic are — at any rate for me — in their spiritual implications a search and a cry in the wilderness protesting against the fate of their own faithlessness."[24]

It seems as though O'Neill saw himself fated to unbelief. Yet even without Catholicism and its mysteries and Christianity and its commandments, there remained a body of knowledge that could inspire belief in notions of nobility and the soul's struggle to confront the paradoxes of existence. O'Neill may have used the theater to deal with religious questions. To deal with the glare and grief of the human condition, however, he also turned to classical tragedy despite its absence in American history. O'Neill tried to laugh at death to defy the hold of religion on his mind, but his mind rested more confidently with tragedy than theology..

10

"The Greek Dream in Tragedy
Is the Noblest Ever"

From the Athenean amphitheater to the Elizabethan stage, and up to recent times and the modern playhouse, tragedy has made its appearance before a variety of audiences, and each gathering of stage-fixed viewers has expected a play with an inevitably sad ending. The spectator knows that knowledge itself is futile in overcoming tragedy, for knowledge arrives too late, after the action has runs its course. But in American history, beginning with the Enlightenment of the eighteenth century, the Transcendentalism of the nineteenth, and up to the philosophy of Pragmatism of the twentieth century, tragedy would be fatal to liberty unless knowledge could comprehend and control events. Tragedy insults intelligence. Believing the human mind to partake of the divine, Emerson wrote an essay on "The Tragic," advising his fellow Americans that while pain, suffering, and terror exist, a true relation with nature rests on equilibrium and self-trust. "Tragedy is in the eye of the observer, and not in the heart of the sufferer." Emerson's vision allowed him to imagine the harmony and beauty of all things; O'Neill's stared deep into the heart of the suffering soul.

In classical drama tragedy implied the aristocratic passions of nobility and ecstasy. Nietzsche's *The Birth of Tragedy* insisted that the ancient Greek theater was born of music and died of reason, the Dionysian world of freedom and passion overtaken by the Apollonian world of prudence and proportion. Nietzsche doubted that modern democracy would ever know the meaning of tragedy. Did tragedy have a place on the American stage?

Eugene O'Neill's friend and admirer, Joseph Wood Krutch, thought not, at least at first. In *The Modern Temper* Krutch denied that classical tragedy could find expression in modern society. An American audience may watch a performance of Shakespeare, only to appreciate on the stage what it cannot experience in life. The democratic masses shun suffering and thus cannot feel the pain that can give rise to exultation. In a chapter titled "The Tragic Fallacy," Krutch argued that in contemporary life tragedy is seen as fallacious, for it is based on assumptions about God, Nature, Moral Order, or something beyond the human condition that serves to justify the suffering of that condition. The tragedian, Krutch noted, need "not believe in God, but must believe in man." Nietzsche "was the last of the great philosophers to attempt a tragic justification of life"—Nietzsche returned to the Greeks, the playwrights who wrote of tragedy in heroic terms, but the philosopher "was palsied by the universally modern incapacity to conceive man as noble." Tragedy can no longer be written once the living faiths that sustained it have died.[1]

A decade after Krutch wrote *The Modern Temper* he published *The American Drama Since 1918,* and chapter 3 bears the title, "Tragedy: Eugene O'Neill." Krutch now conceded that modern America could be the setting for genuine tragedy and not merely for clever melodrama or sentimental fancy and flight. Evaluating the *oeuvre* of O'Neill, he praised the playwright for raising problems for which there are no answers, depicting characters as obsessed by something stronger than themselves, describing the need to belong that cannot find its dwelling in a homeless world. O'Neill's plays may lack grandeur to the extent his characters are without belief and long for they know not what, but tragedy can still make itself felt even when there is no rising to consciousness or reconciliation with reality. "The tragedy of Dion," Krutch wrote of *The Great God Brown,* "is fundamentally the tragedy of frustration, not the complete tragedy of fulfillment." George Bernard Shaw observed, in *Man and Superman,* that "there are two tragedies in life. One is not to get your heart's desire. The other is to get it." The sentiment expressed the familiar adage that those who get what they wish for could well be cursed. But the "complete tragedy" of fulfillment implies that the story is carried out to the point that the protagonist attains an awareness of his or her predicament, sometimes called a "recognition scene," or in ancient Greek drama *anagnorisis,* which takes the play beyond the crisis to offer some measure of resolution.

Alexis de Tocqueville's *Democracy in America* offers a study in the tragedy of frustration. Here we discover that the American people assume that they can attain their hearts' desires, but tragedy inheres in the very formulation that Jefferson bequeathed to America: the premise that all men are created equal and entitled to the pursuit of happiness. In the era of Jacksonian democracy, the setting of some of O'Neill's historical plays, all men are not born with equal talents and abilities or equal claims to recognition and respect; instead, all have the same opportunity to participate in a competitive society of individualism and self-assertion. Thoreau understood what Tocqueville described and saw Americans animated by a "fantastical uneasiness" as they led desperate lives. Emerson, admired by Nietzsche, believed Americans had no time for tragedy as they busied themselves making money. America could never reach enlightenment or equipoise and its mind remained "half-conscious." Tocqueville traced this fevered restlessness to democracy itself, which feeds the dream of wealth, power, and status. Of that dream that compels Americans to prove themselves, Tocqueville wrote that "they see it close enough to know its charms, but they do not get near enough to enjoy it, and before they have fully relished its delights, they die."[2] With the tragedy of frustration, there is no recognition scene, no awakening of self-knowledge, no understanding or realization. Americans strive, get ahead, perhaps succeed, and then "die."

To O'Neill tragedy reflected primarily the desperation of desire unaware of which forces are driving it to self-destruction. In ancient thought, nobility may be the height from which one experiences a tragic fall. In modern society, democracy may be the theater in which desire expresses its tragic struggle to rise. In a letter to the theater scholar Arthur Hobson Quinn, O'Neill explained why his plays can readily be misunderstood:

> Where I feel myself most neglected is just where I set most store by myself—as a bit of a poet, who has labored with the spoken word to evolve original rhythms of beauty, where beauty apparently isn't [in his plays of race and class]—and to see the transfiguring nobility of tragedy, in as near the Greek sense as one can grasp it, in seemingly the most ignoble, debased lives. And just here is where I am a most confirmed mystic . . . for I'm always, always trying to interpret Life in terms of lives, never just lives in terms of character. I'm always acutely conscious of the Force behind—Fate, God, our biological past creating our present, whatever one calls it—Mystery certainly—and of the one eternal tragedy of Man is his glorious, self-destructive struggle to make the Force express him instead of being, as an animal is, an infinitesimal incident in its expression. And my profound conviction is that this is the only subject worth writing about and that it is possible—or can be—to develop a tragic expression in terms of transfigured modern values and symbols in the theatre which may to some degree bring home to members of a modern audience their

enobling identity with the tragic figures on the stage. Of course, this is very much a dream, but where the theatre is concerned, one must have a dream, and the Greek dream in tragedy is the noblest ever![3]

What stood against the possibility of a tragic sense of life in America was the type of people Nietzsche called "the last man," those who clung to the certain, preferring complacency to conviction, the American character that Emerson and Thoreau protested as indifferent to truth, beauty, and genius. O'Neill reminded the public that a profound pessimism is preferable to a "skin deep optimism." Shunning a lesser success for the challenges of a "greater failure" demonstrates again that "the noblest is eternally the most tragic."[4]

At the time of O'Neill's youth at the turn of the twentieth century the leader of American letters was William Dean Howells, a genial human being and a talented novelist who did much to usher in realism in American prose fiction. But pessimism and tragedy he thought better left to Europe, especially the Russia of Fyodor Dostoevski. In this country the writer should deal with "the smiling aspects of life," which are the "more American."[5]

By no means was O'Neill the first to challenge the sunny optimism of Howells by bringing a sense of tragedy to bear upon American life. The novelist Theodore Dreiser did so with *Sister Carrie* in 1906, and Herman Melville's *Billy Budd,* written in 1890, came to public light in 1924, a time when O'Neill was the most exciting name in the American theater. "I have an innate feeling of exultance about tragedy," O'Neill commented in 1923, referring to his first successful major play, *Beyond the Horizon.* "The tragedy of man is perhaps the only significant thing about him. . . . What I am after is to get the audience to leave the theatre with an exultant feeling from seeing somebody on the stage facing life, fighting against the eternal odds, not conquering, but perhaps inevitably being conquered. The individual life is made significant just by the struggle." Tragedy teaches the wisdom of irony, pathos, and pity, of unintended consequences, actions at cross-purposes, and empathy toward suffering and guilt:

> The struggle of man to dominate life, to assert and insist that life has no meaning outside himself where he comes in conflict with life, which he does at every turn; and his attempt to adapt life to his own needs, in which he doesn't succeed, is what I mean when I say that Man is the hero. If one out of ten thousand can grasp what the author means, if that one can formulate within himself his identity with the person in the play,

then the theatre will get back to the fundamental meaning of the drama, which contains something of the religious spirit which the Greek theatre had. And something of the exultance which is completely lacking in modern life.[6]

In his attempt to make America appreciate the meaning of tragedy, O'Neill set out on an uphill struggle against an American culture that settled for the practical and useful, much in the way he defiantly exclaimed in the face of his father, "Life is tragedy, hurrah!" Not only O'Neill's family but America itself needed to be reminded that the true human spirit struggles against life to stand above it, even if such struggle requires "enmity and death and the cross of the martyr." Such a figure, remarked O'Neill, "is necessarily tragic, but to me he is exhilirating."[7]

MOURNING BECOMES ELECTRA

O'Neill's greatest work of tragedy, which led to his winning the Nobel Prize, was *Mourning Becomes Electra*. It opened in New York in 1931, in the depths of the Great Depression. Before the curtain rises the mood is wistful, elegiac, pensive, as the audience hears the music of grief and longing. A band in the distant background is playing "John Brown's Body," and then, more audibly, the poignant, haunting chantey "Shenandoah" is heard, sung by a age-wearied baritone, a "song that more than any other holds in it the brooding rhythm of the sea":

> Oh, Shenandoah, I long to hear you
> A-way, my rolling river
> Oh, Shenandoah, I can't get near you
> Way-ay, I'm bound away
> Across the wide Missouri.
>
> Oh, Shenandoah, I love your daughter
> A-way, you rolling river.

Tocqueville's pre–Civil War America seemed free of tragedy since the country was united and the family intact: "There are no subjects for drama in a country which has seen no great political catastrophes and in which love always leads by a direct and easy road to marriage."[8] But in the America depicted in O'Neill's *Mourning Becomes Electra,* the country has endured a political catastrophe, and love has no easy road to or from marriage. American history would witness the assassination of four of its presidents; O'Neill was thirteen at the time of William McKinley's assassination in 1901 — no more than the family can democracy itself avoid death.

The play is set in a northeast seacoast town in 1865–1866, the years immediately following the Civil War in which the future of the republic remained uncertain. The fate of the American republic and that of the Mannon family share a common destiny; neither the country nor the household will ever be the same after the ravages of war. Tocqueville believed that with the widespread acceptance of democratic values in America both the country and the family would thrive, but O'Neill's play opens with the prospect that death has overtaken both institutions. The Civil War was a family war, a fraticide and patricide, a slaughter of brother by brother and of fathers by sons. The opening scenes of the play evoke an ending rather than a beginning, as though the American republic is attending its own funeral. The anticipation of Ezra Manning's return to his mansion occurs as the final battles of the war have been fought. His family has been in emotional disarray, the country itself has politically disintegrated. Mannon has been longing to rejoin his wife, whose affections for him are no longer there and probably never were. The union of husband and wife is based neither on love nor even a vow but instead on the devotion of one person and the disgust of the other. The republic, too, had been founded on "the defect of better motives," as James Madison put it, and thus America was to be preserved by the calculations of the head rather than the promptings of the heart, by the balance of power and not the adhesion of human affections. Ezra Mannon returns home right after the assassination of Abraham Lincoln, and addressing his daughter Lavinia and wife Christine, he wonders what victory can mean if it entails death:

MANNON: Peace ought to be signed soon. The President's assassination is a frightful calamity. But it can't change the course of events.
LAVINIA: Poor man! It's dreadful he should die just at the moment of his victory.
MANNON: Yes! (*then after a pause — somberly*) All victory ends in the defeat of death. That's sure. But does defeat end in the victory of death? That's what I wonder.

Ezra senses that his wife has come to hate him, and such thoughts have haunted him as he lay awake on the battlefield. He was ready to face death, he tells Christine, if only he could know why matrimonial happiness had eluded him. The wife feigns never to have known any barrier between them and, lying in bed, she shuts her eyes as he wonders aloud what has happened to their marriage. Christine advises him not to allow himself to become overwrought about a subject better left to silence. But for Mannon it "was seeing death all the time in this war that got me to thinking these things. Death was so common, it didn't mean anything. That freed me to think of life. Queer, isn't it? Death made me think of life. Before that life had only made me think of death!"

Greek wisdom looks to the grave to discover the meaning of life. That consciousness of death arises from life itself is a conviction of modern existentialist thought. One philosopher who influenced O'Neill, Arthur Schopenhauer, saw death as the true aim of life. Without the "terrifying certainty of death," wrote Schopenhauer, men and women would have little impulse to philosophize to get to the bottom of life's meaning. Death is the theme of O'Neill's first successfully performed play, *Bound East for Cardiff,* written years before the deaths of his father, mother, and brother. In liberal political philosophy aversion to death is the motive that compels people to turn to political institutions to preserve life. In O'Neill's play, the death of family members, by murder or suicide, comes close to suggesting that the human subject is less interested in preserving life than in realizing longings, whether romantic dreams or unconscious psychological drives. The American republic, like the Mannon family, also chose the course of violence and death in the Civil War. Lincoln's Gettysburg Address, a commemoration of the loss of fallen soldiers, southern as well as northern, could have been titled "Mourning Becomes America." But while Lincoln believed America could rededicate itself to the "proposition" of 1776 that had given birth to freedom, O'Neill's play leaves America unreconciled with its own history. Lincoln hoped the "family of man" would be magnanimous, "with malice toward none and justice toward all." In the Mannon family, there is spite, cruelty, and punishment with no suggestion of redemption.

O'Neill's tragedy dramatizes a family at war with itself. Ezra Mannon had been a judge and elected town mayor before going off to war. He is stiff, brusque, and authoritative, qualities O'Neill associated with New England Puritanism. The Mannon household itself symbolizes the coming together of commercial success and public duty that once characterized American civic virtue. Ezra's wife Christine is a tall, voluptuous women of forty who looks much younger and "moves with a floating animal grace." Daughter Lavinia is twenty-three but looks much older and accentuates her unattractiveness by wearing black dresses and pulling her hair back tight.

Devoted to her father, Lavinia suspects that her mother is having an affair with Adam Brant, a handsome sea captain to whom she is also powerfully attracted, so romantically drawn that her suppressed love for him turns to jealousy and hatred of the mother. But the emotions run in the opposite direction with the mother and her lover. The relationship of Brant and Christine repeats a theme in other O'Neill plays: Brant at first resents Christine, the wife of the man who had mistreated his mother, and sleeps with her to accomplish his revenge; yet he falls madly for her, and hence genuine love grows from the depths of hatred.

The lovers Adam and Christine plot to murder Ezra, who has begun to intuit that his wife is awaiting his death so that she can be set free. Christine goads him by admitting her adultery, and Ezra, staggering as though he has been stabbed, has a heart seizure and asks for his medicine. She hands him a pellet and no sooner does he swallow it than he realizes he has been poisoned and cries out for his daughter, uttering, "She's guilty — not medicine!"

Shortly after Ezra's death his son Orin returns home and instantly asks for his mother. Christine assures her son of her undying love for him and warns him not to listen to jealous Lavinia and her mad stories about murder in the family. To Lavinia he denies vehemently that their mother could possibly have murdered their father, but Lavinia sets a trap that convinces him. Orin takes revenge by killing Adam Brant on his ship, smashing apart his cabin to make it look like a robbery. Orin and Lavinia then taunt their mother with Adam's death. But while the guilt-stricken son, convinced that it was Brant who suggested murdering his father, ultimately tries to seek his mother's forgiveness, the fierce Lavinia torments their mother, driving her to death as Christine rushes up to her bedroom where a shot rings out.

In Aeschylus' *Oresteia,* the death of the mother Clytemnestra by her son Orestes concludes the play. But O'Neill felt that the daughter Electra deserved punishment as well, and by his treatment of Lavinia in his own play he would show how every member of the Mannon family was fated to a tragic end. Of all the family members, Lavinia is the most dishonest with herself, claiming that the death of Brant was simple justice and her mother nothing more than an adulteress. Yet while on a trip to the South Pacific with Orin, Lavinia herself starts taking on the sensual persona of her mother and flirts with men; when they return, Orin sees her embracing and kissing her longtime suitor Peter. He is incensed by his sister's romantic impulses since it convinces him of what he has suspected: Lavinia talked him into murdering Brant because the handsome captain had spurned her love in favor of that of her mother. She angrily denies it, but Orin is anguished to realize he has betrayed his mother and been betrayed by his sister. He takes his life with a pistol.

From the beginning of the play to the next to last scene, Lavinia has been in a state of denial about her deepest feelings, claiming to be acting from principles of justice while suppressing the passions of love, jealousy, and revenge. But in the arms of Peter, truth outs itself from layers of repression. "Can't you forget sin and see that all love is beautiful?" Lavinia insists to Peter, kissing him "with desperate passion":

Kiss me! Hold me close! Want me! Want me so much you'd murder anyone to have me! I did that—for you! Take me in the house of the dead and love me! Our love will drive the dead away! It will shame them back into death! (*at the topmost pitch of desperate, frantic abandonment*) Want me! Take me, Adam! (*She is brought back to herself with a start by this name escaping her—bewilderedly, laughing idiotically*) Adam? Why did I call you Adam? I've never heard that name before—outside of the Bible! (*then suddenly with a hopeless, dead finality*) Always the dead between! It's no good trying any more!

"Death becomes the Mannons!" Orin had earlier remarked looking upon his father's body in the casket. Only Lavinia, who has forsworn any possibility of love in her lifetime, chooses to live, but she reenters the mansion and orders that all the flowers be removed and all the shutters nailed closed. She disappears into a tomb. She walks, O'Neill wrote in the final stage direction, as if the closing of the shutters "were a word of command" to shut out life. Mourning becomes Lavinia, as befits the living dead.

*

Mourning Becomes Electra was an instant success and the decisive achievement in O'Neill's winning the Nobel Prize in 1936. In ill health, O'Neill never went to Oslo to deliver his acceptance speech, but in his prepared address he acknowledged the influence of the Swedish playwright August Strindberg and of the German philosopher Friedrich Nietzsche. O'Neill spoke openly of the "original inspiration" and the "influence" of other writers that ran through his plays. "I have never been one of those who are so timidly uncertain of their own contribution that they feel they cannot afford to admit ever having been influenced, lest they be discovered as lacking all originality."[9] Never one to look over his shoulder, O'Neill was seldom bothered by what Harold Bloom called the "anxiety of influence," a writer's fear that he or she can only borrow from the great thinkers of the past instead of surpassing them. In *Contempt*, Alberto Moravia's novel, *Mourning Becomes Electra* sets off a controversy between two screenwriters debating how to do a film of Homer's *Odyssey*. One insists that O'Neill lacked the nerve to give his play a modernist interpretation by drawing upon the insights of Freud and other explorers of the unconscious, and the other writer defends O'Neill for remaining faithful to the classical format. *Mourning Becomes Electra* derived directly from Aeschylus and his trilogy of the *Oresteia,* written in 458 B.C. O'Neill first tried to write his play in verse but, perhaps a little intimidated by Aeschyulus, decided on prose.

"Is it possible," O'Neill asked while thinking about writing *Mourning Becomes Electra,* "to get a modern psychological approximation of the Greek sense of tragedy into such a play, which an intelligent audience of today possessed of no belief in gods or supernatural retribution, could accept and be moved by?"[10] Surveying the classical canon, he chose the *Oresteia* trilogy of Aeschylus as his model, believing its fundamental theme "has greater possibilities of revealing all the deep hidden relationships in the family than any other" of the ancient tragedies. In O'Neill's play there is no blood sacrifice of the daughter by the father as a means of satisfying the gods, as in the Greek variations, and thus the father's death at the hands of the wife has no revenge motive. Nonetheless, Aeschylus's Clytemnestra is an adulterous wife who murders her husband and then is slain by her son Orestes, who is urged on by her daughter Electra; O'Neill's Christine is a faithless wife who poisons her husband and then is driven to suicide by her daughter's vicious taunts. The American house of Mannon is similar to the Greek house of Atreus, serving as, in O'Neill's words, a setting for the "best possible Greek plot of crime and retribution" based on the "chain of fate."

The historian Herodotus regarded warfare as a perversion of the natural order of things, a carnage in which the fathers buried the sons, the old live, and the young die. Some Greek playwrights also saw war as the march of folly and the scene of sorrow. O'Neill similarly pondered the psychological perils of combat. Orin discusses with his sister Lavinia his experiences in the Civil War and General Ulysses Grant's complimenting their father's tenacity on the field of battle. Lavinia is shocked by her brother's callousness. You cannot take death so solemnly, Orin replies. On the battlefront it is "only a joke! You don't understand, Vinnie. You have to learn to mock or go crazy." Lavinia reminds him he had been awarded for bravery; Orin sets the story straight:

> I'll tell you the joke about that heroic deed. It really began the night be-
> fore when I sneaked through their lines. I was always volunteering for
> extra danger. I was so scared anyone would guess I was afraid! There was
> a thick mist and it was so still you could hear the fog seeping into the
> ground. I met a Reb crawling toward our lines. His face drifted out of

the mist toward mine. I shortened my sword and let him have the point under the ear. He stared at me with an idiotic look as if he'd sat on a tack—and his eyes dimmed and went out—(*His voice has sunk lower and lower, as if he were talking to himself. He pauses and stares over his father's body fascinatedly at nothing.*)

LAVINIA: (*with a shudder*) Don't think of that now!

ORIN: (*goes on in the same air*). Before I'd gotten back I had to kill another in the same way. It was like murdering the same man twice. I had a queer feeling that war meant murdering the same man over and over, and that in the end I would discover the man was myself! Their faces keep coming back in dreams — and they change to Father's face — or to mine.

The denial of guilt, the repetition of visions and dreams, and the repressions of thoughts about mother and father all make for a Freudian undercurrent in *Mourning Becomes Electra*. Yet O'Neill's play appears, at first, a twist on the theme of the Oedipal complex. Orin harbors no lethal thoughts toward his father out of lust for his mother; instead, he and Lavinia drive their mother to suicide. But earlier he confesses to his mother that he is not sorry to see his father dead in the casket, and Christine admits that she too is relieved that he is no longer alive. Orin now feels close to his mother, about to relive the childhood fantasies of possessing her, reminding her of how he used to brush her hair and dreaming of running off to the "blessed isles" with the love of his life. What drives Orin to despair is not that his mother has murdered his father but that she has taken a lover. To be hurt and deceived by the mother is a theme in many of O'Neill's plays, as it was a reality in his own life. For personal as well as theatrical reasons, he turned the fifth-century B.C. Oresteian legend into a nineteenth-century American experience.

When Barrett Clark wrote O'Neill about *Mourning Becomes Electra* and suggested his "introspective tragedies of man and woman" may be appreciated in light of the "modern science" of Freud and Jung, the playwright responded impatiently that critics "read too damn much Freud into stuff that could very well have been written exactly as it is before psychoanalysis was ever heard of":

Imagine the Freudian bias that would be read into Stendahl, Balzac, Strindberg, Dostoievsky, etc. if they were written today! . . . In short, I think I know enough about men and women to have written *Mourning Becomes Electra* almost exactly as it is if I had never heard of Freud or Jung or the others. Authors were psychologists, you know, before psychology was invented. And I am no deep student of psychoanalysis. As far as I can remember, of all the books written by Freud, Jung, etc., I have only read four, and Jung is the only one who interests me. Some of his suggestions I find extraordinarily illuminating in the light of my own experience with hidden motives.[11]

Elsewhere O'Neill noted that he had only read two of Freud's works, *Totem and Taboo* and *Beyond the Pleasure Principle*. The one book that may have influenced him was Jung's *Psychology of the Unconscious*, O'Neill acknowledged. "But the 'unconscious' influence stuff strikes me as always extremely suspicious! It is so damned easy to prove! I would say that what has influenced my plays the most is my knowledge of the drama of all time—particularly Greek tragedy—and not any books on psychology."[12]

THE CIVIL WAR AS CLASSICAL TRAGEDY

The background of the American Civil War resonates in *Mourning Becomes Electra,* a triology of thirteen acts divided into three parts, "The Homecoming," "The Hunted," and "The Haunted." In part one Orin returns from the war as hardened, cynical, obsessed with death. As in the Civil War, nothing in the play can be solved by open, rational dialogue. The household as well as the state knows no law other than domination and deception. Inadvertently Orin tries to bring home the meaning of the war, unaware that his own mother's hands are as soiled as any soldier's. Protesting the pseudo-patriotism that had wives and sweethearts waving their men onto war, Orin explodes: "Sometime in some war they ought to make the women take the men's place for a month or so. Give them a taste of murder!" Christine gasps, "Orin!" The war continues within the household even after peace is being declared on the battlefield.

"The drama, more than any other form of literature," wrote Tocqueville, "is bound by many close links to the actual state of society."[13] The links here are made through the Mannon household's caretaker, gardener, and relatives, who serve as a Greek chorus, supplying the necessary observations and appropriate gossip. Did the war have political significance for the ordinary worker? The sharp-eyed Seth, who more than anyone else is aware of the secrets of the Mannon family's background, feels no need to conceal his racial prejudices. "That durned nigger cook is allus askin' me to fetch wood fur her! You'd think I was her slave! That's what we get fur freein' 'em!"

Prominently displayed in Ezra Mannon's study is a large painting of George Washington and two smaller ones of Alexander Hamilton and John Marshall. Washington led the colonies to victory in the American

Revolution; Hamilton helped frame the Constitution and inaugurated the country's economic policies; Marshall established the authority of the Supreme Court with his doctrine of judicial review. Absent from the pantheon is Thomas Jefferson, author of the Declaration of Independence and champion of states' rights, ideas that did much to bring on the Civil War. But the war itself resulted from America's inability to do what the Constitution had promised to do: prevent factional discord from escalating into violence. And the plight of the Mannons suggests that even when war comes to an end, strife continues by yet fouler means. The play's two protagonists, Lavinia and Christine, are determined to prevail. Out of love for another person—Lavinia for her father and Christine for Adam Brant—the two come to hate one another. The family, like the country, succumbs to emotions that tear it apart.

In the play as well as in the events leading up to the Civil War, there is little awareness of the story unfolding, few moments of recognition of what is going on. The significance of human experience remains beyond the grasp of those who live through it   at least until the very end. History takes its toll without the consent of the people. Authority is murdered: Ezra Mannon poisoned and Abraham Lincoln assassinated. The country as well as the family will be haunted by ghosts; love will no longer be permitted while the dead live on in guilty memory, and America must somehow punish itself before it can ask for redemption.

Mourning Becomes Electra deals with two contrary impulses that divide the Mannon family as it had in some respects divided American history in the antebellum era. Ezra Mannon expresses the conscience of Calvinism: duty, probity, self-interrogation, judgment, and family responsibility. Christine Mannon expresses the impulses of romanticism: freedom, escape, self-assertion, and erotic fulfillment. On the one side, the perils of sin; on the other, the promise of happiness. The Civil War has been depicted by historians as a cultural confrontation between "Yankee and Cavalier," the stern citizen and the debonair hedonist, the energetic merchant and productive manufacturer in the North in opposition to the lazy plantation owner and his leisure-class pretensions in the South. While Ezra and Christine express these vying temperaments, the son Orin and the daughter Lavinia vacillate from one to the other, each feeling the romantic impulse to love and escape and also the duty to see justice done even if mingled with revenge.

What was O'Neill's purpose in hanging portraits of Washington, Hamilton, and Marshall on his stage set? Since their brooding presence has no effect on the characters' thoughts and actions, O'Neill may have sought to remind us, as did the historian Henry Adams, that the Civil War represented the breakdown of the Federalist system established in the Constitution of 1787. "Our theory of government is a failure," wrote Adams in response to the Civil War. The Constitution failed to do what it promised to do: balance power and control conflict. The "new science of politics," in countervailing interest against interest and passion against passion, promised to deal with desire itself, especially the human drive to dominate others.[14] Although the republic would survive the Civil War, it would do so by the exercise of power, not reason and persuasion. The Federalist portraits gaze down upon a household at war with itself, a domestic scene that also dramatizes the ruin of the country's political foundations that had once aimed to rid America of the violence that afflicted the Old World. Hamilton had hoped that the Constitution would discipline "desire" and thereby control "the unruly passions of the human heart."[15]

The issues that divide the Mannon family — love, lust, envy, revenge — are not the same issues that had eaten away at the foundations of the Union — tariffs, internal improvements, westward expansion, and, above all, slavery. But if the country at large had solved by acts of political compromise all but the issue of slavery, reason and deliberation could play no role in the Mannon household. Private matters of the heart could rarely be made public. The Mannon children deeply desire the affections of their parents, while the mother seeks to be free from her dour husband and to be in the arms of her lover. The play ends with all but Lavinia dead, and even she entombs herself in a final act of recognition and self-punishment. In the Civil War, too, the affections that once held together different sections of the country collapsed in acrimony. The tragedy of the Civil War is that the men who fought each other had at one time esteemed the Union, and southerners could even take pride in the Virginia dynasty (Washington, Jefferson, Madison, Monroe) that guided the republic in its path to greatness. But the sentiments of duty and honor proved less unifying when each section of the country followed the logic of geography as a filial devotion, and northerners and southerners alike killed the Union they once loved.

Had O'Neill remained faithful to the classical sources he drew upon to write *Mourning Becomes Electra*, he might have provided a political resolution to a personal tragedy. Aeschylus has his protagonist move out of the household into the city of Athens where public deliberation and trial and judgment can deal successfully with deeds of revenge and justice, where reason can prevail over passion, "and the brutal strife / the civil war devouring men / . . . never rages through our city."[16] How to break the cycle of vengeance and revenge that sets off war? In Greek philosophy what rescues society from feuds and strife is politics and law. But O'Neill's Lavinia shuts herself in the house and orders the blinds drawn. Her plight is too private to be shared and submitted to public judgment. O'Neill's play concludes precisely where Tocqueville feared the American character would end up: "the danger that he may be shut up in the solitude of his own heart."

SORROW, TEARS AND BLOOD: *A LONG DAY'S JOURNEY INTO NIGHT*

O'Neill drew upon Aeschylus's *Oresteia* to bring a tragic sensibility to bear upon American history. Other Americans regarded Athens as a beacon, the poet and philosopher Emerson relishing the thought that his mind and that of the ancient Greeks met in common perceptions. Could O'Neill also enjoy such a rapturous affinity?

In classical thought, genuine social relations become possible through dialogue, and human beings as "political animals" realize themselves to the extent that they leave the *oikos* (the household) and participate in the larger *polis* (the local city-state). But O'Neill rarely considered the possibility that politics can solve the problems confronting the human condition in America. O'Neill would have us look to the family and household not as a solution to our problems but as the site where conflict continues without resolution. The *Oresteia* concludes with the ways of Athens justified as private vices are judged against public virtues. O'Neill's tragic plays, however, never move beyond the household; on the contrary, to venture from the farm to the city is to succumb to sin and corruption. Not that life on the farm enables characters to achieve a conscious recognition of their predicament — O'Neill is no Jeffersonian upholding the values of rural life. His tragic plays open and close within the bosom of the household to dramatize the family as fate itself.

A Moon for the Misbegotten opens with the son of Phil Hogan sneaking away from the family farm as if it were a prison house, this son being the third to run away from home to escape what each feels is his father's tyranny. The audience is left with the father Hogan and his daughter Josie. Despite brusque exchanges and witty put-downs, the father and daughter actually have affection for one another. Josie, a large, muscular woman, intimidates men by creating the impression she is wanton and has slept with numerous men, married and single. Actually she is a virgin deeply in love with her neighbor James Tyrone. Although Hogan has depended on his daughter for companionship and help around the farm, he very much wants her to marry Tyrone, in part because it would relieve his financial situation but also because he wants to see his daughter happy. To watch the father and daughter make a fool of an intruding neighbor complaining about stray pigs is comedy serving the cause of class consciousness. The appearance of Tyrone toward the end of Act One continues the light-hearted banter of the dialogue. But as the play develops in Acts Two and Three, the comic interludes disappear and the mood turns solemn and sorrow finds its character. James Tyrone is one of the most pathetic figures in modern drama; he is also, in many respects, a portrait of Eugene's O'Neill's brother.

James O'Neill Jr. (Jamie) was ten years senior to Eugene, who in his youth had the adolescent's fascination for an older brother, the man about town who knew the ropes. Handsome, witty, charming, Jamie knocked around with Broadway actresses and prostitutes and was popular among the local smart set of young New London. Good looks and intelligence, F. Scott Fitzgerald used to say, was all one needed. But to know Jamie was to know how talent can turn the individual into what Nietzsche called an "inverted cripple," one who allows ability to degenerate into soothing delusions that appease the dread of failure. "His habitual expression of cynicism," O'Neill wrote of his brother, "gives his countenance a Mephistophelian cast." Jamie even warned Eugene that he was leading him through the door of damnation. A squandered life is the curse of the Irish American, and James O'Neill senior, a self-made man, would often criticize his elder son only to see Eugene come to his defense. In *Long Day's Journey into Night,* the father explodes after learning that his younger son has shared with his brother the money he had given to him alone:

TYRONE: Well, if you split the money I gave you with him, like a fool—
EDMUND: Sure I did. He's always staked me when he had anything.
TYRONE: Then it doesn't take a soothsayer to tell he's probably in the whorehouse.
EDMUND: What of it if he is? Why not?
TYRONE: (*Contemptuously*) Why not, indeed. It's the fit place for him. If he's ever had a loftier dream than whores and whiskey, he's never shown it.

Eugene the romantic idealist would not allow his brother the hardened cynic to suffer the recriminations of the father. Jamie symbolized much that had haunted the ill-fated O'Neill household. A drunk who could never reform himself, a once-attractive youth now losing his eyesight, his hair thin and turned white, legs wobbly, speech slurred, a dissolute who never knew intimate love or peace of mind, Jamie reminded Eugene O'Neill of the destructive tendencies within himself and others he had seen on Skid Row. The demon-ridden Jamie died in a sanitarium in 1923, the year that *A Moon for the Misbegotten* is set. O'Neill wrote a filial-love play to come to grips with the memory of his tortured brother.

O'Neill's mother had died the previous year in California, and her body arrived in New York accompanied by Jamie on the evening that *The Hairy Ape* opened. In *A Moon for the Misbegotten,* Jamie confesses to Josie that he spent the nights crossing the country in the train in the company of a prostitute, with his mother's casket in the baggage compartment. He is overwhelmed with guilt as he recounts the trip, and looks to Josie for the forgiveness he can no longer obtain from his mother. Josie's outpouring of love is absolution enough, but Jamie cannot respond, ashamed that he needs her love to comfort his anguish. Josie cannot bear to see Jamie going back to the city and his wayward life, and she asks him to remember that her love gave him peace at least for a while. He claims not to remember:

JOSIE: (*sadly*) All right, Jim. Neither do I then. Good-bye, and God bless you. . . .
TYRONE: (*stammers*) Wait, Josie! I'm a liar! I'm a louse! Forgive me, Josie. I do remember! I'm glad I remember! I'll never forget your love! (*He kisses her on the lips.*) Never! (*kissing her again*) Never, do you hear! I'll always love you, Josie. (*He kisses her again.*) Good-bye — and God bless you!

Tyrone leaves the farm without looking back, and Josie knows he is going to his death; her final words in the play come as a beatitude not only for Jamie but for the whole O'Neill family:

May you have your wish and die in your sleep soon, Jim, darling. May you rest forever in forgiveness and peace.

The tragedy that marked the life of James O'Neill Jr. involved no struggle between conflicting forces or a fall from high station. Moreover, the defeat of noble actions may leave us with exultation as well as sorrow. The theme in *Moon for the Misbegotten* is more Catholic than classical and deals with the weakness of will rather than the furies of fate. What Eugene O'Neill felt deeply in sympathy, his brother felt in guilt: the recognition of tragic waste.

*

The play had a short run in 1947 and disappointed the critics. O'Neill wrote it shortly after completing his masterpiece and most revealing work, *A Long Day's Journey into Night.* Here he wrote, in what some critics consider the greatest American play, a psychotherapeutic memoir. It deals with his entire family, each member with a tale of woe.

While working on the play in 1939–1941, O'Neill was deeply troubled by the world situation, hearing on the radio accounts of western Europe teetering before the forces of fascism. This play, as well as the later *Moon for the Misbegotten,* was written when O'Neill's health was severely declining. Later he would also be distressed at hearing that his young daughter Oona was to marry the much older Charlie Chaplin. O'Neill never thought much of actors and even less of one who had too many ex-wives. He would endure the sorrow over the suicide of his elder son and the death of a grandchild and then discover that his younger son had become a heroin addict. These intense private griefs O'Neill felt too personally to discuss publicly, and he ordered that *A Long Day's Journey into Night* not be seen by the public until twenty-five years after his death. He died in November 1953, but Carlotta allowed a Swedish production of the play to be performed three years later, and it opened to a smashing success in New York that same year.

The play presents two different intellectual worlds that O'Neill deliberately drew within his household to delineate the separation of his mind from that of his father's. In the stage directions O'Neill poses two bookcases on each side of the living room holding volumes whose titles are too small for the audience to read. One bookcase has a picture of Shakespeare above it and below "novels by Balzac, Zola, Stendahl, philosophical and sociological works by Schopenhauer, Nietzsche, Marx, Engels, Kropotkin, Max Stirner, plays by Ibsen, Shaw, Strindberg, poetry by Swinburne, Rossetti, Wilde, Ernest Downson, Kipling, etc." The other bookcase is glassed in and contains "sets of Dumas, Victor Hugo, Charles Lever, three sets of Shakespeare, the World's Best Literature in fifty large volumes, Hume's History of England, Thiers' History of the Consulate and Empire, Smollett's History of England, Gibbon's Roman Empire and miscellaneous volumes of old plays, poetry, and several histories of Ireland. The astonishing thing about these sets is that all the volumes have the look of having been read and reread."

In the play arguments break out between father and son over which authors are to be regarded as exemplary. The father idolizes Shakespeare and has even convinced himself that the Bard was partly Irish Catholic as well as the teacher of great moral truths. The nineteenth-century authors in the glasscase represent the flower of Victorian optimism about progress and the promises of life, the novelists Dumas and Hugo characteristic in assuming that literature could both penetrate and represent life. Yet the son reads Nietzsche, who concluded that life resists representation and awaits interpretation by those best prepared to question it, and Schopenhauer, who tried to overcome the self to see the world only to conclude that man's greatest guilt is to have been born.

*

O'Neill's was a book-nurtured mind, and his reading preferences took him beyond what George Santayana called "The Genteel Tradition in American Philosophy." In an address delivered around the same time as the setting for O'Neill's family play, Santayana saw the once-rich currents of American intellectual life running dry as commerce triumphed over culture and the practical replaced the philosophical. With the life of the mind having lost its "inquiring spirit" and "agonized conscience," the philosopher described modern America as taking on the values that O'Neill's father represented: piety, comfort, respectability, and real estate.

The American audience had long been used to the length of O'Neill's dramas, and no one was surprised to sit through the four and a half hours of his posthumous play. It takes place during a single day and early evening in August 1912, at the moment the Greenwich Village rebellion was about to assault the genteel verities of older generations. In the play the conflicting tensions that drive apart the O'Neill household are, to be sure, personal, psychological, even pathological. They are also intellectual and reflect the crisis of authority that troubled America as it entered the era of modernity. The father cannot impose the older ideals he derived from his reading on his two sons, one a mordant wastrel, the other a somber anarchist. "Among those who no longer believe in the religion of their fathers," wrote Walter Lippmann, another figure to emerge at the dawn of the Greenwich Village rebellion, "some are proudly defiant, and many are indifferent. But there are also a few, perhaps an increasing number, who feel there is a vacancy in their lives."[17] Vacancy, absence, emptiness, nothingness — such was the abyss into which the two young O'Neills stared when at home.

The play unfolds as though the family were coming out of the closet: James senior wondering why he has forsaken his career as a Shakespearean actor and pondering, having become rich, "What the hell was it I wanted to buy?"; the elder son Jamie lost, embittered, and craving his mother's love; the younger son Edmund ill, bewildered, and angry at his father for skimping on medical care; the mother Mary tense, nervous, complaining that her husband and sons are watching her every move. The father is as much in love with his wife as the sons are with their mother, and they wonder whether they have lost her in trying too much to possess her. But they also know what no one wants to acknowledge openly: she is possessed by her own morphine habit. "Christ," Jamie explodes, "I'd never dreamed before that any women but whores took dope!" Jamie, who blames his mother's addiction on the pain she suffered from giving birth to his brother, claims he had set out "to make a bum" of Edmund and that he distorted the telling of his life to do so. "My putting you wise so you'd learn from my mistakes. Believed that myself at times, but it's a fake. Made my mistakes look good. Made getting drunk romantic. Made whores fascinating vampires instead of poor, stupid, diseased slobs they really are. Made fun of work as a sucker's game. Never wanted you to succeed and make me look even worse by comparison. Wanted you to fail. Always jealous of you. Mama's boy, Papa's pet!"

In the course of several acts, Mary usually makes a delayed entrance, and even when she is upstairs or in another room the thoughts of her husband and sons stay fixed on her. Their state of mind turns on her psychological condition, and her entrance into various scenes only dramatizes her physical presence and mental absence. Edmund is convinced that his mother deliberately seeks to build a "blank wall" around herself so she will not need to deal with her family, especially him, who bears the burden of guilt for having brought into the world the birth pain that led the doctor to prescribe morphine. "I don't blame you," she assures Edmund:

> How could you believe me—when I can't believe myself? I've become such a liar. I never lied about anything once upon a time. Now I have to lie, especially to myself. . . . I've never understood anything about it [her addiction], except that one day long ago I found I could no longer call my soul my own.

In several of O'Neill's plays the son suffers a psychic wound at the hands of a mother who betrays her maternal nature by shunning him. In psychoanalytic theory, the "separation anxiety" begins with birth itself and the ejection from the womb. In O'Neill's case, however, the phobia goes beyond the infant's wrenching from the body of the mother. The playwright's ordeal is closer to Jacques Lacan's theory than that of Freud. The loss of the mother remains into adulthood and becomes part of the phenomenon of desire itself, compelling the self to feel alienated from the object for which it longs. Edmund fears that his mother will take to morphine and once again retreat into her own world, leaving him more alone than ever. For Lacan it is not the primal birth separation that introduces anguish but that the separation never really completes itself and the adult remains in phobic distress about the mother because she is both absent and omnipresent at the same time. Edmund, and no doubt Eugene O'Neill, felt deeply desire's dependence on the Other. In notes to the play,

O'Neill remarks that the mother's worry over her son's illness "had started her off again," as though once more it was his existence even as an adult that led her to return to drugs. "Dead son becomes only child she can love," he writes in the notes concerning his brother who died as an infant, "because living sons cause too much pain." O'Neill could rarely prevent thoughts about his mother from rushing in on him. "It is the nature of grief," observed Edmund Burke, "to keep its object perpetually in its eye."[18] Even when thinking of others the object would be forever there. Years earlier young Eugene O'Neill poured out his soul to Beatrice Ashe, expressing his undying love and pleading that she become his wife; she turned him down and told him that he was looking for a mother.

*

The play has a dreamlike atmosphere: a foghorn groaning in the background; puffs of white fog wafting across the open porch; emotions charging the room with outbursts of anger, touches of tenderness, moments of despair. James recalls his misspent life; Jamie lapses into whiskey talk; Edmund drifts off into reveries about the South Seas; Mary wanders the upstairs from room to room — the family is cut off from the outside world. Edmund's tuberculosis makes him as fearful about the future as the other family members are regretful about the past. All are fighting the demon of depression, and O'Neill makes the audience feel it, "stabbed to our depths by the importance of this feeling to him."[19]

The pain lies in the hurtful self-interrogation that each family member submits the mind to, forever troubled by the thought that they have been brought down not by fate or circumstances but by their own decisions and mistakes. Remorse, guilt, pity—such emotions walked across the stage of other O'Neill plays. But the story of his family is history from the inside out, truth recollected in writhing, with the long day's journey morphing into the Day of Judgment that consumes the household by what it cannot get rid of—conscience. Memory, which is supposed to be an attribute of the intellect, becomes in O'Neill an ordeal of anxiety. Forgetfulness and oblivion only come from drink and drugs. "Whenever man has thought it necessary to create a memory of himself," wrote Nietzsche, "his effort has been attended with torture, blood, and sacrifice."[20]

In memory begins the pangs of responsibility. Why, Edmund asks his mother, did she "jump on Jamie all of a sudden?" She answers "bitterly":

Because he's always sneering at someone else, always looking for the worst weakness in everyone. (*Then with a strange, abrupt change to a detached, impersonal tone.*) But I suppose life has made him like that, and he can't help it. None of us can help the things life has done to us. They're done before you realize it, and once they're done they make you do other things until at last everything comes between you and what you'd like to be, and you've lost your true self forever.

Many of O'Neill's characters come to feel that they have betrayed the promises of a true self. But it is never clear whether it is "what life has done to us" or whether it is what we have done to life that leads to our predicament. Mary's story is all the more poignant since her ambitions once aimed at virtuosity and spirituality, or so she claims. In her youth she aspired to become a concert pianist and then of entering the convent in the hope of becoming a nun. When she fell in love with James Tyrone she accepted his marriage proposal and accompanied him on his exhausting acting tours and looked forward to a social life among the "best people." The love between husband and wife remained strong enough to break through from time to time, and while Mary never forgot how society gave her the cold shoulder for marrying an actor, she also reminisced about the "great matinee idol" that was her husband and relished the day of her wedding and her beautiful white wedding gown. But Mary suffers from an inner loneliness, and she worries that she can only endure by telling lies to herself, wondering how and when her estrangement from her very being started, how she lost her soul without knowing it.

Eugene O'Neill gave his mother the dominant role in his play as she had been in his early life. He describes her as youthful even in her later years, wearing a "marble mask of girlish innocence." The soul she has lost she hopes to find when the family becomes well again, when her husband and older son cease their heavy drinking, her younger son is cured of tuberculosis, and she herself breaks the long morphine habit. But under the influence of the drug, she speaks openly of her fears, resentments, confusions, and past hopes — and voicing one remaining hope, for "some day when the Blessed Virgin Mary forgives me and gives me back the faith in Her love and pity I used to have in my convent days, and I can pray to Her again." She gave up the idea of her vocation, the audience discovers, when the Mother Superior told her to go out into the world to experience the normal pleasures of existence to be sure she was worthy to give her life up to God. But an unexpected event came between her and her religious devotion: "Then in the spring something happened to me. Yes, I remember. I fell in love with James Tyrone and was so happy for a time."

*

Giving up her life to the Blessed Virgin held out the hope of entrance into heaven and a future of eternal bliss; marriage to her husband made Mary happy—but only "for a time." The fulfillment of life escapes O'Neill's mother figure as it does so many of his other characters. But O'Neill cannot allow his characters to hide from themselves, and even in bar-room scenes with drunken sots there occur moments of self-revelation. O'Neill's elegiac vision reminds us of what has vanished, of unconsummated desire. *Long Day's Journey into Night* was a deeply personal play, a memoir of pain and sorrow. But even in works that are political rather than personal, the elegy remains, a mourning for what has been lost and can never be restored. We come to the last play that O'Neill lived to see performed, *The Iceman Cometh.*

11

Waiting for Hickey

"I'M THROUGH WITH THE MOVEMENT"

After O'Neill saw *The Hairy Ape* performed in 1922, and gave several interviews in which he expressed his sympathies for the working class, he seldom thought about the social issues that had once animated the radical Left. The "Lost Generation" of the twenties, having witnessed the bitter outcome of the First World War and the Red Scare, no longer had much interest in politics — except perhaps those who bade farewell to its causes and convictions. But historical developments themselves, particularly in the thirties and forties, compelled O'Neill to return to the subjects of politics and society. In the decades when freedom was being threatened by totalitarianism, the playwright pondered the awful question of whether humanity desired freedom or dreaded it.

In the years between the two world wars, America experienced the ravages of world depression, the menacing rise of Hitler, bitter controversies over Stalin's dictatorship, and the ultimate "wound in the heart," the Spanish Civil War, which brought the subject of anarchism back into discussion. During these years O'Neill wrote no play that addressed politics specifically or the plight of the working class, although he later worked on an unfinished text describing the visit to America of Errico Malatesta, the legendary Italian anarchist of the late nineteenth century. Yet curiously, the arrest, trial, and execution of the two Italian-American anarchists, Nicola Sacco and Bartolomeo Vanzetti, brought no response from O'Neill, even though the American literati wrote poems and marched in picket lines in protest of sentencing the two to the electric chair for allegedly murdering a guard in a bank holdup. In the late twenties and early thirties, O'Neill instead was writing plays both comic and tragic dealing with religion, science, women, and even ancient biblical tales, while struggling with the breakup of his marriage to Agnes Boulton.

During the Spanish Civil War, roughly from 1936 to 1939, the American Left divided sharply between those who supported the communists in Spain and those who grew suspicious after hearing rumors of Stalin's ordering the liquidation of anarchist leaders fighting on the Loyalist side, if not to save the Republic, at least to prevent its falling to the forces of fascism. O'Neill began writing *The Iceman Cometh* in 1939, the year in which Spain fell to the reactionary Falange, a war with Hitler seemed inevitable, and the destiny of Western civilization imperiled. Yet much of the American Left, whether socialists, anarchists, Trotskyists, or even progressive liberals, hesitated in calling for America to take up arms against the Third Reich. If Hitler were to be defeated, it would not be by ideas that once inspired the American Left, particularly the idea of class consciousness and social revolution. Long before a defeatist mentality gripped some members of the Left in the forties, and well before "the end of ideology" was proclaimed in the fifties, O'Neill's play depicted radicalism dying out decades earlier.

*

O'Neill chose 1912 as the period for *The Iceman Cometh,* a year personally depressing and at the same time politically exhilarating. It was the year in which he attempted suicide in a New York flophouse, yet also the year of American socialism's most exciting moment, when presidential candidate Eugene Debs obtained close to a million votes in a country that had dozens of socialists serving in Congress and in state legislatures. The year in which the play was performed, 1946, was also — or so it seemed to the "New York Intellectuals" — a year of radical hope. After the defeat of fascism, communist parties dominated French and Italian politics, and the Soviet Union had established hegemony throughout Eastern Europe by virtue of the presence of the Red Army. "It's 1919 all over again!" *Partisan Review* editor Philip Rahv claimed for 1946, just before the brutal realities of the cold war surfaced.

Whatever the postwar optimism of the Left, *The Iceman Cometh* hinted that not only revolution but even radical politics must be seen as a misplaced dream, especially when activists themselves cannot tell the horrible truth about their own political motives. Larry Slade, the disillusioned rebel, cannot put up with the rationalizations of Donald Parritt, the anarchist youth from the West Coast. Parritt insists upon telling Slade why he gave up on radical politics, and fears that others, who have their own motives to hide, might correctly suspect his. Slade refuses to listen and is about to leave the room when Parritt accuses him of having already guessed his motives:

> Don't go! (*Larry lets himself be pulled down on his chair. Parritt examines his face and becomes insultingly scornful.*) Who do you think you're kidding? I know damned well you've guessed—
>
> LARRY: I've guessed nothing!
>
> PARRITT: But I want you to guess now! I'm glad you have! I know now, since Hickey's been after me, that I meant you to guess right from the start. That's why I came to you. (*hurrying on with an attempt at a plausible frank air that makes what he says seem doubly false*) I want you to understand the reason. You see, I began studying American history. I got admiring George Washington and Jefferson and Jackson and Lincoln. I began to feel patriotic and love this country. I saw it was the best government in the world, where everybody was equal and had a chance. I saw that the ideas behind the Movement came from a lot of Russians like Bakunin and Kropotkin and were meant for Europe, but we didn't need them here in a democracy where we were free already. I didn't want this country to be destroyed for a damned foreign pipe dream. After all, I'm from old American pioneer stock. I began to feel I was a traitor for helping a lot of cranks and bums and free women plot to overthrow our government. And then I saw it was my duty to my country—
>
> LARRY: (*nauseated—turns on him*) You stinking rotten liar! Do you think you can fool me with such hypocrite's cant! (*then turning away*) I don't give a damn what you did! It's on your head—whatever it was! I don't want to know—and I won't know!

The Iceman Cometh was a decade ahead of its times. Written in 1939, it captures precisely the reasoning that would be used by many writers and intellectuals in the McCarthy era to explain their retreat from radicalism.[1] Yet in the play O'Neill makes clear that the claim of embracing American ideals may be far from the real reasons that lead activists to renounce radicalism. "We didn't need them here in a democracy," Parritt says of foreign ideas, "where we were free already." The relationship of democracy to authentic freedom troubled O'Neill as much as it did his heroes Emerson, Thoreau, and Nietzsche. And like the New England Transcendentalists, O'Neill could hardly see the American people behaving as though they were "free already" and able to act with reflective self-knowledge rather than with "quiet desperation."

The Iceman Cometh indicts people who are quick to judge and convert others and reluctant to face themselves. Parritt thinks that Slade will sympathize with him since they have both been spurned by the same woman, Rosa Parritt: the son neglected by a mother who throws all her energy into the movement, and the lover rejected by a rebel who sees in a life of promiscuity the hope for women's freedom. "The Movement is her life," complains Parritt of his mother, who has no actual role in the play but whom O'Neill fashioned after the anarchist Emma Goldman. The son protests the "great incorruptible Mother of the Revolution, whose only child is the Proletariat." The audience discovers at the end of the play that Parritt actually abandoned radical politics and turned in his mother because she neglected him and left him alone to look into the abyss, a maternal betrayal that aroused his hatred and revenge. Parritt thinks Slade will understand since he has also been spurned by the same woman in the name of free love. But to be free and to be in love had always been a quandary to the anarchist, as Emma Goldman honestly observed in her writings. The urge to be free and liberated easily gives way to the urge to possess and dominate. The hope of the anarchist was to see humanity acting rather than allowing itself to be acted upon, asserting the self rather than submitting. But the presence of desire contradicts conscience as the will lusts after objects alien to the self. "I'm through with the Movement long since," declared Slade. "I saw men didn't want to be saved from themselves, for that would mean they'd have to give up greed, and they'll never pay that price for liberty."

In modern liberal thought, greed as the pursuit of self-interest made liberty possible as the individual put one's own desires ahead of church and state. With O'Neill, however, we are frozen in the world of liberalism that can never reach the goal of radicalism: that new world free of the past, the world promised by socialism and anarchism, a world no longer greedy for riches, power, and status, a world graced with "a touch of the poet." But while O'Neill curses radical politics for its self-deceptions about the promises of revolution, he still holds political activists to principles of loyalty and comradeship. Thus his character Slade cannot believe that anyone he associated with would betray the movement and inform the authorities: "By God, I hate to believe it of any of the crowd, if I am through long since with any connection with them. I know they're damned fools, most of them, as stupidly greedy for power as the worst capitalist they attack, but I'd swear there couldn't be a yellow stool pigeon among them."

And "the worst capitalist," what has O'Neill to say about that creature? If radical politics cannot extirpate material greed while still espousing honesty of convictions, the realm of economics can do neither. The character Theodore Hickman, or "Hickey," the play's long-awaited protagonist, represents a nihilism so complete that it is oblivious of itself. Hickey tells us how he became such a good salesman under the spell of his evangelist father. "I didn't fall for the religious bunk. Listening to my old man whooping up hell fire and scaring those Hoosier suckers into shelling out their dough only handed me a laugh, although I had to hand it to him, the way he sold them nothing for something." Economics, like religion, plays upon the hopes and fears of the human race. Seduced by the seller, the buyer acquires objects to prove his spiritual as well as social status. Praying is desiring, purchasing is fulfilling. Economics, even more than politics, is a con game in which trust is established by manipulating emotions as the salesman becomes a performer whose aim is to please and to profit. Capitalism depends upon credit, which in turn amounts to credibility (as Max Weber reminded us). "It was a cinch for me to make good," Hickey boasts. "I had the knack. It was like a game, sizing people up quick, spotting what their pet pipe dreams were, and then kidding 'em along that line, pretending you believed what they wanted to believe about themselves."

Yet Hickey's life of dissimulation does him in. *The Iceman Cometh* is about betrayal and deception toward others and toward one's self. The characters would have us believe that they are motivated by high ideals, yet it is hate and resentment that is driving them. Both the radical activist and the conservative capitalist are incapable of consciousness, of a self-knowledge that could compel them to face what they fear and thereby confront their own desperate claims of innocence. And Hickey is no less self-loathing as a salesman than as a husband who has killed his wife. For eventually the seller hates the buyer for forcing him to lead a life of serial lying. Hence the salesman who arrives at the bar to buy the house rounds of free booze becomes, after he's off the bottle, the messiah who claims he wants to save their souls out of love and pity. But the false messiah cannot even save himself.

The Iceman Cometh could well be described as an antipolitical play, a text and performance that sought to register the exhaustion of political ideas at the end of the thirties, on the eve of World War II. Although O'Neill would continue to sympathize with many political causes, including the status of women and the plight of African Americans, he, like many anarchists, had no notion of a solution since they refused to look to the state, where resides the doctrine of natural rights and the equal protection of laws found in the U.S. Constitution. A powerful state loomed as the very monster the movement dreaded. O'Neill identified too much with the beautiful losers, such as the mystic bohemian Terry Carlin, to be able to show the Left the way to political success. When O'Neill described himself as "a philosophical anarchist," and told radicals that they could "go to it, but leave me out of it," he was subscribing to an ethic of conviction to keep his conscience clear of the untoward consequences that violent anarchists had brought about through history—their resort to terror and assassination.

"THE LONG SLEEP OF DEATH"

The audience watching *The Iceman Cometh* may well have understood that the play promised no political message of deliverance. America emerged victorious from World War II, having defied the views of numerous radical intellectuals, who had predicted that an economy that refused to collectivize would remain too inefficient to stand up against the Third Reich. But under President Franklin D. Roosevelt, American capitalism did collectivize as the national government organized a planned economy that went on to help defeat Hitler's Germany. One subject hovers over the play, however, one that has no end even with the end of ideology, and it has less to do with winning than dying. Slade complains that the barroom stinks with the stench of death. Shortly after the Second World War, O'Neill was interviewed by Hamilton Basso, a southern novelist who had spent some time in Europe. He asked O'Neill what he thought of the philosophy of existentialism that was coming out of France. O'Neill replied that he continued to admire three German thinkers: Nietzsche, Spengler, and Schopenhauer.[2] They reinforced O'Neill's conviction that no one can easily accept the approach of one's own death, to contemplate being no more, to pass away forever. O'Neill's one religion play was titled *Days Without End,* a yearning by a fallen Catholic author to be assured of eternity; in *The Fountain* the imminence of death casts the individual back upon himself, with recollections of youth the only response to the cessation of life. The play with which O'Neill enters the world of modern drama, *Bound East for Cardiff,* is also about death's arrival in the person of the "dark lady." Schopenhauer insisted that the fear of death proves all the more that the deepest truth about humanity is the will to live, even if life itself only amounts to enduring and suffering. This philosophical message finds its echo in the drab barroom of *The Iceman Cometh.* Hickey tells Larry to stop lying to himself:

LARRY: You think when I say I'm finished with life, and tired of watching the stupid greed of the human circus, and I'll welcome closing my eyes in the long sleep of death—you think that's a coward's lie?

HICKEY: (*chuckling*) Well, what do you think, Larry?

LARRY: (*with increasing bitter intensity, more as if he were fighting with himself than with Hickey*) I'm afraid to live, am I?—and even more afraid to die! So I sit here, with my pride drowned on the bottom of a bottle, keeping drunk so I won't see myself shaking in my britches with fright, or hear myself whining and praying: Beloved Christ, let me live a little longer at any price! If it's only for a few days more, or a few hours even, have mercy, Almighty God, and let me still clutch greedily to my yellow heart this sweet treasure, this jewel beyond price, the dirty, stinking bit of withered old flesh which is my beautiful little life! (*He laughs with a sneering, vindictive, self-loathing, staring inward at himself with contempt and hatred. Then abruptly he makes Hickey the antagonist.*) You think you'll make me admit that to myself?

HICKEY: (*chuckling*) But you just did admit it, didn't you?

At the conclusion of the play Larry announces that he is the only one in the room that Hickey has made a "convert to death," but he makes no effort to come to a final reckoning and there is no suggestion he is to take his life. In O'Neill's own life, just after he wrote the play he was stricken with a disease that left his hands trembling, and, no longer able to write, he thought of suicide. He once played on a recording the passage where Larry "is forced to admit, while refusing to admit, that saving dream that he is finished with life and sick of it and will welcome the long sleep of death is just a pipe dream." Replaying the passage — "I'm afraid to live, am I?"—O'Neill recalled many moments when he longed for death yet pleaded to God to let him live just a little longer, "a few hours even, . . . let me still clutch greedily to my yellow heart this sweet treasure, this jewel beyond price, the dirty, stinking bit of withered old flesh which is my beautiful little life!" Shocked to hear the words, O'Neill wrote to a friend: "It wasn't Larry, it was my ghost talking to me, or I to my ghost."[3] To regard clinging to life as an act of greed implies that thought cannot guide the emotions; that, indeed, classical philosophy has failed to teach humankind how to die and modern philosophy to teach how to live. Life may have no meaning, but it sustains itself by the fear that death is the ultimate terror, the dread of annihilation.

Almost a half-century earlier, in a letter to his sweetheart Jessica Ripkin, young O'Neill boasted that he had been lifted up into "the lofty ether of Nietzsche and Schopenhauer." No matter how much the philosophers may have influenced him, they could do little to help him face his later demons. Schopenhauer might have taught O'Neill to ask himself a consoling question. When he had attempted suicide, would not death have been simply that split second when life leaves the body? Yet consciousness does not fear death as much as the will, which struggles against death as the very expression of the indestructible desire to live. Nietzsche also asserted the primacy of will as the essence of life. O'Neill, however, had been brought up a Catholic and taught to believe that the will is forever corrupted by sin. While Nietzsche fought against "sickness of will," Schopenhauer was perhaps closer to O'Neill in seeing will as an expression of unfulfilled desire. "Now the nature of man," observed Schopenhauer, "consists in this, that his will strives, is satisfied, and strives anew. . . . For the absence of satisfaction is suffering, the empty longing for a new wish, langour, ennui."⁴ The denizens of Harry Hope's dive are certainly suffering and longing for a new wish, but they do nothing about it, except to await the ennui of sleep.

The Iceman Cometh promises to lay bare the "secrets of the soul." Aristotle declared that the "proper function of man is the activity of the soul according to reason." In Harry Hope's saloon Schopenhauer replaces Aristotle. It is not reason but "pipe dreams" that represent the rage of life to live no matter what the conditions of existence. In their retreat to the saloon, the drunks will not admit to themselves how much they are part of the world or how responsible they are for their past conduct. But even with the illusionary distinction between the self and the world there still remain the dread of death and the desire to live.

The Iceman Cometh appeared in America only a year after the American people mourned the death of President Franklin D. Roosevelt and the four hundred thousand soldiers lost on the battlefields of World War II. There is a touch of the Gothic in introducing the subject of death and dying, once called "the king of terror." In the Middle Ages, the subject was on everyone's lips, but rarely were carnal thoughts expressed. In modern times, however, discussion of death is taboo while the subject of sex flourishes in conversation and in public entertainment. But the characters in the play can neither face death nor enjoy sex. They are beyond desire, with no ends to live for and no causes to die for. In political philosophy, fear of dying was regarded as an anxiety, with the primal fear of extinction compelling humankind to accept civil society and its laws. But O'Neill's characters are more natural than social, less civil than cynical. What they want most of all is to go back to sleep, to drink themselves into a stupor, to find peace in oblivion. O'Neill leaves America where a later radical generation would find it — dead from the neck up.

If the world is, as O'Neill assumed with Schopenhauer, a vast emptiness asking to be filled with ideas, one can only wonder if O'Neill really believed he could get at the "roots" of his country's sickness. In *The Iceman Cometh* O'Neill insists upon the necessity of sustaining illusions, so much so that he refused to shorten his four and a half-hour play. A "drastic condensation," he wrote to Kenneth Macgowan, would defeat the play's purpose: "After all, what I've tried to write is a play where at the end you feel you know the souls of the seventeen men and women . . . as well as if you read a play about each of them." It is essential to build up a complete picture of the group in the beginning, as well as "the atmosphere of the place, the humor and friendship and human warmth and *deep inner contentment* of the bottom." Moreover, each of the characters had to be challenged to leave the bar on the shared assumption that they can return to real life, even if they end up scurrying back inside for a quick drink. "Take for example," O'Neill pointed out to Macgowan, "your point about the part near the end where each character tells his face-saving version of his experience when he went out to confront his pipe dream. I don't write this as a piece of playwrighting. *They do it. They have to.* Each of them! In just that way! They *must* tell these lies as a first step in taking up life again."[5]

Life is bearable, O'Neill seems to be saying, only when we contrive not to look at truth. Yet O'Neill himself cannot look at anything else. The character Larry Slade tells us in an opening scene why he had to end his thirty-year devotion to the cause of revolutionary anarchism. "I was born condemned to be one of those who has to see all sides of a question. When you're damned like that, the questions multiply for you until in the end it's all question and no answer. As history proves, to be a worldly success at anything, especially revolution, you have to wear blinders like a horse and see only straight in front of you. You have to see, too, that this is all black, and that is all white."

The disjunction between the necessity of unquestioning illusions in life and the imperative of question-raising truths in politics barely begins to capture O'Neill's richly complex stance. *The Iceman Cometh* may have as its theme humanity's need to survive by virtue of life-sustaining hopes, however hopeless they may be. But even Larry, who tells us that he is condemned to see too much, complains that it doesn't matter how things are seen. "To hell with the truth! As the history of the world proves, the truth has no bearing on anything. It's irrelevant and immaterial, as the lawyers say. The lie of a pipe dream is what gives life to the whole and misbegotten mad lot of us, drunk or sober." Acknowledging such "philosophical wisdom," the bar bums affectionately call Slade "de old Foolosopher."

Although his character Slade cries out that "truth has no bearing on anything," O'Neill, in his own self, could only stare truth in the face as though it bore on everything, and this meant coming to terms with two interrelated histories, that of his family and that of his nation. However lenient and forgiving O'Neill was toward the characters in his plays, he was hard and demanding on himself. As his close friend Saxe Commins put it: "Tormented as Gene was by his past and the tragic events in his family's history, he never denied reality. Indeed, his need to confront his past and deal with it as honestly as possible was a primary impulse at the root of his art."[6]

If O'Neill allowed the characters in *The Iceman Cometh* their comforting pipe dreams, he himself sought, as he put it, "to give pain a voice." In doing so he met one of George Santayana's definitions of beauty as the exaltation of anguish: "The more terrible the experience described, the more powerful must the art be that is to transform it."[7] O'Neill presented characters who can neither live with doubt nor die with dignity, and many of his plays come close to tragedy in allowing the audience to witness souls in agony. A modernist who knows the value of truth precisely because he cannot find it, O'Neill has revenge upon the contemporary poststructuralist, particularly Roland Barthes's "Death of the Author" thesis, which holds that writing is a discursive game with its own rules and results apart from the writer's intentions and purposes, that there is, in short, only the text and no truth beyond it. But O'Neill's is a presence that is not to be denied, an author who lived with experiences too deep and personal to be reduced to language and its limitations. The problem of life, O'Neill taught us, lies in our will, not in our words. O'Neill believed in the truths of experience and he asked himself how much truth could he accept. With Nietzsche, O'Neill understood that the will cannot will backward and hence the past cannot be changed. Happiness may be impossible when we cannot completely unburden ourselves of our own history, but the capacity to live historically gives life its tragic justification. "Life is good *because* it is painful," wrote Nietzsche, and the American playwright elevated pain into a noble emotion, no small feat in a country dedicated to pleasure and the pursuit of happiness. With O'Neill we are, at last, aware that truth—today an idea so ridiculed that it often appears within inverted commas—bears precisely on what actually occurred in the past, and the more the hurt the more the truth.

Yet those who believe in the philosophy of Hegel and Marx see truth not as painful but as progressive, always unfolding and rising, about to appear over the horizon to deliver us from alienation and oppression. Marx built his philosophy of history on the foundations of Hegel's dialectical reasoning, and thus history becomes a succession of progressive stages governed by logic, moving by an intelligible necessity to higher and higher syntheses, from classical antiquity to feudalism to bourgeois capitalism and, finally, to the world of socialism. Hegel depicted the self as a slave to the passions of desire, and to the extent that self is bound up with an object beyond itself, the whole meaning of history is the self's struggle to be recognized by another and hence, at last, the reconciliation of all conflict.

Was such a vision only another "pipe dream" that might be fulfilled simply by waiting for tomorrow? O'Neill agreed with Nietzsche that the idea of truth could well be more an emotional construction than a real product of the processes of history. Once truth is no longer regarded as an object of discovery or as a possibility of deliverance from experience, why wait for it? In *The Iceman Cometh* the desperate derelicts wait for Hickey, the messiah who turns out to be a murderer. O'Neill also waits, even while knowing there will be no arrival, no deliverance from the human condition. Can life have a purpose if it must end in death? O'Neill's challenge was to master what his mind could not grasp and to forgive what it could not forget.

But *The Iceman Cometh* is truly the end of history. Marx's whole idea of struggle derived from Hegel's conviction that the deepest desire in human beings is the desire for recognition, and that it is humanly natural to desire what others desire and to wish to love and be loved. Hegel insisted that only with the presence of others does the self feel desire and the mind awaken and give birth to self-consciousness. But Nietzsche also insisted that to listen to others could revive the pains residing in memory, and thus the best strategy for survival is forgetfulness, which he called "a positive checking faculty." In *The Iceman Cometh* the characters prefer to sleep and pass out rather than to listen and learn. As Hickey is holding forth on the fate of his wife, Harry Hope's head lifts from the table and he complains:

> Get it over, you long-winded bastard! You married her, and you caught her cheating with the iceman, and you croaked her, and who the hell cares? What's she to us? All we want is to pass out in peace, bejees! (*A chorus of dull, resentful protest from all the group. They mumble, like sleepers who curse a person who keeps awakening them,* "What's it to us? We want to pass out in peace!" *Hope drinks and they mechanically follow his example. He pours another and they do the same. He complains with a stupid, nagging insistence*) No life in the booze! No kick! Dishwater. Bejees, I'll never pass out!

In Harry Hope's saloon, desire is dead.

POLITICS AND REMEMBRANCE

Eugene O'Neill's political philosophy defies categorization. Too disdainful of the powerful to be a conservative, he was also too skeptical of reason to be a liberal and too obsessed with the past to subscribe to a Marxism that regards history as a series of stages that are progressively surpassed. Let us juxtapose the playwright to America's favorite political philosopher.

If only Thomas Jefferson were right, Eugene O'Neill's worries would be over. Jefferson believed that each generation is sovereign unto itself and that the past cannot be allowed to bind the present. It was a scientific "axiom" to Jefferson that "the dead have no rights; they are nothing, and nothing cannot own something."[8] O'Neill and his characters, however, felt the presence of the dead almost as though they were still living and memories of things past would haunt them like a curse. For the playwright the past is overdetermined in that events rarely happen as a result of choices made in the present. Yet the past has significance to the extent we must live with its consequences. Nowhere is this historical consciousness of the unbearable weight of history better dramatized than in *The Iceman Cometh*. "This dump is the Palace of Pipe Dreams!" announces Slade, and the audience is asked to consider that politics cannot solve a human condition that may only be relieved by forgetfulness, pity, sleep, booze, and death, with the ghost of anarchism lingering in the barroom like the stench of stale whiskey.

In the play there is no possibility of liberalism, no suggestion that the mind enters the world as a *tabula rasa,* as John Locke propounded; or that America has it in its power to start the world "all over again," as Tom Paine exhorted. Nor is there any hope for even a glimpse of radicalism, no vision of a world being transformed by subjects who cannot even rise from the table to change themselves, not to mention their environment. Anarchism, a theory that could never actualize itself, died before it was born. In O'Neill's play, America has no second act in history, for the country cannot liberate itself from itself. Jefferson had promised that America could be free from the tyranny of the past; the playwright insists that we cannot escape history.

In conservative political thought, the presence of the past is to be commemorated rather than lamented. The philosophers David Hume, Edmund Burke, and G. W. F. Hegel would base a political regime on the solid ground of human experience. Nevertheless, even conservative philosophers believe that humankind cannot take too much reality. Hegel taught that the origins of government must be veiled in secrecy. Burke favored employing "drapery" to cover up the void behind our habits and prejudices. Hume insisted that we should not pretend to know the cause and origins of human behavior lest we proudly claim to be able to control that which we do not understand. In terms that a playwright would appreciate, Hume suggested that humans exist in the world as an audience in a theater. The spectator sees the show and enjoys the performance but the "true springs and causes of every event" remain concealed.[9]

Why should the explanation and understanding of events be left in darkness? Knowledge is supposed to make us free, and with modern intelligence we are supposedly better prepared to cope with life. As a playwright, O'Neill could hardly follow the philosopher and hide from the audience the motives of the actors. Nor could he allow our thoughts to be shaped by the dominance of the foreground when life had already been determined by the background. O'Neill saw past experience as traumatic, almost a struggle between life and death, with his subjects trying to deny what they cannot face. Like James Joyce, O'Neill viewed history as a "nightmare" because memory of the past restricted the possibilities of the present.

But must memory always be negative? In the novels of Marcel Proust, remembrance is pleasurable rather than painful. The difference between the two emotions in the two writers may have to do with the difference between devotion and deprivation in early childhood, with Proust's mother lavishing attention on him and O'Neill's withdrawing into a morphine-induced seclusion. In Proust forgetfulness and even oblivion serve to heighten the delectability of memory when it occurs. Memory is to be cherished because it reconciles past with present experience, making us aware that "true paradises are those which one has lost."[10]

With O'Neill the past is a purgatory that is never lost; it weighs like a "tumor" on the brain of the living, as Marx put it. What makes the past so heavy in *The Iceman Cometh* is a theme with unmistakable political implications: betrayal, the violation of some moral principle that leaves the conscience singed with guilt. In the play revelations of unfaithfulness involve both ideas and people, politics and the personal, the forsaking of the ideological convictions of anarchism and the cheating on one's spouse. In O'Neill's life itself betrayal was everywhere. His mother forsook her maternal responsibility in neglecting her children; his father gave up his career as one of the country's leading Shakespearean actors to take on the more commercially successful *The Count of Monte Cristo;* and his brother surrendered himself to alcohol. But in American history the thought of betrayal was far from personal.

The thought was present at the birth of the republic, with colonists convinced that the British parliament had violated the social contract by denying the right of representation and revolution (the Declaration of Independence reads like a series of broken trusts); and it continues into our contemporary era, when a president can be impeached for violating the oath of office. At the coming of the Civil War, both North and South saw each other as traitors to the foundations, apostates to the very meaning of America. Abraham Lincoln, who urged Americans to live up to "the mystic chords of memory," accused southern slaveholders of betraying the Declaration's affirmation of equality, and they accused him of betraying the Constitution's protection of slavery as a species of property.

The idea of betrayal may have philosophical as well as political implications. It could, for example, compel us to think twice about an idea that is everywhere on the American campus, the idea of poststructuralism, which has made us aware of the false "metaphysics of presence," that is, our normal assumption that when we write and speak we are referring to something actually "out there" beyond our words and utterances. But, to borrow from Gertrude Stein, there may be no there there. If not, why worry? In truth, the impression of betrayal presupposes the presence of a principle that has been violated. To turn one's back on an ideal would be no great offense if that ideal could be seen simply as a "social construction" born of contingency and having no intrinsic reality. Why be obedient to a principle based on convenience instead of truth? The opposite of the act of betrayal is the act of loyalty, a fidelity and constancy to some principle entailing a prior commitment. Loyalty to what?

It may seem strange that a playwright absorbed in the philosophical outlook of Friedrich Nietzsche would allow himself to be troubled by disloyalty. In *The Iceman Cometh* the act of betrayal is admonished as disobedience to the political conscience; yet Nietzsche insisted that reinterpretation and self-creation could take the place that obedience had once occupied in political philosophy. An obsession about the past "mummifies" life itself.[11]

In *The Genealogy of Morals* Nietzsche argued that forgetfulness is the first step toward freedom and memory the beginning of responsibility if kept in check. The truly liberated person is he or she who bears the burden not of fulfilling promises but instead of enjoying the right of making them. The autonomous individual should be too strong to suffer from guilt and a bad conscience and too wise to feel responsibility for society's virtues. Significantly, O'Neill's play deals with the fate of the anarchist movement, a political philosophy that once told us that there are no tyrants but only submissive slaves and that there would be no state had there not been willing subjects. *The Iceman Cometh* presents the spectacle of weakness and defeat as the audience witnesses a humankind too fearful to forget, too guilty to create its own morality, and too much in a hazy stupor to even be aware of the narrative of betrayal unfolding in the tavern.

The deed of betrayal in the play is no moral parable; it had its own actual history, both in the period in which O'Neill is writing the play, and of the period about which he is writing. In 1939 O'Neill interrupted his writing of his autobiographical *Long Day's Journey into Night* to work on *The Iceman Cometh,* and while jotting down notes for the latter he was up until three in the morning listening to Hitler's declaration of war against Poland.[12] Hitler could move against Poland because of the nonaggression pact that he had just negotiated with the Soviet Union, which came as a blow to the Left throughout the world. Earlier the Kremlin's "Popular Front" policy, announced by the Comintern in 1935, had called upon all political elements, including anarchists as well as liberals, conservatives, and Christian democrats, to take a united stand against Hitler and fascism. The diplomacy of the late thirties was fraught with betrayals, particularly the failure of the liberal West to come to the aid of democratic Czechoslovakia. But the nonaggression pact came as the ultimate shock, throwing the Left into bitter disillusionment. All the older causes and ideologies died at the outbreak of the war.

In *The Iceman Cometh* the theme of betrayal goes back two decades before the play was written, and its stigma is personal as well as historical. O'Neill intends Rosa Parritt as the historical figure of Emma Goldman and Donald Parritt as her son though, in reality, he is based on the son of Goldman's close friend Gertie Vose. The audience is unaware that Parritt had turned on his radical mother by letting detectives know where she was hiding after a bombing. As the play opens Rosa is in jail and no one knows who is to blame for her incarceration. Actually, the real Goldman used her publication *Mother Earth* to denounce Vose, the son of her friend, as a "Judas Iscariot" for informing on two anarchists wanted in the 1910 bombing of the Los Angeles Times building. Vose "cold-bloodedly, deliberately betrayed the two men," Goldman raged. "It was the most terrible blow in my public life of twenty-five years. Terrible because of the mother of that cur; terrible because he grew up in a radical atmosphere."[13] Although Vose turned spy for the silver ($2,500), in the play Parritt betrays his mother out of hatred toward one who gave her whole life to "the Movement" and had no time for her son. Whatever the motive, O'Neill felt the shock of betrayal as much as Goldman, and the "yellow stool pigeon" is denounced as the vilest of creatures.

Larry Slade thinks backward as well as forward, dwelling on the past, present, and future as a continuum of pain and sorrow. Many of the other characters, however, regard their past lives as the best of times and look to the future to bring back what has been lost to the present. They all have what Larry terms "a touching credulity concerning tomorrows" since their sentimentalized version of the past projects itself into the future. So oriented, the derelicts claim to be capable of changing themselves any time they choose to do so. Herewith *The Iceman Cometh* raises another idea with political significance, the question of reform, a problem that has preoccupied history and political philosophy as much as its solution has eluded us.

*

Hope of reform goes all the way back in American history. The first settlers in New England sought to escape the corrupting compromises of the established Church in England in order to lead more purified lives in the New World. In the eighteenth century the colonists rebelled against the power and corruptions of the British monarchy and the "pestilence" of the court intrigues in Parliament so that virtue could be rescued from the clutches of vice. The imperative of reform reached a crescendo in the Populist and Progressive eras of the late nineteenth century, when the American people turned to the national government to save America from the power of big business. The sentiment of reform often carried with it a restoration motif, as though the demand for new changes would return America to the more wholesome ways of older times. Curiously, the characters in *The Iceman Cometh* partake of that very same outlook. Tomorrow must be better than today because the past was better than the present. "Pipe dreams" are born of the need to believe that we can think forward to go backward. In reform the future does not yet exist; it is to be brought into being, and when it is it will be consonant with the past that has been lost but can be regained. To reform is not to begin all over or to adapt to change but to be reborn back into the past. How, then, is reform to take effect?

The question was apparently on O'Neill's mind when writing *Iceman*, for he then had profound second thoughts about the whole project of society's reformation. "When an artist starts saving the world, he starts losing himself," he wrote to George Jean Nathan in 1939. "I know, having been bitten by the salvationist bug myself at times. But only momentarily, so to speak, my true conviction being that the one reform worth cheering is the Second Flood, and that the interesting thing about people is the obvious fact that they don't really want to be saved — the tragic idiotic ambition for self-destruction in them."[14]

In Western history, ever since Jean Jacques Rousseau, reform has been a matter of institutional rearrangements, a change in the environment that has hindered human development. In *The Iceman Cometh* that prospect calls for nothing more than walking out the barroom door. Urged to return to respectable society, the broken-down characters do shape up and don clean clothes in order to exit the tavern — only to scurry right back in the next scene. O'Neill leaves us with a troubling question: how can society be reformed if its subjects cannot save themselves from themselves?

A PARABLE OF PITY

The answer appears to be offered by Theodore Hickman, the salesman and onetime drunk who arrives at the tavern to tell the barmates that he has sworn off liquor and, letting go of his "pipe dreams" about a better tomorrow, has finally found peace and is living a new life free of demons.

The loquacious, irrepressible Hickey wants Larry to challenge the illusions of his fellow drunks, particularly those of the anarchist Hugo Kalmer. "Leave Hugo be!" Larry lashes back. "He rotted ten years in prison for his faith! He's earned his dream! Have you no decency or pity?" Hickey, startled that the taciturn Larry has burst forth, replies: "Of course, I have pity. But now I've seen the light, it isn't my old kind of pity—the kind yours is. It isn't the kind that lets itself off easy by encouraging some poor guy to go on kidding himself with a lie—the kind that leaves the poor slob worse off because it makes him feel guiltier than ever." Then Hickey turns his attention to Parritt, the guilt-ridden fictional son of Emma Goldman, and concludes: "He's licked, Larry. I think there is only one possible way out you can help him to take. That is, if you have the right kind of pity for him." Uneasily, Larry asks, "What do you mean?" and then pretends to be uninterested in pursuing the matter.

In a private letter O'Neill, accounting for the play's length, notes, "If I did not build up the complete picture of the group as it now is in the first part . . . you wouldn't feel the same sympathy for them, or be moved by what Hickey has done to them."[15] O'Neill asks us to feel sympathy, not pity, to identify with those in trouble and suffering, to share their pain, not to indulge in condescension toward those who are weak and dissolute.

The nature of the "right kind of pity" is never overtly explained by Hickey in the play. The subject, however, is one of the most perplexing in intellectual history. Against those older drama critics who claimed that O'Neill had no talent for offering a "theater of ideas," *The Iceman Cometh* reverberates with ideas of religious and political significance. The play may be read as a dramatic discourse on the idea of pity and on the doctrinal contradictions of Christianity itself. Both subjects were pondered by O'Neill's intellectual hero Nietzsche. In *The Anti-Christ* the philosopher wrote:

> Christianity is called the religion of *pity*. Pity stands in opposition to all the tonic passions that augment the energy of the feeling of aliveness: it is a depressant. A man loses power when he pities. Through pity that drain upon strength which suffering works is multiplied a thousandfold. Suffering is made contagious by pity; under certain circumstances it may lead to a total sacrifice of life and living energy. . . . If one measures the effects of pity by the gravity of the reactions it sets up, its character as a menace to life appears in much clearer light. Pity thwarts the whole law of evolution, which is the law of natural selection. It preserves whatever is ripe for destruction; it fights on the side of those disinherited and condemned by life; by maintaining life in so many of the botched of all kinds, it gives life itself a gloomy and dubious aspect.

Noting that pity had been elevated into a virtue, Nietzsche observed that Schopenhauer was right to see it as a shield that denies the will and stands against "all those instincts which work for the preservation and enhancement of life: in the protector of the miserable, it is the prime agent in the promotion of *decadence.*" Schopenhaur had no quarrel with pity, according to Nietzsche, because he was "hostile to life."[16] But Nietzsche would expose the emotion as the destroyer of the will to power.

In *The Iceman Cometh* the miserable find their protection in "pipe dreams," the wishes of the heart that dull the mind and incapacitate the will. In scolding Hickey for trying to arouse Hugo from his drunken slumbers, Slade comes close to implying that the Czech anarchist deserves pity for all the suffering he had endured in prison. But Hickey accuses Slade of not having the "right kind of pity"—Slade's being the kind that lets people off the hook by allowing them to continue with their illusions, which leaves the "poor slob worse off because it makes him feel guiltier than ever." Such pity may have more to do with those who bestow it than with those who receive it, for it does nothing to relieve the condition of suffering, not to mention its causes.

The audiences that watched the Tyrone family undergo their *Long Day's Journey into Night* experienced a pathos and sorrow, an empathy for those living in agony and remorse. But the mother and father, however deeply they felt their Catholic religion, could hardly feel the overriding Christian commandment to love others as they love God and themselves. Compassion may be felt but it is seldom expressed in an atmosphere of accusation, with the mother lamenting that we cannot help who we are or what we do. It is as though God made us an object of pity rather than love. Writing about the Catholic novelist Graham Greene, Conor Cruise O'Brien, noting that "he who is addicted to pitying others may be exalting himself above them," suggested that this condition indicates a conflicting state of mind within Christianity itself. We are the creations of a "religion that exhorted its followers to love without the aid of admiration or desire. Christ told men to love; the most they could manage was pity; it was something." Perhaps the only thing. Nietzsche, after declaring that God is dead, made it clear that He "died out of pity for man." God commanded humanity to love even though He himself could only pity his own creations.[17]

In 1939, the year O'Neill began writing *The Iceman Cometh,* the Austrian novelist Stefan Zweig's *Beware of Pity* was published in London. It tells the story of a military officer who takes pity on a young woman confined to crutches and a wheelchair. A doctor tries to warn him to beware of what seems to be among the "best possible motives," the impulse to feel solace for the invalid:

Pity—that's all right. But there are two kinds of pity. One, the weak and sentimental kind, which is really no more than the heart's impatience to be rid as quickly as possible of the painful emotion aroused by the sight of another's unhappiness, that pity which is not compassion, but only an instinctive desire to fortify one's own soul against the sufferings of another; and the other, the only kind that counts, the unsentimental but creative kind, which knows what it is about and is determined to hold out, in patience and forbearance, to the very limits of its strength and even beyond.[18]

The doctor believes in only the second kind of pity, "unsentimental but creative," and it turns out that he has married a blind woman to console her for his failure to cure her, and she fills his life with gloom and depression. In O'Neill's play, Hickey declares there are two kinds of pity, one that keeps the subject wallowing in guilt, the other going unspecified. But secretly Hickey pities his wife for his failure to cure himself of his own moral sickness that she must bear. With bravado Hickey assures the miserable drunks in the bar that he has given up his "pipe dream" and taken control of his life. Actually, the pity he expressed toward his own wife, which, like that of Zweig's doctor, would be determined to "hold out in patience and forbearance," failed to do so. He asked his wife to be pitied for the sins of the flesh he committed with other women, and she continued to forgive him his infidelities. "The crown of Christian ethics is the doctrine of forgiveness," wrote the theologian Reinhold Niebuhr. But in *The Iceman Cometh*, Christian ethics confronts a contradiction. The mind can readily forgive others but to forgive one's own conscience requires convincing oneself that temptation can be conquered. Christianity commands us to do what we are incapable of doing, leaving us with no resources of intellect but with only what Nietzsche called "the bite of conscience."[19]

Hickey sets out to reform others as though he has the right to do so after having reformed himself; assuming to know the "right kind of pity," he continues to tell those he intends to redeem how much he had loved his dear wife. But Hickey must repress what he himself knows, that pity turns into emotional blackmail. His twisted mind comes to see his wife's pity for him as a strategy of manipulation. Her loving kindness and forgiveness made him promise to reform, yet only she knew what he gradually came to understand, that his need for absolution for playing around with other women made him dependent upon her. Eventually he begins to hate himself, but there is "a limit to the guilt you can feel and . . . you have to begin blaming someone else, too." Enraged by his need for her, his self-hatred is projected onto his wife. After he shoots her, he shouts: "Well, you know what you can do with your pipe dream now, you damned bitch!"

Hickey expresses Nietzsche's idea of decadent Christianity, the mind wracked with guilt that has been brought up on the idea of sin. Such a mind suffers from impotent resentment and needs to seek a cause for its suffering, someone or something to blame. Unable to change one's ways, and unable, like the anarchist and socialist, to blame society for his misery, the morally decadent takes revenge on those morally superior and without sin. Religion can so fill the mind with sin and guilt that "the Christian wants to get rid of himself," observed Nietzsche, and resentment derives from "the desire to stun the pain."[20]

Does the same repressed hatred compel Hickey to try to convince the drunks that they must give up their pipe dreams and cease longing for the promises of tomorrow and accept the realities of today? Hickey believes that the forlorn bums can be saved and that his kind of pity will produce "real results." Larry counters that his desperate comrades are too weak to change and must cling to their illusion that change somehow will occur on its own. The juxtaposition of the two characters of Hickey and Larry raises the question of social reform and spiritual redemption. Ralph Waldo Emerson, who pondered such issues, would perhaps have seen Hickey as another example of the reformer who seeks to redeem others out of the delusion that he has redeemed himself. Of such efforts, Emerson warned, "hypocrisy and vanity are often the disgusting result." Emerson witnessed the many political reforms and religious revivals of the 1840s, and while he supported many causes, he had his doubts about the zealous missionary. "Many a reformer perishes in his removal of rubbish; and that makes the offensiveness of the class. They are partial; they are not equal to the work they pretend. They lose their way." Emerson continues as though he anticipates O'Neill's character. "In the assault on the kingdom of darkness they expend all their energy on some accidental evil, and lose their sanity and power of benefit."[21]

Although *The Iceman Cometh* may be regarded as a successful theatrical entertainment that belongs to popular culture, some of its themes have serious ramifications for political philosophy and intellectual history. The presence or absence of pity may be an emotion that not only comes between men and women but goes beyond human relations to affect historical outcomes. It has even been suggested that the American Revolution was a success because, unlike the French Revolution, pity played no role.

Hannah Arendt's *On Revolution* dealt not only with the ideas that inspire a revolution but its deeper emotions as well. Drawing upon Melville and Dostoevski in addition to some of the philosophers of the French and American revolutions, Arendt probes the meanings of compassion, goodness, solidarity, suffering, and happiness. All such sentiments are wrought with ambiguities but the most troubling is "pity." Compassion is aroused by the plight of others and solidarity seeks to unify the interests of all:

> Solidarity, because it partakes of reason, and hence of generality, is able to comprehend a multitude conceptually, not only the multitude of a class or a nation or a people, but eventually all mankind. But this solidarity, though it may be aroused by suffering, is not guided by it, and it comprehends the strong and the rich no less than the weak and the poor; compared with the sentiment of pity, it may appear cold and abstract.... Pity, because it is not stricken in the flesh and keeps its sentimental distance, can succeed where compassion always will fail; it can reach out to the multitude and therefore, like solidarity, does not look upon fortune and misfortune, the strong and the weak with an equal eye; without the presence of misfortune, pity could not exist, and it therefore has a vested interest in the existence of the unhappy as thirst for power has a vested interest in the existence of the weak. Moreover, by virtue of being a sentiment, pity can be enjoyed for its own sake, and this will almost automatically lead to a glorification of its cause, which is the suffering of others.[22]

According to Arendt, the American Revolution, taking place in an environment free of hunger and poverty, succeeded because it aimed at achieving political liberty and had no need to overcome human misery. O'Neill had thought of writing plays dealing with the Revolution and its aftermath, yet his anarchist convictions would lead him to see the Revolution as a failure, and his tragic sense of life precluded him from thinking about the possibilities of politics. Nonetheless, the characters in *The Iceman Cometh* compel us to think about politics in regard to political agency.

All the characters have some quarrel with society and with others who have crossed their paths; and the stage, perhaps even more than the state, is the arena where people are asked to face the truth about themselves. The play deals with what philosophers call "action theory," the challenge of figuring out the explanation of human behavior, the motives at the bottom of social conduct. Like the philosopher, the playwright considers the gap between what people say and what they truly feel, and between what they really want and what they actually do — especially when they do nothing.

While remaining passive, the inhabitants of the "No Chance Saloon" put forth stories about themselves that can be self-contradictory. The Harvard graduate's father either ruined the son's life because he was a disreputable crook, or the son let the father down and then himself sank into dissipation. The wife of Jimmy Tomorrow drives him to drink by the depression brought on by her adultery, or he lost his job and took to the bottle because life was too much for him. The proprietor Harry Hope's wife was either a solid inspiration who enabled him to run for office, or a shrew who pushed him further than his talents could take him to the point of facing failure. As the play develops, O'Neill makes us understand how easy it is for the down and out to entertain visions of their own victimhood, complaining about what life has done to them and seldom considering what they have done to themselves.

The Iceman Cometh makes us aware that language itself may be irrelevant in explaining what is going on, that conversation and chatter may be excuses and speeches and pronouncements mere rationalizations. With the modern playwright history is not only what occurs but what is remembered, and memory may be as unreliable as truth is unknowable. Thus the play's characters tell each other how much they had loved their long-gone dear wives only later, after rounds of drinks, to blurt out their venomous recollections of the "nagging bitch." To move from the personal to the political, one might well ask whether the anarchist acts in the spirit of freedom when he denounces the state and upholds the individual, or does the urge to destroy conceal a deeper will to dominate. In the play O'Neill has Hugo, a character based on a Greenwich Village anarchist, the Czech Hippolyte Havel, get up on a table and hold forth in a drunken stupor:

Hello, leedle peoples! Neffer mind! Soon you vill eat hot dogs beneath the villow trees and trink free vine — (*abruptly in a haughty fastidious tone*) The champaigne vas not properly iced. (*with guttural anger*) Gottamned liar, Hickey! Does that prove I vant to be aristocrat? I love only the proletariat. I vill lead them! I vill be like a Gott to them! They will be my slaves! (*he stops in bewildered self-amazement — to Larry appealingly*) I am very trunk, no, Larry? I talk foolishness. I am so trunk, Larry, old friend, am I not, I don't know vhat I say?

O'Neill enables us to see that human action and intention may have little to do with the words uttered by those who think they are explaining themselves when they are actually repressing their deepest urges. In our era when public discourse is touted as the democratic solution to democratic problems, one may well be suspicious that reason and its linguistic expressions truly account for what people want to do and why they do it. If reasons were causes and words would faithfully represent acts, then no one would have to say, "I don't know vhat I say." With O'Neill we see how language can hide our thoughts when truth remains subverbal.

The eighteenth-century Enlightenment rested much of its hopes on the rational, prudent mind that knows its needs as it sets out to satisfy its interest in the pursuit of happiness. O'Neill's *Iceman* characters are beyond interest and desire, without appetite, ambition, or even lust. Neither a good meal, a possible opportunity, nor even a sensual thought moves them to do something about their lives. Ideas die along with emotions. Emerging disillusioned from the anarchist movement, O'Neill's Larry Slade has nowhere to go politically. The Marxist, to the extent that he or she can ward off doubt, looks to science and philosophy for hope, to the progressive "laws" of historical development and to the "dialectic" as the keys to why capitalism carries its own self-destructive "contradictions." But for O'Neill and his anarchist comrades, the Wobblies and the rebels of the Lyrical Left of Greenwich Village, only the masses can bring reason and justice into the world. Thus *The Iceman Cometh* questions both the liberal assumption that revolution and the struggle for freedom have their sources in human nature and the Marxist assumption that the downfall of capitalism and the overcoming of human alienation have their sources in history and its inexorable stages. In an earlier play, *Days Without End* (1933), written during the Depression, O'Neill describes the American people cringing in the face of insecurity. "They have lost the ideal of the Land of the Free. Freedom demands initiative, courage, the need to decide what life must mean to oneself. To them," O'Neill observed, waxing Nietzschean, "that is terror."

Eugene O'Neill was not the only modern playwright who doubted that history rises from the bottom up. Anatoly Lunacharsky, the Russian playwright with whom O'Neill corresponded, discerned similar reservations in a few of Maxim Gorky's plays. The Russian writer also depicted workers fueling their dreams with vodka and remaining incapable of translating their desires into reality. In Russia, too, dreams of revolution remain stuck in a saloon. Such men, wrote Lunacharsky of Gorky's characters, "turn out to be whining neurasthenic intellectuals, who are absolutely unfit for struggle."[23]

One need only compare O'Neill's *The Iceman Cometh* to Clifford Odets' *Waiting for Lefty* to sense how the rich complexity of art can undermine the easy clarity of politics. In Odets' play, the audience feels the drama of class conflict, the upward movement of social consciousness, and, as the labor strike is about to take place, the exciting acceleration of history. O'Neill knew the working class more intimately than most communist writers. He shipped out on freighters, hung out in working-class dives, and labored with hand and shovel in the mines of Honduras. Yet O'Neill could see no revolutionary potential in the working class. While sharing a genuine comradeship with fellow workers, he refused to endow them with a special role and mission in history, what the French Left called *ouvrierisme,* a labor metaphysic (to use C. Wright Mills' apt formulation) that promised deliverance from alienation and oppression, a hope that was as much a figment of the intellectual class as a fact of the working class. That Odets' characters are up and marching and O'Neill's sitting and slumbering may suggest that *The Iceman Cometh* is closer to Marx's recognition that modern capitalist society puts people to sleep. The masses cannot awake from their collective enchantment until they face what has happened to themselves. Marx could well have shared O'Neill's haunting reminder of humanity's clinging to "pipe dreams" when he wrote that "the reform of consciousness consists *solely* in . . . the awakening of the world from its dream about itself," and if the playwright identified desire as some kind of sin, the philosopher identified it with "crude communism," the embittered rivalry in which people find themselves resentful, envious, and overcome with the "desire to level" distinctions of any kind.[24] But O'Neill was too much steeped in Nietzsche to have his barroom characters awaken from dreams to see the truth about themselves as an object of discovery.

*

O'Neill wrote *The Iceman Cometh* in the years 1939–1941, a period when Western intellectual history and political philosophy seemed on the verge of collapse as war raged in Europe. At that time the Enlightenment "project" was questioned not only by German "critical theorists" who came to America from Frankfurt but by some conservative militant realpolitik theorists as well. With the crisis of liberalism in mind, James Burnham would later write a book with the frightening title, *Suicide of the West.* While the ex-Trotskyist Burnham believed that the American intellectual didn't have what it takes to face Stalin, the philosopher John Dewey earlier advised his fellow liberals that they ought not to face Hitler. "No matter what happens," he advised Americans at the outbreak of the war in 1939, "stay out!"[25]

In view of these defeatist stances on the part of many American intellectuals, O'Neill's politics stand up well. After the fall of France he supported American intervention, though he did not wish to see Ireland entering the war on the side of England. At the time he was sketching out plays on the threat of totalitarianism ("The Last Conquest"), and an eleven-play cycle on American history beginning with a script on "The Rights of Man 1775." He praised President Roosevelt in 1944 for "the guts and courage he has shown in overcoming his physical handicaps and for the way he has borne the terrible, killing responsibility of a War Commander," adding, "occasionally in this role, he attains the semblance of genuine stature and dignity. But all the same, if I was voting this fall, I'd vote for Norman Thomas."[26]

A man of the Left, O'Neill sympathized with the democratic socialists while distrusting American communism. He resisted appeals by communist-sponsored organizations to lend his name to various causes. When the League of American Writers asked him to donate manuscripts for a fund-raiser, O'Neill told a friend that the organization "strikes me as a phony—one of those communist inspired organizations which use sucker names for a fake front." If his manuscripts ever fell into the hands of the Soviets, "they would promptly ban everything I've written and take all I've got and send me to a local Siberia or shoot me." O'Neill was both amused and appalled when a Russian reviewer of *Iceman* thought there was a communist in the play. It "isn't true," O'Neill protested, "because there is a world of difference between a Communist and a Communist-Anarchist." "The latter," he noted, referring to the followers of Peter Kropotkin, "is shot on sight in Russia." As did Emma Goldman and Carlo Tresca, O'Neill was well aware of the grim fate of the anarchists in the Soviet Union.[27]

Although O'Neill has been accused of succumbing to a hopeless pessimism, he never lost hope in the early years of World War II even when the Third Reich had conquered almost all of western Europe. The Office of War Information asked the Nobel laureate for a statement to bolster morale at a time when the outcome of the struggle was in doubt. After describing the nihilistic, murderous nature of fascism, O'Neill wrote: "It is against this intolerably hideous and sadistic leader-dream of a world deformed and tortured, lashed back into a past of ignorant serfdom, its culture dead and spat upon, that the United States is waging war. . . . The free men and women of Europe, whose allies and friends we are, cannot be conquered in spirit. They know a terrible day of reckoning will come for their oppressors. . . . They will win because the longing of the human spirit for the dignity and self-respect of freedom is imperishable and unconquerable. All things, including leaders, have their day and pass, but the aspiring soul of Free Man remains, and will remain as long as there is Man."[28]

Other than believing in the Allied cause, O'Neill never fooled himself into predicting that the war would be a complete victory for the future of freedom. He could never forget the outcome of the First World War, and he wondered what the "greedy politicians and monkey diplomats" would do to conclude the present war. He wished for an earlier day "when the foxes like Talleyrand, Metternich, and Castlereagh cooked up the relatively intelligent Vienna treaty," which brought the Napoleonic wars to an end. He had no patience with the pacifists and noninterventionists, and he advised his son that America had only two choices, "kill or be killed, crush or be crushed."[29] O'Neill remained strongly sympathetic toward the working class but far from sentimental about its capacity for political action. During the war he also expressed a new respect for a middle class that he saw as threatened due to the Depression. The Greenwich Village rebels had derided the bourgeoisie as hopelessly respectable and, as upright as it was uptight, too conservative for its own good. But O'Neill, with his anarchist suspicion of organized power, saw a saving remnant in the unorganized:

> What particularly gripes me is the growing ruin of the class between Big Business and Unionized Labor—the small business man, shop keeper, white collar worker, professional man, small farmer, etc. We see so many instances of that in this neighborhood [northern California]. The people who are the finest type of American are pushed to the wall, while the lousiest type uses Defense work to get rich quick as lazily as possible, hoping the war will go on indefinitely. Of course, some of this ruin of the Forgotten Class may be necessary in total war, but I am convinced there is a deliberate plan by a Washington clique to use the war to smash this class—in order to achieve the true democracy of the future, when without this class democracy cannot live![30]

Years earlier O'Neill had expressed similar sentiments in his only comedy, *Ah, Wilderness!* (1933). The play is a testament to the country's character, especially the "homely decency" of the much-maligned middle class. O'Neill's entire *oeuvre* cries out for America to take freedom seriously. The framers of the Constitution gave democracy its "machinery"; the playwright asked the people to give it dignity so that it will remain an instrument of freedom as long as there is "Free Man." But freedom, as the Conclusion to this book suggests, is complicated by desire. To crave for that which one does not possess is to feel freedom controlled by passions the intellect cannot command. An American government that was conceived without relying on classical virtue or Christian love asks the people to face what James Madison called the "defect" of better motives and Lincoln lamented as the absence of the "better angels" of our nature. The playwright faced that fallen human condition.

Conclusion:
The Theater as Temple

"The theatre to me is life — the substance and interpretation of life," O'Neill stated in an interview in 1922. "Life is struggle, often, if not usually, unsuccessful struggle; for most of us have something within us which prevents us from accomplishing what we dream and desire. And then, as we progress, we are always seeing further than we can reach."[1]

Life as struggle. That outlook could well be endorsed on all sides of the political spectrum. The radical left sees history and freedom struggling to rise from below; the conservative right sees truth and morality struggling to be preserved from above; and the liberal center sees hope and progress struggling to be free of the past. But O'Neill's outlook on life defies all these familiar categories and calls into question how we think about politics, religion, and economics.

In *The Hairy Ape* and in other O'Neill plays, the worker is incapable of class struggle, politics remains at the level of platitudes, religion is indifferent to sin and guilt, and economics is more about profit and possession than productivity and progress. Religion, instead of compelling the powerful to know themselves, insulates them from reality and delivers them from what Christianity had assumed it had implanted in a fallen human nature: a bad conscience. Christianity taught the poor and powerless to invent morality so that they would see themselves as morally superior to the rich and powerful. A Christian ethical sense, however, rarely kept the ruling classes in moral awe of Christ and the cross. In O'Neill's outlook, the rich and powerful feel nothing other than their egoism.

Was O'Neill's preoccupation with the specter of desire unwarranted?

The founding theorist of capitalism, the eighteenth-century philosopher Adam Smith, might convince us that O'Neill's obsession with desire was an unnecessary fixation. Egoistic selfishness need not be a problem as long as the free market is allowed to work out its laws of supply and demand and the universal human impulse of "sympathy" opens the mind to the needs of others. Smith hoped that the need to be looked up to and praised would compel people to restrain their selfishness and behave honorably in order to command respect. But society on its own would be insufficient to carry out such a role. Smith acknowledged that his psychology of human behavior rested on religion and the presence of the Deity as a moral judge. Centuries later, with the shock delivered by Nietzsche, God fades into the twilight as humankind decides to be its own judge of what is right and wrong and creates its own values independently of Christianity. Historically the rise of the free market counted upon the moral sentiment of sympathy, but the decidedly unsympathetic and selfish Deborah Harford, in *More Stately Mansions,* believes that "the only evil is to deny oneself," and in the play her son says, facetiously, that the genuine expression of sympathy is to be found in the murderer who "possesses the true quality of mercy" by putting people out of their misery. If O'Neill rejected the idea of a liberating class consciousness arising from the lower depths, so too did he scoff at the idea that market capitalism as a social institution would generate any semblance of moral behavior radiating from the heights of society. And there is little indication in O'Neill that the weak have the capacity to inflict guilt upon the strong, the old illusion of Christianity that led the poor to think themselves spiritually superior to the rich and and more worthy to enter the gates of heaven.

Many of the American Founders, especially the framers of the Constitution, and those who defended it, like the *Federalist* authors and John Adams, would not only have understood what was troubling O'Neill but possibly have believed that they had a solution to the problem of desire. They saw the "interests and passions" as endemic to liberty and at the same time as necessary to freedom as "air is to fire." In *Federalist* number six, Hamilton asked: "Is not the love of wealth as domineering and enterprising a passion as that of power and glory?" Like O'Neill, the framers of the Constitution were steeped in the classics, and like the playwright they did not believe that desire, which they often called "self-love," could be disciplined by reason to generate the will to control power. Instead they turned to the "machinery of government" to keep factions in check. Just as democracy would work by countervailing "interests to interests, and passion to passion," so would desire be controlled either through institutional arrangements or through responsible leadership in the office of the presidency. Unenlightened, direct democracy would be the arena of unreflective, immediate desire, and thus government must deal not with what people want but what they need in light of the public good. It is the role of representative government to "enlarge and refine" the desires of the people and channel them toward constructive ends. This was the Federalist solution proposed in the Constitution of 1787.

By the 1830s, however, the anti-Federalist Jeffersonian view came to prevail in America's political culture. Henceforth many of the checks and controls eroded with the rise of unrestrained democracy, and no politician dared to stand in the way of the people's wishes and demands. Several of O'Neill's plays take place in Jeffersonian-Jacksonian America, and the Federalist portraits of Washington, Hamilton, and Marshall hang on the wall in *Mourning Becomes Electra* as relics of a forgotten past that America has left behind. The Federalist believed that an effective government could deflect the will of the people and sublimate private vices toward public ends. Yet as Tocqueville noted, the idea of a "mixed government" that would juxtapose passion against passion proved illusory as all Americans entertained the same passionate pursuits. In O'Neill's historical plays, democracy becomes the very expression of desire.

*

The dialectic between past and present runs through O'Neill's plays. A Jeffersonian America, however, believed that each generation was sovereign unto itself and that the "dead" could not control the "living"; Tocqueville informed Americans that democracy looks ahead so that "the woof of time is ever being broken and the track of past generations lost."[2] Democracy offers freedom, choice, possibilities attainable through the force of the imagination. But O'Neill saw something preventing people from attaining their dreams and desires, and for many of his characters it was the burden of history. Thus he saw the present and future foreordained by the past. "Well," exclaims Hickey in *The Iceman Cometh*, "it's all there, at the start, everything that happens afterwards." "You can go along as if nothing had happened," Nina Leeds tells her father in *Strange Interlude*, "and really, nothing will have happened that hasn't already happened." It was once believed that one could look to history to understand it so that humankind would no longer be its victims but instead its masters. But with O'Neill, as with other modernists such as T. S. Eliot, we are the creatures of history, never its creators.

Historical fatalism—that which happened had to happen—may be too deterministic to leave room for freedom. So too the burden of memory. To some thinkers memory could be redemptive and serve as a source of identity and even authority. With the Declaration of Independence in mind, Lincoln invoked "the mystic chords of memory" to remind Americans that the country was founded upon the "proposition" of human equality. But memory for O'Neill conjured up pain, and he would remind Americans of how they have betrayed their professed principles: land taken from Native Americans, explorers searching for God but settling for gold, slavery and the exploitation of another's labor, radicals turning stool pigeon, his own father leaving art behind out of avarice. Once O'Neill remarked in jest that he was "a minor anti-Christ" who must judge others as severely as he judged himself. "God is Dead! Long Live — What?"[3]

Long Live Democracy! In America, liberal democracy is esteemed for guaranteeing freedom, the exercise of rights, and the possibility of opportunity for all. Yet moving within the parameters of democracy is the specter of power, the drive to expand, subdue, control. "If the mind wills anything with enough intensity of love," declares Deborah in *More Stately Mansions,* "it can force life to its desire, create a heaven, if need be, out of hell!" The equation of love and power is telling. With O'Neill's characters, love for another person or for a piece of property gives one the right to take by whatever means possible. Deborah's son Simon denounces Andrew Jackson whose administration is standing in the way of allowing market capitalism to rip freely in a free environment: "Conditions are becoming worse every day. (*with a flash of vindictive anger*) That mad fool, Jackson! What does he know of business — an ignorant, mob-rousing, slave-dealing plantation owner! The cowardly tariff compromise he accepted coupled with his insane banking policy are ruining the country!"

O'Neill's Simon vacillates between the idealistic poet and the crass profiteer only to reach a conclusion almost nihilistic. "But you're quite right," he says to his wife Sara. "My old romantic obsession with Rousseau's fake conception of the inner nature of man was a stupid mistake. Rousseau, as I see him now, was a weak, moral sentimentalist — a coward who had neither the courage nor the ability to live in a world of facts and accept the obvious truth about man — which is that man is compounded of one-tenth spirit to nine-tenths hog." Those who think with Rousseau hide themselves in their dreams and pretensions about a better self in a better world: "All you have to do to see how sentimentally naive Rousseau's conception [of happiness] was, is to study history — or merely read your daily newspaper and see what man is doing with himself. After all, his deeds constitute the true relation of his nature. What he desires is what he is. (*with a bitter enthusiasm*) There's a book that ought to be written." Simon contemplates a new basis of morality that would acknowledge that the natural instincts are selfish rather than benevolent, a perfect society of imperfect creatures who know themselves as such.

Significantly, the framers of the Constitution also concluded that Rousseau would mislead our republic with his innocent views of human nature. The *Federalist* authors sought to tell the dark truths about humankind that would later trouble O'Neill, and Nathaniel Hawthorne and Herman Melville would make us feel not only the guilt of our desires but the guilt of denying them. Desire plays havoc with freedom, which cannot exist as an authentic experience because the divisions and factions the Constitution was designed to control pale before the divisions within human nature itself, where liberty seeks its opposite and succumbs to that which destroys it. "All in the name of Freedom!" exclaims Simon. "As if Freedom could ever exist in Reality! As if at the end of every dream of liberty one did not find the slave, oneself, to whom oneself, the Master, is enslaved!" With the surging presence of desire, the will cannot take itself as its own object and instead gives itself over to some force other than itself.

There is, O'Neill suggests, no real freedom in formal freedom, which at best can exist as resistance to domination but cannot realize a completeness of being when human nature is divided at its core. O'Neill discerned an American character wherein unchecked ambition would struggle to realize itself and the will would allow itself to be determined by the urge to possess, whether it be wealth, status, power, beauty, or love itself, not the love that gives but that which takes. "He loves me!" exclaims Nina Leeds to herself. "He is mine!" It was not only O'Neill's anarchism that led him to conclude that government could rarely serve as a source of authority that would restrain the passions. Alexis de Tocqueville reached the same conclusion when he saw sovereign authority in the United States escaping political institutions and lodging itself in society and its sentiments, where the "feverish ardor" aroused by the "love of money" subordinates the self to the dominant culture of possessive acquisitiveness.[4]

O'Neill studied the classics, which raises the question whether he considered that the spirit of tragedy could serve to guide a young democracy as a political proposition. According to some scholars, Aeschylus's *Oresteia* served the civic purposes of Athens by showing how resolution and harmony could emerge from suspicion and conflict and how the passions could be tempered.[5] Similarly, "Aeschylean justice" aimed at the double goal of the reconciliation of differences and at the same time the recognition of other points of view that would legitimate pluralism.[6] O'Neill's characters, however, remain different from one another and have little capacity for transcendence so that they might see things from another's point of view. The mind is bonded to the self and its desires, and thus the theater of O'Neill leaves democracy not in harmony with itself but in conflict, inflamed with the possessive impulses that the Founders had set out to control.

In O'Neill's modern American theater, characters rarely progress toward self-realization or even to the beginnings of a higher order of understanding. There are exceptions, of course: Con in *Touch of the Poet* undergoes a new identity as an aristocratic manqué turned Jacksonian democrat; Erie in *Hughie* feels a glimmer of insight as to where he is in life; Josie in *Moon for the Misbegotten* attains absolution. But in the two great plays, *Long Day's Journey into Night* and *The Iceman Cometh,* the stories end with neither resolution nor revelation as the audience realizes that the characters will continue their lives in compulsive repetition and repression. The characters are too overcome with discord to achieve a state of being where they are free of the need for others. Hence they can never be sure who they are or where they belong, or what it is that they want or what it is that obstructs them from getting it. Are they thwarted from forces within the self or from without?

Consider O'Neill's explicit and lengthy stage directions. He carefully spelled out in detail every piece of furniture and other aspects of set design. The tables and other fixtures on the stage are real and occupy a space outside the mind. Yet the characters take no notice of their surroundings, as though all reality is mental, a phenomenon of the mind, and the mind is determined by perceptions and distortions of its own making, left contemplating its own constructions. "Something? Outside me?" Deborah Harford replies when asked if she is afraid of what might be in the garden. "No, nothing is there but I. . . . I have never lived except in mind. A very frightening prison it becomes at last, full of ghosts and corpses." She retreats into her mind, conscious that her self is losing control of itself as her desire to continue to possess her son is threatened by her daughter-in-law.

The great hope of older philosophical theories was that the self would come to see itself through the eyes of others. Society could take the place of religion if people began to model themselves in expectation of the opinion of others. This perspective, which began with Adam Smith, received its most recent expression in Rene Girard's theory of the "triangulation of desire" that leads one person to seek an object precisely because another is seeking it or vying for it. Presumably we do not know what we want until we are aroused to acquire what another possesses. Yet for the thinkers O'Neill was familiar with (Rousseau, Emerson, Nietzsche), such social behavior was precisely the problem. To submit to the gaze of others was the beginning of human alienation.

Rarely do O'Neill's characters coincidentally run into someone who has an impact on their thoughts (Yank and Anna Christie are among the exceptions), or suddenly encounter an unexpected idea that comes from nowhere, or come up against an event that occasions a change in the mind's outlook (the failure of a labor strike makes revolution all the fonder). Such an encounter may have happened in the past, in the Civil War, for example, before the story begins, but the audience can only suspect that the experience reinforced the character's prior convictions about life's meaning. What humankind is is basically what it thinks and desires and remembers, an inner predisposition that limits the mind's potential for perception. On the stage, truth makes no entrance as an intruder or even as an invited guest; or if it does, when, for example, Hickey makes his appearance in *Iceman,* the characters return to their same crippled selves upon his departure. Identity, if at all known, is fixed, almost fated, immune to the vicissitudes of experience in later life. You are who you were.

Who, then, was Eugene Gladstone O'Neill? Many scholars answer that question by returning to the playwright's family to remind us of the torturous conditions of his childhood and his coming of age in the symbolically haunted house in New London, Connecticut.[7] In his essay "The Genius of O'Neill," however, the literary critic Lionel Trilling suggested that the playwright's imagination soared from the personal and social to the "transcendental" as he sought to address "the meaning of life" and the "riddle of the universe." Several plays have their sources in O'Neill's personal background, particularly *Moon for the Misbegotten* and *Long Day's Journey.* But Clearly O'Neill was not always thinking about his family when he worked out the characters and plots for his plays. In contrast to religion, the subject of politics rarely became a topic of conversation or contention among members of his family. Yet O'Neill, coming onto the cultural scene during the Greenwich Village rebellion, could hardly avoid politics and its passionate causes, and the Marxists on the Left looked to history to fulfill the role that religion had once promised in redeeming humankind from its alienated condition. In *The Iceman Cometh* O'Neill has Larry Slade, a composite character based upon the bohemian anarchist Terry Carlin and others, explain why a blinding devotion to politics may be the death of intellect:

> You asked me why I quit the movement. I had a lot of good reasons. One was myself, and another was my comrades, and the last was the breed of swine called men in general. For myself, I was forced to admit, at the end of thirty years, devotion to the Cause, that I was never made for it. I was born condemned to be one of those who has to see all sides of a question. When you're damned like that, the questions multiply for you until in the end it's all question and no answer. As history proves, to be a worldly

success at anything, especially revolution, you have to wear blinders like a horse and see only straight in front of you. You have to see, too, that this is all black, and that is all white.

The thirties generation of writers was asked to wear blinders and accept the party line coming on a cablegram from Moscow. O'Neill represents the best of the earlier generation of Greenwich Village rebels who had no interest in taking orders or giving them. But O'Neill himself stood out as unique amid the "Lyrical Left." He could not believe, with the Marxists, that the market economy was history's inevitable stage on the way to socialism; or believe, with the capitalists, that property was the indispensable instrument of freedom that humanizes the world. Nor could he believe, with liberal reformers, that compassion would help uplift the masses. He learned from Nietzsche that pity is condescending and reflects a morbid fascination with failure. "We need, above all, to learn again to believe in the possibility of nobility of spirit in ourselves," announces John in *Days Without End.* But the message of the German philosopher would be as disdained for teaching freedom as Christ was crucified for preaching love. "I'll grant you the pseudo-Nietzschean savior I just evoked out of my past is an equally futile ghost," state's John's alter ego Loving. "Even if he came, we'd only send him to the insane asylum for teaching that we should have a nobler aim for our lives than getting all four feet in a trough of swill."

Or a trough of oil. America's contemporary war in Iraq would have depressed O'Neill but it would not have surprised him. Democratic pride had worried O'Neill as much as it had worried Tocqueville, and the anarchist had always been skeptical of the ballot as a means of realizing liberty, as though an election alone guarantees freedom and makes democracy possible. O'Neill lived through the age of Woodrow Wilson and he knew that the war "to end all wars" and to "make the world safe for democracy" was a utopian fantasy, especially a war declared by a leader who saw himself as a savior after having lost sight of Christ's Sermon on the Mount.

*

Not only did politics set O'Neill apart from the Left. His tragic sensibility had a touch of the metaphysical and even mystical. "O'Neill is unique in the kind of thought we call philosophical," observed Trilling. O'Neill's philosophical temperament led him to explore ultimate questions about the riddle of power, the meaning of existence, and a life that awaits its rendezvous with death. In *Lazarus Laughed* he could invoke philosophy to suggest that there should be nothing to fear from death once we see ourselves as part of a universal nature that continues into eternity. "Be immortal because life is immortal," Caligula is instructed. "Contain the harmony of the womb and the grave within you!" "Be inspired by death!" But such exhortations are more proclaimed than proven, and indeed O'Neill could neither subscribe to the philosophy of life of his beloved Greeks nor to the philosophy of history of his bold comrades — neither Aristotle nor Marx.

Aristotle sought to demonstrate that cognitive reason could lead us to happiness, defined as self-sufficiency, a state of lacking in nothing, the cessation of desire. Marx sought to demonstrate that we could realize in practice what philosophy promised to be the fruit of theory, the "reunification of man with nature," the overcoming of alienation found in a new life of free, joyous, uncoerced labor that would fulfill the human need for wholeness. Aristotle held out the possibility of happiness through thought, Marx the promise of freedom through action. Both thinkers assumed that the problem of desire disappears once life passes over from necessity into freedom.

With O'Neill it is the other way around. Desire becomes all the more intense when the imagination is free to dwell upon it and the will can act upon motives of pleasure and delight. But as an emotional fixation, desire turns out to be boundless, an irresistible passion that leaves the subject experiencing frustration instead of fulfillment. Only when desire has power as its object do O'Neill's subjects delight in a sense of completion, even if it means domination. "I'm too strong for you," Sara shouts to her mother-in-law Deborah in *More Stately Mansions,* who seeks to have her son all to herself and at her command alone. "Life is too strong for you! But it's not too strong for me! I'll take what I want and make it mine!" And in America, Sara reminds the audience, you are free to take what you want.

The play was part of the unfinished "cycle" project, which was to have the theme of "A Tale of Possessor Self-Dispossessed," suggesting that what one seeks to possess comes to possess the seeker. The theme had been on O'Neill's mind perhaps ever since he left the Catholic Church, and years later, in an interview at the time of the production of *The Iceman Cometh,* he reiterated the biblical warning about losing one's soul by trying to possess something outside it. In *A Long Day's Journey,* the father and two sons ache to gain the attention of wife and mother, to possess the thoughts of an addict who no longer knows her own mind. The mother is not an end in herself but a means of satisfying their needs for approbation and forgiveness. Their sole motive of thought and action is desire for the Other, and reason is helpless to redirect it.

Yet O'Neill had to consider that possessive desire itself made democracy possible and even elevated its longings to the level of tragedy. If classical and Christian philosophy sought to discipline the desires that rage within the heart, modern democracy holds out the promise of fulfilling them. Democracy is noble because the dreams of tomorrow that profoundly stir its emotions have no threshold of satisfaction, no consummation. "The higher the dream," O'Neill remarked in 1922, referring to *Beyond the Horizon,* "the more impossible it is to realize fully." But life is not a contract of social convenience; it is a trial of moral character. "A man wills his own defeat when he pursues the unattainable," noted O'Neill. "But his struggle is his success! He is an example of the spiritual significance which life attains when it aims high enough, when the individual fights all the hostile forces within and without himself to a future of nobler values."[8]

Eugene O'Neill used America not only for the material of drama but for the theater of tragedy. He sought to give America "the one true theatre, the theatre of the Greeks and Elizabethans." It would be a demanding theater in which masks could be used to unmask our emotions. "I mean a theater returned to its highest and sole significant function as a Temple where the religion of poetic interpretation and symbolic celebration of life is communicated to human beings, starved in spirit by their soul-stifling struggle to exist as masks among the masks of the living!"[9]

O'Neill may have told Americans more than they wanted to know about themselves. He well knew that many upright citizens would go about their lives unmoved by his own troubles as they continued to wear their masks of contentment. Yet year in and year out the American audience came back for more. To welcome the performance of desire and its discontents before our eyes suggests that many Americans also knew the meaning of a long day's journey. O'Neill would not follow his father's advice and give the American people a dose of cheerfulness that had little basis in their own lives. That he asked America to struggle for an impossible dream and accept an inevitable defeat can only mean that he saw his country containing spiritual resources that cannot be denied. O'Neill may have experienced his own life as "the curse of the misbegotten." But he fought defeat and despair until the very end. He remains a friend of all those who endeavor to clarify their own emotions and know their own reasons and refuse to accept excuses as explanations. To deny desire was the unpardonable sin; to live with it the basis of honesty and the beginning of hope. The playwright Eugene O'Neill sought to convey the quality of understanding that is born only of pain and rises to perception to reach the truths of human passion. For life to be felt as noble, it must be seen as tragic.

Notes

BIBLIOGRAPHICAL NOTE

All those working on Eugene O'Neill are indebted to two comprehensive biographies: Louis Sheaffer's two-volume work, *O'Neill: Son and Playwright* (1968; New York: Paragon, 1989), and *O'Neill: Son and Artist* (1973; New York: Paragon, 1990); and Arthur and Barbara Gelb, *O'Neill* (New York: Harper & Row, 1962), which has been reissued in an enlarged edition with a new preface in the Perennial Library edition, 1987. The Gelbs have also published the first volume of a projected three-volume biography, *O'Neill: Life with Monte Cristo* (New York: Applause, 2000). Though not as comprehensive, an early study by Croswell Bowen, *The Curse of the Misbegotten: A Tale of the House of O'Neill* (New York: McGraw-Hill, 1959), still reads poignantly.

Three major interpretive works are Travis Bogard, *Contour in Time: The Plays of Eugene O'Neill* (rev. ed., New York: Oxford Univ. Press, 1988), which treats the subject in light of Greek and Shakespearean tragedy; John H. Raleigh, *The Plays of Eugene O'Neill* (Carbondale: Southern Illinois Univ. Press, 1965), more concerned to appreciate the dramatist as a "quintessential" American writer (p. 239); and Stephen A. Black, *Eugene O'Neill: Beyond Mourning and Tragedy* (New Haven: Yale Univ. Press, 1999), a psychoanalytical interpretation depicting O'Neill's grief and trauma over his family.

More specialized studies are Doris Alexander, *Eugene O'Neill's Creative Struggle: The Decisive Decade, 1924–1933* (University Park: Pennsylvania State Univ. Press, 1992); Judith Barlow, *Final Acts: The Creation of Three Late O'Neill Plays* (Athens: Univ. of Georgia Press, 1985); Norman & Berlin, *O'Neill's Shakespeare* (Ann Arbor: Univ. of Michigan Press, 1993); Linda Bin-Zvi, *Susan Glaspell: Essays on Her Theatre and Fiction* (Ann Arbor: Univ. of Michigan Press, 1985); Jean Chothia, *Forging a Language: A Study of the Plays of Eugene O'Neill* (New York: Cambridge Univ. Press, 1979); Thierry Dubost, *Struggle, Defeat or Rebirth* (Jefferson, N.C.: McFarland, 1997); Edwin A. Engel, *The Haunted Heroes of Eugene O'Neill* (Cambridge: Harvard Univ. Press, 1953); Doris V. Falk, *Eugene O'Neill and the Tragic Tension* (New Brunswick: Rutgers Univ. Press, 1958);

Virginia Floyd, *The Plays of Eugene O'Neill: A New Assessment* (New York: Ungar, 1985); Floyd, ed., *Eugene O'Neill at Work: Newly Released Ideas for Plays* (New York: Ungar, 1981); Floyd, ed., *Eugene O'Neill: The Unfinished Plays* (New York: Ungar, 1985); Horst Frenz and Susan Tuck, eds., *Eugene O'Neill's Critics: Voices from Abroad* (Carbondale: Southern Illinois Univ. Press, 1984); Donald C. Gallup, *Eugene O'Neill and His Eleven-Play Cycle* (New Haven: Yale Univ. Press, 1998); Joel Pfister, *Staging Depth: Eugene O'Neill and the Politics of Psychological Discourse* (Chapel Hill: Univ. of North Carolina Press, 1995); Laurin R. Porter, *The Banished Prince: Time, Memory, and Ritual in the Late Plays of Eugene O'Neill* (Ann Arbor: Theatre Series, University of Michigan, 1988); James A. Robinson, *Eugene O'Neill and Oriental Thought: A Divided Vision* (Carbondale: Southern Illinois Univ. Press, 1982); Edward L. Shaughnessy, *Down the Nights and Down the Days: Eugene O'Neill's Catholic Sensibility* (Notre Dame, Ind.: Univ. of Notre Dame Press, 1996).

Harold Bloom has edited anthologies of important articles by O'Neill scholars: *Eugene O'Neill* (New York: Chelsea House, 1987); *Eugene O'Neill's Long Day's Journey into Night* (New York: Chelsea House, 1987); and *Eugene O'Neill's The Iceman Cometh* (New York: Chelsea House, 1987). See also *The Cambridge Companion to Eugene O'Neill*, ed. Michael Manheim (New York: Cambridge Univ. Press, 1998); and James J. Martine, *Critical Essays on Eugene O'Neill* (Boston: G. K. Hall, 1984).

For O'Neill's correspondence, see the valuable compilation, *Selected Letters of Eugene O'Neill*, ed. Travis Bogard and Jackson R. Bryer (New Haven: Yale Univ. Press, 1988); and also *The Theatre We Worked For: The Letters of Eugene O'Neill to Kenneth Macgowan*, ed. Travis Bogard and Jackson R. Bryer (New Haven: Yale Univ. Press, 1982); *"As Ever, Gene": The Letters of Eugene O'Neill to George Jean Nathan*, ed. Nancy L. Roberts and Arthur W. Roberts (Madison, N.J.: Farleigh Dickinson Univ. Press, 1987); *"Love and Admiration and Respect": The O'Neill-Commins Correspondence*, ed. Dorothy Commins (Durham: Duke Univ. Press, 1986).

A valuable resource is *The Eugene O'Neill Newsletter* (1977–1988), succeeded by *The Eugene O'Neill Review*, which is edited by Professor Frederick C. Wilkins and can be presently found on webmaster@eoneill.com.

ABBREVIATIONS

These abbreviations are used in the notes to indicate the following sources:

CWON	*Conversations with Eugene O'Neill*, ed. Mark W. Estrin (Jackson: Univ. Press of Mississippi, 1990).
EON mss.	The O'Neill papers in the Beinecke Rare Book and Manuscript Library at Yale University, New Haven CT.
EONR	*The Eugene O'Neill Review*
ONHP	*O'Neill and His Plays: Four Decades of Criticism*, ed. Oscar Cargill, N. Bryllion Fagin, and William J. Fisher (New York: New York Univ. Press, 1961).
SLON	*Selected Letters of Eugene O'Neill*, ed. Travis Bogard and Jackson R. Bryer (New Haven: Yale Univ. Press, 1988).

Tocqueville   Alexis de Tocqueville, *Democracy in America,* ed. J. P. Mayer, trans.
George Lawrence (Garden City, N.Y.: Doubleday, 1969).

PREFACE

1. "The Ordeal of Eugene O'Neill," *Time,* Oct. 21, 1946, 71–78.

2. EON to Lawrence Langer, Aug. 11, 1940, *SLON,* 511.

3. EON to Dudley Nichols, Dec. 16, 1941, *SLON,* 537–38.

4. "Ordeal of O'Neill," 72.

5. Ben Brantley, "Bottoms Up to Illusions," *New York Times,* Apr. 9, 1999, pt. E, 1, 6.

6. "Ordeal of O'Neill," 76.

7. Quoted in Sean Wilentz, "That Century, Yet Again," *New Yorker,* Nov. 9, 1998, 104–105.

8. On *Time* magazine, see Martin Halliwell, *The Constant Dialogue: Reinhold Niebuhr and American Intellectual Culture* (New York: Rowman and Littlefield, 2005), 3–7; O'Neill's "Man is born broken" quotation is taken from his play *The Great God Brown.*

INTRODUCTION

1. Mary B. Mullett, "The Extraordinary Story of Eugene O'Neill," *American Magazine,* 94, Nov. 1922, reprinted in *CWON,* 26–37; EON to Kenneth Macgowan, Dec. 30, 1940, in *The Theatre We Worked For: The Letters of Eugene O'Neill to Kenneth Macgowan,* ed. Travis Bogard and Jackson R. Bryer (New Haven: Yale Univ. Press, 1982), 256–58; Friedrich Nietzsche, *The Birth of Tragedy and the Genealogy of Morals,* trans. Francis Golffing (Garden City, N.Y.: Doubleday Anchor, 1956), 149.

2. EON to Beatrice Ashe, Nov. 8, 1914, *SLON,* 38.

3. Quoted in Croswell Bowen, *The Curse of the Misbegotten: A Tale of the House of O'Neill* (New York: McGraw-Hill, 1959), 114.

4. Dudley Nichols, Introduction to *The Emperor Jones and The Straw* (New York: Modern Library, 1928), ix–xxv.

5. Tocqueville, *Democracy,* 12.

6. Reinhold Niebuhr, *Beyond Tragedy: Essays on the Christian Interpretation of History* (New York: Scribner's, 1965), 205.

7. Tocqueville, *Democracy,* 537.

CHAPTER ONE

1. EON to James T. Farrell, July 28, 1943, *SLON,* 545–46; Virginia Floyd, "Eugene O'Neill: Gift of a Celtic Legacy," *Recorder,* 3 (Summer 1989), 5–14.

2. EON to Eugene O'Neill Jr., May 7, 1945, *SLON,* 569.

3. Quoted in Doris Alexander, *The Tempering of Eugene O'Neill* (New York: Harcourt, 1962), 211–18.

4. Friedrich Nietzsche, *The Birth of Tragedy and the Genealogy of Morals,* trans. Francis Golffing (Garden City, N.Y.: Doubleday Anchor, 1956), 192.

5. Kirby A. Miller, *Emigrants and Ethics: Ireland and the Irish Exodus to North America* (New York: Oxford Univ. Press, 1985), 280–568.

6. George Orwell, *A Collection of Essays* (New York: Harcourt, 1946), 230.

7. *Irish Hunger: Personal Reflections on the Legacy of the Famine,* ed. Tom Hayden (Boulder: Rinehart, 1997).

8. Agnes Boulton, *Part of a Long Story: Eugene O'Neill as a Young Man in Love* (Garden City, N.Y.: Doubleday, 1958), 198–200; Louis Sheaffer, *O'Neill: Son and Playwright* (Boston: Little, Brown, 1968), 171.

9. See the valuable study by Stephen A. Black, *Eugene O'Neill: Beyond Mourning and Tragedy* (New Haven: Yale Univ. Press, 1999).

10. EON to Sophus Keith Winter, July 7, 1933, *SLON,* 416–17.

11. Christopher Murray, *Sean O'Casey: Writer at Work* (Dublin: Gill & MacMillan, 2004), 301.

12. Boulton, *Part of a Long Story,* 198–200; Sheaffer, *Son and Playwright,* 171.

13. Dorothy Day, *The Long Loneliness: An Autobiography* (New York: Harper & Row, 1952), xi.

14. Boulton, *Part of a Long Story,* 200–204.

15. EON to Mrs. George Pierce Baker, Jan. 20, 1935, *SLON,* 443; EON, "Professor George Baker," *New York Times,* Jan. 3, 1935.

16. Ralph Waldo Emerson, "Inspiration," in *Letters and Social Aims* (1875; Boston: Riverside Press, 1904), 269–97; Tocqueville, *Democracy,* 489–93.

17. Ralph Waldo Emerson, "The Tragic," in *The Portable Emerson,* ed. Mark Van Doren (New York: Viking, 1946), 216–23. Curiously, in 1920, in the aftermath of World War I, many American writers and intellectuals, disillusioned with the outcome of the war, but equally estranged from an America that had yet to "come of age," decided to leave the country for Paris and the Left Bank and elsewhere. The poets T. S. Eliot and Ezra Pound became permanent expatriates while the novelists F. Scott Fitzgerald and Ernest Hemingway prowled about Europe until the economic crash of 1929. The story has been thoughtfully chronicled in Malcolm Cowley's *Exile's Return,* first published in 1929, revised in 1934, with numerous editions since then. The many critical analyses in Harold Stearn's *Civilization in the United States,* which included contributions on subjects ranging from architecture to literature, music, philosophy, and the theater, all advised aspiring American thinkers and creative intellects to head abroad to find more fertile grounds for their talents. No one, it seemed, anticipated that America was about to witness the flowering of literary life. At the very time that O'Neill was coming on the American intellectual scene with his playwrighting, the consensus held that America was intellectually dead. This "lost generation," ironically, produced four Nobel Award winners (Sinclair Lewis, Ernest Hemingway, William Faulkner, and O'Neill).

18. Eugene O'Neill, "Damn the Optimists!" originally in the *New York Tribune,* Feb. 13, 1921, reprinted in *ONHP,* 104–107.

19. Glaspell, quoted in Arthur and Barbara Gelb, *O'Neill* (New York: Harper & Row, 1962), 309.

20. Quoted in *A Mencken Chrestomathy: Henry Louis Mencken,* ed. Lucia Bergamasco et al. (Paris: Armand Colin, 2003), 63.

21. Mary B. Mullet "The Extraordinary Story of Eugene O'Neill," *CWON,* 26–37; John MacPhee, *Looking for a Ship* (New York: Farrar Strauss, 1990), 37; Max Eastman, *Enjoyment of Living* (New York: Harper & Row, 1948), 566; Ingrid Bergman, "A Meeting with O'Neill," in *Eugene O'Neill: A World View,* ed. Virginia Floyd (New York: Frederick Ungar, 1979), 294.

22. Quoted in Louis Scheaffer, *O'Neill: Son and Artist* (1973; New York: Paragon, 1990), 632.

23. Quoted in Black, *Beyond Mourning and Tragedy,* 494–505.

24. EON to George C. Tyler, Dec. 9, 1920, *SLON,* 143.

CHAPTER TWO

1. Quoted in Croswell Bowen, *The Curse of the Misbegotten,* 309.

2. Mary McCarthy, *Theatre Chronicle: 1937–1962* (New York: Noonday, 1963), 81–88.

3. Francis Ferguson, "Melodramatist," and Bernard De Voto, "Minority Report," both in *ONHP,* 271–82, 301–306.

4. Eric Bentley, *The Playwright as Thinker* (1946; New York: Harcourt, 1986), 318–22.

5. Harold Bloom, "Foreword," Eugene O'Neill, *Long Day's Journey into Night* (New Haven: Yale Univ. Press, 2002), viii.

6. Edmund Wilson, *To the Finland Station: A Study in the Writing and Acting of History* (1940; New York: New York Review of Books ed., 2003), 274.

7. Friedrich Nietzsche, "Thus Spoke Zarathustra," in *The Portable Nietzsche,* ed. Walter Kaufmann (New York: Penguin, 1959), 251; Bakunin, quoted in Max Eastman, *Marxism: Is It Science?* (New York: Norton, 1940); for a discussion of anarchism, see Chapters 3 and 11.

8. Thomas Mann, "Schopenhauer," in *Essays of Three Decades,* trans. H. T. Lowe-Porter (New York: Knopf, 1947), 372–410.

9. *Schopenhauer et la creation litteraire en Europe,* ed. Anne Henry (Paris: Meridiens Klincksieck, 1989), 61.

10. Edmund Wilson, *Shores of Light: A Literary Chronicle* (New York: Vintage, 1952), 100.

11. Quoted in Bentley, *Playwright as Thinker,* 321–22.

12. Quoted in Joshua Mitchell, *The Fragility of Freedom: Tocqueville on Religion, Democracy, and the American Future* (Chicago: Univ. of Chicago Press, 1995), 80.

13. The subject of desire has been with us since men and women left the caves, or the Garden of Eden, and felt that something had been lost that had to be regained. In much of recent literature, the subject has been addressed by feminist scholars, for the most part questioning the view, first formulated by Sigmund Freud and amplified by Jacques Lacan, that desire is the result of a dyad relationship of child to parent, especially the young girl's yearning for the identity and approval of the father. On a more philosophical level, desire is seen as either a need to return to an impossible origin in the self or an emotion that is moved by something other than the self. The phenomenon of desire derives from the human subject that lacks self-sufficiency; hence the subject is constituted through a process of identification with images other than

itself, and images are shaped by the structures of language or constructions of a given culture. For valuable critical evaluation of the literature, see Jessica Benjamin, "A Desire of One's Own," *Feminist Studies/Critical Studies,* ed. Teresa de Lauretis (Bloomington: Indiana Univ. Press, 1986), 78–101; Judith Butler, "Desire," in *Critical Terms for Literary Study,* ed. Frank Lentricchia and Tomas McLauglin (Chicago: Univ. of Chicago Press, 1990), 369–86; *Philosophy and Desire,* ed. Hugh J. Silverman (New York: Routledge, 2000); Warren B. Irvine, *On Desire: Why We Want What We Want* (New York: Oxford Univ. Press, 2006); and, most recently, the special issue, "Le désir de Platon à Gilles Deleuze," *Le Magazine littéraire,* 455 (juillet–août 2006), 28–64.

A psychoanalytical approach to O'Neill had been applied with much skill and insight by Stephen A. Black, *Eugene O'Neill: Beyond Mourning and Tragedy* (New Haven: Yale Univ. Press, 1999). Black sees an Oedipal tension in O'Neill's life as well as in his plays. He particularly focuses on a school of thought known as "object relations," a process by which the child grows from the total dependency of the infant to mature independence and autonomy, an effort involving separating the images of one's own self from the mental representations of others, from the me to the not-me. There is no doubt that O'Neill struggles with this ordeal since in his very last plays he is still dealing with his mother and other members of his family. But his was an Irish-Catholic family, where religion, philosophy, and theology weighed heavily. Catholic teaching also instilled the view that the human soul is obscure to itself. Moreover, the memories of many of O'Neill's characters do not necessarily return to childhood as the site of a traumatic experience but often to youth and adulthood where the mind confronts failure, death, and despair.

14. EON to Brooks Atkinson, June 19, 1931, *SLON,* 389–91.

15. *The Political Philosophy of John Locke,* ed. David Wooton (New York: Mentor, 1993), 242–387; John Locke, *Questions Concerning the Law of Nature,* ed. Robert Horowitz, Jeremy Strauss, and Diskin Clay (Ithaca, N.Y.: Cornell Univ. Press, 1990), 12–169.

16. EON to Grace Dupre Hills, Mar. 21, 1925, *SLON,* 194–95.

17. EON to Arthur Hobson Quinn, May 29, 1927, *SLON,* 245.

18. Tia De Nora, *Beethoven and the Construction of Genius* (Berkeley: Univ. of California Press, 1995).

19. Carlotta Monterey to Joseph Wood Krutch, n.d., EON mss., Box 2; EON to Petre Comanescu, February 1947, *ibid.* Box 1. O'Neill was referring to Richard Dana Skinner's *Eugene O'Neill: The Quest of the Poet* (1935: New York: Russell & Russell, 1969) and Sophus Keith Winther's *Eugene O'Neill: A Critical Study* (1934: New York: Russell & Russell, 1969).

20. Lionel Trilling, "The Genius of O'Neill," *ONHP,* 292–300; "Introduction," *Eugene O'Neill: Three Plays* (New York: Modern Library, 1937), vii–xix.

21. Tocqueville, *Democracy,* 507.

22. George Wilson Pierson, *Tocqueville in America* (1938; Baltimore: Johns Hopkins Univ. Press, 1996), 119.

23. Robert Fagles and W. B. Stanford, "Introductory Essay," *Aeschylus: The Oresteia* (New York: Penguin, 1977), 69–70.

24. John Patrick Diggins, *The Promise of Pragmatism: Modernity and the Crisis of Knowledge and Authority* (Chicago: Univ. of Chicago Press, 1994).

CHAPTER THREE

1. Bertrand D. Wolfe, *Strange Communists I Have Known* (New York: Bantam Books, 1967), 11–35.

2. EON to Louise Bryant (n.d., 1918–1919, Provincetown); these letters along with some poems were discovered by Professor Paul Roazen in the papers of diplomat William C. Bullitt, in the latter's papers in the Beinecke Library, Yale University. Bullitt became the husband of Louise Bryant, and they lived together in Europe before divorcing in the early thirties.

3. EON to Bennett Cerf, June 15, 1940, *SLON,* 506.

4. EON to Harry Winberger, Jan. 11, 1940, *SLON,* 496–97.

5. Quoted in Irving Howe, *Politics and the Novel* (Cleveland: Meridian, 1957), 15.

6. "The Earth Is the Limit," n.d., EON mss., Box 45.

7. Quoted in Croswell Bowen, *The Curse of the Misbegotten,* 315–16.

8. Malcolm Cowley, "A Weekend with Eugene O'Neill," *ONHP,* 41–49.

9. Dorothy Day quoted in Louis Sheaffer, *O'Neill: Son and Playwright* (Boston: Little, Brown, 1968), 403–404.

10. Friedrich Nietzsche, *The Genealogy of Morals and Ecco Homo* (New York: Vintage, 1989), 130.

11. EON to Jessica Rippin, May 7, 1914, *SLON,* 21–24.

12. Joel Pfister, *Staging Depth: Eugene O'Neill and the Politics of Psychological Discourse* (Chapel Hill: Univ. of North Carolina Press, 1995).

13. H. L. Mencken, *Nietzsche* (1913; Baltimore: Johns Hopkins Univ. Press, 1993), 236.

14. A thorough investigation of this subject may be found in Winifred L. Frazer, *E.G. and E.O.: Emma Goldman and The Iceman Cometh* (Gainesville: Univ. of Florida Press, 1974).

15. Reinhold Niebuhr, *Children of Light, Children of Darkness* (New York: Scribners, 1944), 86.

16. Jean Paul Sartre, *Being and Nothingness* (1956; New York: Citadel, 2001), 340.

17. Emma Goldman, "The Tragedy of Women's Emancipation," in *The Feminist Papers: From Adams to de Beauvoir,* ed. Alice S. Rossi (1973; Boston: Northeastern Univ. Press, 1988), 508–16.

18. EON to Benjamin De Casseres, June 22, 1927, *SLON,* 245–46.

19. The anarchist who has wrestled with this issue is the late philosopher Gilles Deleuze; see his *Nietzsche and Philosophy,* trans. Hugh Tomlinson (1962; New York: Columbia Univ. Press, 1983); see also *Philosophy and Desire,* ed. Hugh J. Silverman (New York: Routledge, 2000).

20. EON to George Jean Nathan, Jan. 2, 1933, *SLON,* 161.

21. Quoted in Travis Bogard, *From the Silence of Tao House: Essays About Eugene and Carlotta O'Neill and the Tao House Plays* (Danville, Calif.: Eugene O'Neill Foundation, 1993), 109–111; Barrett H. Clark, *Eugene O'Neill: The Man and His Plays* (1926; New York: Dover, 1947), 84–85.

22. EON to Alexander Berkman, Jan. 29, 1927, *SLON,* 232–33; Bruce Mann, "The FBI Memorandum on O'Neill," *EONR,* 15 (1991), 59–64.

23. Quoted in Clark, *O'Neill,* 84.

24. Quoted in Doris Alexander, "Eugene O'Neill as Social Critic," in *ONHP*, 390–407. Alexander's essay, which first appeared in the *American Quarterly* a half-century ago (1954), still remains one of the most astute analyses of O'Neill's social thought.

25. Carol Bird, "Eugene O'Neill—The Inner Man," first appeared in *Theatre Magazine* (June 1924), reprinted in *CWON*, 50–55.

CHAPTER FOUR

1. Niall Ferguson, *Empire: The Rise and Demise of the British World Order and the Lessons for Global Power* (New York: Basic Books, 2002); Robert J. Bliwise, "American Imperialism," *Duke Magazine*, 89 (Mar.-Apr. 2003), 34–41. I am indebted to Linda Ben-Zvi for knowledge of Carlotta Monterey's role in *Bird of Paradise* from a paper she delivered to an O'Neill conference in Tours in June 2003.

2. "French Revolution Dates," EON mss., Box 77.

3. Karl Schriftgisser, "Interview with O'Neill," *New York Times,* Oct. 6, 1946.

4. Travis Bogard, *Contours in Time: The Plays of Eugene O'Neill* (rev. ed., New York: Oxford Univ. Press, 1988), xv.

5. Normand Berlin, *O'Neill's Shakespeare* (Ann Arbor: Univ. of Michigan Press, 1993).

6. EON to Malcolm Mollan, Dec. 3, 1921, *SLON,* 158–60.

7. "Work Diary," Sept. 3, 1939, EON mss., Box 78.

8. Oswald Spengler, *The Decline of the West* (1926; New York: Knopf, 1939), II, 469–96.

9. Mary B. Mullett, "The Extraordinary Story of Eugene O'Neill," *CWON,* 26–37.

10. EON to Sister Mary Leo, Feb. 6, 1925, *SLON,* 192–93.

11. Edward Said, *Orientalism* (New York: Vintage, 1979), 1–110.

12. John Larner, *Marco Polo and the Discovery of the World* (New Haven: Yale Univ. Press, 2001). Larson informs us that Marco Polo was an outsider who went about his trying adventures with a "stoical silence" and carried out his tasks and wrote his journal "with no easily identifiable self-interest at stake" (p. 183).

13. John Mason Brown, "Marco Millions," in *ONHP,* 181–183.

14. EON to Kenneth Macgowan, Mar. 18, 1921, *SLON,* 150–51; and Mar. 29 and Apr. 8, 1921, in *The Theatre We Worked For,* ed. Travis Bogard and Jackson R. Bryer, 21–24; Louis Shaeffer, *O'Neill: Son and Artist,* 52–54.

15. Quoted in Bogard, *Contour in Time,* 233–34.

16. Agnes Boulton, *Part of a Long Story: Eugene O'Neill as a Young Man in Love* (Garden City, N.Y.: Doubleday, 1958), 61.

17. James A. Robinson, *Eugene O'Neill and Oriental Thought: A Divided Vision* (Carbondale: Southern Illinois Univ. Press, 1982).

CHAPTER FIVE

1. EON to Grace Dupre Hills, Mar. 21, 1925, *SLON,* 194–95.

2. EON to Mr. Perlman, Feb. 5, 1925, *SLON,* 192.

3. EON to Kenneth Macgowan, Aug. 19, 1924, *SLON,* 189–90.

4. Friedrich Nietzsche, *The Gay Science,* trans. Walter Kaufmann (New York: Vintage, 1974), 88–89.

5. Hannah Arendt, *Love and Saint Augustine,* trans. Joanna Vecchiarelli Scott and Judith Chelius Stark (1929; Chicago: Univ. of Chicago Press, 1996).

6. Tocqueville, *Democracy,* 628.

7. George Wilson Pearson, *Tocqueville in America* (1937; Baltimore: Johns Hopkins, 1996), 158–59.

8. Tocqueville, *Democracy,* 631.

9. EON to George Jean Nathan, in *"As Ever, Gene": The Letters of Eugene O'Neill to George Jean Nathan,* ed. Nancy L. Roberts and Arthur W. Roberts (Madison, N.J.: Farleigh Dickinson Univ. Press, 1987), 53–54.

10. EON to Barrett H. Clark, n.d.; to Kenneth Macgowan, Dec. 28, 1938; to John Mason Brown, n.d.; to Lawrence Langner, n.d., EON mss., Boxes 1 and 2.

11. Arthur and Barbara Gelb, *O'Neill,* 938.

12. I am much indebted to the late Donald C. Gallup for his valuable *Eugene O'Neill and His Eleven-Play Cycle* (New Haven: Yale Univ. Press, 1998).

13. *Eugene O'Neill at Work: Newly Released Ideas-for Plays,* ed. Virginia Floyd (New York: Ungar, 1981), 251–55.

14. "Robespierre: An Interpretation," n.d., EON mss., Box 77.

15. EON to Lawrence Langer, Aug. 12, 1936 *SLON,* 452; Hamilton Basso, "Profiles: The Tragic Sense," *CWON,* 224–36.

16. There have been, of course, interpretations of America by Catholic intellectuals, especially Orestes A. Brownson in the nineteenth century and Garry Wills in the twentieth. But O'Neill is closer to Tocqueville, another Catholic whose lapsed religion is more agony than faith.

17. Quoted in Joshua Mitchell, *The Fragility of Freedom: Tocqueville on Religion, Democracy, and the American Future* (Chicago: Univ. of Chicago Press, 1995), 80.

CHAPTER SIX

1. EON to Lawrence Langner, Aug. 12, 1936, *SLON,* 452.

2. Jane Austen, *Pride and Prejudice* (1813; New York: Penguin, 1972), 67.

3. Friedrich Nietzsche, *Genealogy of Morals and Ecce Homo,* ed. and trans. Walter Kaufmann (New York: Vintage, 1967), 232.

4. *Tocqueville in America,* ed. George Wilson Pierson (1938; Baltimore: Johns Hopkins Univ. Press, 1996), 91–92.

5. See Roger Boesche, "Hedonism and Nihilism: The Predictions of Tocqueville and Nietzsche," *The Tocqueville Review/La Revue Tocqueville,* 8 (1986–1987), 165–85.

6. Ann Douglas, *The Feminization of American Culture* (New York: Knopf, 1977); George Santayana, "The Genteel Tradition in American Philosophy," in *Santayana on America,* ed. Richard Colton Lyon (New York: Harcourt, 1968), 36–56. That sexual identities actually merge in the play renders even more complicated the feminization

thesis; see the astute analysis by Laurin Porter, "The Banished Prince Revisited: A Feminist Reading of *More Stately Mansions," EONR,* 19 (1995), 7–28.

7. Margaret Gilman Bower, ed., "Introduction," *Eugene O'Neill's More Stately Mansions: The Unexpurgated Edition* (New York: Oxford, 1988), 3–19.

8. *Tocqueville in America,* 71.

9. Joshua Mitchell, *The Fragility of Freedom: Tocqueville on Religion, Democracy, and the American Future* (Chicago: Univ. of Chicago Press, 1995).

10. Tocqueville, *Democracy,* 433.

11. Ibid., 536–38.

12. Karl Marx, "Economic and Philosophic Manuscripts of 1844," in *The Marx-Engels Reader,* ed. Robert C. Tucker (New York: Norton, 1978), 133–35.

13. *Social Theories of Jacksonian Democracy,* ed. Joseph Blau (Indianapolis: Bobbs-Merrill, 1954), 21–37, 183–98; *Ideology and Power in the Age of Jackson,* ed. Edwin C. Rozwenc (Garden City, N.Y.: Anchor, 1964), 3–90.

14. Charles Sellers, *The Market Revolution: Jacksonian America, 1815–1846* (New York: Oxford, 1991), 3–69.

15. Tocqueville, *Democracy,* 403.

16. Ralph Waldo Emerson, "Self-Reliance," *The Selected Writings of Ralph Waldo Emerson,* ed. Brooks Atkinson (New York: Modern Library, 1992), 132–53.

17. Tocqueville, *Democracy,* 586–89.

CHAPTER SEVEN

1. I am paraphrasing the critique of James Baldwin, in *Notes of a Native Son* and elsewhere in his writings, and that of other black scholars.

2. Kenneth Burke, *Philosophy of Literary Form* (Berkeley: Univ. of California Press, 1974), 361.

3. Quoted in "Notes," *Opportunity,* 2 (Apr. 1924), 114.

4. Iver Bernstein, *The New York City Draft Riots: Their Significance for American Society and Politics in the Age of the Civil War* (New York: Oxford, 1990). See also the insightful novel by Peter Quinn, *Banished Children of Eve* (New York: Penguin, 1994).

5. "Negro Play," n.d., EON mss., Box 77; see also *Eugene O'Neill at Work,* ed. Virginia Floyd, 175–76.

6. Orlando Patterson, *Slavery and Social Death: A Comparative Study* (Cambridge: Harvard Univ. Press, 1982).

7. Deborah Wood Holton, "Revealing Blindness, Revealing Vision: Interpreting O'Neill's Black Female Characters," *EONR,* 19 (1995), 29–44.

8. See Adolph L. Reed, Jr., *W. E. B. Du Bois and American Political Thought: Fabianism and the Color Line* (New York: Oxford, 1997).

9. W. E. B. Du Bois, *The Souls of Black Folk* (1903; New York: Dover, 1994), 2–3.

10. O'Neill almost never allowed anyone to change lines in his plays or experiment with settings or scenes that departed from his explicit stage directions. Gilpin was so bold as to try variations on his own lines, which brought out an ire in O'Neill that resulted in racist remarks. With other plays there arose the implication that O'Neill's

knowledge of black life in America was inadequate in both characterization and vernacular. Paul Robeson, however, respected O'Neill's fidelity to detail and when arranging for a production of *Jones* in 1940, he asked O'Neill's permission to use a Hammond organ to accompany the drum beat so as to "enhance atmosphere and mood without obtruding on text or action." Paul Robeson to Eugene O'Neill, July 31, 1940, EON mss., Box 8.

11. Gabriele Poole is skeptical of the religious interpretation in the valuable "'Blarsted Niggers!': The Emperor Jones and Modernism's Encounter with Africa," *EONR,* 18 (1994), 21–37.

12. Travis Bogard, *Contour in Time,* 139.

13. *The Life and Selected Writings of Thomas Jefferson,* ed. Adrienne Koch and William Peden (New York: Modern Library, 1944), 278.

14. Arthur and Barbara Gelb, *O'Neill,* 551.

15. T. S. Eliot, "All God's Chillun Got Wings," in *ONHP,* 168–69.

16. Doris V. Falk, *Eugene O'Neill and the Tragic Tension* (New Brunswick: Rutgers Univ. Press, 1958), 90.

17. Quoted in Richard Brucher, "O'Neill, Othello, and Robeson," *EONR,* 18 (1994), 45–58.

18. Paul Robeson, "Reflections on O'Neill's Plays," *Opportunity,* Dec. 1924, 368–70.

CHAPTER EIGHT

1. Henry Adams, *The Education of Henry Adams* (New York: Modern Library, 1930), 353; Simone de Beauvoir, *The Second Sex* (1952; New York: Vintage, 1989), xii; H. L. Mencken, *In Defense of Women* (New York: Star Books, 1922), 210.

2. Richard Ellmann, *Oscar Wilde* (New York: Knopf, 1988), 9

3. Mabel Dodge Luhan, *Intimate Memoirs,* vol. 3, *Movers and Shakers* (New York: Kraus, 1936), 39, 83.

4. Joseph Wood Krutch, *The Modern Temper* (New York: Harcourt, 1929), 1–38, 58–78. Whereas Krutch believed that science destroyed the illusion of love, Floyd Dell, a Greenwich village comrade of O'Neill, expected that science would expose the neurosis that stood in the way of its fulfillment; see Floyd Dell, *Love in the Machine Age* (New York: Farrar and Rinehart, 1930).

5. Nietzsche, quoted by Gilles Deleuze in "Nomad Thought," in *The New Nietzsche,* ed. David B. Allison (Cambridge: MIT Press, 1985), 164.

6. O'Neill's remarks to Macgowan are quoted in Margaret Ranald's unpublished paper, "Carlotta Monterey"; EON to Kenneth Macgowan, Feb. 22, 1928, *SLON,* 177–78; EON to Mike Gold, Aug. 15, 1928, *SLON,* 308.

7. Nathan quoted in *CWON,* 123.

8. "Nietzsche Quotations," n.d., EON mss., Box 77.

9. Quoted in Arthur and Barbara Gelb, *O'Neill,* 367.

10. The correspondence with Beatrice Ashe is in *SLON,* 27–74.

11. The EON-Louise Bryant letters, not dated, were discovered by Paul Roazen in the papers of William C. Bullitt, Beinecke Library, Yale University. Bullitt had

been ambassador to Russia at the time of the Bolshevik Revolution, and he later married Louise Bryant. Roazen was a professor of political theory who became interested in Bullitt because of his collaboration with Sigmund Freud on a psychoanalytic interpretation of the presidency of Woodrow Wilson. All O'Neill scholars are indebted to Professor Roazen, who passed away in 2005, for these letters.

12. Emma Goldman, "The Tragedy of Women's Emancipation," in *The Feminist Papers: From Adams to de Beauvoir,* ed. Alice S. Rossi (1973; Boston: Northeastern Univ. Press, 1988), 506–17.

13. Ralph Waldo Emerson, "Fate," in *Ralph Waldo Emerson: Selected Prose and Poetry,* ed. Reginald L. Cook (New York: Rinehart, 1966), 254–82.

14. See the special issue on "O'Neill and Gender," edited by Bette Mandl, *EONR,* 19 (Spring/Fall 1995).

15. F. Scott Fitzgerald, *The Crack Up* (New York: New Directions, 1956), 297.

16. EON to Louis Kanter, Jan. 28, 1921, *SLON,* 146.

17. O'Neill, "Damn the Optimists!" *ONHP,* 104–106.

18. *New York Times,* Apr. 11, 1920.

19. Denis de Rougemont, *Love in the Western World,* trans. Montgomery Belgium (1946; New York: Pantheon, 1956), 282.

20. EON to George Jean Nathan, Feb. 1, 1921, in *"As Ever, Gene,"* ed. Nancy L. Roberts and Arthur W. Roberts, 44.

21. Travis Bogard, "Anna Christie: Her Fall and Rise," in *O'Neill: A Collection of Critical Essays,* ed. John Gassner (Englewood Cliffs, N.J.: Prentice Hall, 1964), 62–71.

22. "Ideas, Scenarios, Notes, 1920s–30s," EON mss., Box 77

23. Paul Roazen used to try to persuade me that O'Neill's character Nina Leeds was based on Louise Bryant. The time period of World War I is the right context, and Louise lost her husband John Reed at the conclusion of the war. But the differences between the two women are telling. Whereas Louise was unfaithful in having affairs with O'Neill and others, Nina is devoted to her fiancé, and has affairs only after he is killed in the war. Moreover, after the deaths of the men, the two women go on to lead entirely different lives. Louise had a brief, troubled marriage with ambassador Bullitt, was divorced, turned to alcohol and drugs, and was seen stumbling around Paris before she died in 1936. Nina's life, in contrast, is a study not in dissipation but in utter control.

24. Quoted in John H. Houcin, "Eugene O'Neill's 'Woman Play' in Boston," *EONR,* 22 (1998), 48–62; see also Bette Mandl, "Gender Design in Eugene O'Neill's *Strange Interlude,*" *EONR,* 19 (Spring/Fall 1995), 123–28; Otis W. Winchester, "History in Literature: Eugene O'Neill's *Strange Interlude* as a Transcript of America in the 1920s," *Literature and History,* ed. I. E. Cadenhead, Jr. (Tulsa: Univ. of Tulsa Press, 1970), 43–58.

CHAPTER NINE

1. See the valuable study by Edward L. Shaughnessy, *Down the Nights and Down the Days: Eugene O'Neill's Catholic Sensibility* (Notre Dame, Ind.: Univ. of Notre Dame

Press, 1996). Stephen Black has pointed out to me that the story of young O'Neill on the stairs struggling with his father has been repeated in the literature but, while it may have been told by the playwright to an interviewer, it has not been documented. Myself once a young falling-away Catholic, I would like to believe the story is true.

2. A conversational remark made to Joseph Wood Krutch, used in his "Introduction" to *Nine Plays by Eugene O'Neill* and reprinted in *ONHP,* 115.

3. Croswell Bowen, "The Black Irishman," in *ONHP,* 64–84.

4. Day quoted in Shaughnessy, *Down the Nights and Down the Days,* 7.

5. EON to Sister Mary Leo, Mar. 26, 1929, *SLON,* 332–33.

6. *The Writings of William James,* ed. John J. McDermott (New York: Modern Library, 1968), 717–34.

7. EON to Richard Dana Skinner, Feb. 1934, Box 8, EON mss.

8. Eugene O'Neill, "Tomorrow," *O'Neill: Complete Plays,* ed. Travis Bogard (New York: Library of America, 1988), III, 952.

9. Joseph Wood Krutch, *The Modern Temper* (New York: Harcourt, 1929), 153.

10. Cyrus Day, "The Iceman and the Bridegroom," *Modern Drama,* 1 (1958), 3–9; Travis Bogard discusses skeptically the "Last Supper" theme in *Contour in Time,* 417–19.

11. EON to George Jean Nathan, Aug. 26, 1928, in *"As Ever, Gene,"* ed. Nancy L. Roberts and Arthur W. Roberts, 83–86.

12. Brenda Murphy, "Fetishizing the Dynamo: Henry Adams and Eugene O'Neill," *EONR,* 16 (1992), 85–90.

13. EON to Saxe Commins, Apr. 1929, in *"Love and Admiration and Respect": The O'Neill-Commins Correspondence,* ed. Dorothy Commins (Durham: Duke Univ. Press, 1986), 50–51.

14. Quoted in Walter Kauffmann, *The Portable Nietzsche* (New York: Viking, 1954), 285.

15. Conor Cruise O'Brien, *Maria Cross: Imaginative Patterns in a Group of Modern Catholic Writers* (New York: Oxford Univ. Press, 1952), 251.

16. *The Confessions of St. Augustine,* trans. John K. Ryan (New York: Image Books, 1960), 97–99.

17. See Doris Alexander, *Eugene O'Neill's Creative Struggle: The Decisive Decade, 1924–1933* (University Park: Pennsylvania State Univ. Press, 1992), 86–88.

18. Quoted in Virginia Floyd, *The Plays of Eugene O'Neill: A New Assessment* (New York: Ungar, 1985), 333.

19. EON to Arthur Hobson, May 29, 1927, *SLON,* 245.

20. Bogard, *Contour in Time,* 286–87.

21. Reinhold Niebuhr, *The Nature and Destiny of Man* (New York: Scribner, 1944), II, 293.

22. Shaughnessy develops his thesis from O'Neill's remark about all his plays dealing with sin and redemption. *Down the Nights and Down the Days,* 1–52.

23. Louis Shaeffer, *O'Neill: Son and Artist,* 412.

24. EON to Mr. Danda [?], ca. 1934; and to William E. Brooks, Mar. 5, 1934, EON mss., Box 1.

CHAPTER TEN

1. Joseph Wood Krutch, *The Modern Temper* (New York: Harcourt, 1929), 79–97.

2. Tocqueville, *Democracy,* 536–38.

3. EON to Arthur Hobson Quinn, Apr. 3, 1925, *SLON,* 195.

4. O'Neill, "Damn the Optimists!" *ONHP,* 104–106.

5. Alfred Kazin, *On Native Grounds: An Interpretation of Modern American Prose Literature* (San Diego: Harcourt Brace, 1995).

6. Quoted in Arthur and Barbara Gelb, *O'Neill: Life with Monte Cristo* (New York: Applause, 2000), 638.

7. Mary B. Mullett, "The Extraordinary Story of Eugene O'Neill," *CWON,* 26–37; Malcolm Mollan, "Making Plays with a Tragic End: An Intimate Interview with Eugene O'Neill," *CWON,* 13–20; Joseph Wood Krutch, "Tragedy: Eugene O'Neill," in *The American Drama Since 1918* (New York: Harcourt, 1939), 75–133.

8. Tocqueville, *Democracy,* 493.

9. Quoted in Arthur and Barbara Gelb, *Life with Monte Cristo,* 814.

10. O'Neill, quoted in *"Love and Admiration and Respect,"* ed. Dorothy Commins, 79.

11. Quoted in Barrett H. Clark, *O'Neill: The Man and His Plays* (New York: McBride, 1929), 136.

12. Louis Shaeffer, *O'Neill: Son and Artist,* 244–45; Arthur H. Nethercot, ""The Psychoanalyzing of Eugene O'Neill," *Modern Drama,* 16 (1973), 35–48.

13. Tocqueville, *Democracy,* 493.

14. John P. Diggins, *The Lost Soul of American Politics: Virtue, Self-Interests, and the Foundations of Liberalism* (New York: Basic, 1984).

15. *The Federalist,* no. 31; see also the valuable analysis by John Alvis, "On the American Line: O'Neill's *Mourning Becomes Electra* and the Principles of the Founding," *The Southern Review,* 22 (Winter 1986), 69–82.

16. Aeschylus, *The Oresteia,* trans. Robert Fagels, ed. and introd. W. B. Stanford (New York: Penguin, 1977), 274.

17. Walter Lippmann, *A Preface to Morals* (New York: MacMillan, 1929), 3.

18. *Eugene O'Neill at Work,* ed. Virginia Floyd, 281–98; Edmund Burke, *A Philosophical Inquiry into the Origins of Our Ideas of the Sublime and Beautiful* (London: Univ. of Notre Dame Press, 1968), 37.

19. The drama critic Stark Young's response to a previous play, quoted by Kenneth Tynan, who reviewed *Long Day's Journey* in the London *Observer,* excerpted in *File on O'Neill,* ed. Stephen Black (London: Methuen, 1993), 77–78.

20. Friedrich Nietzsche, *The Birth of Tragedy and The Genealogy of Morals,* trans. Francis Golffing (Garden City, N.Y.: Doubleday Anchor, 1956), 192–93.

CHAPTER ELEVEN

1. John P. Diggins, *Up from Communism: Conservative Odysseys in American Intellectual History* (New York: Harper, 1975).

2. Hamilton Basso, "Profiles: The Tragic Sense," *CWON,* 224–36.

3. EON to Lawrence Langer, May 13, 1944, *SLON,* 555–57.

4. Arthur Schopenhauer, *The World as Will and Idea,* trans. T. B. Haldane and J. Kemp (1883; London: Routledge & Kegan Paul, 1948), 1, 336.

5. EON to Kenneth Macgowan, Dec. 30, 1940, in *The Theatre We Worked For,* ed. Travis Bogard and Jackson R. Bryer, 256–58.

6. "*Love and Admiration and Respect,*" ed. Dorothy Commins, 3.

7. George Santayana, *The Sense of Beauty* (New York: Dover, 1985), 39.

8. Thomas Jefferson to Sanuel Kercheval, July 12, 1816, in *The Life and Selected Writings of Thomas Jefferson,* ed. Adrienne Koch and William Peden (New York: Modern Library, 1944), 673–76.

9. David Hume, *Essays Moral, Political and Literary,* ed. T. H. Green and T. H. Grose (London, 1898), II, 316.

10. Quoted in Roger Shattuck, *Proust's Way: A Field Guide in Search of Lost Time* (New York: Norton, 2000), 122.

11. Freidrich Nietzsche, "On the Uses and Disadvantages of History," in *Untimely Meditations,* ed. Daniel Breazeale, trans. R. J. Hollingdale (1873; New York: Cambridge Univ. Press, 1997), 57–124.

12. "Work Diary," Aug. 31, 1939, EON mss., Box 78.

13. Quoted in Arthur and Barbara Gelb, *O'Neill: Life with Monte Cristo,* 511–515.

14. EON to George Jean Nathan, May 13, 1939, *SLON,* 486–87.

15. Quoted in *The Theatre We Worked For,* 257; for some of this treatment I am indebted to Michael Hinden, "'The Right Kind of Pity': Notes on O'Neill's Revisions for *The Iceman Cometh*" (paper delivered to the International Eugene O'Neill Conference, Bermuda, 1998).

16. Freidrich Nietzsche, *The Anti-Christ,* trans. H. L. Mencken (Tucson: See Sharp Press, 1999), 24–25.

17. Conor Cruise O'Brien, "Graham Greene: The Anatomy of Pity," Chapter 2 in *Maria Cross: Imaginative Patterns in a Group of Modern Catholic Writers* (New York: Oxford Univ. Press, 1952), 63–94. (O'Brien's book was published under the pseudonym "Donar O'Donnell.")

18. Stefan Zweig, *Beware of Pity,* trans. Phyllis and Trevor Blewitt (London: Pushkin Press, 2000), 250.

19. Reinhold Niebuhr, *An Interpretation of Christian Ethics* (New York: Meridian Books, 1956), 201.

20. Quoted in George Allen Morgan, *What Nietzsche Meant* (New York: Harper, 1941), 149–50.

21. Ralph Waldo Emerson, "New England Reformers," in *The Portable Emerson,* ed. Mark Van Doren (New York: Viking, 1946), 110–36.

22. Hannah Arendt, *On Revolution* (New York: Viking, 1962), 84.

23. Anatoly Lunacharsky, "A Portrait," in *Maxim Gorky,* trans. Alex Miller (Moscow: Progress, n.d.), I, 10.

24. Karl Marx, "Economic and Philosophical Manuscripts of 1844," in *The Marx-Engels Reader,* ed. Robert C. Tucker (New York: Norton, 1978), 283–337.

25. See, for example, Max Horkheimer, "The End of Reason," in *The Essential Frankfurt School Reader,* ed. Andrew Arato and Eike Gebhart (New York: Continuum,

1993), 26–48, and James Burnham, *The Managerial Revolution* (New York: John Day, 1940); on Dewey and World War II, see John Patrick Diggins, *The Promise of Pragmatism: Modernism and the Crisis of Knowledge and Authority* (Chicago: Univ. of Chicago Press, 1994), 250–79.

26. EON to Eugene O'Neill Jr., Aug. 13, 1944, *SLON,* 562–63.

27. EON to George Jean Nathan, Aug. 2, 1940, in *"As Ever, Gene,"* ed. Nancy L. Roberts and Arthur W. Roberts, 205–06; EON to Saxe Commins, Oct. 31, 1939, in *"Love and Admiration and Respect,"* 184–85.

28. EON to L. F. Gittler, Oct. 23, 1942, *SLON,* 534–35.

29. EON to Eugene O'Neill Jr., June 1, 1942, *SLON,* 528–39; EON to George Jean Nathan, Oct. 24, 1942, in *"As Ever, Gene,"* 219–20.

30. EON to Sophus Keith Winther, Dec. 26, 1944, *SLON,* 538–40.

CONCLUSION

1. EON, "What the Theatre Means to Me," *ONHP,* 107.

2. Tocqueville, *Democracy,* 507; see also Daniel J. Boorstin, *The Lost World of Thomas Jefferson* (Boston: Beacon, 1948).

3. EON to Benjamin De Casseres, *SLON,* 316–18.

4. Tocqueville, *Democracy,* 611–12.

5. See the valuable "Introductory Essay" by Robert Fagles and W. B. Stanford, *The Oresteia* (New York: Penguin, 1977), 13–97.

6. Peter J. Euban, *The Tragedy of Political Theory: The Road Not Taken* (Princeton: Princeton Univ. Press, 1990), 268–72.

7. See, for example, Maria T. Miliora, *Narcissism, the Family, and Madness: A Self-Psychological Study of Eugene O'Neill and His Plays* (New York: Peter Lang, 2000).

8. Mary B. Mullett, "The Extraordinary Story of Eugene O'Neill," *CWON,* 26–37.

9. EON, "Memoranda on Masks," *ONHP,* 116–22.

Index

Christianity (*continued*)
    about suffering, 186. *See also*
    Calvinism; Puritanism; Roman
    Catholicism
Christophe, Henri, 144
Cicero, 1
Civilization in the United States (Stearn),
    23, 270n17
Civil War: betrayal in, 243; conflict of
    right against right in, 15; as about
    different concepts of property, 103;
    draft riots of 1863, 139; as failure of
    American system of government for
    Adams, 219–20; as family war, 212;
    Mourning Becomes Electra and, xv, 212,
    216–17, 218–21; as Yankee-Cavalier
    confrontation, 219
Clansman, The (Dixon), 138
Clark, Barrett H., 62–63, 106, 217–18
class: and draft riots of 1863, 139; as in
    flux in America, 102, 130; Jacksonian
    democracy and, 116. *See also* class
    consciousness; middle class;
    working class (proletariat)
class consciousness: defeat of Hitler
    requiring more than, 232; Marx on,
    34; in *Moon for the Misbegotten,* 222;
    O'Neill as skeptical about masses
    rising to, 35, 36, 75, 76, 258; socialist
    assumption that masses can rise to,
    35, 72
classical philosophy: Aristotle, 5, 23,
    42–43, 112, 238, 265; in *Days Without
    End,* 203; as moral force, 45; on
    overcoming desire, 42, 50; on
    politics, 221
cold war, xiii, 232
Columbus, Christopher, 87–88, 91
Comanescu, Petre, 47
Commins, Saxe, 193, 239
communism: Bolsheviks, 60, 68, 76, 78,
    203; cold war, xiii, 232; in *Days
    Without End,* 203; Lenin on
    withering away of the state in, 60;
    Marco Millions and, 87; Marx on
    crude, 254; O'Neill and John Reed,
    24, 35, 51; O'Neill on, xiv, 34–35, 52,

76, 255; postwar successes in Europe,
    232; Spanish Civil War and, 232. *See
    also* Soviet Union
Confident Years, The (Brooks), 143
Conrad, Joseph, 20, 147
conscience, 84, 123
consciousness, problem of, 40
conservatism: on desire, 50, 64; on life
    as struggle, 257; and O'Neill's later
    political opinions, 52; on the past,
    242; Reaganism, 52, 104
Constitution of the United States, 219,
    220, 256, 261
Contempt (Moravia), 215–16
Cooper, James Fenimore, 132
Count of Monte Cristo, The (Fechter), 14,
    22, 43, 243
Cowley, Malcolm, 23, 56, 270n17
Crane, Hart, 23
critical theory, 254
culture, high versus low, 33, 37
cummings, e. e., 58
cycle project (O'Neill), 105–9; "And
    Give Me Death," 108; "The Calms
    of Capricorn," 107–8; "The Career
    of Bessie Bowen," 108; difficulties
    of, 28, 106; "The Greed of the
    Meek," 108, 109; as history of a
    family, 111–12, 127; Leda Cade
    character, 108; manuscripts
    destroyed, 106, 107; O'Neill's
    preparatory reading for, 109; "The
    Rights of Man 1775," 254;
    Shakespeare's tetralogies compared
    with, 81; spiritual undertheme of,
    115; surviving parts of, 111; as "A Tale
    of Possessors Self-Dispossessed,"
    105, 128, 265; "Twilight of
    Possessors-Dispossessed," 131–32.
    See also *More Stately Mansions; Touch
    of the Poet, A*

Darwinism, 184, 190–91
Davies, Howard, xii
Day, Dorothy, 21, 56, 185
Days Without End (O'Neill): on
    Americans losing sense of freedom,

entail, 102

equality: and American fondness for nobility, 117; and dueling in *A Touch of the Poet*, 116; Emerson and Tocqueville concerned about, 23; Jefferson's egalitarianism, 122; rural life associated with, 173; Tocqueville on status and, 131; and tragedy of frustration, 209

eternal recurrence, 21, 92, 195

Euripides, 5

Exile's Return (Cowley), 270n17

existentialism, 236

Falk, Doris, 155

false consciousness, 72, 75, 84

family: Aeschylus's *Oresteia* and, 216; Civil War as family war, 212; as fate in O'Neill plays, 221; in *Mourning Becomes Electra*, 212, 216, 219; O'Neill's cycle project as history of a, 111–12, 127; as subject of O'Neill plays, xiv; Tocqueville on American, 134. *See also* O'Neill family

Farrell, James T., 11

fatalism, historical, 259

Federalists, xiv, 3, 104, 220, 258–59, 261

feminism: on *Diff'rent*, 168–69; Ibsen and, 166; on marriage, 169; and *Strange Interlude*, 181; as subject of O'Neill plays, xiv, 19; and *Welded*, 169; when O'Neill arrived on theatrical scene, 158, 166, 181; on women in work force, 170

feminization of American culture, 119

Ferguson, Francis, 32

Fernandez, William (Spanish Willie), 56

Finnegan's Wake (Joyce), 40

Fiske, John, 88

Fitzgerald, F. Scott, 15, 55, 158, 167, 177, 222, 270n17

Flowering of New England, The (Brooks), 120

Fordism, 74

Fountain, The (O'Neill), 87–93; as continuous with American history, 94; and death, 236; desire as positive in, 4; lust for gold in, 95; O'Neill's idea in writing, 90; Ponce de Leon, 88–89, 90, 91–92

Frankfurt school, 254

Franklin, Ben, 45

"Fratricide" (O'Neill), 57–58

freedom: America as land of the free, 4, 9, 109, 112, 253; Americans lacking concepts to guide it, 42; anarchists on, 35; democracy and authentic, 233; democracy distinguished from, 4; desire as playing havoc with, 3, 8, 15, 44–45, 256, 261; formal, 261; the future required for, 48; as giving way to possession, 127–28; individual versus social conception of, 60; institutional, 131; in liberalism, 43, 234; mental suffering resulting from, 8; in *Mourning Becomes Electra*, 219; Nietzsche on, 60; O'Neill on free will, 111; O'Neill on human aspiration for, 255; as power in America, 3, 8; and private property, 120; state rights and, 123; the state seen as antithesis to, 104; totalitarian threat to, 231; wealth and power seen as means to, 122; will of majority versus individual, 123; women as renouncing their own, 181

free love, 25, 167, 234

free market, 258. *See also* capitalism

Freud, Sigmund: *Beyond the Pleasure Principle*, 218; on desire, 271n13; man no longer in center of universe for, 196; O'Neill influenced by, 5, 38, 39; seen as intellectual emancipator, 64, 100; *Totem and Taboo*, 218. *See also* Freudianism

Freudianism: and *Diff'rent*, 168; extirpation of religion sought by, 190; Freudian criticism of O'Neill, 5–6; and *Mourning Becomes Electra*, 217–18; popular allusions to in the twenties, 177; on repressed drives, 26. *See also* psychoanalysis

Irish (*continued*)
history, 39–40; Con Melody of *A Touch of the Poet,* 113; in cycle project, 115; as driven off land in old country, 17, 173; O'Neill as Black Irishmen, 185–86; James O'Neill on immigrant experience, 13–14, 16; O'Neill's Irish ancestry and family, 11–16, 111; squandered lives as curse of, 222; and suffering, 30
I.W.W. (Industrial Workers of the World; Wobblies), 24, 50, 65–69, 73, 253

Jackson, Andrew: Bank of the United States vetoed by, 133; in *More Stately Mansions,* 120, 123, 260; in *A Touch of the Poet,* 46, 113, 114, 116, 262. *See also* Jacksonian democracy
Jacksonian democracy: equality and tragedy of frustration in, 209; as freeing Americans from interference and domination, 120; in *More Stately Mansions,* 123, 133; rural life associated with, 173; as shaping future of republic, 116; spoils system of, 113, 120; traditional view of, 122
James, William, 33, 38, 80, 123, 142, 185, 186
Jefferson, Thomas: children by Sally Hemings, 149; on consequences of slavery, 148; on each generation as sovereign, 241–42, 259; egalitarian humanism of, 122; on government as threat to property, 104; and *Mourning Becomes Electra,* 219; and natural right versus popular sovereignty, 123; O'Neill plans play on, 104, 107; promise of equality as leading to tragedy, 208–9; replacing "property" with "happiness" in Declaration of Independence, 102; in Virginia dynasty, 220
Jeffersonianism, 57, 106, 170, 221, 259
Jenkins, Kathleen (wife), 20, 161
Jimmy the Priest's, 20–21, 55

Johnson, Jack, 149
Josephson, Matthew, 109
Joyce, James, 40, 243
Jung, Carl G., 39, 168, 217, 218

Kanter, Louis, 168
King, Clarence, 149
Kipling, Rudyard, 79
Kropotkin, Peter, 255
Krutch, Joseph Wood: *American Drama Since 1918,* 208; and Carlotta Monterey on interpretations of O'Neill's work, 46; on love, 158–59; *The Modern Temper,* 158, 184, 186, 190, 202, 208; on need for relation to something beyond ourselves, 186; O'Neill's plays supported by, 25; on religion and modernity, 184, 190; on tragedy on American stage, 208
Kublai Kaan, 85, 86, 88
Ku Klux Klan, 138, 149

labor: as driving force of history for Marxism, 72; labor theory of value, 36, 77; Ludlow strike of 1914, 65; ownership seen as based on, 100, 103, 104; socialism on, 35; as subject of O'Neill plays, 105; work ethic, 7, 84, 94, 96, 198. *See also* working class (proletariat)
Lacan, Jacques, 226, 271n13
land: American Indians dispossessed, 133, 260; inheritance in America, 97, 102–3; as permeating American history, 103–4
Langner, Lawrence, 106, 107, 111
Larner, John, 87, 274n12
"Last Conquest, The" (O'Neill), 27, 254
Lawson, John Howard, xiv
Lazarus Laughed (O'Neill), 196–202; on fear of death, 45, 197–202, 264–65; and Heidegger's *Being and Time,* 202; in O'Neill's "God trilogy," 202; and O'Neill's mother, 200; political implications of, 199
League of American Writers, 255

O'Neill, Carlotta Monterey (wife):
allows production of *Long Day's
Journey into Night,* 29, 224; in *Bird of
Paradise,* 80; on destruction of cycle
project manuscripts, 106; guarding
O'Neill against unwelcome visitors,
56; in *The Hairy Ape,* 26; on
interpretations of O'Neill's work,
46; Krutch asked to be O'Neill's
biographer by, 159; marriage to
O'Neill, 27–29; and O'Neill as Black
Irishmen, 185; O'Neill on his love
for, 160; O'Neill talks about his love
affairs with, 161

O'Neill, Edmund (brother), 18

O'Neill, Eugene
on America: on America as failure,
xiii; on American democracy as
betraying its own values, 7–9, 260;
on American history as tragic, xv; on
democratic pride, xv, 264; on getting
to the roots of America's sickness,
105–6, 238; Nietzschean reading of
American history of, 3; and
Progressive Historians, 107
biography of, 11–30; birth of, 18; death
of, 29; early life of, 19–24; education
of, 19, 22, 57, 161; father supporting
while at Princeton, 55; first trip to
brothel of, 40, 161, 177; health
problems of, 27, 28, 237; Irish
ancestry and family of, 11–16, 111;
Krutch as biographer of, 159; last
years of, 27–29; living on Cape Cod,
24, 25–26; property acquired by, 100;
as reclusive in later years, 56; as
seaman, 20; suicide attempt of, 21,
232; at tuberculosis sanitarium,
21–22, 161
children of: daughter Oona, 28, 29;
son Eugene Jr., 11, 12, 21, 28, 82, 224;
son Shane, 12, 28, 224
family of. *See* O'Neill family
friendships of: Dorothy Day, 56; John
Reed, 24, 35, 51, 57, 60; and "lost
generation," 23

influences on, 215; Emerson, 46, 48,
93, 119; European dramatists, 22–23;
Freud, 5, 38, 39; Goldman, 60–62;
Ibsen, 5, 21, 165, 166, 224; Nietzsche,
3, 36, 38, 48, 59–60, 62–63, 92, 93,
215, 236, 237; Schopenhauer, 20, 36,
38, 59, 60, 62, 63, 189, 236, 237;
Spengler, 36, 38, 81–82, 236;
Strindberg, 5, 21, 165, 215; Thoreau,
46, 48
personal characteristics of: as
attracted to wealth and elegance, 55;
betrayal seen everywhere by, 243; as
Black Irishman, 185–86; drinking by,
21, 25; humorous side of, 26–27;
physical appearance of, 27; tragic
view of life of, 26–27
as playwright: African Americans in
plays of, 139–40; American history
in plays of, 47–49; on Aristotle's view
of tragedy, 42–43; begins to write
plays, 21–22, 56–57, 162; characters
carrying burden of history, 39–40;
characters having little capacity for
transcendence, 261–62; characters
incapable of thinking beyond
themselves, 47; criticism of, 31–46;
desire in plays of, 4; dialectic
between past and present in plays of,
259; dialogue of, 6, 33, 41, 46; divided
self of characters of, 1; as dramatist
of ideas, 36; early plays ending with
pistol shots, 53; as emphathizing
with his characters, 37; Freudian
criticism of, 5–6; on Greek tragedy,
5; Hegelian notion of tragedy of, 15;
as historical dramatist, 79–94; home
in plays of, 17; Irish immigrant
experience and work of, 16–19;
length of plays of, 225; melodrama of
early plays of, 32, 33, 41, 53; memory
in plays of, 3, 19, 40, 41–42, 196;
mourning and grief in plays of, 19;
Nobel Prize for, xi, 23, 26, 32, 47, 211,
215, 270n17; plays as haunted by
history, 41–42; political philosophy

O'Neill, Eugene, as playwright (*cont.*)
for understanding plays of, 43,
49–50; praise for plays in mid-1920s,
25; property in plays of, 16–17;
psychoanalytic approach to, 272n13;
Pulitzer Prizes for, xi, 23, 25, 29, 170,
176; the sea as inspiration for, 20;
self-revelation in plays of, 229; sex in
plays of, 177–78; social-political basis
of plays of, 53–56; stage directions
of, 262; subjects of plays of, xiv, 19,
25, 105; on theater as life, 257; on
theater revealing to us who we are, 1;
on tragedy, 209–11; women in plays
of, 165–82
politics of, 51–78; on all authority as
oppressive, 50; as anarchist, 46, 52,
54, 59–65, 133, 193, 235–36, 261;
apparent contradiction in, 62; on
class consciousness, 35, 75, 76, 258;
on communism, xiv, 34–35, 52, 76,
255; as defying categorization, 241;
on economic determinism, 111–12;
on electoral politics, 54, 65, 264; on
freedom as distinguished from
democracy, 4; in Greenwich Village
"Lyrical Left," xiv, 264; knowledge of
working class of, 75, 253; left-wing
associations of, 24, 54; as left-wing
mystic, 47, 264; on revolutionary
potential of working class, 253–54,
256, 257; on Russian Revolution, 68,
69; sympathy for working class,
77–78, 133, 231, 256; and World War I,
56–59; World War II supported by,
254–56
relationships with women, 161–65;
affair with Carlotta Monterey, 26;
affair with Louise Bryant, 24, 51–52,
163–64, 167; breakup with Agnes
Boulton, 26, 232; crush on Marion
Welch, 161; divorce from Agnes
Boulton, 26; divorce from Kathleen
Jenkins, 21; on his love for Carlotta,
160; living in Bermuda with Agnes
Boulton, 26; living in Boston with

Carlotta, 28–29; living in East Bay
with Carlotta, 27–28, 55; living in Sea
Island with Carlotta Monterey, 26;
marriage to Agnes Boulton, 25, 169;
marriage to Carlotta Monterey, 26;
marriage to Kathleen Jenkins, 20,
161; relationship with Beatrice Ashe,
1, 162–63, 166, 227; relationship with
Catherine Mackay, 22, 161;
relationship with Maibelle Scott, 161
and religion, 183–205; Bible quoted by,
189; ceases going to mass, 183–84,
278n1; on faith, 181; Roman Catholic
background of, 4–5, 17, 39, 84, 93,
109, 182, 183, 189, 196, 204–5, 237–38,
272n13; yearning to be at one with
nature and spirit, 187
as thinker, 31–50; on dualism, 186; on
history as a nightmare, 243; on
history as tragic, xiii–xiv, xv; on life
as struggle, 257; multicultural
sympathies of, 55, 84–85, 93; and
pragmatism, 186; reading
preferences of, 225; and science, 190;
on self-knowledge, 1–2, 19;
transnational curiosity of, 55
works of: *Abortion,* 55; *Anna Christie,*
173–75, 178, 180, 262; *Before Breakfast,*
167; *Bound East for Cardiff,* 22, 24, 213;
Diff'rent, 167–69; *The Dreamy Kid,*
140–42, 149; *Dynamo,* 190–94, 202;
"Fratricide," 57–58; "God trilogy" of,
202; *Hughie,* 38, 187, 262; "The Last
Conquest," 27, 254; *The Moon of the
Caribbees,* 80; *Now I Ask You,* 167; *The
Personal Equation,* 65–69; *Recklessness,*
53; *Servitude,* 166, 181; *Shell Shock,*
58–59; *Sniper,* 58, 59; *The Straw,* 161;
The Web, 22; *Welded,* 160, 169–70, 181.
See also *Ah, Wilderness!; All God's
Chillun Got Wings; Beyond the
Horizon;* cycle project; *Days Without
End; Desire Under the Elms; Emperor
Jones, The; Fountain, The; Great God
Brown, The; Hairy Ape, The; Iceman
Cometh, The; Lazarus Laughed; Long*

Day's Journey into Night; Marco
Millions; Moon for the Misbegotten;
More Stately Mansions; Mourning
Becomes Electra; Strange Interlude;
Touch of the Poet, A

O'Neill, Eugene, Jr. (son), 11, 12, 21, 28,
82, 224

O'Neill, James (father): as bad Catholic,
189; betrayal by, 243; in The Count of
Monte Cristo, 14, 22, 43, 243; death of,
25, 197; as dying broken and bitter,
30; as embodying what went wrong
with America, 14–15; on Irish
immigrant experience, 13–14, 16;
leaving art behind for avarice, 11, 14,
22, 43–44, 243, 260; in Long Day's
Journey into Night, 4, 5, 13–14, 43,
187–88, 222, 225, 228; O'Neill as
unforgiving toward, 14; and O'Neill
ceasing to go to mass, 183; and
O'Neill's marriage to Kathleen
Jenkins, 20; on O'Neill's success, 24;
on people going to theater to forget
their troubles, 4; on son Jamie, 222;
supporting O'Neill while he was at
Princeton, 55; telling O'Neill truth
about his mother, 184; unfulfilled
desire of, 11; values represented by,
225

O'Neill, James, Jr. (Jamie) (brother), 18;
betrayal by, 243; death of, 25, 197, 222;
in Long Day's Journey into Night,
187–88, 225, 226, 227; in Moon for the
Misbegotten, 221–22, 223; squandered
life of, 222; telling O'Neill truth
about his mother, 184

O'Neill, Kathleen Jenkins (wife), 20,
161

O'Neill, Mary Ellen Quinlan (Ella)
(mother): death of, 25, 197, 201, 223;
difficulty accepting O'Neill as he
was, 163–64; drug addiction of, 18,
184, 196, 225–26, 228; and Dynamo,
193–94; and Lazarus Laughed, 200; in
Long Day's Journey into Night, 18, 165,
178, 225–29; marriage to James

O'Neill, 18; as not there for young
O'Neill, 162, 243; and O'Neill's
outlook on women, 166; ordeal of
giving birth to O'Neill, 18, 180;
suicide attempt of, 184

O'Neill, Oona (daughter), 28, 29, 224

O'Neill, Shane (son), 12, 28, 224

O'Neill family: "curse of the
misbegotten" of, 11; and cycle
project, 127; deaths of, 25, 197, 201,
202; Edmund, 18; in Long Day's
Journey into Night, 18, 29–30, 224;
talk used as weapon by, 49. See also
O'Neill, James; O'Neill, James, Jr.
(Jamie); O'Neill, Mary Ellen
Quinlan (Ella)

On Revolution (Arendt), 250–51

Oresteia (Aeschylus), 48–49, 214, 216,
217, 220, 221, 261

original sin, xiii, 39, 103

Orwell, George, 17, 51

ouvrierisme, 254

Paine, Thomas, 62, 104, 107, 117, 242

parental authority, 134

Parrington, Vernon Louis, 106–7

Pascal, Blaise, 37–38, 128

Peguy, Charles, 196

Personal Equation, The (O'Neill), 65–69

philosophy: linguistic turn in, 49;
O'Neill on existentialism, 236;
Stoics, 102. See also classical
philosophy; Hegelianism;
Nietzsche, Friedrich; pragmatism;
Schopenhauer, Arthur

pity: The Iceman Cometh as parable of,
246–51; Nietzsche on, 247–48, 264

politics, 51–78; Henry Adams on, 53;
classical philosophy on humans as
political animals, 221; electoral, 54,
65, 264; reform, 245–46, 249, 250; as
remaining at level of platitudes, 257;
and remembrance in The Iceman
Cometh, 241–46; as subject in O'Neill
plays, 263–64. See also conservatism;
radicalism

65–69; social-political basis of O'Neill's plays, 53–56; World War I as crisis for, 57. *See also* anarchism; communism; Marxism; socialism

Rahv, Philip, 232

Reaganism, 52, 104

Recklessness (O'Neill), 53

Reds (film), 51–52, 163

Reed, John: in Beatty's *Reds,* 51; on Bolshevik Revolution, 60, 68, 69, 78; as cultural nationalist, 57; as founder of American communism, 24, 35; friendship with O'Neill, 24; and Louise Bryant, 24, 51, 163, 165, 167; *Ten Days That Shook the World,* 24, 35, 68; as war correspondent, 58, 60

reform, 245–46, 249, 250

religion, 183–205; in *Days Without End,* 184, 202–5, 236; as difficult to reconcile with science, 184; "God is dead," 36, 53, 184, 187–88, 201, 248, 258, 260; in *The Great God Brown,* 194–96; *The Iceman Cometh* as religious play, 190; as insulating powerful from reality, 257; in *Lazarus Laughed,* 196–202; Mill on, 184; modern temper and problem of unbelief, 186–90; O'Neill on faith, 181; sanctification of money in America, 83; and science in *Dynamo,* 190–94; as subject of O'Neill plays, 25, 105; Tocqueville on American, 6–7, 130. *See also* Christianity

Ripkin, Jessica, 59, 60, 237

Roazen, Paul, 273n2, 277n11, 278n23

Robards, Jason, 32

Robber Barons, The: The Great American Capitalists (Josephson), 109

Robeson, Paul, 144, 155, 276n10

Robespierre, Maximilien, 107

Roman Catholicism: Adams studying, 196; in *Days Without End,* 27; interpretations of American history by Catholic historians, 275n16; Jansenist themes in, 37–38, 109; O'Neill ceases going to mass, 183–84; O'Neill's Catholic background, 4–5, 17, 39, 84, 93, 109, 182, 183, 189, 196, 204–5, 237–38, 272n13; on original sin, 39; sin, damnation, and suffering in imagination of, 196

romanticism, 219

Roosevelt, Franklin D., 27, 236, 238, 254–55

Roosevelt, Theodore, 80

Rorty, Richard, 49

Rougemont, Denis de, 172–73

Rousseau, Jean-Jacques, 64, 120, 125, 246, 260–61, 262

R.U.R. (Capek), 74

Russian Revolution: Bolsheviks, xiv, 60, 68, 76, 78, 203; intellectuals as carried away with, 68–69

Sacco, Nicola, 231

Said, Edward, 84

Sam, Guillaume, 144

Santayana, George, 15, 83, 119, 225, 240

Sartre, Jean Paul, 61

Schaeffer, Louis, 204

Schopenhauer, Arthur: on death, 213, 236, 237; in *Long Day's Journey into Night,* 224, 225; Nietzsche influenced by, 189; O'Neill influenced by, 20, 36, 38, 59, 60, 62, 63, 189, 236, 237; on overcoming desire, 42; pessimism of, 37; on pity, 248; on sin of being born, 39; on will as expression of unfulfilled desire, 238; on will to life, 21, 201; on women, 157

science: Marxists looking to, 253; O'Neill's attitude toward, 190; religion as difficult to reconcile with, 184; and religion in *Dynamo,* 190–94

Scopes trial, 190

Scott, Maibelle, 161

secular humanism, 190

self, divided. *See* divided self

self-determinism, 112, 123

self-interest, 107, 129, 133, 234

self-knowledge: in *All God's Chillun Got Wings,* 155; the Greeks on rational

Toomer, Jean, 144
totalitarianism, 231, 254
Totem and Taboo (Freud), 218
Touch of the Poet, A (O'Neill), 112–18;
    avarice in, 45; as at center of cycle
    project, 115; Con Melody, 112–13;
    democratic conformity in, 46, 116;
    desire in, 4; on failure of American
    democracy, 111, 112; new identity
    achieved in, 262; Nora, 113–15; Sara,
    114–15; Simon Harford, 115–16, 119;
    successful posthumous production
    of, 28; time of, 113
tragedy, 207–29; American history
    lacking sense of, xv, 211; on American
    stage, 207–11; Hegelian, 15; nobility
    and, 266; O'Neill allowing audiences
    to witness souls in agony, 240;
    O'Neill and Nietzsche finding joy in,
    27; O'Neill on, 209–11; opposition
    in, 93; pre–Civil War America as free
    of, 211. *See also* Greek tragedy
"Tragedy of Woman's Emancipation,
    The" (Goldman), 61–62
Transcendentalists, 2, 3, 120, 134–35, 207,
    233
Tresca, Carlo, 255
triangulation of desire, 262
Trilling, Lionel, 25, 47, 107, 263, 264
truth: in *Hughie,* 187; modern temper
    questioning, 186–87; O'Neill facing
    up to, 239–41; as painful, 240
Tucker, Benjamin R., 62, 63
Turner, Frederick Jackson, 104, 106–7
Twain, Mark, 137
two-party system, 65
tyranny of the majority, 4

Vanzetti, Bartolomeo, 231
Veblen, Thorstein, 57, 108
Vose, Gertie, 245

Waiting for Lefty (Odets), 253–54
Walpole, Horace, 26
war, Greek view of, 216
Warren, Joseph, 62

Washington, George, 218–19, 220, 259
waterfront taverns, 20–21, 27, 49, 55, 70
wealth. *See* money (wealth)
"Wealth" (Emerson), 124
Web, The (O'Neill), 22
Weber, Max, 45, 77, 196, 235
Welch, Marion, 161
Welded (O'Neill), 160, 169–70, 181
"white man's burden," 79
"whiteness," 150
Whitman, Walt, 7, 57
Wilde, Oscar, 36, 157, 224
will: in bondage to desire, 122;
    democracy as victory of will over
    birth, 131; as helpless to change the
    past, 42; Nietzsche on, 38, 123, 238;
    Schopenhauer on, 21, 38; will to
    believe, 33, 38, 123, 185; will to desire,
    38; will to power, 3, 36, 40, 75, 109,
    123, 124, 156
Williams, Tennessee, 94
Wilson, Edmund, 25, 34, 40
Wilson, Woodrow, 50, 57, 264
Wobblies (Industrial Workers of the
    World; I.W.W.), 24, 50, 65–69, 73, 253
Wolfe, Bertrand D., 51
women, 157–82; in *Anna Christie,* 173–75;
    feminization of American culture,
    119; as functioning biologically not
    professionally in O'Neill's plays, 170;
    new woman, 181; as Nietzscheans in
    O'Neill's plays, 156; O'Neill on
    nesting instinct of, 171; O'Neill's
    relationships with, 161–65; as
    renouncing their own freedom, 181;
    in *Strange Interlude,* 159, 175–81; as
    subject of O'Neill plays, xiv, 19, 160,
    165–82. *See also* feminism
Woolf, Virginia, 40
work ethic, 7, 84, 94, 96, 198
working class (proletariat): alienation
    of, 76–77; as "body" of revolution for
    Marx, 65; Gramsci on oppression of,
    74; in *The Hairy Ape,* 70–72; O'Neill
    on revolutionary potential of,
    253–54, 256, 257; O'Neill's knowledge